THE KURILLIAN KNOT

The Kurillian Knot

A History of Japanese-Russian Border Negotiations

HIROSHI KIMURA

Translated by Mark Ealey

Stanford University Press
Stanford, California

Stanford University Press
Stanford, California

English translation ©2008 by the Board of Trustees of
the Leland Stanford Junior University. All rights reserved.

Updates and additional material by the author ©2008 by the
Board of Trustees of the Leland Stanford Junior University.
All rights reserved.

The Kurillian Knot was originally published in Japanese in 1993 under the
title *Nichiro Kokkyo Kosho Shi* ©1993, Chuo-koran-sha, Tokyo.

The book was published in Russian in 1996 under the title *Kuril'skaia
problema: Istoriia iapono-rossiiskikh peregovorov po pogranichinym voprosam*
©1996, Iurinkom, Kiev.

The updated and expanded edition of the book was published in Japanese
in 2005 under the title *Shinpan [revised new edition] Nichiro Kokkyo Kosho Shi*
©2005, Kadokawa-shoten, Tokyo.

Printed in the United States of America on acid-free, archival-quality paper.

Library of Congress Cataloging-in-Publication Data
Kimura, Hiroshi, 1936-
    [Nichi-Ro kokkyo koshoshi. English]
    The Kurillian knot : a history of Japanese-Russian border negotiations /
Hiroshi Kimura ; translated by Mark Ealey.
        p. cm.
    Originally published in Japanese under the title: Nichi-Ro kokkyo koshoshi,
1993.
    Published in Russian under the title: Kuril'skaia problema, 1996.
    Includes bibliographical references and index.
    ISBN 978-0-8047-5835-2 (cloth : alk. paper)
    1. Japan—Boundaries—Russia (Federation)—History. 2. Russia (Federation)—
Boundaries—Japan—History. 3. Japan—Boundaries—Soviet Union—History.
4. Soviet Union—Boundaries—Japan—History. 5. Kuril Islands (Russia)—
International status—History. 6. Japan—Foreign relations—Russia (Federation)
7. Russia (Federation)—Foreign relations—Japan. I. Ealey, Mark. II. Title.
    DS849.R7K53413 2007
    327.52047—dc22   2008001982

Typeset by Classic Typography in 10.5/12 Bembo

To my two mentors,
Professors
Masamichi Inoki
and
John N. Hazard

Contents

List of Illustrations

Figures

Maps

I.William Zartman, an international authority on the study of negotiations and professor of international organizations and conflict resolution at the Johns Hopkins University, suggests that the process of negotiation is divided into three phases. First is the *diagnostic* phase, the stage when a judgment is made regarding whether to enter into negotiations. Second is the *formula* phase in which specific formulas or rules that could provide a basis for agreement are defined. In the third or *detail* phase, the specific elements of an agreement are finalized.[1]

What happens if we apply this three-stage formula to Japanese-Russian border delimitation? President Gorbachev's visit to Japan in 1991 saw Japanese-Russian border negotiations enter their first phase. Gorbachev agreed with Prime Minister Toshiki Kaifu to commence negotiations on the sovereignty of the islands of Etorofu, Kunashiri, Shikotan, and Habomai. The process of negotiation entered its second stage when President Yeltsin visited Japan in 1993. With regard to how the negotiations over these four islands should be carried out, President Boris Yeltsin and Prime Minister Morihiro Hosokawa agreed upon what formula should be used.

So what is the formula that represents the second phase of Japanese-Russian negotiations? It is found in Article 2 of the Tokyo Declaration signed by the top leaders of Japan and Russia in 1993: "Both sides agree that negotiations toward an early conclusion of a peace treaty through the solution of this issue on the basis of historical and legal facts and based on the documents produced with the two countries' agreement as well as on the principles of law and justice should continue."

That is to say, the formula is represented by "historical and legal facts," "documents produced with the two countries' agreement," and "law and justice." Of those, the "documents produced with the two countries' agreement" refers to the Joint Compendium of Documents on the History of the Territorial Issue Between Japan and Russia, hereinafter referred to as the Joint Compendium. This compendium was compiled jointly by the Japanese and Russian Ministries of Foreign Affairs and is a collection of historical documents that both sides have agreed to include. Previously, the territorial dispute between Japan and the Soviet Union featured a pointless string of interactions in which each would selectively quote historical documents to suit their own case, refuting and denying the other side's assertions. However, things have changed. Now, when Japan and Russia discuss the border delimitation issue, neither questions the credibility of the documents in the Joint Compendium, and they may be quoted and used as the basis of negotiations. In that respect, the Joint Compendium has become one aspect of the *formula* of Japanese-Russian border negotiations.

The problem is how this kind of compendium should be used. Apart from the short preface, it is a collection of forty-two documents arranged in chronological order. There is no doubt that apart from a mere handful of specialists, no one would have any idea of the documents' significance. Be that as it may, the Joint Compendium is a set of fundamental materials that I hope are read by as many people as possible. So, what needs to be done?

In this book I have attempted to give a historical description of Japanese-Russian relations with regard to the Northern Territories (in Russia these islands are referred to as the Southern Kuriles) from the seventeenth century to the present day. It is my hope that by referring to specific historical occurrences on both a domestic and international level I have produced a chronicle of Japanese-Russian history that is more easily digestible for the reader. To the maximum extent possible I have included reference to the relevant items among the forty-two documents of the Joint Compendium and have gone on to explain their significance. I have also explained the reasons why some of these documents have not been available to the general public until the publication of the Joint Compendium, and I have provided an explanation of the significance of the documents being released. In the Appendix to this volume I have included, in their entirety, all forty-two documents from the Joint Compendium. More enthusiastic readers will be able to refer to these documents, but the main text will suffice for most. A lack of agreement between the Japanese and Russian Ministries of Foreign Affairs has ruled out some other documents from appearing in the Joint Compendium, and for those that I consider to be important, I suggest reasons why they were not included and explain their content.

Acknowledgments

The first Japanese version of this book was published in September 1993 by Chūō-Kōron Co. Ltd., Tokyo. Thanks to the support of the Japan Foundation, a superb Russian translation by Megumi Suezawa of Heisei International University and by Valentin Yakushik of the Faculty of Law, Kiev University, was then published in 1996: Hiroshi Kimura, *Kuril'skaia problema:*

Istoriia Iapono-rossiiskikh peregovorov po pogranichinym voprosam (Kiev: Iurinkom, June 1996).

The first Japanese edition covered the period up to Yeltsin's visit to Japan in 1993, so I felt that the need to bring the work up to date by adding coverage of subsequent developments. The revised and enlarged edition in Japanese was published by Kadokawa-shoten, Tokyo, in 2005. Kenjirō Kumagai of Kadokawa-shoten has offered invaluable assistance after the draft was handed over. The English translation of second Japanese edition was carried out by Mark Ealey, a highly skilled translator specializing in works of diplomatic history. I am greatly indebted to Mark for his devotion to such a major task. Two of his research students, Stephen Albrow and Jason Allen, also contributed to the translation of Chapter 8. Special gratitude goes to Mr. Geoffrey Jukes, professor emeritus at the Australian National University, who generously edited the entire manuscript, making numerous comments and suggestions, particularly in the military-strategic field. Proofreading of the text was carried out by Dr. Peter Berton, professor emeritus at the University of Southern California (USC), a leading authority in Russo-Japanese relations, Ms. Tatiana White, a graduate student at the USC, and Dr. Brad Williams, a young and promising specialist in Russo-Japanese relations at the National Singapore University, Singapore. I am particularly indebted to Daniel Okimoto, professor at Stanford University, who was kind enough to recommend my manuscript to the Stanford University Press. I am also grateful to Professors Peggy Falkenheim Meyer, Kimie Hara, Archie Brown, and Arthur Stockwin for their recommendations for publication.

Without the kind support of the people mentioned here, this project would not have reached fruition.

Introduction: Territorial Conflict

Definition of Globalization

We are now said to be in the age of globalization. However, the word "globalization" does not necessarily mean the same to everyone.[1] Here it will be used to mean the flow of people, goods and services, capital, information, ideas, values, and technology around the globe on a level transcending state boundaries.[2] Globalization has been facilitated by rapid strides in development of communications, freight and transport systems, and the huge cost reductions that have resulted, particularly with the "revolution in information technology (IT)."

The word "internationalization" is often used as a synonym for "globalization," but the nuance is slightly different.[3] Internationalization does not negate national borders, and indeed, it is premised on the existence of countries divided from each other by clearly marked state boundaries and territories. Its focus is on the increase in frequency and scale of exchange between those states and their peoples. In contrast, "globalization" places emphasis on issues that transcend the preexisting doorstep to states, namely, national borders.[4] One might even say that the authority and function of nation-states and state-centric agencies is reduced.[5] In their place, nonstate entities such as individual citizens, groups, corporations, and international organizations create the procedures and global standards for making reasonable choices. As a consequence of such processes, "social relations acquire relatively distanceless and borderless qualities, so that lives are increasingly played out in the world as a single place."[6] All this suggests "the shrinking of distance,"[7] "the world as a single place," and in the most extreme of terms, the advent of the "global village,"[8] as envisaged by the likes of Marshall McLuhan.

So when did globalization start? This is a difficult question to answer. Some like to suggest that in the broadest sense of the word it started more or less at the same time as the history of mankind.[9] Others consider that the establishment of the Silk Road as a route for economic and cultural exchange between Asia and Europe marks the advent of globalization.[10] However, this represents what could be termed "thin globalization."[11] "Thick globalization" or "contemporary globalization,"[12] which is more intensive as well as extensive, affecting the lives of many more people, began in the latter half of the twentieth century.[13] To be even more specific, it should probably be seen as a phenomenon that began in the early 1990s when the walls separating the East and West camps crumbled.

Globalization does not occur at the same speed and scale in every sphere of human activity.[14] This is one reason why it is difficult to determine when globalization actually began. Some areas (for example, technology and the economy) have been globalized more smoothly and rapidly than others (for example, politics), where the influence of globalization has been slow and less remarkable. Some areas, such as social and cultural activities (for example, customs and fashion), would fall somewhere between these two extremes.[15]

Also, globalization does not have a uniform influence.[16] Generally speaking, its impact is greater in the "North" than the "South"; in the younger generation rather than the older; in the professional class than among manual laborers. For example, at this point in time, when we have just entered the twenty-first century, as many as one-quarter of the population of the United States is availing itself of the benefits of the World Wide Web (www.); the corresponding figure in South Asia is no more than 0.01 percent. Even by 2010, it is thought that as much as 70 percent of the world's population will still not have access to the Internet through computers and cellular phones, and approximately 50 percent still will never have made a telephone call.[17]

It is therefore important for us to make it clear which fields or dimensions of globalization we are talking about. Failing to do so merely confuses the issue and leads to unproductive discussions.

As a political scientist, I feel obligated to ask the following questions: Does globalization reduce the role of "nation-states," thereby eroding their meaning?[18] Will the advent of the borderless age that is expected to result from globalization render those key components of "nation-states," such as "territory," "national borders," and "sovereignty" meaningless? These two questions are mutually related, as nation-states control set areas of territory, and within the national borders that define such territory, in principle, they claim to exercise exclusive authority, for example, "sovereignty" over the residents. The concept of the nation-state is based on this thinking.

Globalization and the Nation-State

Does globalization, by rendering the concepts of "territory," "national borders," and "sovereignty" obsolete, therefore lead to the dissolution of nation-states?[19] In particular, does the trend toward borderlessness, or to use a slightly more difficult term, "supraterritoriality," erode the raison d'être of one of the key elements of the nation-state, namely, "territory"?[20]

Broadly speaking, there are three ways of responding to these questions.[21] "Globalists" would answer in the affirmative. In other words, they suggest that advances in globalization, in particular in the IT field, have overcome geographical limitations and that, as a result, the significance of political borders as the artificial barriers that previously divided nation-states, has diminished, and therefore territorial sovereignty is becoming obsolete.[22] In contrast, "traditionalists" would say "no."[23] They consider that the process of globalization is occurring within the parameters of the nation-state system; therefore, the notion of national sovereignty will not be eroded in the foreseeable future. The third group is that of "transformationalists," those who occupy the middle ground between the other two.[24] They argue that while as a result of globalization the notion of territorial sovereignty will not necessarily disappear, in terms of power and function it will undergo significant transformation. Personally, I tend to take the third "tranformationalist" view. Let me explain why.

First of all, territorial instincts are rooted in human nature. Any theory that shrinks from this fact immediately distances itself from reality. We all desire to secure for ourselves a certain territory where we feel free and unfettered by others. This is merely a reflection of our animal instincts.[25] The expression "elbow room" best illustrates this inherent desire in man. In his work, *Hōjōki* (My ten-foot-square hut), the thirteenth-century Japanese literary recluse Kamo no Chōmei philosophized that a human being does not require a large amount of space to lead his life. He did qualify this, however, by stating that to survive, a human being must have at least a ten-foot-square space. That securing a certain amount of space is essential for human survival is also illustrated by the appearance of deep vein thrombosis syndrome among airline passengers. Being confined to a small space in an aircraft for long periods of time not only results in psychological discomfort but also manifests itself as a physical problem.

Apart from shelter from the elements, human beings need to secure and control a certain amount of space in which to hunt or farm, and a "love space" for breeding activities to preserve the species.[26] Normally, the larger that physical space is—whether as "territory" or "sphere of influence"—the more free and comfortable we feel.

Secondly, we must remember that territory is not just a living space that provides us with the food, clothing, and shelter to facilitate basic survival. To put it another way, it does more than merely allow us to achieve physical and material security. It plays another important function. It is endowed with nonmaterial value. "Territory" supports a certain distinctive "lifestyle" that reflects the language, culture, and customs of those who belong to its component groups. This also means that it is an area that confirms one's own identity or sense of belonging.[27]

For example, terms such as "home," "fatherland," and "motherland" are deeply stored in the collective memories of families, ethnic groups, and nations.[28] While the feelings attached to a particular area may, in some cases, be somewhat irrational, their psychological or symbolic significance cannot be easily dismissed. This land gives birth to and fosters feelings of affection and comradeship toward other members of the same group. It is the basis of love for one's hometown, patriotism, and nationalism. Should such a "sacred land" be lost, the displaced souls will often suffer from a "loss of home," a feeling of being *déraciné*, and even an identity crisis.

To recapitulate, territory is inherently linked to man's basic desires in terms of existence on a physical and cultural level.[29] When these basic desires are denied, or prevented from being realized, humans possess an innate desire to defend the territory or sphere of influence under their control. In his book *On Aggression*, Konrad Lorenz, winner of the Nobel Prize for physiology and medicine, wrote that "in every individual the readiness to fight is greatest in the most familiar place, that is, in the middle of its territory."[30] In other words, the threshold value of fight-eliciting stimuli is at its lowest where the animal feels safest, that is, "where its readiness to fight is least diminished by its readiness to escape."[31] Thus, "In nearing the center of the territory the aggressive urge increases in geometrical ratio to the decrease in distance from the center."[32]

It therefore becomes understandable, and even justifiable, to have police and military to defend one's territory by ejecting the invader. In return for protection of these territories, we agree to grant sufficient control (sovereignty) to the organ possessing the power to force such issues. With these background factors and reasons, a state with territorial sovereignty is born and legitimized, and it continues to exist until now.

Will Territorial Sovereignty Become Obsolete?

A nation-state is defined as an entity, which possesses its own fixed, demarcated territory, within which it exercises exclusive authority (sovereignty) over its nation. What, then, is the impact of globalization on the sovereignty and autonomy of nation-states? Here again, there is a diversity of judgment.

Globalists argue that global change will make both territorial sovereign states and the systems comprised of sovereign states increasingly vulnerable, even obsolete.[33] They suggest that instead of the nation-state system, nonstate or nongovernmental entities, especially multinational and suprainternational organizations, are emerging and increasing their significance. These newly emerging organizations are a "challenger" to the nation-state in the sense that they are trying to deprive nation-states of their roles and even replace them.[34]

Globalists often support their claims by citing (1) the development of multinational organizations; (2) trends toward unification of states; and (3) proposals for "joint-sovereignty" or "joint-administration." But I would like to suggest that these do not necessarily provide a sufficient basis to justify globalist arguments. Let me explain.

Multinational Corporations

In today's world, nonstate actors, such as multinational corporations, are assuming increasing prominence. Multinational corporations are huge international enterprises that carry out the majority of their business activities across national borders. All over the world they have subsidiary companies, through which they carry out international investment, production, management, and sales activities. This phenomenon started in the 1960s, as a result of huge, mainly American, corporations setting up overseas in order to sidestep trade barriers. Similarly, Japanese corporations have, almost en masse, transferred their production bases to China and South-East Asia in search of cheap labor, leading to the hollowing out of Japanese industry. These days there is little point in asking about the nationality of certain products. Being able to label a product as completely "Made in Japan" or "Made in the USA" is rapidly becoming a thing of the past. At least in the economic sphere, globalization undeniably diminishes the controlling power of nation-states. Yet it is premature to jump to the conclusion that such active and prosperous development of multinational corporations will, before too long, lead to the demise of nation-states or the nation-state system. Let me explain three related reasons why one should doubt the validity of such a conclusion.[35]

The first lies in the fact that nation-states have been displaying considerable ability to stand up to multinational corporations. It is true that when multinational corporations began their activities in the 1950s and 1960s, nation-states were completely defenseless to deal with the inroads these organizations made into state affairs. But as awareness of the economic impact of the situation has grown, a reaction has set in that demonstrates the survival capacity of nation-states. Nation-states began to counter by implementing a range of criteria to which multinationals must adhere in order to gain access to national territory. In other words, "political imperatives" have initiated defensive countermeasures against "economic infringement."

Secondly, the development of multinational corporations does not necessarily lead to reduction or denial of the power of nation-states. These two organizations are not in a zero-sum relationship. Let me quote the excellent explanation given by Professor Samuel Huntington of Harvard University.

Predictions of the death of the nation-state are premature. They overlook the ability of human beings and human institutions to respond to challenges and adapt themselves to changed environments. They seemed to be based on a zero-sum assumption about power and sovereignty: that a growth in the power of transnational organizations must be accompanied by a decrease in the power of nation-states. This, however, need not be the case . . . an increase in the number, functions, and scope of transnational organizations will increase the demand for access to national territories and hence also increase the value of the one resource almost exclusively under the control of national governments.[36]

The third reason is that multinational corporations tend to move into geographical areas where peace and security are sufficiently assured thanks to the authority of nation-states. Nation-states protect their domestic order and guarantee property rights from both internal and external threats, through the use of police, armed forces, and other institutions. Multinational corporations assume this of nation-states and organize their activities on this premise. (In that sense, the power of modern-day multinationals pales compared to that of the East India Company of years gone by, which boasted its own army and territory.)

If we were to divide sovereignty into two, internal and external components, we see that they are closely linked.[37] For example, Stephen Krasner had the following to say: "If a state cannot regulate what passes across its borders, it will not be able to control what happens within them."[38] The opposite is also true. Even looking at it in these terms, as Huntington suggests, not only should we avoid seeing multinationals and nation-states as mutually exclusive, we could even say that they can only coexist, but actually rely on each other's support.

On close inspection, we see that while multinational corporations are multinational and transnational in terms of their activities and personnel, their administrative authority and headquarters, which effectively monitor, regulate, and police their activities, particularly final decision-making power, are located in the United States or other major nations.[39] This has nothing to do with where the corporations want to pay taxes.[40] They differentiate between the location of the base for decision making and the geographical scope of operations, and in this sense, there is no great difference between, say, the World Bank and the U.S. Air Force.[41] The latter maintains a clear national base in terms of control and personnel, yet qualifies as a transnational organization in terms of its scope of operation. This is more or less applicable to the former as well.

Intergovernmental Organizations

In recent times, there has been an undeniable trend for nation-states to integrate into larger units, as intergovernmental organizations. Of course we have not yet succeeded in creating (and are never likely to create) a world government. While the United Nations may appear to have that potential, at present it is merely a collection of individual states that possess sovereignty within their territories.[42] Be that as it may, we have the following supranational, global, or regional bodies, which deal with matters that cut across national borders: NATO, EU, ASEAN, African Unity (AU), the Organization of American States (OAS), the Central American Common Market (CACM), the International Monetary Fund (IMF), the World Bank, the World Trade Organization (WTO), and so on. These governmental organizations, or even institutions, have taken over some of the aspects of sovereignty previously held by sovereign states.

However, this does not mean that these organizations will look to deny states their sovereignty. In fact, the opposite is the case, in that the activities of intergovernmental organizations are actually based on the premise that nation-states exist. In this respect, the relationship between these organizations and nation-states differs little from that between multinational corporations and nation-states.

Let us take the European Union (EU) for example. The EU has had its own money (Euro) as a standard currency since July 1, 2001. This means that it has removed currency sovereignty from its participating member-states. It does not mean, however, that the EU intends to strip those states of their sovereignty in its entirety and bring about the collapse of the nation-state system. Britain, for example, is still using the pound.

The EU is a collective entity, comprising states that have similar historical and cultural backgrounds. In this respect, the EU can be seen as an exceptional case, one that could probably only come about in Europe. The formation of the EU thus represents neither "the retreat of the state" nor "the twilight of the nation-state system."[43]

Furthermore, the establishment of an international organization such as the EU only becomes possible with the consent of the member-states. It was formulated after the countries that sought to create it agreed of their own volition to do so. Denmark, for example, joined the EU after its inception. Also, member-states transfer only some parts of their sovereignty to the EU. Speaking of the extremes, the EU's activities are based on the wishes of its member-states and are an extension of their own national agendas.[44] By the same token, if a member-state is unhappy with the EU's operations, it can freely withdraw from membership.

Which is larger then, the degree of sovereignty that member-states have transferred to the EU, or the part that they have retained? It goes without saying that the latter is far more significant. In the soccer World Cup, held in Korea and Japan in June 2002, about the time that the Euro was introduced, the participant teams were from states such as Germany, France, Italy,

Spain, or even smaller units than that, for example, England. Players who normally played in foreign club teams appeared for the country of their nationality. Fans followed their national teams, supporting them with bold displays of patriotic fervor.

The EU neither ignores nor denies the existence of national borders dividing its member-states. On the contrary, it takes for granted the notion that borders serve as the geographical boundaries between nation-states. We might even say that the EU could not exist without its acceptance of the concept of territorial borders.

Let me give an example. The future position of Kaliningrad provides a good illustration. In November 2002, it was decided that Lithuania and Poland would join the EU in 2004. In a departure from the past, the EU will surely require these two countries to make their customs controls at their borders with the Russian enclave of Kaliningrad tighter than now. Without this stipulation, the EU would be unable to prevent illegal goods and immigrants being smuggled into its domain via these new member-states from Kaliningrad and even from Russia and Belarus. Kaliningrad has twenty-three border-crossing points with its neighbors and is notorious as a center for the smuggling of cigarettes, drugs, and used cars, as a hub of human traffic and prostitution, and as a breeding ground for HIV and AIDS. President Putin agreed that Russians traveling to and from Kaliningrad will require a "transit permit." While these transit permits allow multiple entry during a set period, they are, nevertheless, a kind of visa. So while the EU might be looking to liberalize the flow of people and goods among its member-states by lowering the height of the "doorstep"—borders—between members of the EU, it is at the same time trying to increase its height between EU member-states and nonmembers.[45]

Even if we see Kaliningrad as a special case and put it aside for the moment, there is little need to explain that the EU is hardly opening its doors to all the people and goods that are ready to flow in from nonmember states. For a range of reasons, including humanitarian grounds and liberal multiculturalism, the EU and its members do not reject out of hand people or goods from nonmember states. But they are opposed to the unlimited flow of refugees and illegal immigrants. If this were allowed to happen, the EU would run the risk of provoking unnecessary friction and conflict with the residents of the region. The flow of illegal immigrants has become such a serious problem in countries such as Holland, Germany, and France that it has helped extremist right-wing political parties rapidly increase their influence.

It thus becomes necessary for us to distinguish clearly between the following two things.[46] First, in recent years, there has been a trend for nation-states to transfer to international organizations some *parts* of the powers and functions they used to possess. This is one thing. But, second, this does not mean that a state relinquishes *all* its powers and functions to such supranational institutions. Indeed, a state can even withdraw from an international organization it once decided to join (for example, the EU), and by so doing recover the powers it had previously ceded. That is to say, the transfer of sovereign power does not amount to its relinquishment.[47] Moreover, even when grouping together, at least now nation-states retain far more sovereignty than they cede.

It has also to be pointed out at this conjunction that so many new nations-states have come into existence since the end of the Cold War. For instance, fifteen independent states were created from the former Soviet Union; the Yugoslav federation was divided; Czechoslovakia has broken up into separate Czech and Slovak republics. Also, but for the Russian Federal Government's use of military force, the Chechen Republic would undoubtedly break away to become an independent nation. In the thirteen years since the end of the Cold War, at least twenty new states have been created. The number of countries that join the United Nations continues to increase (as of mid-2006 the total was 192).

Joint Sovereignty

Recently some have advocated such schemes as "joint sovereignty," "shared sovereignty," and "joint administration." In other words, apportioning sovereignty to a number of states, rather than just one. This too presses for revision of the traditional concept of a nation-state, for example, "one sovereignty-state presiding over one territory." For instance, in November 2002 the British government held a referendum in Gibraltar on the question of putting it under joint sovereignty of UK and Spain. Since about 90 percent of Gibraltar's 30,000 population are of British descent, an overwhelming 99 percent of voters rejected the proposal.[48]

The notion of "joint sovereignty" or other forms of joint control over a particular territory may sound quite acceptable to the uninitiated, but it soon becomes clear how unrealistic an ideal it is when we try to put it into practice. Suppose, for instance, that some conflict or trouble were to occur in an area governed in this way. Which state would have the right to exercise judicial control over those concerned? Some might say that those involved should come under the jurisdiction of the participating state to which they belonged, but if so clear discrepancies would be likely to occur in handling people of different nationalities who have committed the same act. Also, if individuals of one nationality received different legal treatment in the area under joint administration from what was the norm in their home country, this would invite criticism as violating the principle of equal treatment under the law.[49] Another question to raise here is to which state would a resident of such an area pay taxes? In short, "shared sovereignty" cannot provide acceptable solutions to basic issues with regard to jurisdiction and taxation, matters closely connected to state-sovereignty.

This may not pose a serious problem over joint use of rivers and pasture land in border areas where nobody resides, but in a place with even just one resident, complications would be unavoidable. Karafuto (now Sakhalin) prior to 1875 provides an excellent illustration of this. At that time the island was a sort of condominium under Russo-Japanese joint sovereignty, where Russians, Japanese, and Ainu lived side by side. Because of such a legal limbo, there were constant conflicts between these groups, and it was not uncommon for them to explode into violence, murder, and arson.[50] This was one of the main reasons why in 1875 Japan and Russia concluded the Treaty of St. Petersburg, giving Russia sovereignty over Sakhalin in exchange for ceding the entire Kurile Islands chain to Japan.

In short, joint administration, at best, is nothing more than an interim measure put in place until a definitive solution can be reached. At worst, it is an attempt to avoid facing the problem that is at the core of territorial disputes. Though it may be conceived as a wise means of settlement, in reality it frequently creates potential bases for new and probably even more complicated sources of conflict.[51]

Despite all these defects, Moscow governments under Yeltsin and Putin repeatedly made proposals to Tokyo to conduct "joint economic development [*sovmestnoe khoziaistvennoe osvoenie*]" on and around the disputed Northern Territories. If this would contribute to finding a final solution to the territorial dispute, the Japanese government would have seriously considered it. However, if it only helped consolidate the current de facto Russian ownership of the disputed islands, then Tokyo would not accept the idea at all.[52]

Summary

Let me summarize the argument thus far.

1. It is safe to say that the traditional notion of territorial sovereignty is, to a certain extent, changing because of globalization. The trend that sees sovereign states cede part of their powers and function to nonstate entities (multinational organizations, NGOs, international organizations, and so on) is likely to continue.

2. However, this trend cannot be cited as evidence that the process of globalization leads to the demise of nation-states, as strategically they transfer only certain aspects of their powers and functions to transnational or nongovernmental organizations.[53]

3. The usual understanding of the relationship between nation-states and globalization as a dichotomy is an illusion in the first place.[54]

Such thinking does not reflect the realities of contemporary international society. Indeed, not only do nation-states and globalization coexist at the same time, but also they can be said to complement each other.[55]

4. It is far too early to suggest that the recent expansion of "supraterritoriality" is consigning the concept of the sovereign state to the past. Nation-states, founded on territory, are as important now as they have ever been. That a number of new states have been born one after another is surely testimony to this. It is likely that both territorial and state consciousness, as well as the nationalism based on them, will continue to exist for some time into the future.

5. This means that we need to pay close attention to both the outbreak and continuation of territorial conflict. Those who suggest that such interest has been rendered inappropriate in what has become a borderless and globalized world run the risk of being criticized as Utopians ignoring reality.

6. In post-Cold War international society, two forces are progressing simultaneously. One is a centripetal or unifying force, which looks to bring things together at a level involving units larger than the state. It could also be described as movements toward globalism. The EU is a prime example of this force. The other force is of a centrifugal nature, conversely acting to divide the state into even smaller pieces. This is a trend rooted in nationalism. The dissolutions of the Soviet Union, Czechoslovakia, and Yugoslavia are typical examples.

Centrifugal and centripetal forces are coming to bear at the same time. Alvin and Heidi Toffler explain it as "'glocalism'—the decentralist shift of political control downward from nation-states to local communities and, simultaneously, upward to the European Union, the United Nations and other supranational agencies."[56] These two forces could just as easily be described as "integration" and "fragmentation,"[57] or "fusion" and "fission." However we describe them, the important issue is that these two mutually contradictory trends are occurring simultaneously and in parallel.[58]

If we accept this, we can safely draw the following conclusions about the relationship between globalization and nation-states. Both "globalization" (the demise of the state) and "sovereign nation-state" arguments are extreme forms of their respective logic. A view somewhere between these two extremes, one that reflects the current "transformationalist approach," is an appropriate form of analysis both for current circumstances and for the foreseeable future.[59] This may seem yet another example of an academic fence sitting, but today's complex international environment requires us to view matters in terms of a more multifaceted and multidimensional paradigm than simplified or overgeneralized concepts.[60]

Territorial Conflict as a Cause of War

Territorial conflict can easily lead to war. That is to say, conflict over territory, be it land, air, or sea, involves a contest for sovereignty over something that there is only one of. It therefore tends to assume the nature of a zero-sum game (a conflict in which one party gains only through the other's loss). In extreme cases, zero-sum game situations lead to war.

The relationship between territory and war is close and complex. Territorial conflict, first of all, can lead to war. Next, it cannot be solved by resorting to war. Yet, it also sometimes occurs as a result of war. Be that as it may, it can be described as the most widespread and significant cause of wars in the past two or three centuries. Why is this? Between what kinds of nations are wars most common? Many wars occur because of conflict over the national border dividing adjacent countries.[61] Paul Diehl has discovered a close correlation between wars and territorial "proximity or contiguity." Of the thirteen significant wars fought between the world's major powers from 1816 to 1980, twelve (92 percent) were between nations that shared a national boundary. In that same period, of fifty-four disputes between nations that did not share a border, only one (2 percent) escalated to open warfare.[62] That of course was Japan's war against the United States, the British Empire, and the Netherlands from 1941 to 1945. Also, according to research by Lewis F. Richardson (1960), a close correlation exists between shared frontiers and external wars.[63] Richardson's research focuses on wars involving the world's thirty-three major nations during the period 1825–1946. He found a clear correlation between the number of wars a country was involved in and the number of national borders it had.[64]

There is no doubt that since World War Two there has been a dramatic decrease in the number of wars fought with the objective of occupying or acquiring *all* of another country's territory, but unfortunately the world has not seen the end of wars aimed at *partial* expansion of one country's territory.[65] In recent times there have been armed conflicts between Israel and neighboring Arab nations, China and Russia over Damansky (Chenpao) Island, the Iran-Iraq War, the Falklands (Malvinas) War, to name just a few examples of fighting sparked by conflict over territory. Military clashes between India and Pakistan over Kashmir were frequent.

Countries that share national boundaries or are geographically close to each other have more opportunities to become involved in armed clashes or wars than more distant countries. Let us take China as an example. It is more likely to fight a war against Russia, Vietnam, or India than Tunisia or

Paraguay.[66] Richardson used the analogy of domestic violence to explain this. Murders and other violent acts are frequently committed by the victim's friends, relatives, neighbors, or acquaintances, but violence by strangers with whom one has little chance of contact is rare.[67] With this, we can conclude that conflict over national borders "has been probably the most significant cause of wars between nations in the past two or three hundred years."[68]

Of course this does not mean that countries sharing national borders are constantly in conflict with each other, causing armed clashes and wars. The 7,600-kilometer border between China and the Soviet Union at that time, the world's second longest, did tend to heighten tension between these two nations. This was one cause of antagonism between them and did in fact lead to bloodshed near Damansky (Chenpao) Island. But, by the same token, the United States and Canada share the longest border (8,900 kilometers), but maintain a very friendly relationship.[69] In other words, shared borders or geographical proximity do not by themselves automatically lead to conflict or international cooperation. That is to say, the former factors are not a direct cause of either of the latter outcomes. However, the former does at least function as a catalyst to amplify relationships that involve conflict or cooperation based on other reasons. As Professor Bruce M. Russett of Yale University commented, "Except in some sense for border disputes, countries do not fight each other *because* they are physically close; they merely happen to have the *opportunity* to fight because they are close. Proximity becomes the catalyst."[70]

The Need for Research on Territorial Disputes

The above analysis helps confirm that territorial disputes are an important source of conflict that, in extreme cases, even results in armed clashes and wars. Despite the significant role territorial disputes play in international politics, they have to date received little more than perfunctory attention as an area of research in study of international affairs. It is truly astonishing that the concept of territoriality as a basic cause of conflict has been so neglected and so little studied by students of international politics.[71] The reason for this is that, up to now, mainstream research has emphasized ideological factors in the conflict between East and West, in particular the nuclear weapons debate and the shift to remote warfare, with the result that territorial or border disputes have tended to be seen as geographical or localized clashes, of minor importance for research.

However, the changes brought about by the end of the Cold War have forced us to amend our approach. That is to say, it has greatly alleviated the conflict centered on the ideological gap between the United States and former Soviet Union, the world's two nuclear superpowers, or their respective caches of nuclear weapons. It has, instead, seen the reemergence of territorial disputes, which for a time at least seemed to have disappeared from history's center stage. During the Cold War, certain types of territorial disputes between the blocs were bottled up and frozen by the fear of nuclear war, the solidarity of the Western camp, and the firm establishment of Soviet hegemony.[72] But from 1989 to 1991 the collapse of communist ideology, the breakup of the Eastern European bloc, and the disappearance of the Soviet Union as a military superpower, rekindled the flames of pent-up disputes over territory, seeing them burst forth and rage rampant, for example, the civil wars in Bosnia-Herzegovina, Kosovo, and Macedonia in former Yugoslavia. Conflict within or strife between the republics that made up the former Soviet Union such as between Armenia and Azerbaijan, South Ossetia and Georgia, Moldova and the Republic of Transdniestria, as well as the civil war in Tajikistan, are but a few examples of such border or territorial disputes.

Territorial conflict can be traced back to a broad range of causes related to racial, ethnic, political, economic, and national security issues. Psychological or symbolic factors concerning the dignity or honor of the nation or its people also have an important role to play.

Methods for solving territorial conflict are also many and varied. Broadly speaking, they can be divided into two means: use of force to expand the territory of one country and therefore change national borders; and those involving peaceful talks to reach agreement.

Military solutions involve bloodshed, and on top of being expensive exercises, they give birth to feelings of hatred that lead to acts of revenge. Thus in the long term, they provide no true solution to the dispute. In particular, use of military force does not produce a normal and stable situation acceptable to both parties. One of the main reasons why the Germans—normally known for their wisdom—could be incited by Hitler to cause World War Two is that after defeat in World War One they not only had harsh reparations forced on them, but they also had to cede territory to neighboring countries, most notably to Poland. In other words, the seizure of territory by military force tends to lead to a vicious cycle.

Realizing this to be the case, in the Atlantic Charter (1941) and the Cairo Declaration (1943), the Allied Powers in World War Two declared their stance on seeking "no aggrandizement, territorial or other." That is to say, they attempted to bring a stop to this cycle by stating the principle of "territorial nonexpansion," namely that the victorious nations shall not, neither as revenge nor punishment, seize territory from the defeated nations. Unfortunately, however, Stalin chose to ignore this new code of ethics, and under his guidance the victorious Soviet Union expanded its territories before and after the end of World War Two. Those nations, which became victims of the same "aggression and greed" cited by the Allies as a reason for stripping Japan of territory, amounted to eleven countries. In 1939–45 the USSR annexed Estonia, Latvia, and Lithuania and took territory from Finland, Poland, Germany, Hungary, Czechoslovakia, Romania, Outer Mongolia, and Japan. It obtained in total some 670,000 square kilometers of land in the postwar turmoil, equivalent to the combined area of Great Britain, Italy, and Greece. What I want to emphasize particularly here is that means of solving territorial disputes without resorting to war were already starting to be explored by mankind in the mid-twentieth century.

Modern international political theory sees the solution to territorial issues and conflict in the above-mentioned two ways. Even though times change, for the most part, human thought and ideas remain the same. Our ancestors in both Japan and Russia will have been absorbed—although they did not necessarily clearly appreciate the fact—by the sort of problems and solutions summarized above. Now, sufficiently armed with an awareness of the issues involved, it is time for us to shift our attention to an examination of the actual history of negotiations between Japan and Russia.

MAP 1. Map of Japan.

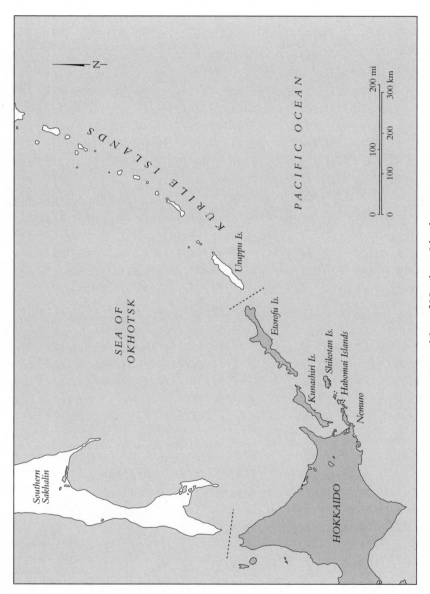

MAP 2. Map of Northern Islands.

CHAPTER 1

Waking Up to the Concept
of National Borders

In the Fog

In the Northern Territories (which the Russians call the Southern Kuriles), mist and fog are indivisible. In protest against the Soviet seizure of the Habomai group of islets, along with the islands of Shikotan, Kunashiri, and Etorofu (hereafter for brevity described as "the four islands") between August 28 and September 5, 1945, that same period is annually designated "Northern Territories Reversion Month," and protest meetings are held in and around Nemuro City in Hokkaido. Ironically, every year about half of those who plan to attend these meetings find themselves foiled because thick fog causes cancellation of flights into Kushiro Airport, forcing them to give up or rush to find ground transport and arrive after the meetings have started.

In fact the Northern Territories, and the Kurile Archipelago stretching north from there, are notorious for thick fogs. These originate in the North Pacific in March and April, and by mid-May have started edging northwest to cover the Kuriles, stubbornly clinging to them through the summer months before eventually dissipating in autumn. July has an average of twenty-five and August normally more than twenty "fog days." This fog, called "gas" by Hokkaido locals, begins to dissipate in September–October, drifting away across the Sea of Okhotsk. It rarely appears from November onward.

Tsarist Russian Captain Vasilii Mikhailovich Golovnin, commander of the sloop-of-war *Diana*, and very familiar with both the Kurile region and the Japanese, wrote in his *Memoirs of Captivity in Japan: 1811–1813*, "All navigators who have sailed in the seas I had to traverse complain of the cloudy weather and excessively thick fogs, which prevented them from approaching the coasts, and consequently from making any observations of them." When in the area in 1810, he wrote, "I was convinced by experience of the truth of the complaint." He later added, "Both on the way there and back we had rough and hazy weather, and the horizon was constantly hidden by heavy clouds. All, therefore, that convinced me that fogs might be considered as proper to that sea . . . and that there was in no season good and clear weather for more than a week together."[1]

A Swedish zoologist, Sten Bergman, who traveled in the vicinity of the four islands in autumn 1922, described in the opening passages of a book "the dense fog unique to the Kuriles" and "the impenetrably thick fog." He wrote, "This must be the thickest fog around any group of islands in the world." He continued:

Those of us on the Ministry of Agriculture and Forestry survey vessel *Hakuho* soon warmed to Captain Yamamoto and his crew. The captain and most of his senior staff spoke excellent English and told us that they have sailed the waters around the Kuriles many times and that this region is known for having the thickest fog of any area in the world, making navigation around the islands an extremely difficult and indeed dangerous task. The cruise schedule is completely determined by the weather, and the largest impediments to traveling in the region are posed by the persistent fog in summer and the blizzard conditions in winter. . . . I awoke at 7 a.m. the next day just as the ship pulled up the anchor. . . . Before long, Nemuro disappeared from sight, and within an hour we were enveloped in a bank of that dense fog unique to the Kuriles.[2]

Now let me explain why I have chosen to open the first chapter of this book with this topic of impenetrable fog around the Kuriles.

Who first discovered the Kurile region and the island of Sakhalin? Who first settled them on a permanent basis? When did they come under a specific nation's sovereignty? All three are reasonable and justifiable questions, and also of immediate relevance in the contemporary context. Today, national boundaries in every corner of the globe are delimited so strictly that mere centimeters of inexactitude are unacceptable. To this day, the sovereignty of the four islands northeast of Hokkaido remains a contentious issue between Japan and Russia. Difficult though it may be to believe, a clear perception of national borders in the Kuriles, Sakhalin, and their surrounding region took root among the peoples of Japan and Russia not much more than one hundred years ago. Until then, however, this region was seen as murky and indistinct, like its interminable fogs.

Because the Northern Territories issue has been the subject of intense political conflict between Japan and tsarist Russia, the Soviet Union, and now the Russian Federation, a mistaken perception has arisen that both countries have been at each other's throats over national borders since the very beginning of their respective histories. This view has come about as a result of seeing the histories of both countries, and of the region itself, in the context of current perception of the problem. If we view this region solely in terms of the modern notion of national borders, and through a "prism of territorial rivalry," we risk seeing only a distorted image.[3]

Professor Toshiyuki Akizuki, formerly of the Law Faculty of Hokkaido University and the most preeminent researcher into early Russo-Japanese relations, considers that the Japanese did not come to consider the notion of national boundaries until the end of the eighteenth century. He wrote, "One would think that by the mid-seventeenth century, when the Tokugawa *Bakufu* (shogunate government) issued the Order for National Seclusion, forbidding both travel to foreign countries by Japanese and the entry to of foreigners to Japan, Japan's national boundaries, surrounded as they were by sea on all sides, must have been clear. However, in actual fact . . . north of Japan, there lay a boundless expanse of land unfettered by national boundaries."[4] Akizuki continued, "Certainly, until the eighteenth century . . . with regard to Yezo (Hokkaido), the Japanese did not have any 'clear perception of their own territorial borders'—and more accurately speaking, it can be presumed they did not even possess the notion of national borders. Yezo, in the broad sense, represented the land where the Ainu lived, the Japanese of the day had only the vaguest knowledge about its expanses, and it is doubtful that they even viewed their own outposts in Yezo as their own country's territory."[5]

The same applies equally to the Russians of the day. Again according to Akizuki, the first wave of fur trappers moving eastward toward Siberia at the end of the sixteenth century had already reached the Pacific seaboard by the mid-seventeenth century, from which time on they would have known of Japan as the "country over the sea." But at this stage, the Russians "would have had only the vaguest perception of the expanse of sea in front of them, knowing nothing of how far it stretched, what countries could be found at its outer limits and who might be living in such lands."[6] The only information the Russians possessed about Japan at this time came from Mercator maps imported from the Netherlands. It was even thought that the "Famous Great Japanese Islands" stretched from the Amur River in the north to the Chinese coastline in the south.[7]

A Western authority on early Russo-Japanese relations, Professor John Stephan of the University of Hawaii, holds the same view as Akizuki: "A Russo-Japanese frontier developed almost imperceptibly over a period of years, during which national boundaries in the modern sense of the word did not exist. Until the nineteenth century, neither Russia nor Japan had a clear conception of how far its sovereignty extended in the Kuriles."[8]

Both countries awoke to the notion of national boundaries as the result of external stimuli.[9] Where there was no contact with the outside world, there was no need to draw clear lines between oneself and others, or between inside and outside, but when broader international forces began to intrude into one's sphere of activity, the notion of adjoining only something out there in the fog no longer sufficed.[10] This created a need to delimit one's own territory and in turn gave birth to the notion of national boundaries. One task involved in deciding the physical extent of national territory was the making of maps, and that necessitated dispatching survey teams and expeditions.

The Birth and Development of Territorial Awareness

The Matsumae clan (*han*), given control over Hokkaido during the shogunate, differentiated between the areas where Japanese (*Wajin*) and Ainu resided, terming the former "Land of Matsumae," and the latter "Land of Yezo." Then, just how far north did the Matsumae clan judge the Land of Yezo to extend?

History has it that in 1599 the first domain chief of the Matsumae clan, Yoshihiro Matsumae, presented to Shogun Ieyasu Tokugawa, as a mark of his fealty, a map titled Matsumae Chizu (Map of Matsumae), featuring Yezo in its entirety. Unfortunately this map has not survived, so how Yezo was depicted is beyond our imagination.[11]

In later years the Matsumae clan frequently submitted maps of the region on orders from the shogunate. The oldest of those was drawn in response to a shogunate directive of 1644 for all clans to contribute to a national project to create a map of the entire country. While this also does not survive, it is represented as part of a later Map of Japan from the Shohō Period.

In 1633, eleven years before submitting this map, the Matsumae clan had surveyed tracks in Yezo in preparation for the first inspection tour by shogunate representatives, and in 1635 clan retainers were dispatched on an "island tour," instructed to create a map of the Land of Yezo. We can safely say that by then preparations for drafting the map ordered by the shogunate in 1644 had already been completed. The Map of Japan from the Shoho Period was judged the most authoritative cartographical depiction of the northern regions at that time, and for many years it, or later revised versions, was used whenever there was need to refer to maps of the Land of Yezo. Later revisions, such as the map the Matsumae clan submitted to the shogunate in 1700, as part of the Genroku National Map, were little changed. The late Shinichiro Takakura (professor emeritus of Hokkaido University and renowned authority on northern region maps) thought the Matsumae map of the Land of Yezo currently in Hakodate Municipal Museum to be closest to the original Map of Japan from the Shoho Period.

In short, as effectively drafted by the sole executive power on Hokkaido, the Matsumae clan, and used in the national map compiled by the shogunate, it is reasonable to assume that the Map of Japan from the Shoho Period was the most authoritative map of that time. Indeed this was the first map drawn by Japanese that included Karafuto and the Kurile Archipelago. This is likely to be the reason why it appears as Item 1 in the Joint Compendium of Documents on the History of the Territorial Demarcation Between Russia and Japan compiled by the Japanese and Russian Ministries of Foreign Affairs. The Joint Compendium is the collaborative work of the Japanese and Russian foreign ministers. It was originally scheduled to be signed by the two countries' leaders during Yeltsin's visit to Tokyo in September 1992, but since Yeltsin did not go to Tokyo at that time, it was simultaneously released by the two governments in September 1992. This compendium originally contained thirty-five documents, then seven more were added. These historical documents were formulated on the basis of mutual agreement between Russia and Japan, and they not only date from the pre-1956 Soviet Union but also from tsarist Russia. English translations of all forty-two documents are found in the Appendix in this book.[12]

However, its historical significance aside, in cartographical terms the Map of Japan from the Shoho Period is extremely inaccurate. Although records state that the cartographers made an "island tour," in fact they did so not by surveying the coastline from points on land, but by sailing around the islands. Places that could not be reached, particularly inland locations, were depicted on the basis of interviews with local Ainu or others familiar with those areas. So, apart from the southern tip of Hokkaido, the Matsumae domain, the map is inaccurate. The area denoted as the Land of Yezo is particularly poorly represented, and Sakhalin is depicted as much smaller than Hokkaido. The Kuriles are drawn not as an Archipelago but as one entity, and although the islands' names are included, depiction of their order and size is random.

The years 1772 to 1786, when Okitsugu Tanuma was a chief senior councilor to the shogunate, may have gone down in history as a period dominated by corruption, but those years were also a time when Japanese awareness of and interest in Russia to the north was refined. Tanuma was a mercantilist who sought to enrich the nation by promoting trade with the outside world. He chanced to be sent a book, *Akayezo fusetsu ko* (1783; A study of Red-Yezo [i.e., Russian] reports) by Heisuke Kudo, a court physician from Sendai Domain and medical practitioner in Edo. Kudo's book was based on information acquired from Genzaemon Minato, former superintendent of Matsumae clan finances, about the arrival of Russians in the Land of Yezo and knowledge of Russia that the renowned interpreter of Dutch, Kogyu Yoshio, had gleaned from Dutch books. It represented the first Japanese book about Russians, called "red people" because they arrived in the Land of Yezo in scarlet clothing.

One background factor behind Kudo's writing this book was a letter sent in 1771 to the officers-in-chief of the Factory of the Dutch East India Company (*opperhoofd*) in Nagasaki by Hungarian Baron Mauritius von Benyowsky, warning that the Russians were preparing to seize the islands close to the Land of Yezo.[13] The content of this letter was clearly false, as at that stage the Russians had neither capability nor intention to invade Japanese territory, but the Dutch in Nagasaki may have used it in an attempt to deter the Japanese from entering into a trading relationship with Russia, and Kudo in fact suggested in his book that this was their motivation.[14] He argued that on the contrary, by actively seeking to enter into trade with Russia, the Japanese would develop an understanding of it, thus enabling them to put in place appropriate policies for dealing with encroachment from the north. This suggestion struck a chord with Tanuma's mercantile thinking.

Shihei Hayashi of the same Sendai clan as Kudo wrote both the Illustrated Survey of Three Countries (1785) and *Kaikoku Heidan* (Military discussion for a maritime nation) (1787–91), not only proposing that Japan acquire the Land of Yezo before Russia, but also vigorously advocating a strong naval defense. In 1785 Hayashi compiled the Map of the Island of Yezo, which Professor Takakura describes as "a blend of old Japanese and new Western-made maps"—a combination of traditional Japanese cartographic skills with European geographical and other information imported via China.

It was during the Tanuma years that the first Japanese explorers were dispatched to Yezo. The most famous member of these expeditions was Tokunai Mogami, protégé of the Edo-period political economist Toshiaki Honda. Mogami surveyed Kunashiri, Etorofu, and Uruppu before creating A Map of All the Islands of Yezo (1790). This map gives the Russian names of islands in the Kurile chain, learned through direct contact with Russians there. This map was far superior to any Western or Russian map of the area at that time, and it gave a generally accurate representation of Japan's northern regions. However, with Tanuma's downfall and replacement by Sadanobu Matsudaira in 1786, the shogunate's attention moved for the time being to domestic affairs, interest in the northern regions faded for a while, and further expeditions to the Land of Yezo were cancelled.

Russian Interest in the Kuriles

What about Russia? Russia's interest in its eastern regions began in the reign of Peter the Great (1682–1725). By the mid-seventeenth century Russia already knew of Japan's existence from Dutch maps, and its interest deepened when firsthand information began to come from Japanese castaways.

There are three main reasons why castaways were so common during the Edo period. Firstly, in keeping with the policy of national seclusion, regulations forbade building large ships capable of sailing outside Japanese waters. This meant that if Japanese vessels suffered broken rudders in storms, their masts would fall, and they would drift at the mercy of the currents. Secondly, with the remarkable expansion in domestic commerce this age saw a sudden increase in sea-borne freight. Thirdly, if Japanese ships sailing with that season's rice harvest experienced the strong northwesterly winds common in early winter, they would often be blown far off course into the Pacific.[15] Some of them were carried north by the Kuroshio current, their crews castaway on the Kamchatka Peninsula or Aleutian or Kurile Islands, and the survivors rescued by local Russians.

The first Japanese castaway to meet with Russians was an Osaka merchant's clerk named "Denbei," found in 1698 by the Cossack commander Vladimir Atlasov, otherwise known as the "Conqueror of Kamchatka," and taken to Moscow, where he was presented to Peter the Great.[16] The tsar had heard about Japan from Dutch sources and showed great interest in Denbei.[17] The second castaway was a man called "Sanima" (Sanaemon), washed ashore on Kamchatka in 1710. He in turn provided the local Cossacks with information about Japan.[18] The next were two men, "Sōza" and "Gonza," rescued from a Satsuma ship wrecked near Cape Lopatka in Kamchatka, and taken to St. Petersburg for an audience with Empress Anna Ivanovna (1730–40).[19] From that time on, Japanese castaways were relatively common, the most famous of them being Kōdayū Daikokuya (set sail in 1783, shipwrecked and returned to Japan in 1792).[20] The information gained from such castaways not only deepened Russian interest in Japan and the region in general but also strengthened desires to enter into trade with it.

The tsarist Russian flag's double-headed eagle symbolized Russia as a Eurasian nation, standing astride Europe and Asia, with a foreign policy looking both east and west. While Peter the Great established his new capital St. Petersburg, at the mouth of the River Neva, as a "window on Europe," he was also greatly interested in the East. He was particularly excited by reports from Atlasov about fur trapping in Kamchatka and by Denbei's grandiose descriptions of Japan. In 1702 he ordered the conquest of Kamchatka and the gathering of information that might be useful in preparing to initiate trade and commerce with Japan. Exemplifying his avid interest in the region, a series of expeditions went to the Kurile Archipelago, and by the mid-eighteenth century the chain of islands had literally come to be seen as a set of "stepping stones to Japan."[21]

The first serious expeditions to the Kuriles were launched in 1771, and one of the key figures in organizing them was the Kamchatka Cossack Ivan P. Kozyrevskii. He crossed to Shumshu, the northernmost island in the Kuriles, then to Paramushir, where he gained information about the remaining islands from Ainu from the Southern Kuriles. This was without doubt a great achievement; for many years after that, even into the late 1830s, Russia's southward advance was limited to a few of the northern islands of the chain, and their knowledge of the rest of the archipelago was limited to what was known from Kozyrevskii's reports. The information he gathered was extremely accurate in many respects. The Complete Map as Far as Matsumae Island that he submitted in 1713 was the first non-Japanese map of the full Kurile chain. It was subsequently referred to in composition of many eighteenth-century Russian and European maps, but unfortunately no longer exists.

By talking to Kurile Ainu, Kozyrevskii acquired information about the main Kurile Islands as far south as Matsumae Island (Hokkaido). For example, he describes Etorofu Island thus:

It is a large island with a substantial population. The inhabitants are known as Cych-Kuril by those living in the more northern islands mentioned earlier. This is the same as what the Japanese call "Ezo." Their language and customs are different from those of the people in the Northern Kurile Islands, and they shave their heads and sit down to make greetings. There is deep forest on the island, giving home to all sorts of wild animals, in particular a large number of bears. In some places, there are river mouths that provide safe anchorage for large vessels. This is particularly noteworthy, as the northernmost islands have little forest and few places appropriate for large vessels to drop anchor.[22]

An extract from Kozyrevskii's description of Kunashiri is included as Item 2 in the Joint Compendium. The Russian Foreign Ministry probably insisted on its inclusion, as the earliest description of a Northern Territories island by a Russian. His description is as follows:

It is inhabited by the same foreigners as Iturup and Urup; the same religion is observed there; I did not find out whether they speak the same language or have their own; they travel to the island of Matsumae, on which the castle of Matsumae is located, and people from the island of Matsumae come to Kunashir every year to trade their goods. This island is larger than Iturup and Urup and more populous. I did not find out whether the inhabitants of Kunashir are subjects of Matsumae or not. But, the inhabitants of Iturup and Urup are living their own lives, not subject to anyone, and engage in free trade.[23]

Professor Stephan indicates that there are two conflicting schools of thought on the circumstances surrounding Kozyrevskii's expedition and subsequent evaluation. The first, more traditional view sees the Cossacks led by Ivan Kozyrevskii and Danila Antsiferov as unscrupulous rogues, trying to "atone" for their involvement in the murder of three Kamchatka leaders, including Atlasov, by crushing the "treacherous" aboriginals. The second view, espoused mainly by Soviet-era historians, is that these explorers were implementing orders from the Governor of Yakutsk—originating from the tsar himself—and should therefore be hailed as heroically playing a part in Peter the Great's grand geopolitical strategy. Professor Stephan concludes that both interpretations contain elements of truth. Directives from the tsar certainly would have existed. However, while Peter the Great was interested in the

East, the reality was surely that Kamchatka and the Kuriles were too far from Moscow and St. Petersburg to rate highly in his mind. Therefore it is wrong to see the Russian eastward advance extending down through the Kuriles as an orchestrated part of a centrally planned grand design. Kozyrevskii and Antsiferov were motivated to undertake a dangerous mission by feelings stronger than mere patriotic fervor. Their instinct for survival could well prompt them to seek a feat remarkable enough to annul the horrible punishment awaiting them for murdering their superiors.[24]

Whatever their motives, the Cossacks' expedition was the first to shed light on this previously unknown world. Encouraged by Kozyrevskii's reports, Peter the Great dispatched an expedition under navigator-geodesists Ivan Evreinov and Fedor Luzhin to survey the Okhotsk region (1721).[25] Their objective was ostensibly to ascertain whether the American and Asian continents were separate or connected. But it is also suggested that their real aim was to find out how advanced Japanese mining (gold, silver and copper, and so on) was in the Kuriles, and to gather information about possibilities for commencing trade with Japan. When the long Northern War with Sweden (1700–21) ended, Peter again acquired some leeway to further the eastern advance. Before he died in 1725, he commissioned an expedition under Captain Vitus Bering, a Dane serving in the Russian Navy.[26] Peter's wife and successor, Catherine I, confirmed his decision, and Bering proved the existence of the passage between Asia and America later named the Bering Strait. From 1739 to 1742 one of his lieutenants, another Dane, Captain Martin Spanberg, and the British mariner William Walton, sailed to the Kuriles and Japan.[27]

The Roots of Russian-Style Expansionism

Russia's geographical environment has at least the following features. Firstly, it is not surrounded by ideal natural barriers (sea, large rivers, or mountain ranges). Secondly, being mostly in the higher northern latitudes, it has severe climatic conditions, with long winters and great snowfalls. Thirdly, most of its land is not suited to agriculture.

Such a harsh natural environment cannot adequately support large concentrations of population. As a result, in order to achieve even the slightest improvement in their living environment, Russian people are prepared to move to the periphery of as yet undeveloped areas. In particular, they are subject to a strong impulse to migrate southward to lands with warmer climates.

Such latent urges are brought to the surface by the anarchistic temperament of the Russian people. Russians are strong-willed people who detest being subject to political authority, preferring instead to free themselves from it by migrating to remote areas where there is little or no regulation by the authorities. One of the roots of Russian colonial expansion can be found in this aspect of the Russian psyche. British historian Bernard Pares wrote, "The Russian enjoys space, and what he likes before all things is elbow room—elbow room, brotherhood with his fellowman, but without compulsion, which he is always seeking to avoid. Russian life is fluid—that is how, quite apart from government action, it has come to spread itself over so great a part of the world. The Russian was always a born wanderer."[28]

Sooner or later authority catches up with, and penetrates into, what the Russians had thought to be their land of freedom. This is just a matter of time, an inevitable development from which there is no escape. Nevertheless, when this happens, Russians again look to flee, moving in search of an area subject to a lesser degree of governmental constraint. As this cycle repeats, the territory of the Russian state naturally expands. The land settled and cultivated thanks to the toil of guileless citizens falls under the political and military authority of the state that simply followed afterward. The government, at least sometimes, deliberately used this to its advantage. For example, when Nicolas II was told that many Russian peasants were ignoring laws governing residency and secretly looking for "good land" to which the entire village could be relocated, the minister for the interior advised him that the wisest approach would be to encourage this movement, rather than repress it.

Of course there were also colonial and territorial expansionist policies that the state actively pursued, and even in such cases normal citizens were frequently used as the advance guard. That is to say, first of all a handful of pioneers and settlers were dispatched to the area in question. It goes without saying that these people were required to pay tax. After a while, on the pretext that these settlers had asked for protection, the government would send in the military, thereby cementing its control of the region. In the end, the land would be incorporated into imperial Russian territory.

At least to outsiders, this approach appeared as though the Russian people and state were effectively colluding or acting as one in this campaign of territorial expansion. Be that as it may, territorial expansion through colonization is a consistent theme in the history of Russia. In the opening section of his *A History of Russia*, one of Russia's greatest historians, Vasilii Kliuchevskii, clearly stated that "the history of Russia is the history of a country forever undergoing colonization. The principal, fundamental factor in Russian history has been migration or colonization."[29]

This more or less applies to the advance into Siberia and the Far East. Spurred by the prospect of wealth from trade in sable, fox, otter, and fur seal pelts, the Cossacks pushed ever eastward along rivers, through the taiga, across the tundra and steppes of Siberia, until they eventually reached the Sea of Okhotsk, the Arctic and Pacific Oceans. Wherever possible they traded with the indigenous people they came across along the way, such as the Ainu. Although Russian state authority offered the fur traders protection, it also required them to collect *iasak*, or pelt-tax, from the locals, and in this respect, "the fur trade was synonymous with the conquest of Siberia."[30]

Russian Approaches to Japan

In the former Soviet Union, there was a popular joke to the effect that "communism is like the horizon. However close you might think you are getting, you cannot reach it." For Russia, during the two hundred and more years spanning the seventeenth to nineteenth centuries, Japan seemed to be never any closer than the horizon. Just when Russians thought they had managed to get a little closer to Japan, she again seemed to drift away toward the horizon. Indeed the renowned Soviet Japanologist S. Znamenskii went one step further, likening Japan not to the horizon, but to a mirage. In his book *In Search of Japan*, published in 1929, he wrote, "For a long time, for Russia Japan was like a mirage that would fade away when approached."[31] To summarize what I have written so far, let us borrow a little more of Znamenskii's poetic figuration from his description:

Across the sea from his vantage point at the southern tip of Kamchatka, the land he had conquered, Atlasov could make out something that looked like land. Thanks to the reports of Atlasov and Denbei this mirage had taken on a form clearly identifying it as Japan, and by this stage it was even visible from Moscow. Plans were now afoot to make approaches to this land. But when Kozyrevskii and his party set foot on the first island of the Kurile chain (Shumshu) they found that this was not Japan after all, and that the mirage had drifted on to the second island. When Kozyrevskii took one step further, onto that second island (Paramushir), he found that the image of Japan had again moved off into the distance, somewhere at the end of this chain of islands. Spanberg finally transformed the mirage into reality by reaching the shores of Japan and seeing real Japanese people, but two years later, when he again tried to return to those shores, he was unsuccessful, and Japan again disappeared into the Pacific Ocean, once more becoming a mirage in people's minds. The only thing that reminded Russians that Japan did exist was the fact that, as had been the case from earlier times, Japanese ships would occasionally be wrecked on the Russian coast after being carried by the currents from somewhere on the other side of the mist.[32]

While Peter the Great was interested in Asia, the Russian Far East, and Japan, he was so preoccupied with wars being fought to the north, west, and south that he died before he could effectively turn his attention eastward. Subsequent Russian emperors and empresses shared Peter's interest and in particular, as though impelled to honor his wishes, Empress Catherine II (1729–96) attempted to make approaches to Japan. For Russian merchants and for the state itself, Japan represented a potential market for furs, a route from Siberia across the Pacific to North America, a source of food and other supplies, and a place for Russian seafarers to rest before setting sail again. Therefore opening the door to Japan became a target of great importance. Nevertheless, during her reign Catherine II was preoccupied with wars against European powers such as Turkey, Poland, and Sweden, as well as internal problems such as the Pugachov Rebellion. As a result, she was unable to de-vote her full attention to establishing relations with Japan. In other words, with the empress, as with Peter, there was again clearly a gap between inten-tions and reality.

The "Instruction from the Collegium of the Admiralty to Grigorii I. Mulovskii" (1787), Item 3 of the Joint Compendium, can be said to repre-sent a good example of intentions not translated into action. This "Instruc-tion" ordered Captain Mulovskii to organize an expedition to undertake Russia's first circumnavigation of the globe. It specifically states that he should "sail around and describe all the small and large Kurile Islands from Japan to Cape Lopatka of the Kamchatka Peninsula, identify them on the map as precisely as possible, and formally include all the islands from the is-land of Matsumae to Cape Lopatka under the possession of the Russian state." In other words he was instructed to claim not just the Kurile Archi-pelago but also Hokkaido as Russian territory, and such was obviously be-yond his capabilities.

It is very difficult to understand why the Russian Ministry of Foreign Affairs insisted on including this document in the Joint Compendium. Firstly, it was no more than a statement of intent and was never put into ac-tion. In other words, as Catherine II was obliged to focus her attention on Russia's wars against Turkey and Sweden, the expedition never materialized. As S. Znamenskii describes it, "Plans were made for circumnavigation of the world by an expedition to be led by Mulovskii, which would have included surveys of the southern areas of the Sea of Okhotsk, as well as attempts to establish relations with Japan. By the end of 1787 preparation for the expe-dition was almost complete, but in the end the plan was cancelled because of the wars with Sweden and Turkey."[33]

Secondly, if that was indeed the plan, recording that the tsarist government intended to include Hokkaido in the Russian domain would serve as proof of Russian expansionist ambitions at that time. This surely would not be de-sirable for Russia, as it immediately reminds us of Benyowsky's letter of 1771 to the officers-in-chief of the Dutch factory in Dejima, warning that the Russians were preparing to seize the islands near Yezo. The existence of this "Instruction" therefore suggests that we cannot discount the warnings in that letter or from Dutch sources as completely unwarranted. At risk of repeating myself, I find it puzzling as to what the Russian Ministry of Foreign Affairs intended by including a document of this nature in the Joint Compendium.

My third point is that even if Catherine II had been able to secure the Kurile Islands as Russian territory, evidence exists suggesting that she did not think it possible to control and administer them. For example, an Imperial Edict she sent to the governor of Irkutsk in 1779 contained the following decision on the Kuriles: "With regard to difficulties encountered in exercising control over the newly conquered lands and abuses, the hairy Kurillians subjugated are to be left free, and no collection of any kind of taxes shall be demanded of them."[34]

It is noteworthy that an almost contractual arrangement was thought to exist, whereby *iasak* (pelt-tax) was accepted in return for the grant of protection. In other words, Catherine's edict suggests that even if the Kurile Archipelago were brought under Russian control, the residents could not realistically be offered any protection, so attempts to claim control over them should be abandoned. In his book *Kuriles* (1871), Russian historian A. Polonskii explained, "As Catherine II desired that commercial relations with the Japanese would continue indefinitely, in general she permitted free trade and looked to encourage friendship and avoid acts of needless violence which might anger the Japanese."[35] Znamenskii added, "At that time, the people in the center had little enthusiasm for imperialist ventures in the Far East because they were exclusively absorbed by huge imperialistic aspirations in the West."[36]

"Shock Therapy"

Let us turn our attention back to the Japanese side. When Sadanobu Matsudaira replaced Okitsugu Tanuma (1787), he assumed the task of cleansing the nation's political scene. As the shogunate became preoccupied with internal matters, further expeditions to the Land of Yezo were cancelled. However, this was destined to be little more than a temporary interruption in Japan's interest in the north. That is to say, the Russians showed no signs of reducing their interest in Japan, or of relenting from knocking on Japan's door.

In 1792, making use of a lull in the European wars, Empress Catherine II moved to seek trade relations with Japan actively, by dispatching what can be seen as the first official delegation to Japan. The appearance of Kōdayû Daikokuya in St. Petersburg provided the stimulus, and indeed the pretext, for Catherine the Great to seek contact with Japan. Kōdayû was a ship's captain who had sailed from Ise Province (now Mie Prefecture) in 1782 with the freighter *Shinshō maru*, only to be blown off course and castaway on Amchitka Island in the Aleutians, whence he was transported to St. Petersburg for an audience with the empress. After ten years of hardship in Russia, he was taken back to his homeland by a delegation headed by Adam Laxman, whose real intentions involved more long-term goals than the mere repatriation of a castaway. Laxman's ship, the *Ekaterina*, arrived in Akkeshi, Hokkaido, in 1792. The shogunate's chief senior councilor of the day, Sadanobu Matsudaira, applied the law that trade and commercial relations with the outside world were permitted only in Nagasaki, and he sent Laxman and his delegation on their way with nothing to show but a permit to enter that port. After this, the Russian government again became engrossed in internal matters and diplomatic wranglings within Europe, and so lost the leeway to dispatch further official delegations to Japan.

However, ten years later, in 1803, Emperor Alexander I entrusted Nikolai Rezanov, son-in-law of fur-trader Gregorii Shelikhov, and a director of the Russian-American Company, to lead an expedition to Japan. His diplomatic mission traveled on board the vessel *Nadezhda* (Hope), captained by a naval officer, Ivan Krusenstern. As Rezanov carried imperial credentials from Alexander I, it can be said that his was the first official diplomatic mission sent to Japan. The *Nadezhda* entered Nagasaki in 1804, but after waiting for six months Rezanov was obliged to leave empty-handed. By this stage, the shogunate attitude toward foreign approaches was unbending. Not only did the delegation find it difficult to gain permission to go ashore, but when they were granted a permit to leave the ship for health reasons, they were permitted to go no farther than the building allocated to them in Kibachiura. The reception the shogunate afforded the Russian delegation was not only rude, it lacked the courtesy Rezanov would expect to be shown to official representatives of another nation.

To add insult to injury, their diplomatic overtures were rejected. They had been under the impression that if they followed the shogunate's instructions and made their way to Nagasaki, their wishes would be met. Instead, they found to their dismay that Japan's stance on national seclusion had hardened rather than eased. Rezanov was incensed by the discourteous treatment and rejection of his approaches regarding trade so that his feelings of humiliation and indignation against the shogunate made him think of "revenge" and "scaring the Japanese a little" (Anton Chekhov).[37] Force, it seemed, was the only means left to bring Japan around. He wrote a letter to that effect to Emperor Alexander I, and before there was time for any reply to arrive, he ordered his subordinates, Lieutenants Nikolai Khvostov and Gavriil Davydov, to launch attacks on Japanese settlements in Sakhalin and the Kuriles. In other words, retribution for what had happened in Nagasaki was to be exacted on inhabitants of Sakhalin and the Kuriles.[38] In 1806 these two young naval officers led raiding parties that struck at the Japanese settlement of Kushunkotan in Southern Sakhalin. The following year they made repeated attacks on the village of Naibo and the garrison at Shana on Etorofu, plundering and burning these Japanese settlements.[39]

Khvostov's and Davydov's attacks on Sakhalin and the Kuriles had a significant impact on Japan. The exact extent to which these Russian officers' piratical acts were carried out on orders from Rezanov is unknown. Another point shrouded in uncertainty is the connection between Rezanov's intent in using force and the tsarist government's stance. It is highly unlikely that Alexander I gave any orders sanctioning these acts of violence, and had Khvostov's and Davydov's plans been known beforehand, they would probably not have been approved. Therefore, it may be mistaken to seek to implicate the Russian government in this use of force against Japan. Perhaps these violent incidents should be seen as no more than one aspect of an unfortunate episode in the two countries' history.

As it happens, putting aside the issue of responsibility for the moment, we can safely say that the impact of the "Russophobia" these attacks implanted in the psyche of the insular Japanese of the day was of momentous proportions. Up to that time Japanese had referred to Russians as *Aka-hito* (red people), possibly because some had red hair, or because many wore scarlet cloaks. Be that as it may, after the attacks some Japanese began to call the Russians *aka-oni* (red devils).[40]

According to the late Professor Hayao Shimizu of Tokyo University of Foreign Studies, the Khvostov-Davydov incident resulted in an "awareness that Russia (or the Soviet Union) is an undetachable element in any consideration of Japanese national security" and that the attacks represent the first experience of what would go on to form what Shimizu called Japan's "Russia-complex."[41] This might be a slightly overstated assessment, but it is the only flaw in his book, which is otherwise an invaluable treatise on the history of Russo-Japanese negotiations. Making allowances for that point, Shimizu's work is still extremely significant, as the general principles and truths it alludes to are manifested in negotiations and international relations. In other words, Shimizu writes that in order to achieve our goals, humans—or groups of humans represented by states—will at first approach the other party for talks in a peaceful manner, but when this does not produce the desired results, they are prone to become impatient and resort to use of force to resolve the matter. In such cases, the use of force will actually have the opposite effect and serve to thwart the original objective. Only on rare occasions will it act as shock therapy.

During the period between Laxman's and Rezanov's visits, the Russians' attitude toward Japan in negotiations about the opening of trade was courteous and gentlemanly in every way, leaving no room for criticism. In response, the shogunate's representatives vacillated, prevaricated, and played for time, in the end turning the delegations away in a manner that could only harm Russian national pride. That being so, Rezanov sought to rectify his failure in the negotiations by resorting to force. Those members of the shogunate who favored opening the country to the outside world indicated some degree of understanding toward Rezanov's actions.[42] "By Word and By Sword" is the title the late Professor George Lensen chose for chapter 5 of his classic work, *The Russian Push Toward Japan* (1959).[43] As his choice of words suggests, during the period in question Russia was persistent in its attempts to pry open Japan's door, using both methods—negotiations and force.

In the context of our interest in Russo-Japanese territorial disputes, Khvostov's and Davydov's attacks in 1806 and 1807 highlight one more important factor. In those days Japanese were already living on Etorofu and Kunashiri, islands now referred to as part of the "Northern Territories," as well as, of course, on Sakhalin. It is a fact that since 1799 the shogunate had already stationed five hundred clansmen each from the Tsugaru and Nanbu domains on Etorofu and Kunashiri as frontier garrisons. According to Lensen, "Etorofu had been a Japanese colony for over a decade. It boasted a population of over a thousand Ainu and a garrison of over three hundred Japanese of the Nambu and Tsugaru domains."[44] Item 4 in the Joint Compendium confirms this.

As well as immediately heightening Japanese wariness toward Russia, the attacks on Sakhalin and the Kuriles served to alert Japan to the need to defend her northern frontiers. In 1798, against a backdrop of this increased wariness, Jūzō Kondō joined an expedition assembled to explore and survey Japan's northern frontier region and together with Tokunai Mogami visited Kunashiri before crossing to Etorofu. There they erected a post with the inscription, "Dai Nippon Etorofu" (Etorofu of Great Japan), proclaiming the island Japanese territory. In 1800, Kondō commissioned Kahei Takadaya, a trader with a thriving shipping business servicing the routes between the Yezo region and Honshu, to survey the sea route to Etorofu. Takadaya subsequently established a total of seventeen fishing grounds around that island. The shogunate came to realize that the administration of the Land of Yezo and policy toward Russia could no longer just be left to the Matsumae clan alone, and from 1799 to 1804 he took steps to see the region placed under the central government's direct control.

Furthermore, mindful of the need to clarify Japan's sphere of influence in the region, particularly in respect of the interior of Sakhalin, the shogunate ordered Denjūrō Matsuda and Rinzō Mamiya to explore Sakhalin. In 1809 Mamiya discovered that it was an island separated from the continent by a strait, a full forty years before the Russian explorer Gennadii I. Nevelskoi made the same observation in 1849.

A number of years passed before Japan had the opportunity to exact retribution for Khvostov's and Davydov's attacks. In 1811, when Vasilii Golovnin—commander of the sloop-of-war *Diana* and leader of a Russian expedition commissioned to conduct the first general scientific survey of the entire Kurile chain—came ashore on Kunashiri, as though stepping into a trap he was seized by clansmen of the Nanbu garrison. With his seven subordinates Golovnin was held captive for two years and three months. This was the nadir in relations between Russia and Japan. Fortunately, however, Golovnin's lieutenant, Peter Ricord, was an officer of great perspicacity. With the cooperation of the Hakodate merchant Kahei Takadaya, who had been seized by a Russian ship in 1812 in retaliation for Golovnin's detention, Ricord presented evidence to the shogunate that the Khvostov-Davydov attacks in no way reflected the will of the Russian government and eventually succeeded in securing the exchange of Takadaya for Golovnin and his survey team. After his return to Russia, Golovnin's work, *Memoirs of Vasilii Mikhailovich Golovnin, who was prisoner of the Japanese in 1811, 1812, 1813*, became a bestseller and represents a classic ethnographic study of the Japanese people.

The Golovnin incident is significant in at least two ways. First, it indicated the importance of assuming a calm but determined approach to talks as peaceful means of solving disputes. The attitudes adopted by Golovnin, Ricord, Kahei Takadaya, and others directly involved in this incident were wise, composed, and astute, particularly in the trust and courtesy each party displayed toward the other. This attitude could even be used as a model for negotiating behavior these days. For example, what would have happened had Golovnin died in captivity at Matsumae, either at the hands of his Japanese jailers, or through illness? Founding his argument on such a worst-case scenario, Lensen saw Golovnin's captivity as an important milestone in Russo-Japanese relations.[45] Certainly had Golovnin died in captivity, whatever the cause, Russo-Japanese relations would have taken a turn for the worse.[46] Russia would not only have been provided with an excuse for assuming a harder, more antagonistic attitude toward Japan but also would have been tempted to react accordingly. Golovnin's amicable release, by contrast, improved relations between the two countries.[47]

Lensen paid particular tribute to the composed and astute Japanese judgment. Golovnin's interrogators and interpreters could have easily compromised their Russian captives in the circumstances of the day. But to the contrary, Golovnin's captors did their best to help the Russians. For example, when interpreter Teisuke Murakami found a note in Golovnin's pocket that included disparaging comments about Japan, he omitted those remarks from his translation and instead expanded the portion emphasizing that Khvostov's and Davydov's attacks did not have the tsar's approval.[48] This may be only one example, but Golovnin's diary also contains entries, such as "the Japanese are kind, generous and peace-loving,"[49] that suggest he could not hide his feelings of goodwill toward the Japanese.

The second significance of the Golovnin incident is that it highlighted the vagueness of the national boundary between Russia and Japan. It served as a painful lesson that to prevent a recurrence, the border between the two nations must be clearly delimited.

CHAPTER 2

Black Ships from the North

The Period of Preparation for Territorial Demarcation

On the surface, the forty-year period between Golovnin's release in 1813 and Putiatin's arrival to Nagasaki in 1853 was relatively calm. While both Russia and Japan continued to maintain high levels of mutual interest, they were basically preoccupied with other matters. This in itself allows us to identify another aspect of Russo-Japanese relations that has continued to the present day: neither country has necessarily given priority to their mutual relations, and each has tended to pay attention to the other only when diplomatic developments with other powerful nations have permitted. After all, diplomatic affairs are not necessarily prioritized according to primary and secondary considerations, and where possible diplomacy is practiced on a concurrent and parallel basis. With this in mind, it might be more advisable for us to see these forty years as a period of skillful behind-the-scenes maneuvering in preparation for the next major development. Perceptively turning his attention to this, Professor Stephan remarked that these four decades were "deceptively quiescent."[1]

Be that as it may, in the West Russia dissipated her energies first in the war against Napoleon (1812–14) and forty years later was obliged to turn her attention to war in the Crimea (1853–56) against the Ottoman Empire and its allies, Great Britain and France. During that period, the course of the Russian–American Company's growing activities bypassed Japan and headed toward Hawaii, Alaska, and California. For Japan too, with the Russian menace temporarily allayed, and the Nanbu and Tsugaru clans both appealing that the financial burden of maintaining troops in the Land of Yezo was exhausting their resources, the shogunate in 1814 withdrew its garrisons from all areas outside Matsumae and Hakodate, later, in 1821, abolishing direct rule of Yezo, and returning administrative control to the Matsumae clan.

Khvostov's and Davydov's raids and Golovnin's incarceration highlighted the necessity to decide the border between Japan and Russia. In fact, that was among the main reasons why Golovnin had been sent to Japan. On his return to his homeland, Golovnin proposed the border be set between Uruppu and Etorofu, and gradually this idea became widely accepted in Russia. For example, in 1813 the governor of Irkutsk, Nikolai Treskin, wrote to the governor of the Matsumae clan, proposing that Uruppu become a neutral commercial center between Russia and Japan. Although the shogunate showed no inclination whatsoever toward wanting to enter into trade with Russia, it welcomed the fact that the proposal was based on the premise that both Etorofu and Kunashiri were Japanese territories. In 1814 it was decided by the shogunate that Uruppu would be a neutral zone, with the islands south of and including Etorofu Japanese, and those north of and including Simushir, Russian:[2] "With regard to the establishment of a national boundary, both Japan and Russia agree that Japanese territory shall be deemed to be the islands as far as, and including, the island of Etorofu, and Russian territory as far as the island of Simushir. Neither Japan nor Russia shall build dwellings on those islands between these two [Uruppu, Chirpoi, Makanruru]. Inform them that if Russia encroaches upon Etorofu, Japan will take action to repel them."[3]

However, in 1813, 1814, and 1816, thick fog and other bad weather prevented envoys sent by the shogunate from conveying its intention to the Russians. Similarly, Russian vessels dispatched to receive the Japanese response managed to reach Etorofu, but were unable to contact their Japanese counterparts. Although they were unable to manage a rendezvous, we should note that both countries intended to acknowledge that the islands from Etorofu (inclusive) south were Japanese territory, and that formal agreement on this point was in train.[4]

It is also important to remember that Governor Treskin saw matters the same way. In 1814, after questioning Golovnin and Ricord about the border issue and Russo-Japanese relations in general, Treskin wrote an eight-point report to the governor-general of Siberia, Ivan Pestel, proposing specific policy lines toward Japan. His sixth point stated that the channel between Uruppu and Etorofu was the natural boundary between Russia and Japan. The specific wording was:

Six: Regarding what is proposed as the border between Russia and Japan. Golovnin has confirmed that the Japanese government sees the natural border with our side as being between the 18th island of Uruppu from where Russian territory extends northwards, and the natural border with Japan as the 19th island of Etorofu which is inhabited by Japanese. In the current circumstances, it would be counterproductive to seek to expand the Russian border further beyond this point, and there is no reason to demand that the Japanese allow expansion of the Russian border.[5]

The late Professor Yoshimitsu Kōriyama of Kagoshima University commented thus on the significance of this sixth point: "This represents the opinion of Governor Treskin in his position as the highest ranking official of the day in the Russian Far East. . . . This established fact became the officially accepted Russian position." In other words: "While no treaty had been concluded between Japan and Russia, the natural limits of each country's authority meant that Russian territory came to be seen as those Kurile Islands north of, and including Uruppu, with those south of there being Japanese."[6] Professor Toshiyuki Akizuki of Hokkaido University also concluded, "It is certain the Siberian authorities of the day acknowledged that the islands south of and including Etorofu were Japanese territory."[7]

Around the time Japanese and Russian attention toward the Kuriles temporarily waned, the United States and Britain, motivated by the thought of profit through whaling and otter pelts, the need for ports in which to restock, and the desire to establish commercial relations with Japan, began to encroach on the islands from the Pacific. Surprised by these developments, Russia reacted by claiming nearly the entire North Pacific Rim coast of North America as the monopolistic preserve of the Russian-American Company and declaring it off limits to foreign vessels. In order to establish this exclusion-zone Russia needed to clarify the extent of her own territory. This led to the issuing, on September 4, 1821, of an *ukaz* (Imperial Decree) by Tsar Alexander I, which is Item 5 in the Joint Compendium. Paragraph 2 of the Second Special Directive issued to the Russian-American Company on September 13, 1821, has exactly the same content.[8]

In attempts to justify Russian claims to the entire chain of islands, Russian academics in Soviet days often quoted these decrees.[9] However, upon closer examination of the original texts, it is quite obvious that both decrees limit the area in question to "the Kurile Islands, *that is [to est'*: Russian] the islands extending from the Bering Straits down to the southern cape of the island of Uruppu, that is as far as latitude 45 degrees 50 minutes North" (italics added).[10] Alexander's decrees are in keeping with Treskin's proposals of 1813 and 1814, and in specifying only the islands from Urup northward as subject to Russian protection, exclude Etorofu and Kunashiri from Russian territory. The Russian government of the day was well aware that Japan had not only set fishing grounds around Etorofu, but had also established an administrative presence there. Akizuki thus wrote that "without exception" Russian and Japanese materials originating from the early years of the nineteenth century acknowledge that the actual border between the two countries fell between Uruppu and Etorofu.[11]

Tsar Alexander I's decrees are also significant as Russian official documents that interpret the Kurile Islands as those north of, and including, Uruppu. This is indeed important for interpreting the extent of the "Kurile Islands" with regard to the Treaty of Shimoda of 1855, the Sakhalin-Kurile Islands Exchange of 1875, and the San Francisco Peace Treaty of 1951. Professor Stephan draws the following thoroughly logical conclusion from this: "Far from confirming Soviet claims, Alexander's decree indirectly supports Japan's rights in the southern Kuriles."[12] In what is probably the best recent example of a Japanese work covering the history of "Russo-Japanese relations in the Bakumatsu Period," Professor Kōriyama judged it entirely appropriate to interpret Alexander I's ukaz of 1821 as signifying the establishment of the border between Russia and Japan. He even went so far as to suggest that the Treaty of Shimoda, concluded thirty-four years later, represents no more than Russian confirmation of this to Japan. He stated:

In Japan it is generally considered that the border between Russia and Japan was established with the Treaty of Shimoda in 1855, but as many as thirty-four years before that, Russia had, by means of internationally proclaimed Imperial decrees, announced that the southern boundary of her territory was the island of Uruppu. While this was well known in the West, the shogunate was completely unaware of this, and predictably it served to complicate the negotiations with Putiatin carried out from 1853 through to 1855.[13]

The preface to the Joint Compendium indicates exactly the same position as Professor Kōriyama. It says, "By the middle of the nineteenth century, a Japanese-Russian border emerged between the islands of Etorofu and Uruppu. This frontier was *legally* [*iuridicheski*] established by the Treaty of Commerce, Navigation, and Delimitation Between Japan and Russia of February 7, 1855" (italics added).

The Dispatch of Putiatin

Russia was aware that China's defeat in the Opium Wars (1842) had led to ports being opened and was witnessing other nations, such as Britain and the United States, placing increasing pressure on Japan to open up to the outside world. Thus she knew that her interests in the Far East and Pacific area were beginning to be threatened. From 1843 onward, Tsar Nicolas I (who ruled from 1825 to 1855) seriously considered the need to send a naval expedition to press Japan to open her doors to the outside world and to conclude a treaty establishing commercial relations. However, as had previously been the case, domestic affairs took precedence, and another ten years were to pass before this was put into effect.

During that decade, while for the main part Russia focused her attention on the Crimean War (1853–56), she also stepped up her activities in Sakhalin, the Amur River area, and toward Japan. At that stage the chief executors of Russian Far East policy were the governor-general of Eastern Siberia, Nikolai

Muraviev, and a naval officer, Gennadii Nevelskoi, who had earned Muraviev's favor. In 1849 Nevelskoi led an expedition to the Amur River area, discovering that Sakhalin was an island and confirming that the Amur River Bay and estuary could be negotiated by seagoing vessels. However, these "discoveries" were made a full forty-two years after the noted Japanese explorer Rinzō Mamiya had made identical observations. Nevelskoi went on to proclaim Sakhalin and the entire Amur River Russian territory, and in 1851, in recognition of his deeds, Tsar Nicholas I decorated him, uttering in 1855 the famous words, "Where once the Russian flag has been raised, it must not be lowered again."[14] (It did not, however, prevent Alexander II from selling Alaska to the United States in 1867, thereby lowering the Russian flag.) In 1860, Muraviev renamed the city of Haishenwai, ceded by China in the Treaty of Peking, "Vladivostok," that is, "rule" (*vladi*) "the east" (*vostok*). This has tended to be interpreted as an example of Russian expansionism, but at least partially represents a response to Anglo-American encroachment in the region. There are occasions when territorial expansion that includes an element of defense, or was started on the pretext of being for defense, loses its original objective and ends merely as expansion. This, though apparently a contradiction in terms, can perhaps be called "defensive expansionism."[15]

When Nicolas I heard that the United States had dispatched Commodore Matthew Perry with four warships to Japan, he judged further delay out of the question and immediately decided to send Rear-Admiral Evfimii Putiatin as leader of a delegation to China and Japan. Following Laxman's (1792) and Rezanov's (1804) missions, this was Russia's third diplomatic mission to Japan. On October 7, 1852, Putiatin set off from Kronstadt aboard the frigate *Pallada*, on a voyage that would take him about three hundred days. At Chichi-jima in the Ogasawara Islands, the *Pallada* assumed the role of flagship of a squadron of three other Russian vessels, and on August 21, 1853, finally arrived in Nagasaki, approximately one month after Perry's arrival at Uraga.

At Futami Port, on Chichi-jima, a messenger handed Putiatin an additional set of instructions from the tsar. The existence of these previously unreleased instructions, and the nature of their content, were made public in the October 4, 1991, issue of *Izvestiia*, causing great shock waves amongst those involved in Russo/Soviet-Japanese relations. I shall cover their content in some detail. But let me first briefly summarize the document's impact.

These "instructions" represented the first appearance of the terminology Nicholas used (and that appeared later in decrees) for recognizing the Northern Territories as Japanese territory and for authorizing Putiatin to negotiate on that basis. The lengthy *Izvestiia* article was coauthored by Konstantin O. Sarkisov, then head of the Center for Japanese Studies at the Institute of Oriental Studies, Russian Academy of Sciences, and an acknowledged expert on Russo-Japanese studies, and Kiril E. Cherevko, senior fellow at the Institute of Soviet History.[16] That very same day, the evening edition of the *Asahi Shimbun* reported that Professor Koichi Yasuda (Okayama University) had unearthed historical documents with exactly the same content in the naval archives in St. Petersburg, and approximately ten days later, the *Asahi Shimbun* published an article by Professor Yasuda describing their nature.[17] The timing of the release of these articles in Russia and Japan was by no means coincidental. The truth of the matter is that by separate routes Professors Yasuda and Sarkisov had already learned of the existence of these documents in St. Petersburg and Moscow, but Yasuda had acquiesced in Sarkisov's suggestion that politically speaking, it would be preferable for that information to be offered from the Russian side rather than by a Japanese researcher, as it was precisely the kind of announcement that would be obviously favorable to Japan. However, getting wind of this, *Asahi Shimbun* and NHK (7 p.m. and 9 p.m. news on October 4) made a partial announcement.[18] Be that as it may, in the background were the momentous processes of glasnost and perestroika commenced by Gorbachev. In this context, all manner of previously hidden historical truths were being exposed to the light of day.

The Directives to Putiatin

The document in question is the Draft of the Additional Instruction to Admiral Putiatin, issued on February 27, 1853, in the name of Tsar Nicholas I. The front page states, "His Majesty the Emperor wrote the following on this document with his own hand: 'Be it so enacted.' February 24, 1853." In other words, this document regarding the approach to negotiations with Japan on commerce and national borders is not merely something which Nicolas I approved, but is better described as his specific "orders" to Putiatin.

Sarkisov's and Cherevko's article opens with the following explanation of the Imperial Directive: "In order to understand the process of the formation of borders between the two countries, we should remember that Russia was the initiator of their establishment. This basically amounted to 'a demand' to draw the border. To some extent this Russian initiative was the result of tactical considerations. Knowing that the shogunate followed a self-isolationist policy, and would probably refuse to establish contacts and sign a treaty, Russia came up with a proposal on borders."

They go on to move their focus to the substance of the document, which "sheds light on the history of the establishment of borders between Russia and Japan. In order for the reader to get a clear understanding of the following lines, we should remind you that during the whole postwar period Soviet historians actively advertised the idea that the Kuriles, including the Southern Kuriles, have always belonged to Russia. And the fact that in the course of territorial negotiations they had been transferred to Japan was explained as the unjustified concession of a Russian admiral. Where is the truth? Recently discovered documents contain the answer to this question." From here the two authors quote Tsar Nicholas I with the following passage, which features as Item 6 in the Joint Compendium.

On the border issue, it is our wish to be as indulgent as possible (without compromising our interests), bearing in mind that the achievement of the other goal—trade benefits is of vital importance to us. *The southernmost island of the Kurile Islands that belongs to Russia is Uruppu, which we could identify as the last point of Russian authority in the south—so that from our side, the southern tip of this island would be* [as it actually is today] *the border with Japan, and from the Japanese side, the northern tip of the island of Etorofu would be considered to be their border.* (italics added)

The section quoted here, specifically the sentence I have highlighted, is of particular significance. In other words, before the official negotiations with the shogunate even commenced, Tsar Nicholas I had already issued secret instructions to Putiatin to be prepared to acknowledge that the territory south of and including Etorofu belonged to Japan. Almost in one fell swoop, this testimony resolved the issues many Japanese and Russians had disputed. There is little wonder that Sarkisov and Cherevko were so excited by their finding. After revealing the nature of the Imperial Directive, the two go on to reveal their excitement in a way quite unexpected from normally calm and collected researchers, writing, "It seems we have discovered the truth!"

After interpreting that the crux of the tsar's directive to Admiral Putiatin included acknowledgment that Etorofu and the islands south of there were Japanese territory, and Uruppu and the islands north of there Russian territory, Sarkisov and Cherevko go on to state:

The historical documents quoted above make it possible for us to honestly evaluate the history of our relations with our Eastern neighbor [Japan]. Will we lose anything from this? No. On the contrary, freed from false ideas, we will be able to liberate ourselves. The lies that have been instilled in the consciousness of the Russian and Soviet people for decades have poisoned our national consciousness and complicated the resolution of the territorial problem with Japan. They have aroused feelings of pseudo-patriotism and nationalism which have nothing to do with love for one's Motherland.[19]

Delimitation of National Boundaries: The Treaty of Shimoda

After arriving in Nagasaki, Putiatin commenced negotiations on January 18, 1854, with shogunate representatives Toshiakira Kawaji and Masanori Tsutsui. Kawaji and the other Japanese negotiators did their utmost to play for time.[20] They put off the demands of their unwelcome visitors, who, as Putiatin's secretary, Ivan Goncharov (a famous nineteenth-century author of novels such as *Oblomov*) wrote, were "made to feel decidedly unwelcome."[21] As the Russian mission's arrival coincided with the outbreak of war in the Crimea, after proposing a treaty covering friendly relations, commerce, and territorial delimitation, Putiatin took his squadron out to sea again to avoid being attacked by marauding Royal Navy warships. After hearing that on March 31 of the same year Japan had finally been opened through conclusion of the Treaty of Peace and Amity Between the United States and the Empire of Japan (normally referred to as the Kanagawa Treaty) with Commodore Perry, Putiatin sailed the sloop-of-war *Diana* into Osaka and pressed Japan to conclude a similar treaty with Russia. As the shogunate had already promised Putiatin that Russia would receive the same privileges conferred by Japan in any treaties it might conclude with other foreign nations, it was in no position to refuse the admiral's approach. So, on December 22, 1854, Kawaji and Tsutsui recommenced negotiations with the Russian delegation in Shimoda, on the Izu Peninsula.[22]

Right in the middle of the negotiations, the area was struck by a massive earthquake, and the huge tidal wave that followed sank the sloop *Diana*. Both parties worked together to cope with the disaster, and with the cooperation of local Japanese a new vessel, named the *Heda*, was built in the port of the same name.

It is noteworthy that both sets of negotiators at the talks in Nagasaki and Shimoda, although intent on protecting their national interests, were friendly and respectful toward their counterparts. For example, Professor Seizaburō Satō (University of Tokyo) wrote that Kawaji was strong in his praise of Putiatin. "Kawaji was amazed that Putiatin, despite having had his sloop destroyed by a tidal wave, and knowing that Russia's British and French enemies in the Crimean War being fought at that time had a vastly superior presence in the Far East, would attempt to seize a French warship when it happened to enter the port of Shimoda."[23] Also, in the Russians' eyes, Toshiakira Kawaji was judged to possess an intellect discernable beyond the obvious differences in culture and race. Goncharov, who covered the negotiations in minute detail, wrote:

We all liked Kawaji. . . . He was extremely intelligent. We could not help but admire the intellect behind his skillful rebuttals of our arguments. Each and every one of his words, each look in his eyes, each gesture hinted at his sound judgment, keen insight, wit, and skill. Wisdom is unvarying wherever one goes. While differences may exist in terms of race, dress, language and religion, and while even views on life itself may vary, there is a common characteristic amongst wise men.[24]

After five meetings, the Japanese and Russian representatives finally reached agreement on February 7, 1855, and at the Chorakuji-temple, Shimoda, signed the Treaty of Commerce, Navigation, and Delimitation Between Japan and Russia (normally referred to as the Treaty of Shimoda).

Article 2 of the Treaty of Shimoda (see the Joint Compendium, Item 7) describes the border between Russia and Japan in the Kuriles in terms of the islands north of, and including, Uruppu as Russian territory and those south of, and including, Etorofu as Japanese territory, with no border set in Sakhalin, "as has been the case up to this time." Professor Kōriyama saw this as no more than a ceremony between the two countries, marking official acceptance of a position the Russians had previously acknowledged. In 1981 the Japanese government of Zenkō Suzuki set February 7, the day when the border between Russia and Japan was officially established by the Treaty of Shimoda, as "Northern Territories Day." The Treaty of Shimoda, conducted against a peaceful background, is recalled for designating the four islands of the Northern Territories as Japanese territory.

The Theory of "Pressure on Putiatin" Is Mistaken

The view that Japanese pressure forced Putiatin to give up Etorofu, Kunashiri, Shikotan, and Habomai to Japan was prevalent in the Soviet Union during the Brezhnev years. The standpoint of special correspondents to Tokyo of the two main Soviet newspapers, *Izvestiia* and *Pravda*, can be seen as typical of this.

First of all are the comments by Iurii Bandura (then Tokyo correspondent of *Izvestiia*, later deputy-editor of *Moscow News*) in his feature article, titled "Outrage Against History," which appeared in the June 16, 1981, issue of *Izvestiia*. "The person who signed this treaty [Treaty of Shimoda: Kimura] was the Russian diplomat Putiatin, who at the time was effectively being held hostage in Japan under the gun-barrels of warships of Russia's British and French enemies.... Subsequently the tsarist government indicated to Japan that Putiatin's signing of the treaty was in fact contrary to the directive he had received from his homeland, and therefore that the Treaty of Shimoda is not, and never could have been, an instrument by which Japanese 'inalienable rights' [over the Northern Territories] are recognized."[25]

Even in 1989, as many as five years after the advent of the Gorbachev administration, Igor' Latyshev (former special correspondent of *Pravda*, subsequently an affiliated member of the Institute of Oriental Studies) was making comments similar to Bandura's. He commented:

In an attempt to strengthen their own demands on the Kurile Islands in legal terms, those proponents of the Movement for the Return of the Northern Territories normally quote the Russo-Japanese treaties of 1855 and 1875 (Treaty of Shimoda and Treaty of St. Petersburg). However, these two treaties were signed by the tsarist government because of the *pressure* it faced having the British and French navies menacing the Russian Far Eastern borders from their position of predominance in the Pacific. As the tsarist government did not have the ability to defend the Kurile Islands, it was placed in a difficult position, and the Japanese government used that situation to the fullest extent possible. By exerting *pressure* on Russian diplomats who lacked foresight and determination, Japan managed in the first treaty (1855) to have Russia cede the southern islands of the Kurile Archipelago and then in the second treaty (1875) the northern part of the archipelago.[26] (italics added)

As it happens, the stance adopted by the likes of Bandura and Latyshev can only be seen as irrational, in that it flies in the face of the popular view espoused by such Soviet historians as Esfir' Fainberg who was awarded a PhD in history from the Institute of Oriental Studies, Russian Academy of Sciences. Although her book *Russo-Japanese Relations 1697–1875* has been criticized as "full of factual distortions," it heaps praise on Putiatin for finally securing the Treaty of Shimoda from the shogunate and evaluates the treaty itself highly.[27] She stated, "With this, after one hundred years of futile attempts, Russia established a commercial treaty with Japan." Fainberg even went on to state that rather than being prejudicial against Russia, the Treaty of Shimoda was actually unfavorable for Japan. While stating, "The Treaty of Shimoda was effectively an unequal treaty in the same way as the other treaties forced upon feudal Japan by the Western Powers," Fainberg went on to write proudly that in approaching Japan to conclude this treaty tsarist Russia did not put *pressure* on it by a threat of military force. In other words, a foundation for Russo-Japanese friendship was laid before a peaceful background. Putiatin's actions in peacefully concluding this treaty represented a faithful expression of tsarist government policy of the day:

In contrast to the United States, Britain, and France, tsarist Russia did not use the threat of military force to apply pressure on Japan. At that time, Britain and France were resentful of the Treaty of Shimoda being concluded. . . . While some foreign historians repeatedly cast slurs on tsarist Russia for harboring "invasion plans" against Japan, the vast majority of historians see Putiatin's mission as having laid the foundation for neighborly relations between Russia and Japan, and recognize that his activities illustrated the peaceful nature of Russian policies of the day.[28]

More recently, the *Izvestiia* article by Sarkisov and Cherevko (October 4, 1991) makes it clear that the views of the likes of Bandura and Latyshev are completely mistaken. Sarkisov and Cherevko wrote:

The fact that in the course of territorial negotiations they [the four islands of the Kuriles from Etorofu southward: Kimura] had been transferred to Japan used to be explained as an unjustified concession by a Russian admiral. Where is the truth? The following document [Instruction from Emperor Nicolas I to Putiatin: Kimura] contains the answer to this question. "Russia always acknowledged Japan's right to it [the Northern Territories] *voluntarily, without any pressure from outside.*"[29] (italics added)

Sarkisov and Cherevko even go so far as to say, "What were Putiatin's actions? They were brilliant, since he was an experienced negotiator."[30]

Since the early nineteenth century, the border between Russia and Japan has been recognized as falling between Uruppu and Etorofu. Nevertheless, at the negotiations in Nagasaki, Putiatin is recorded as stating, "The Kurile Islands have belonged to Russia from years gone by, and despite it being inhabited only by Russians until fifty years ago, it has since then been taken by Japan." He then went on to say that Russia thereby possessed half the rights to Etorofu. But this represented little more than part of a strategy to put Russia in a position of advantage in negotiations over Sakhalin.[31] That is to say, the Russians would have been well aware that in 1799 the shogunate had taken moves to administer the Land of Yezo directly from Edo, meaning that from that point Etorofu was unmistakably under Japan's control. In the negotiations in Nagasaki and Shimoda, Putiatin's focus was on trade with Japan, and he went so far as saying that if Japan agreed to open trade relations, Etorofu would be ceded to it, and that there was even no need to set a clear border in Sakhalin. This also makes it clear that from the start Etorofu was no more than a "bargaining chip" in the overall negotiations.[32]

Sarkisov and Cherevko correctly interpreted Putiatin's use of Etorofu as no more than a negotiating card and go on to state in their *Izvestiia* article, "Putiatin made a simple but effective move—he presented counter-claims. Not to all the islands, as his compatriots did in the twentieth century, but only to Iturup (Etorofu)." They continue, "Let us give Putiatin the floor," and they cite the old document, Memo on Admiral Putiatin's Activities During his Mission to Japan:[33]

According to the instruction I received from the Ministry of Foreign Affairs, I was supposed to identify Urup [Uruppu] as our border island of the Kuriles, as it happens to be in reality, and to consider the end of Japanese territory to be the island of Iturup [Etorofu]. I also hinted that we had claims on this island, since it is populated by the Ainu and is rarely visited by the Japanese. *The purpose of this announcement, however, was not to actually insist on its transfer, but to relinquish it and thus to ensure that we do not appear completely adamant and inflexible in Japanese eyes.*[34] (italics added)

The Exchange of Sakhalin and the Kuriles

In 1861 an incident took place in which the Russian navy dispatched warships to Tsushima. The tsar's government wanted to force the Tsushima clan to lease land on which to construct a naval base. Dominating the passages between the Sea of Japan and the Pacific Ocean, Tsushima occupies an important strategic position, and in this respect, it had also attracted interest from Britain and France. In years to come Admiral Heihachirō Tōgō's Japanese

Imperial Fleet would intercept and destroy the Russian Second Pacific Squadron in these waters during the Russo-Japanese War at the famous Battle of Tsushima. The Russian attempt to secure land for a naval base has been treated as not only completely unrepresentative of any grand design on the tsarist government's part, but also as merely the reckless and unauthorized action of some Russian naval officers. Be it between Japan and Russia, or other countries for that matter, the possibility of reckless acts occurring overseas always exists. At the same time, however, if that behavior produces dividends, it is more or less the norm for that country's government to go on to use that situation for its own ends.

With the conclusion of the Treaty of Shimoda, official diplomatic relations between Russia and Japan could commence, but the issue of the border in Sakhalin (in Japanese Karafuto) remained vague and unresolved, and as such it was a cause for concern for both countries. The shogunate sent envoys to Russia to discuss the Sakhalin border problem, but the talks ended in failure. In 1867 the governor of Hakodate, Hidezane Koide, signed the Temporary Regulations Relevant to the Island of Karafuto, which recognized that Sakhalin was to be jointly occupied by Russia and Japan, and that citizens of both nations had the right to live wherever they chose on the island.[35] But this opened the way for the Russian military to move southward and was the indirect cause of subsequent complications and Japan's eventual abandonment of Sakhalin. Between the unusual mix of Russian, Japanese, and Ainu living in Sakhalin there were constant conflicts and clashes, frequently leading to serious incidents of violence, murder, and arson. Military and convicts predominately comprised the Russian population; the Japanese had come to work in the fisheries industry or were farmers and artisans sent there in an attempt to establish a "presence" in Sakhalin.

In 1868, after the collapse of the Edo shogunate, the new Meiji government inherited the unresolved problem of the border in Sakhalin. Its first move was to ask the United States to mediate on the issue, and in 1869, when on a visit to Japan, former secretary of state William H. Seward responded to a Japanese approach by recommending that Japan look to buy Sakhalin from Russia.[36] Two years earlier, in 1867, Seward had overseen the American purchase of Alaska from Russia for 7.2 million dollars, so this advice merely reflected his own experience.[37] In 1872, in the negotiations between Japanese foreign minister Taneomi Soejima and Russian minister to Japan Evgenii Biutsov, the Russians proposed that in return for ceding the Northern Kurile Islands except Shumshu and Paramushir to Japan, Russia would gain sovereignty over all Sakhalin. Negotiations were discontinued when Soejima retired from public office after his defeat in the "Seikanron" debate, in which he advocated invading Korea.

The nascent Meiji government, its power base still unestablished and fragile, was surrounded by a number of problems on both the domestic and external scenes. Recommendations of the likes of Kiyotaka Kuroda, a deputy director of the Hokkaido Colonization Office, that out of consideration for such circumstances it would be advisable to avoid conflict with Russia, abandon claims on Sakhalin, and direct all efforts instead on the development of Hokkaido, gradually prevailed. Finally, on May 7, 1875, the Treaty of St. Petersburg, otherwise known as the Treaty for the Exchange of Sakhalin for the Kurile Islands, was signed in the Russian capital by Japanese plenipotentiary Takeaki Enomoto and Russian prime minister and foreign minister Alexander Gorchakov. By this treaty Japan ceded the rights to Sakhalin in exchange for sovereignty over all the Kurile Islands. It was recognized in the articles of the treaty that Japanese and Russian residents of Sakhalin and the Kurile Islands could continue living there and maintain their respective nationalities, and their religious freedom and rights to engage in business and own property were guaranteed. This precedent could serve as a point of reference for guaranteeing the rights of current Russian residents, if at some stage in future the four disputed islands were to be returned to Japan.

Many people, both in Russia and Japan, expressed dissatisfaction with the content of the treaty. Professor Tsuguo Togawa (Sophia University) described the situation succinctly: "In terms of Japanese public opinion, there were many who were critical of the government for exchanging Sakhalin, which they deemed to be extremely valuable both politically and economically, for the Kuriles, which seemed to be little more than 'a row of pebbles' on the map. Some even went as far as to say that this exchange was in effect of one piece of Japanese territory for another Japanese territory."[38] Similarly, in Russia, "This treaty was little more than exchanging Russian territory for Russian territory, and that letting go of the Kuriles, which had taken many years of hard toil to develop, was a result of the Russian government being ignorant of their true value." Even now, some Russian scholars insist that the Japanese government "took advantage of the difficult circumstances Russia found herself in at that stage and forced an unequal treaty on it, making a legally unfounded exchange of Sakhalin for the Russian territory of the Kurile Islands."[39] But, as both Professors Togawa and Lensen have stated, such one-sided feelings of dissatisfaction in both countries were indicative of the lack of understanding of the national circumstances within, and power relationship between, Japan and Russia at the time.[40] At that stage Japan did not possess the financial or military wherewithal to maintain and manage Sakhalin, but the reality of the situation was that Russia had to pay a price to get Japan to give up its rights there. There are no complete victories in diplomatic negotiations, and needless to say, it is unwise to try to judge rights and wrongs of the past from the vantage point of the present.

The important part of the Treaty of St. Petersburg is Article 2 (see the Joint Compendium, Item 8), which reads, "His Majesty the Emperor of all the Russias, for Himself and His descendants, cedes to His Majesty the Emperor of Japan the group of islands, called Kurile which He possesses at present, together with all the rights of sovereignty appertaining to this possession,. . . . The Kurile Islands comprises the following eighteen islands."

In 1895, the Treaty on Commerce and Navigation Between Russia and Japan and the Annexed Declaration were signed (see the Joint Compendium, Item 9). These invalidated and replaced the 1855 Treaty of Shimoda and the 1867 Tentative Regulations Relevant to the Island of Sakhalin. The above-mentioned Annexed Declaration reaffirmed the validity of the 1875 Treaty for the Exchange of Sakhalin for the Kurile Islands.

CHAPTER 3

Territorial Demarcation by Force

IN AN ATTEMPT TO palliate the nation's shock of defeat in the Crimean War, Tsar Alexander II embarked on a program of Great Reforms, epitomized by the emancipation of the serfs in 1861. But the oppressive policies instituted to suppress revolutionary movements born of these reforms eventually led to Alexander falling victim to a bomb planted by members of the terrorist group "People's Will" (Narodnaia volia) in 1881. Succeeding his father as tsar, Alexander III appointed Sergei Witte as minister of finance, promoted industrialization, and implemented a foreign policy that focused on expansion southward in the Far East and Central Asia rather than in Europe.[1] In keeping with Russia's Asian mission, as advocated by Alexander III and Nicolas II, Witte committed himself to policies that saw the construction of the Trans-Siberian Railroad, building and taking control of the North Manchurian (Chinese Eastern) Railroad, and strengthening the Russian Far Eastern Fleet.[2]

Portsmouth Peace Conference

While visiting Japan in April and May 1891, Alexander III's son, Crown Prince and future Tsar Nicholas, was attacked and wounded by an escort policeman, Sanzō Tsuda, in the city of Otsu in Shiga Prefecture. Although the wounds were not life threatening, as an attempt on the life of a foreign dignitary the "Otsu incident" had serious repercussions both at home and overseas. Afraid of Russian retaliation, the Japanese government pressured the Great Court of Cassation to apply Article 116 of the Criminal Code, which prescribed the death penalty for acts of treason against members of the imperial family. However, Chief Justice Korekata Kojima ruled that this did not apply and sentenced Tsuda to life imprisonment for attempted murder, thereby protecting the judiciary's independence.[3] Numerous biographical novels have stated that Nicolas was thereafter unfavorably disposed toward Japan, and in his diary referred to the Japanese as "monkeys."[4] However,

Yasuda, the first foreigner to get direct access to these diaries, states that such popular beliefs were not necessarily correct; the diaries did not in fact contain derogatory comments about the Japanese.[5]

Be that as it may, in 1894, about three and a half years after the Otsu incident, Nicholas ascended the throne as Tsar Nicholas II. He faithfully took over where his father had left off in terms of active and aggressive Far East policies. In 1895, joining forces with France and Germany, not only did the Russian government compel Japan to restore to China the Liaotung Peninsula ceded to Japan as part of the spoils of its victory in the Sino-Japanese War (1894–95), but also in 1898 bullied the Chinese into leasing Port Arthur and Dairen to Russia as naval bases for its Pacific Squadron. Furthermore, in 1900, taking advantage of the fact that the world powers sent troops to quell the Boxer Rebellion (1900), Russian forces occupied Manchuria and refused to withdraw even after the rebellion was suppressed. Japan sensed a menace from Russia as she sought to extend her influence not only into Manchuria but also into the Korean Peninsula. Out of concern that Russian policies of southward expansion posed a threat to the Chinese market and British vested interests there, Great Britain looked to make Japan into a "wave-break against Russian expansion in the Far-East." These newfound common interests saw Great Britain and Japan establish the Anglo-Japanese Alliance in 1902.

However, Japan and Russia were unable to reach a peaceful resolution of the problems relating to Manchuria and developments within Korea, and finally Japan launched the Russo-Japanese War (1904–5).[6] Fierce and skillful fighting by the Japanese upset almost all forecasts of the war's outcome and led to humiliating defeats for the Russian forces. Previously thought impregnable, the Russian fortress of Port Arthur was taken after General Maresuke Nogi stubbornly pressed home attacks, despite great loss of life; the Battle of Mukden ended in victory for Japan. And after a seven-month voyage from the other side of the world, the Russian Baltic Fleet was destroyed at Tsushima by the Japanese Combined Fleet under Admiral Heihachirō Tōgō. But Japanese military success peaked with these battles. As Japan was running out of manpower and money, its government made a secret official request to the United States to mediate. Wary of Japanese expansion and judging America's best interests served by maintaining "balanced antagonism," President Theodore Roosevelt readily accepted the role of mediator.[7] Russia, faced with growing domestic unrest, accepted his proposal of a peace conference.

At this conference, held in Portsmouth, New Hampshire, Foreign Minister Jutarō Komura represented Japan and former Minister of Finance Sergei Witte represented Russia. Though several times close to breakdown, the conference concluded the Treaty of Portsmouth on September 5, 1905. Russia would withdraw her troops from Manchuria and Korea, and cede southern Karafuto (Sakhalin) below the 50th parallel to Japan, but would not be required to pay any indemnity (see the Joint Compendium, Item 10).

The negotiations between Komura and Witte are of historical significance in their own right. Komura managed to achieve Japan's original war aim of removing Russian troops from Manchuria and Korea, despite Japan having already reached the limit of her military and financial resources, and against the background of a Japanese public largely unaware of these facts. Russian witnesses of Komura's manner at the negotiations record that they were impressed that the Japanese plenipotentiary was far more composed than his Russian counterpart.[8] Witte was in a much more precarious position than Komura. Within Russia some factions maintained that the early defeats could be recouped by continuing the war, and it was virtually certain that a breakdown in the talks would bring about Witte's downfall. Also, at this time Russian society was in a state of chaos, just short of exploding into revolution. Resigned to such circumstances, Witte reached an agreement whereby while Japanese troops had occupied all of Sakhalin, Russia would relinquish only the southern portion and would not be required to pay any reparations whatsoever. One particularly conspicuous difference between the two sides was that whereas Witte made skillful use of the American media to manipulate public opinion, the Japanese negotiating stance was marked by a wariness of leaking diplomatic secrets, born of a lack of guile and a desire to let the process follow its natural course.[9]

The nature of the Russo-Japanese War's conclusion led Japanese strategic planners to believe it possible for peace to be concluded when the tide of a war was most favorable.[10] However, the Japanese people, heavily taxed to meet the costs of the war, did not at that time see things quite that way. They had not been told that the economic and military burden of continuing the war was beyond the nation's ability because the government feared public announcements to that effect would encourage Russia to continue the war. Out of concern that the peace process might break down, the Japanese government thus chose not to inform its people of the true situation. This was one of the dilemmas born of entering into peace negotiations at a stage when the war was not completely over. As might be expected, on the day that the Treaty of Portsmouth was signed (September 5, 1905), a mass rally denouncing Komura's "weak diplomacy" was held in Hibiya Park in Tokyo, and violence erupted when the police attempted to disperse the protesters. This led to a riot, in which tens of thousands of people converged on the prime minister's residence, burning a *koban* (police post) in the process, in the "Hibiya incendiary incident."[11] The mob's wrath was also directed toward the United States as mediator in the treaty, and there were attacks not only on its embassy but also on churches known to have American ministers. Nevertheless, President Roosevelt was awarded the Nobel Peace Prize in recognition of his arbitration at the peace conference.

That Japan made territorial gains (Southern Sakhalin) as a result of the Russo-Japanese War is undisputable. From this, it is possible to deduce that

Southern Sakhalin was included among territories described in the Cairo Declaration as "taken by violence and greed." Nevertheless, it was territory acquired legally, based on American mediation, and through a treaty that Russia agreed to and signed. In this respect its situation is fundamentally different from that of the Northern Territories, still occupied illegally by Russia after the Soviet Union forcibly seized these islands, under an agreement made at Yalta, to which Japan was not a party.

The Siberian Intervention

In Russia the February and October Revolutions of 1917 brought tsarism to an end, and the Bolsheviks (the "majority" faction of the Russian Social-Democratic Workers' Party, later the Soviet Communist Party) under Vladimir Lenin established the first Soviet administration. Fearful of the advent of the world's first government based on communist thinking, the Western powers, including Britain, France, the United States, Canada, and Japan embarked on a campaign of blatant interventionism in the Russian Civil War. If circumstances permitted, they even had designs to expand their interests in Russia. On the pretext of protecting Japanese residents in the Russian Far East, Japan in August 1918 landed an expeditionary force in the area around Vladivostok, from where it moved to occupy most of the Trans-Siberian Railway east of Lake Baikal.[12] In the midst of such an intervention the Far Eastern Republic (Dal'nevostochnaia respublika) was created in East Siberia in April 1920. The republic, with its capital in Chita and its head Alexander Krasnoshchekov, was formally independent, recognized as such by the Bolshevik government of Russia on May 14, 1920. It could more accurately be described as the first communist-dominated "people's democracy," used by the Bolsheviks as a buffer state between Russia and Japan, and annexed in November 1922, less than two months after the last Japanese troops left Vladivostok.

In March 1920, in Nikolaevsk (present-day Komsomolsk), near the mouth of the Amur River, there was a series of armed clashes between the Japanese community, comprising garrison and civilian residents, and Russian partisans, in which the Japanese were defeated and 120 of them taken prisoner. As a Japanese relief expedition approached in May, the partisans executed the prisoners and burned the town before withdrawing. The Nikolaevsk incident resulted in the deaths of 384 civilians and 351 soldiers.[13] Out of revenge, Japan then occupied Northern Sakhalin (North Karafuto), and Japanese troops remained there until 1925.

It is not hard to understand how objectionable this foreign intervention was for the Soviet government, occurring as it did just when the nascent Soviet administration was facing one crisis after another. In Russia, as in the West, there is a saying "druz'ia poznaiutsia v bede" (a friend in need is a friend indeed). The Japanese military contribution to the Siberian Intervention was large, involving 72,400 troops, and protracted, lasting from 1918 to 1922 (1925 in Northern Sakhalin). Just as the Japanese find it difficult to forget the long internment of POWs in Siberia after World War Two, the Japanese occupation of Russian soil must be a painful memory for Russians and other ethnic groups who lived in Siberia and the Far East in those days.

Japan Recognizes the Soviet Government

In attempting to extract itself from isolation, it was natural that the nascent Soviet regime would scheme to exploit the rivalries that existed among the Western capitalist powers. In March 1918 it shocked the world by concluding, at Brest-Litovsk, a separate peace treaty with Germany, which aspired to win World War One by concentrating its resources on the Western Front.[14] The next target for Soviet diplomacy was Japan.

The Western nations, particularly the United States, were unhappy that after the Russo-Japanese War Japan had extended her influence in the Far East beyond what they considered necessary. This concern was among the reasons why President Roosevelt agreed to mediate an end to the Russo-Japanese War. The United States was also concerned that Japan had acted alone in the Siberian Intervention, despite having been requested to work in conjunction with the other Allied countries, particularly America. Tokyo also dispatched more troops than the Allies requested, stationed them not only in Siberia but also in Northern Sakhalin, and stayed longer than all the others, despite American requests for their earlier withdrawal. In other words, a clash of interests was born between Japan and the United States.

Soviet Russia was not invited to attend the 1919 Versailles Peace Conference. Japan was invited, but its delegates' views were barely reflected in the decisions made at the conference, further intensifying feelings of frustration in Japan. In the 1920s Japan was hit by an economic crisis, greatly exacerbated in 1923 when the effects of the Great Kanto Earthquake exhausted Japan's national resources to the extent that in many circles pessimism about the prospects of recovery was prevalent. The United States also placed limits on Japanese immigration. In Japan there was increasingly vocal comment that to resist America's political and economic challenge in East Asia, Japan must first cover her back by establishing a friendly relationship with Soviet Russia. In other words, "Japan, essentially, has no other policy that makes sense from the Japanese point of view than to live in peace and harmony with Russia, though painted red."[15] From the Soviet point of view, improvement in relations with Japan was necessary for three reasons: (1) to achieve the withdrawal of Japanese troops from Soviet territory; (2) to terminate Japanese support for antirevolutionary White Russian forces; and (3) to secure Japanese recognition of the communist regime.

From as early as August 1921 Japan and the Soviet Union initiated intermittent negotiations toward normalizing relations, first between Japan and the Far Eastern Republic (1920–22), then between Japan, the Far Eastern Republic, and Soviet Russia, and finally between Japan and the Soviet Union (held December 30, 1922). During that period the Soviet Union concluded the Treaty of Rapallo with Germany, making the German government the first to officially recognize the new Soviet regime.[16]

Japan and the Soviet Union finally signed the Soviet-Japanese Basic Convention in Peking on January 20, 1925. Although the full official name of the treaty is the Convention Embodying the Basic Rules of the Relations Between Japan and the USSR and Japan, it is alternatively referred to as the Peking Convention (Pekinskaia Konventsiia) and often abbreviated to the Japanese-Soviet Basic Treaty (Nisso Kihon Jōyaku).[17] Japan was represented by its minister to China, Kenkichi Yoshizawa, and the Soviet Union by Ambassador Lev Karakhan. Japan ratified the treaty on January 25, the USSR followed suit on February 20, and with this official relations were established between the two countries. By signing this treaty Japan acknowledged Soviet administration as that country's legal government eight years before the United States did so.

Item 11 of the Joint Compendium highlights the relevant sections of the Japanese-Soviet Basic Treaty. That is to say, Article 2 makes it clear that the Soviet Union recognized the *legal* validity of the Treaty of Portsmouth concluded by tsarist Russia, that is, the Soviet Union acknowledged that Southern Sakhalin had been ceded to Japan. A declaration attached to the convention and signed by Ambassador Karakhan qualified this with the statement, "His Government's recognition of the Portsmouth Treaty is not in any way to be interpreted to mean that the Soviet Government shares *political* responsibility with the Tsarist Government" (italics added).

In an interview with a Japanese journalist in August 1925, Josef Stalin, then general secretary of the Soviet Communist Party, made the following boastful statement about Soviet-Japanese relations: "The alliance of the people of Japan with those of the Soviet Union marks a decisive step in our cause to liberate the people of the East. Such an alliance would mark the beginning of the end of great colonial imperialistic powers and of world imperialism. This alliance would be invincible."[18] However, the détente that resulted from signing of the Basic Convention was no more than a modus vivendi, or marriage of convenience, based on each country's view of its interests.

Border Clashes: The Changkufeng and Nomonhan Incidents

The ten-year period following establishment of diplomatic relations was one of relative calm between Japan and the Soviet Union. The revolution, civil war, and Western military interventions all left the Soviet Union exhausted; on top of that, the Soviet government was preoccupied with fierce internal power struggles, the launching of industrialization and agricultural collectivization, leaving little or no leeway to look toward the Far East. After the frustrations of the Siberian Expedition, Japan refocused on moving into China. But new developments in Japan, such as the demise of Taisho democracy, rise of militarism, expansion of the Russo-Japanese border with the establishment of Manchukuo (1932) and conclusion of the Anti-Comintern Pact (1936), which identified the Soviet Union as the main potential enemy, gave rise to possibility of clashes between Japan and the Soviet Union.[19]

In the summer of 1938 the Changkufeng incident occurred. Changkufeng sits at the mouth of the Tumen River, near where the borders of Russia, China, and North Korea meet. In recent times the area has attracted attention for its economic potential, particularly as an outlet for China to the Sea of Japan, but it was formerly little more than a small hill marking the Soviet-Manchurian border. When Soviet troops set up a position on this hill, the Japanese army, judging it to be within the boundaries of Manchukuo, moved to eject them by force. After so doing, they soon bore the brunt of ferocious Soviet counterattacks and were saved from destruction only by the signing of a ceasefire agreement in Moscow.

From May to September 1939, there was a full-scale military clash between Soviet and Japanese forces, this time at Nomonhan/Khalkhin Gol in Mongolia. In May, the Japanese Kwantung Army, alleging frontier violations by troops of the Mongolian People's Republic, invaded Mongolia. In August a major counteroffensive by Soviet and Mongolian forces inflicted a crushing defeat on the Kwantung Army, killing or capturing most of its invading force.[20]

The Japanese-Soviet Neutrality Pact

In that same August of 1939 Hitler and Stalin concluded a Nonaggression Pact. Seven days later Germany initiated World War Two by invading Poland, and in mid-September Soviet forces invaded Eastern Poland.[21] Japan unfolded a policy of southern expansion into the Asian region, and blatant acts of aggression against China and later French Indo-China saw a dramatic deterioration in relations with the United States. After the Nomonhan incident, Japan and the Soviet Union formally demarcated the Soviet-Manchukuo and Manchukuo-Mongolia borders. To safeguard its rear, and somewhat intimidated by its experience of Soviet military power at Nomonhan, Japan in October 1940 sought a nonaggression pact with the Soviet Union. This was also intended to achieve a halt in the support the Soviet Union under Stalin was providing to China against the Japanese invasion.

However, in November 1940 Soviet Foreign Minister Molotov replied that a nonaggression pact could be concluded only if Japan returned "Southern Sakhalin and the Kurile Islands." If Japan would not do this, the Soviet Union would agree only to a neutrality pact. The matter rested there until Japanese Foreign Minister Matsuoka visited Moscow in March and April 1941. At their meeting on April 7, Molotov twice referred to the return of "a group of Northern Kurile Islands" as among the conditions for a nonaggression pact.[22]

Molotov's statement is significant for the Northern Territories issue. The late Professor Lensen focused on Molotov's use of the expression "the Kurile Islands," claiming this probably meant that at that stage, long before they considered making war on Japan, Soviet leaders such as Stalin and Molotov most likely thought the entire Kurile Archipelago had to be recovered from Japan.[23] However, Tsuguo Togawa, formerly a professor at the Slavic Research Center of Hokkaido University, gave more credence to the recollection of Haruhiko Nishi (then Japanese minister to the Soviet Union), who professed to remember that Molotov spoke not of "the Kurile Islands," but of "several islands in the north of the Kurile Archipelago."[24] He said:

I clearly remember Molotov saying, "several islands in the north of the Kurile Archipelago." This supports Japanese claims that the Southern Kurile Islands are inalienably Japanese territory. Molotov must have been well aware of existing treaty arrangements pertaining to the Kuriles, namely the Treaty of Shimoda (1855), which set the islands south of and including Etorofu as Japanese territory, and based upon this, the Treaty of Sakhalin-Kurile Islands Exchange (1875), which applies to neither Kunashiri nor Etorofu. Molotov's statement can be interpreted as being of great significance in future territorial negotiations between Japan and Russia.[25]

After Ambassador Yoshitsugu Tatekawa briefed him on Molotov's proposal, Foreign Minister Yōsuke Matsuoka instructed Tatekawa to offer to buy Northern Sakhalin.[26] This was not the first time the idea of buying Northern Sakhalin had appeared on the Japanese side. In June 1923, during the negotiations leading to the conclusion of the Basic Convention of 1925, the chief Japanese negotiator, Toshitsune Kawakami, told his counterpart, Soviet ambassador to China Adolf Joffe, that the best method for solving the sovereignty problem over Sakhalin would be for Russia to sell its northern half to Japan, and he even suggested a specific price of approximately 150,000,000 yen. Surprisingly, Joffe did not reject this outright. He said he deemed the proposal acceptable in principle, merely upped the "reasonable price" to one billion gold rubles, and subsequently, after receiving instructions from Moscow, further raised it to 1.5 billion.[27] However, with the general military strategic situation in 1940 much more tense than in 1923, Matsuoka's revived proposal to purchase Northern Sakhalin was considered laughable to the Soviet Union. When on November 21, 1940, Ambassador Tatekawa reminded Molotov of the offer, he replied, "In a speech of mine in the Supreme Soviet on March 29, 1940, I joked to those listening that there are people in this world who seek to buy what is not for sale."[28]

The Japanese-Soviet negotiations reached a deadlock. After a Japanese government liaison conference in February 1941, held to review policy toward the Soviet Union, Germany, and Italy, Matsuoka was sent to Moscow, Berlin, and Rome, and in early April 1941, on his way back to Japan, revisited Moscow, where he met with Stalin and Molotov. He again raised the issues of a nonaggression pact and purchase of Northern Sakhalin with Molotov and received a firm refusal to both. He had almost given up hope of concluding even a neutrality pact, when a meeting with Stalin on April 12 removed all impediments. The Japanese-Soviet Neutrality Pact was signed the very next day.[29] As Item 12 in the Joint Compendium indicates, this Pact stated: (1) both parties undertook to maintain peaceful and friendly relations with each other, and mutually respect each other's territorial integrity and inviolability; (2) if one of the contracting parties became the object of military action by one or more third countries, the other party would remain neutral during the whole period of the conflict; and (3) the pact would remain in force for a period of five years, and if not denounced by either contracting party a year before the expiration of that period, would be considered automatically extended for the next five years.

At the post-signing banquet held that night, the following, now well-known exchange is said to have occurred between Stalin and Matsuoka.

Stalin: "You are an Asiatic. So am I. We are all Asian." Matsuoka echoed. "Let us drink to Asian."[30]

When Matsuoka and his entourage left Moscow, Stalin appeared on the station platform to see them off, in what Haruhiko Nishi described as an "unprecedented event," with an openly ebullient Stalin embracing Matsuoka and again speaking of their shared Asian heritage.[31]

Efforts to Eradicate Territorial Conflict: The Atlantic Charter and the Cairo Declaration

The desire for territorial expansion is an impulse not only rooted in the animal instincts of humans but also indivisibly linked with nation-building in modern times. As a result, conflict over borders has become the commonest cause of war. One could even say that modern states have displayed a tendency to constant involvement in wars over territory, as countries that seize territory face the prospect of war when the aggrieved nation seeks to win it back, giving birth to an endless cycle of vengeance, just as in Japan's feudal period. Even where this kind of cycle does not occur, territory ceded as a result of war leads to lingering acrimony between the nations involved. The situation between Israel and Palestine is a good example. They are still fighting for lost territory over fifty-eight years.

How can this vicious circle concerning territory be brought to an end? One effective method requires victorious nations to make sacrifices, and not force a vanquished nation, already suffering from the inferiority complex and other psychological baggage that goes with defeat, to make territorial concessions. Victors should be content with being victorious and restrain their acquisitive instincts. This way of thinking was expressed in concrete form as the "principle of no territorial expansion" agreed by Allied leaders during World War Two.

First of all, Franklin D. Roosevelt and Winston Churchill met on board U.S. and British warships in Placentia Bay of Newfoundland, and on August 14, 1941, issued the joint declaration known as the Atlantic Charter. Its eight common principles, covering such issues as national self-determination, popular sovereignty, international economic collaboration, promotion of social welfare, freedom from fear and want, and abandonment of the use of force, subsequently formed the basis of the United Nations Charter. Article 1 stated that both "their countries seek no aggrandizement, territorial or other." Article 2 further stated, "They desire to see no territorial changes that do not accord with the freely expressed wishes of the peoples concerned" (see the Joint Compendium, Item 13). On September 24, the Soviet government expressed "its agreement with the basic principles of the declaration of the President of the United States Mr. Roosevelt and the Prime Minister of Great Britain Mr. Churchill" (see the Joint Compendium, Item 14). Subsequently, in November 1943, Roosevelt, Churchill, and Chiang Kai-shek met in Cairo, and on November 27 issued the Cairo Declaration. Although its purpose was to "restrain and punish the aggression of Japan," it confirmed the principles of the Atlantic Charter and specified that the Allied powers had no intention to seek territorial expansion. The specific wording is: "They covet no gain for themselves and have no thought of territorial expansion" (see the Joint Compendium, Item 15). The declaration went on to state, "Japan shall be stripped of all the islands in the Pacific which she has seized or occupied since the beginning of the First World War in 1914" and "expelled from all other territories which she has taken by violence and greed."

What is the status of Southern Sakhalin and the Kurile Islands under the Cairo Declaration? As it does not specifically mention them, the only possible interpretation is through the abstract expression, "other territories which she has taken by violence and greed." First of all, Russia ceded the Kurile Islands peacefully and voluntarily to Japan by the Treaty of St. Petersburg in 1875, so they clearly were not "taken by violence and greed." Furthermore, Russia had previously recognized Habomai, Shikotan, Kunashiri, and Etorofu as Japanese territory by peacefully and voluntarily negotiating the Treaty of Shimoda in 1855, so they also were not "taken by violence and greed."[32] What therefore remains is the matter of Southern Karafuto/Sakhalin. Japan acquired this from Russia by a combination of two factors, violent means, through occupying it in the Russo-Japanese War, and peaceful negotiation of the Treaty of Portsmouth. If we choose to emphasize the former, Southern Sakhalin could be seen as "taken by violence and greed," but those who stress the latter will not agree.

Be that as it may, the Cairo Declaration was not a document designed to determine territorial ownership under international law. It was only an expression by Great Britain, the United States, and China of intent to apply a particular policy when making a peace treaty with a defeated Japan, which was not a signatory to it and which was bound to it only by its subsequent acceptance of the Potsdam Declaration, which clearly stated that "the terms of the Cairo Declaration shall be carried out" (see the Joint Compendium, Item 20). In this respect, the content of the Cairo Declaration principle of "no territorial aggrandizement" was binding not only for Japan but for all nations endorsing the Potsdam Declaration, including the Soviet Union.

The Big Three Yalta Conference

Until its very last years, the Soviet Union would always quote the Yalta Agreement as the legal basis for its possession of the Northern Territories. When Soviet politicians, diplomats, and researchers were questioned as to what they meant by the "series of international treaties, agreements, and conventions" resulting in Habomai, Shikotan, Kunashiri, and Etorofu becoming Soviet territory, they would quote the Yalta Agreement and San Francisco Peace Treaty. But could the Yalta Agreement be a sufficient basis for the Soviet Union to claim sovereignty over the Northern Territories?

The Yalta Conference was a summit meeting of Roosevelt, Churchill, and Stalin from February 4–11, 1945, in the quiet Crimean resort town of Yalta, a venue that catered to Stalin's dislike of air travel, and, being in Soviet territory, conferred on the Soviet leader some psychological, logistical, and technical advantages (including, as was later disclosed, the ability to bug the other delegations' discussions). Eight meetings were held, at which creation of a postwar system—subsequently called the Yalta System—was discussed. The Yalta Conference can reasonably be described as the backroom dealings that established the fundamental framework for division and control of the postwar world by the victors.

On the fifth day (February 8), just before the main session attended by all three leaders, Roosevelt and Stalin met to discuss Asian affairs. Stalin wanted to discuss the "political conditions under which the USSR would enter the war against Japan." He claimed that certain political conditions had to be met, so that he could explain to the Soviet people why the Soviet Union should join the war against Japan, which, unlike Germany, had not threatened their country's very existence, and what benefits would result from its doing so.[33]

Roosevelt had been aware of Stalin's intentions for almost a year. For example, the minutes of the Pacific War Council held in Washington on January 12, 1944, note, "President Roosevelt informed the council that his discussions with Generalissimo Chiang Kai-shek and with Marshal Stalin were highly satisfactory—in that both had agreed that Japan should be stripped of her island possessions. . . . He [Stalin] wishes all of Sakhalin to be returned to Russia and to have the Kurile Islands turned over to Russia in order that they may exercise control of the straits leading to Siberia."[34] On December 15 of that year, a telegram to Roosevelt from Ambassador Harriman in Moscow again alerted him to Stalin's conditions for entering the war against Japan. "Top Secret: In my talk with Stalin last night I said that you were anxious to know what political questions he had indicated in October should be clarified in connection with Russia's entry in the war against Japan. He went into the next room and brought out a map. He said the Kurile Islands and Lower Sakhalin should be returned to Russia."[35]

According to Charles E. Bohlen (later U.S. ambassador to the Soviet Union), who was at the February 8 meeting and took notes, "The President evidently thought that both Southern Sakhalin and the Kuriles had been seized by Japan in the 1904 war, and that Russia therefore was only getting back territories that had been taken from her.[36] . . . The President felt that there would be no *difficulty* whatsoever in regard to the southern half of Sakhalin and the Kurile Islands" (italics added).[37] That is how American official records noted Roosevelt's response, but Soviet official publications claimed he said more categorically that "Southern Sakhalin and the Kurile Islands *shall be handed over to* the Soviet Union" (italics added).[38]

To express the slight difference in nuances of these two versions, Item 16 in the Joint Compendium quotes from both. Either way, it is almost certain that Roosevelt intended to grant the Soviet Union "the southern half of Sakhalin and the Kurile Islands" as a reward for entering the war against Japan. According to former Foreign Minister Andrei Gromyko's *Memories*, the day Stalin received Roosevelt's acceptance of the Soviet position on Southern Sakhalin and the Kuriles, he was "extremely happy, walking around his drawing room saying, "Khorosho, ochen' Khorosho" (Good, very good!).[39]

With the benefit of hindsight, some American specialists on the Yalta Conference suggest that had Roosevelt been fully aware of the history of Russo-Japanese relations, and in particular the historical background to sovereignty over the Kurile Islands, the subsequent history of the Northern Territories might have been very different. On the night before the conference began, the State Department provided Roosevelt with a briefing paper compiled by Far Eastern specialist Professor George H. Blakeslee of Clark University.[40] This paper emphasized: (1) Habomai, Shikotan, Kunashiri, and Etorofu were acquired legally by Japan as a result of peaceful negotiations in 1855; and (2) these islands (Southern Kuriles) should be retained by Japan.[41] Unfortunately Roosevelt did not read Blakeslee's report before his meetings with Stalin.[42] In his book *Witness to History 1929–1969* (1973), Charles E. Bohlen wrote about how the fate of the Northern Territories might have been different had Roosevelt read Blakeslee's briefing paper. "If the President had done his homework, or if any of us had been more familiar with

Far Eastern history, the United States might not have given the Kuriles to Stalin so easily."[43]

Roosevelt's blunder on this occasion is a source of great sorrow for me as a Japanese. If he had held out a little longer, Japanese–Russian relations might not have been so unproductive for so many years. Nevertheless, it was not necessarily inevitable that the president would read a briefing paper prepared by a lowly university professor. Moreover, Roosevelt was in very poor health and died only a few weeks later, before the war's end. Besides, even if Roosevelt had read Blakeslee's paper and understood the distinction between the four Northern Territories and the rest of the archipelago, there is no guarantee that he would not have handed over the entire Kurile chain to the USSR.[44]

In this context, we must next ask ourselves whether it was actually *necessary* for the Soviet Union to enter the war in order to defeat Japan.[45] This will probably never be decided one way or the other. There are sufficient grounds for saying that it was *not necessary*. By the summer of 1945 Japan's national resources were completely exhausted, and even if the United States had not dropped the atomic bombs, Japan would probably have capitulated if the Allies had not persisted in demanding unconditional surrender. Moreover, in actual fact Japan's surrender was not necessarily unconditional. Article 13 of the Potsdam Declaration stipulated that the Japanese government order Japan's *military forces*, not the government, to surrender unconditionally.[46] In military terms, rather than *necessary*, Soviet entry into the Far Eastern theater of World War Two was *desirable*, in order to minimize the bloodshed for American troops. Roosevelt wanted the Soviets to enter the war more than anything else, and the larger benefits of securing this far outweighed the value of the Kuriles. Roosevelt was convinced that he was doing the right thing.[47]

American specialists also ask, "Granted that Russian entry into war against Japan was desirable, was the price paid for Soviet help too high? Were the concessions justified?"[48] Before the United States dropped the atomic bombs, they had already planned two major amphibious assaults against the main Japanese islands, but if the Soviet Union were to enter the war before either of these operations were launched, they predicted that American casualties would be reduced by as many as 200,000.[49] Bohlen contends that this estimate is grossly exaggerated, but he does state that Roosevelt's one reason for seeking Stalin's agreement was that Soviet entry into the Asian war would save the hundreds of thousands of American casualties his military experts estimated would otherwise be incurred.[50] No general in the American delegation at Yalta voiced a word of opposition to Roosevelt's acceptance of Stalin's conditions.[51] In fact, according to Harriman, "Nor did the Joint Chiefs of Staff raise the slightest objection when Harriman showed each of them the draft agreement. . . . Marshall, King, and Leahy all agreed with the draft. Even Admiral Leahy, who later wrote that he believed Japan could be defeated without Russian participation, remarked to Harriman, 'This makes the trip [to Yalta] worthwhile.'"[52]

Southern Sakhalin and the Kurile Islands represented the price Roosevelt and Churchill paid at Yalta for Stalin's agreement to enter the war against Japan. Questioning the morality of their acquiescence is merely an academic exercise. Never in their wildest dreams would either have thought of postwar Japan becoming not only a key ally of the United States and Great Britain but also the greatest potential source of economic assistance for a post-Soviet Russia. Nevertheless, dissatisfaction over the nonreturn of the Northern Territories has seen Japan assume a less than positive stance toward contributing economic assistance to Russia. Also, even if these two leaders had made no promises, Stalin might have entered the war against Japan and seized more territory than was promised (for example, half of Hokkaido) or seized the islands as a condition for not entering the war. When considered in this light, maybe Roosevelt and Churchill had little choice but to agree to Stalin's demands.

The Yalta Agreement

Churchill joined Roosevelt and Stalin in signing the Yalta Agreement three days later, on February 11.[53] The part of this secret agreement appears as Item 17 of the Joint Compendium. Article 2 states, "The southern part of Sakhalin as well as the islands adjacent to it shall be returned to the Soviet Union"; Article 3 states, "The Kurile Islands shall be handed over to the Soviet Union."

The Soviet Union cited the Yalta Agreement—in Russia it is called the Crimea Agreement—to attempt to justify its sovereignty over the four islands. Japan put forward the following two indisputable points to repudiate this.

First, the Yalta Agreement was no more than a statement by the Big Three of Allied policy on postwar settlement and as such cannot be judged as representing the final decision of all Allied nations concerned. American official documents on the territorial issue, dated September 7, 1956, confirm this: "The United States regards the so-called Yalta Agreement as simply a statement of common purposes by the then heads of the participating powers, and not as a final determination by those powers or any legal effect in transferring territories."[54]

Second, in addition to the Yalta Agreement being a secret accord, which Japan neither participated in nor signed, there is no legal reason why she should be bound by its provisions. In the Soviet Union, with the advent of the Gorbachev administration and the policy of "glasnost" (openness), the issue of validity of the secret additional protocol attached to the Nazi-Soviet Non-Aggression Pact of 1939 was raised. This protocol determined the respective spheres of influence in Eastern Europe, allocating the Baltic States and Bessarabia to the Soviet sphere, leading to Soviet annexation of them in the following year. Alexander N.Yakovlev, Gorbachev's closest political ally, was appointed chairman of the special commission established at the request of the Baltic States to review the secret protocol. In August 1989,Yakovlev criticized it as "deviating from the Leninist principles of Soviet foreign policy," sentiments echoed by Gorbachev himself in the following month.

This was most likely the reason why from then on there was a dramatic reduction in the frequency with which Soviet Japan specialists quoted the Yalta Agreement to justify Soviet occupation of the Northern Territories. I first became conscious of this at the 14th Conference of Soviet-Japanese Specialists, held in Oiso in June 1989 (since May 1973 jointly hosted by Ichiro Suetsugu, chairman of the Council on National Security Problems, and the Institute of World Economy and International Relations, Soviet Academy of Sciences, IMEMO). A joint paper titled "Soviet-Japanese Relations—Is a Breakthrough Possible?" was presented by two prominent Soviet authorities on Soviet–Japanese relations: Georgii Kunadze, then head of the Research Section of Japanese Politics and Society, IMEMO, subsequently Russian deputy foreign minister, and Konstantin Sarkisov, head of the Center for Japanese Studies, Institute of Oriental Studies; there was, for the first time, no mention of the Yalta Agreement.

Furthermore, in his own paper presented in the summer of 1990, Kunadze said:

What is the Yalta Agreement? It is nothing but a secret agreement among wartime allies concerning territorial and other rewards to the USSR for her entry into the war against Japan. One can add that it is an agreement that did not pass, and could never pass, any process of ratification. Now the Second Congress of the USSR Peoples' Deputies has given a political assessment of the secret protocol attached to the Soviet-German Treaty of 1939, and in his thoroughgoing speech, Alexander Yakovlev has stated that the secret transfer of territory is illegal and unacceptable. In such a context, adherence to the Yalta Agreement can only give rise to annoyance. Needless to say, it does not in any way strengthen our negotiating position and only serves to irritate the other party. The time has come to establish fairness and to announce that the Yalta Agreement, which was not subsequently included in the official documents of the Allies represents no more than a page of our history. Indeed, it is not the best page either.[55]

The following comment is found in the preface to the Joint Compendium of Documents on the History of the Territorial Demarcation Between Russia and Japan: "The Soviet Union *maintained* that the Yalta Agreement provided legal confirmation of the transfer of the Kurile Islands to the USSR, including the islands of Etorofu, Kunashiri, Shikotan, and Habomai. Japan's position is that the Yalta Agreement is not the final determination on the territorial issue and that Japan, which was not a party to this Agreement, is neither legally nor politically bound by its provisions" (italics added).

Whereas Japan's position is clearly stated in the present tense, the Soviet assertion is presented in the past tense, as the day of the Soviet Union belongs to the past. Of course, this does not necessarily mean that the Russian administration gave up, to resort to the Yalta Agreement.

Violation of the Japan-Soviet Neutrality Pact

Just as World War Two was drawing to a close, when Japan was exhausted from her struggle against the Western Allies, Stalin stabbed Japan in the back, entering the Pacific War to secure a place amongst the victors. Not only that, in blatant violation of the "principle of no territorial expansion" espoused in the Atlantic Charter and the Cairo Declaration, in the confusion of the weeks immediately after the surrender, the Soviet Union, like "a thief at a fire" seized from Japan not only Southern Sakhalin and the eighteen islands of the Kurile Archipelago, but also Habomai, Shikotan, Kunashiri, and Etorofu, and even went so far as asking for an occupation zone in the northern half of Hokkaido.[56]

The Soviet-Japanese Neutrality Pact specified that its term would be automatically extended for another five years unless either party renounced it one year before its expiry. The pact came into effect on April 25, 1941, so although the Soviet Union did renounce it in April 1945 (see the Joint Compendium, Item 18), it remained valid until April 25, 1946. Therefore, the Soviet declaration of war on Japan on August 9, 1945 (see the Joint Compendium, Item 19), was clearly in violation of the Neutrality Pact. The preface to the Joint Compendium highlights this:

In the Neutrality Pact between Japan and the USSR of April 13, 1941, the parties had an obligation to mutually respect each other's territorial integrity and inviolability. The pact also stated that it would remain in force for five years and that if neither of the contracting parties denounced it a year before its date of expiration, it would be considered to be automatically extended for the next five years. After the Soviet Union announced its intention to denounce the Soviet-Japanese Neutrality Pact on April 5, 1945, the pact was to have become invalid on April 25, 1946. The Soviet Union declared war on Japan on August 9, 1945.

The Soviet Union entered the war against Japan on August 9, 1945, just five days before the official announcement of the Japanese government's decision to surrender. The date of Soviet declaration of war can be traced back to the fact that Stalin had promised to enter the war against Japan within three months of the defeat of Germany, so as the Nazis surrendered on May 8, the Soviet timing was logical in that context.[57] That the Soviet Union violated the Soviet-Japanese Neutrality Pact is undeniable.

A feature of the wartime U.S.-Soviet alliance was that the two nations shared very little other than their main objective of defeating Nazi Germany.

As soon as hostilities ceased in the European theater, not only did the "strange alliance" disappear into the clouds, but it was immediately replaced by antagonism.[58] Similarly, the Soviet-Japanese relationship represented by the Neutrality Pact was no more than a marriage of convenience, to continue only so long as mutual interests required. Some scholars thus contended in the Soviet period that Japan might have violated the Neutrality Pact, citing a conversation between Foreign Minister Matsuoka and Soviet Ambassador Konstantin Smetanin. On June 23, 1941, the day after Germany invaded the Soviet Union, Smetanin went to Matsuoka to seek assurance that Japan would observe the recently signed Neutrality Pact despite its membership of the Tripartite Pact with Germany and Italy.[59] Matsuoka replied that if the Neutrality Pact clashed with Japan's Tripartite Pact commitments, the Neutrality Pact would "have no force" (Smetanin's notes). But Matsuoka, who had convinced himself that Germany was unlikely to attack the Soviet Union, made this statement at a moment of surprise when the news of the invasion was just breaking.[60] He was considered Hitler's greatest admirer in Japan,[61] had no authority to commit Japan to support Germany's war, and knew that the option of intervention in Siberia had lost favor in Japanese military circles.[62] He may also have thought that Soviet resistance would not continue for long, so there would be no need to conciliate Smetanin. Be that as it may, the facts are that Japan neither renounced nor violated the Neutrality Pact. The Soviet Union did both.

The Occupation of the Four Northern Islands

On August 14, 1945, the Japanese government accepted the Potsdam Declaration and thereby surrendered (see the Joint Compendium, Items 20 and 21). The Potsdam Declaration stated that the "terms of the Cairo Declaration shall be carried out"; the Japanese government was therefore under the impression that those terms would include "no territorial expansion" by the victors.

The U.S. government immediately issued General Order No. 1 to the supreme commander for the Allied Powers, General Douglas MacArthur, regarding the detailed arrangements for the surrender of the Japanese armed forces. Although Stalin basically approved the content of this order, he made two additional requests:

1. To include in the area of surrender of Japanese armed forces to Soviet troops all the Kurile Islands that, in accordance with the decision of the three powers at the Yalta Conference, would be handed over to the Soviet Union; and

2. That the Northern part of Hokkaido, as divided by a line from Rumoi to Kushiro, would become a Soviet-occupation zone.

President Truman agreed to the first request but flatly refused the second.[63]

Stalin ordered Marshal Alexander Vasilevskii, commander-in-chief of the Soviet Forces in the Far East, to occupy the Kurile Islands. Japanese troops laid down their weapons and surrendered—except for some fighting on Shumshu and Paramushir—so the Soviet occupation of Southern Sakhalin and the Kurile Islands was carried out smoothly. All the islands from Shumshu down to and including Uruppu were occupied by August 31. Soviet troops commenced landing on Etorofu on August 28, and the 13,500-strong Japanese garrison surrendered without resistance. Processing this unexpectedly large number delayed the landings on Kunashiri and Shikotan (where 4,800 surrendered) until September 1. All subsequent Soviet publications, including *A History of the Second World War* and *The Military Encyclopedia* claimed that the occupation of all the Kurile Islands was completed by September 1, the day before Japanese government representatives signed the instruments of surrender on board the USS *Missouri*. In fact, after Etorofu, Kunashiri, and Shikotan were occupied, the Soviet High Command decided also to occupy the Habomai group of islets, and this was undertaken on September 3–5.

The details in the preceding paragraph are summarized from an article, titled "The Landing of Soviet Forces on Hokkaido and Southern Kuriles," which appeared in the May 12, 1992, edition of *Izvestiia*.[64] The author was the late Boris Slavinsky, a Russian researcher of Asia-Pacific affairs, who was also deputy editor-in-chief of the journal *Far-Eastern Affairs*, published by the Institute for Far Eastern Studies, the Russian Academy of Sciences. The article was based on primary sources he found in the Central Army-Navy Archive in Moscow. The facts he brought to light for the first time are of major significance. To make this point, I cite them in chronological order.

1945

August 15:   Imperial Edict ending the war

August 28:   Soviet forces land on and occupy Etorofu

September 1:   Soviet forces land on and occupy Kunashiri and Shikotan

September 2:   Japanese Foreign Minister Mamoru Shigemitsu signs the instruments of surrender on board USS *Missouri*

September 2:   Order issued to occupy Habomai group of islets

September 3:   Soviet forces began landing on Habomai islets

September 5:   Occupation of Habomai islets completed

As this list shows, the Soviet occupation of Japan's Northern Territories was conducted between August 28 and September 5. That this was after Japan accepted the terms of the Potsdam Declaration, and that the Habomai islets were seized after September 2, is important. Slavinsky commented, "The occupation of the 'Northern Islands' was nothing but a military occupation conducted without any bloodshed after Japan had surrendered, accepted the conditions stipulated by the Allies, and ceased military action."[65]

The dates of the Soviet landings on the Northern Territories established by Slavinsky from official Soviet documents precisely match those recorded in previously available testimony from former Japanese residents of the islands, who were forcibly repatriated after the landings.[66] Before this material was published, the War Victims' Relief Bureau's position was that "the occupation of the Northern Territories of Etorofu, Kunashiri, Habomai, and Shikotan was carried out between August 29 and September 3."

There is one more important point. Slavinsky wrote that on August 18, Truman agreed to Stalin's request for confirmation that "all of the Kurile Islands" would become Soviet territory.[67] But a problem remains over the meaning of "all of the Kurile Islands." There are strong indications that, at least to Soviet commanders in the field, "all of the Kurile Islands" meant the islands down to and including Uruppu, not Etorofu and islands south of it. Proof of this can be found in statements by Japanese Major Mitsuru Suizu, who was stationed with the Northern Kurile Divisional Command at the end of the war and who was made to serve as a pilot on board a Soviet destroyer as it sailed southward. He recalled that it went only as far as Uruppu and then turned back northward. When he asked Chief-of-Staff Volonov why this was so, he was told emphatically that "the Americans are in charge south of here, so the Soviet Union won't touch them."[68] On returning to Japan, after five years in a Soviet labor camp, Major Suizu was apparently shocked to learn that the Soviet Union had occupied the Northern Territories. Based on his experience, he concluded that the Soviet Union had not initially planned to occupy them, but had acted like "a thief at a fire" on realizing that U.S. forces had not taken them.[69] This fits in with the testimony of contributors to *Former Islands Residents Speak: Our Northern Territories*, who virtually all stated that the first thing Soviet troops said to them after landing was "Have any American troops landed?"[70] If we accept Major Suizu's and the former residents' testimony, it seems that, whatever Stalin intended, the Soviet military on the spot did not see the four islands as part of "all of the Kurile Islands."

On September 2, 1945, Stalin delivered his famous speech marking victory over Japan. He made it very clear that a long-awaited opportunity had come, to be avenged for defeat in the Russo-Japanese War—and that he desired a geographical exit to the Pacific:[71]

As is well known, at that time Russia suffered defeat in the war with Japan. Japan took advantage of tsarist Russia's defeat to wrest south Sakhalin from Russia, to strengthen her hold over the Kurile Islands, thus locking all outlets for our country to the ocean in the east. . . . Today, Japan has acknowledged her defeat and signed the act of unconditional surrender. This means that south Sakhalin and the Kurile Islands will pass to the Soviet Union, and from now on will not serve as a means for isolating the Soviet

Union from the ocean and as a base for Japanese attacks on Far East. They will now serve instead as a means of direct communication of the Soviet Union with the ocean and as a base for the defense of our country against Japanese aggression.[72]

On top of that, after 1947 Stalin ordered the removal of not only all Japanese residents of Southern Sakhalin but also the 17,291 residents of the Northern Territories. Although Article 9 of the Potsdam Declaration stated, "The Japanese military forces, after being completely disarmed, shall be permitted to return to their homes with the opportunity to lead peaceful and productive lives" (see the Joint Compendium, Item 20), Stalin had 609,000 Japanese soldiers and others transported to forced labor in Siberia and kept them there for up to eleven years in harsh conditions that claimed the lives of 62,000 of them. The last of the survivors did not return until the signing of the Soviet-Japanese Joint Declaration in 1956.

On January 29, 1946, General Douglas MacArthur, Supreme Commander Allied Powers (SCAP), issued Directive No. 677, which stated, "Japan is defined to include the four main islands (Hokkaido, Honshu, Kyushu, and Shikoku) and the approximately 1,000 small adjacent islands, . . . excluding . . . the Kurile (Chishima) Islands, the Habomai Island Group, and Shikotan Island." The directive, however, included a disclaimer, that it was not to "be construed as an indication of Allied policy relating to the ultimate determination of the minor islands referred to in Article 8 of the Potsdam Declaration" (see the Joint Compendium, Item 22).

Between 1946 and 1948 the Soviet authorities issued decrees unilaterally integrating Southern Sakhalin and the Kuriles into the Soviet Union. First, a decree of February 2, 1946, declared Southern Sakhalin and the recently seized Kurile Islands to be a district within Khabarovsk Region (see the Joint Compendium, Item 23). Subsequently, on January 2, 1946, this district was abolished and merged into Sakhalin Province. On February 25, 1947, the Soviet constitution was amended to proclaim Sakhalin Province, including Southern Sakhalin and the aforementioned Kurile Islands, part of the Russian Republic. With this, the Soviet Union acquired the region Russia lost to Japan after the Russo-Japanese War (Southern Sakhalin), the region it exchanged with Japan in the 1875 Treaty of St. Petersburg (eighteen Kurile Islands), and the region acknowledged as Japanese by the Treaty of Shimoda in 1855 (the islands south of and including Etorofu).

FIGURE 1. A post with the inscription, "Dai Nippon Etorofu" (Etorofu of Great Japan), proclaiming that Etorofu Island is Japanese territory; post erected by Juzo Kondo in 1798. (This picture was taken in 1930 when the post was repaired and resurrected.)

SOURCE: All photographs are reproduced from the pamphlet "Our Northern Territories" by the Japanese Ministry of Foreign Affairs' Bureau of Public Relations.

FIGURE 2. Rear-Admiral Evfimii Putiatin (1804–83).

FIGURE 3. Toshiakira Kawaji (1801–68).

FIGURE 4. Three Allied leaders at the Yalta Conference, Winston Churchill, Franklin D. Roosevelt, and Joseph Stalin.

FIGURE 5. Japanese Prime Minister Shigeru Yoshida signing at the San Francisco Peace Treaty Conference, September 8, 1951.

FIGURE 6. Japanese Prime Minister Ichiro Hatoyama and Soviet Premier Nikolai Bulganin signing the Soviet-Japanese Joint Declaration in Moscow, October 19, 1956.

FIGURE 7. Japanese Prime Minister Kakuei Tanaka and CPSU's General Secretary Leonid Brezhnev discussing Japanese-Soviet Joint Communiqué in Moscow, October 7–10, 1973.

FIGURE 8. Japanese Prime Minister Toshiki Kaifu and President of the USSR Mikhail S. Gorbachev signing the Japanese-Soviet Joint Communiqué in Tokyo, April 18, 1991.

FIGURE 9. Japanese Prime Minister Morihiro Hosokawa and President of the Russian Federation Boris N. Yeltsin signing the Tokyo Declaration on Japan-Russia Relations in Tokyo, October 13, 1993.

FIGURE 10. "No-necktie" summit meeting between Japanese Prime Minister Ryutaro Hashimoto and President of the Russian Federation Boris N. Yeltsin held at Krasnoyarsk, November 1–2, 1997.

FIGURE 11. "No-necktie" meeting between Ryutaro Hashimoto and Boris N. Yeltsin at Kawana, Japan, April 18–19, 1998.

FIGURE 12. Japanese Prime Minister Keizo Obuchi's official visit to Moscow, November 11–13, 1998.

FIGURE 13. Russian President Vladimir Putin's first official visit to Japan, September 3–5, 2000.

FIGURE 14. Russian President Vladimir Putin and Japanese Prime Minister Yoshiro Mori signing the Irkutsk Joint Statement in Irkutsk, March 25, 2001.

FIGURE 15. Japanese Prime Minister Junichiro Koizumi's official visit to Russia, January 9–12, 2003.

FIGURE 16. Vladimir Putin's second official visit to Japan, November 20–22, 2005.

FIGURE 17. Meeting between Japanese Prime Minister Shinzo Abe and Putin in Hanoi, Vietnam, November 18, 2006.

FIGURE 18. Kaigara Islet, one of the Habomai group; a Japanese fishing boat and the lighthouse on the islet, which was built by the Japanese in 1936.

FIGURE 19. Kunashiri Island.

FIGURE 20. Symbolic statue, wishing for the return of the Northern Islands to Japan; statue called "Bridge to the Four Islands," in Nemuro, Hokkaido.

CHAPTER 4

Toward Normalization of Relations

NOT LONG AFTER World War Two ended, the world was divided into two separate camps, led by the United States and Soviet Union. The ensuing "Cold War" saw both employ all means short of outright war to gain the upper hand. For many years thereafter relations between Japan, the United States, China, and the Soviet Union could be described as parts of an extremely simple equation. In other words, until the Sino-Soviet dispute erupted in the 1960s, the equation represented discord and conflict between two large camps, with the United States and Japan on one side, the Soviet Union and China on the other, and for a long time most developments in Asia could be at least partially explained in terms of this confrontation.

Successive governments in Tokyo judged that they could glean the greatest benefit by sitting firmly under the American umbrella and could secure a place in the international community through a security treaty with the United States. Indeed, at least until the 1970s, it was rare for Tokyo to undertake any foreign policy initiative before Washington had taken the lead. With this overriding context in mind, let us take a closer look at Soviet–Japanese relations during this period.

A Relationship Without Relations

For ten years after World War Two Soviet-Japanese relations could not have been more clear-cut. Until Prime Minister Ichiro Hatoyama visited the Soviet Union in 1956 to sign the Soviet-Japanese Joint Declaration, diplomatic relations between the two countries did not exist, so for that decade the relationship can only be described as without relations. Hostilities had ceased, but there had been no normalization of relations and no peace treaty between the two nations, so in terms of international law they were, strictly speaking, still at war. It is no exaggeration to describe this decade as the years preceding Soviet-Japanese relations.

For more than a decade after World War Two, the philosophy of Shigeru Yoshida (Japanese prime minister 1946–47 and 1948–54), now known as the Yoshida Doctrine, played a major role in framing decisions on the fundamental direction of Japanese foreign policy.[1] From before the war, Yoshida had firmly believed that Japan should maintain harmonious relations with Britain and the United States, and the Cold War's advent so soon after World War Two undoubtedly strengthened this belief. His *Memoirs* include these comments, in describing his visit to West Germany in 1954: "I found myself in complete agreement with West Germany's leaders. . . . Since the United States and the Soviet Union, the two major Powers, are in opposition to each other, one supported by a group of free countries, the other by satellite Communist nations, the only logical policy for both West Germany and Japan to adopt in foreign affairs is cooperation with the United States as members of the group of free nations."[2] In the context of U.S.-Soviet discord, there was no knowing how long Japan might have to wait until it became possible to make peace with all nations. No responsible statesman would choose to make foreign policy decisions contingent on such a remote and unlikely scenario. Probably thinking this way, Yoshida opted not for a "total" peace settlement, including communist nations such as the Soviet Union, but for a "majority"—or "separate" or "one-sided" peace settlement with the United States, Britain, and other nations of the "Free World."[3]

At the same time, Stalin looked to obstruct the process that was steadily drawing Japan into the American camp.[4] But Soviet attempts to do this, by for example demanding control over half of Hokkaido, and by seeking to exercise influence in the Allied Council for Japan, were thwarted at every turn by American leaders such as Truman and MacArthur. Illustrative of this unproductive decade for the Soviet Union is that while it participated in the San Francisco Peace Conference in September 1951, it refused to sign the resulting peace treaty.[5] Let me explain this in greater detail.

The San Francisco Peace Conference

North Korea initiated the Korean War by invading South Korea on June 25, 1950. There is still no accepted explanation regarding Stalin's role in Kim Il Sung's decision to launch it. One version has it that Stalin ordered him to do it, but the more likely scenario is that this was Kim Il Sung's initiative. Although Stalin was noncommittal at first, he likely did not oppose it in principle and went on to provide some support, short of committing Soviet ground or naval forces.[6] Boris Slavinsky made these observations: "As North Korea was reliant on the Soviet Union both economically and militarily, we must of course acknowledge that policy decisions were made jointly with Moscow," and "The fact that in 1949 the People's Liberation Army had destroyed Chiang Kai-shek's forces despite huge injections of American military aid probably led Stalin to believe the same was possible in Korea."[7] Be that as it may, the Korean War engendered a need to reconsider the nature of U.S.–Japanese relations. The United States came to think it prudent to make Japan into an anticommunist bulwark in the Far East. In the words of one of Dulles's biographers, the background to the peace treaty with Japan and the U.S.-Japanese Security Treaty that went with it "represented an American determination to strengthen the peace and security in the Pacific against the ambitions of Red imperialism."[8]

For the San Francisco Peace Conference John Foster Dulles, the chief American delegate and principal architect of peace with Japan, eschewed the standard strategy of gathering representatives of the nations wishing to make peace with Japan and discussing a peace treaty. Instead, he employed a sort of Japanese-style *nemawashi* diplomacy, doing the groundwork by visiting all the main participating nations, explaining the U.S.-British draft, and requesting their approval. As a result, the main task was completed before the invitations to the Peace Conference in San Francisco were issued, and it was conceived as "merely a formal procedure of signing."[9]

Judging from the outcome, Dulles adopted one other significant strategy, in that Japan was forced to relinquish the "Kurile Islands," but to which country it relinquished them was intentionally left unstated. This subtle approach sowed the seeds of enduring conflict between Japan and the Soviet Union over the Northern Territories (see the Joint Compendium, Item 24). Stalin and the Soviet Union fell into the trap.[10] Had the Soviet Union refused to participate in this conference, set up as it was "as a formal procedure of signing the American-British draft already prepared by the United States," its position might have been more consistently persuasive.[11] But despite receiving insufficient preparatory information from the United States, the Soviet Union surprised most by opting to participate in the peace conference, officially justifying its decision by a desire for "exposing the true character of the peace treaty and the American policy of reviving Japanese militarism."[12] Although the Soviet leadership did not consider itself able to exert any direct influence on the U.S. or Japanese governments, it sought to promote the legitimacy of the Soviet position to world opinion, particularly to allies or quasi allies in Asia, such as China and India.

So a Soviet delegation, headed by Andrey Gromyko, took part in the San Francisco Peace Conference, but left without signing the treaty, on the grounds that the Soviet position had not been sufficiently considered. In hindsight it might have been wiser to have signed. To do so could have strengthened the Soviet position on the Northern Territories issue, because as a signatory, it could have cited Article 2, clause C of the treaty, to the effect that Japan had relinquished sovereignty over the "Kurile Islands." Japan would still have been able to claim that Habomai and Shikotan were an extension of Hokkaido, not part of the "Kurile Islands" relinquished under the treaty, and demanded them, but might have had more difficulty in relation to Kunashiri and Etorofu. Granted they had been acknowledged as Japanese territory by the Shimoda Treaty of 1855, their geographical appellation as the "Southern Kuriles" would have made it harder for Japan to argue that they did not belong to the "Kurile Islands" mentioned in the peace treaty.

The Provisional Draft and the Final Draft

In this way, not only did the Soviet Union miss a one-in-a-million chance to undermine Japan's claims for the return of the Northern Territories, but it effectively went out of its way to lend weight to Japan's case. In his speech at the peace conference and in proposals for amendments to the treaty, Gromyko himself publicly acknowledged that the Northern Territories issue was not "resolved," as the Soviet Union would subsequently insist, but very much "unresolved."

For example, in his speech on September 5, 1951 (see the Joint Compendium, Item 25), Gromyko first of all clearly stated, "The peace treaty with Japan should, naturally, resolve a number of *territorial questions* connected with the peace settlement with Japan" (italics added).[13] This statement therefore officially confirmed that the Soviet Union also recognized the international law principle that territory can be legally transferred only by a treaty, and not "as a result of the Second World War" as the Soviet Union would subsequently claim. Gromyko went on to state:

Similarly, by attempting to violate grossly the sovereign rights of the Soviet Union regarding Southern Sakhalin and the islands adjacent to it, as well as the Kurile Islands already under the sovereignty of the Soviet Union, the [American–British] draft also confines itself to a mere mention of the renunciation by Japan of rights, title, and claims to these territories and makes no mention of the historic appurtenance of these territories and the indisputable obligation on the part of Japan to recognize the sovereignty of the Soviet Union over these parts of the territory of the USSR.[14]

Therefore, according to Gromyko, the content of the American–British draft peace treaty was "in contradiction to the obligations undertaken by the United States and Great Britain under the Yalta Agreement regarding the return of Sakhalin and transfer of the Kurile Islands to the Soviet Union."[15]

Actually the United States had initially intended to confirm the Yalta Agreement and to acknowledge the transfer of the Kurile Islands to the Soviet Union, but it moved away from this position during the conference and opted for the less conclusive formula of having Japan relinquish the Kuriles, without defining the country to which sovereignty over them was devolved. This situation is painstakingly described in research by Akira Shigemitsu—nephew of former Foreign Minister Mamoru Shigemitsu—who was not only an outstanding diplomat but also possessed high academic analytical abilities. I shall rely entirely on his work to explain the situation.[16]

The provisional U.S. draft of a Japanese peace treaty, as it stood in March 1951, stated, in keeping with the Yalta Agreement, that "Japan will hand over to the Soviet Union the Kurile Islands."[17] However, it had an additional clause, stating that "the present treaty shall not confer any rights, title or benefits to or upon any State unless and until it signs and ratifies, or adheres to, this treaty."[18] So if the Soviet Union agreed with this draft and was party to the peace treaty, the United States was prepared to settle the issue with the Kurile Islands becoming Soviet territory. Therefore, if the Soviet Union had agreed with that provisional draft, it would have achieved its war aims for the period subsequent to the Yalta Agreement, and its acquisition of the Kurile Islands—despite the remaining problem over their definition—could have been finalized both internationally and legally.

However, although the Soviet Union had no objections to the provisional draft where it concerned the Kurile Islands, it strongly opposed other aspects of it (for example, that it ignored the People's Republic of China's existence, did not contain sufficient barriers to possible reemergence of Japanese militarism, and provided for U.S. forces to remain in Japan). From this response, the United States judged the Soviet Union very unlikely to endorse the kind of peace treaty it desired and switched its approach to one indifferent to Soviet participation. An amended Anglo-American draft was compiled in July 1951 and presented virtually unchanged for signature at the conference.

One of the main differences between the March and July drafts was that whereas the former specified that the Kurile Islands would be handed over to the Soviet Union in accordance with the Yalta Agreement, the latter only stated that Japan would relinquish them and did not name the country to which it would do so. The Potsdam Declaration had stated, "Japanese sovereignty shall be limited to the islands of Honshu, Hokkaido, Kyushu, Shikoku, and such minor islands *as we determine*" (italics added). The wording of the peace treaty meant that while Japan renounced all title and claim to the Kurile Islands vis-à-vis the other signatory nations, she did not renounce them with regard to nonsignatories, leaving determination of the jurisdiction over the islands in a strange state of limbo. This wording is completely removed from the normal approach to territorial settlement in peace treaties, and from a legal point of view, it could only produce an indefinite result.

"Physical Possession Does Not Mean the Acquisition of Sovereignty"

Continuing to refer to Shigemitsu's analysis, I note that essentially treaties about transfer of territory are incomplete unless they determine the title to relinquished territory. Therefore the inconclusive legal situation resulting from the San Francisco Peace Treaty is a transitory one and must in future somehow be brought to a proper conclusion. That was implicit in Dulles's explanation of the draft treaty at the peace conference, when he said, "Clearly, the wise course was to proceed now, so far as Japan is concerned leaving the future to resolve doubts by invoking international solvents *other than this treaty*" (italics added).[19] The issue of jurisdiction over Taiwan, that the San Francisco Peace Treaty similarly left undecided, was solved by the Treaty of Peace Between Japan and the Republic of China in 1952. Subsequently, Japan and the Allied nations indicated that they had no intention of adding a separate agreement, in other words amending the San Francisco Peace Treaty, in order to bring closure to the current incomplete legal relationship. With this in mind, Shigemitsu concluded that the only realistic way forward over the issue of title to the Kurile Islands was for the nations directly involved, Japan and Russia, to resolve it themselves.

Returning to the matter of the San Francisco Peace Conference itself, the American position of promising at Yalta to give the Soviet Union the Kurile Islands, only to renege on this in the peace treaty by not specifying to whom the islands would ultimately belong, can surely be interpreted as an intrigue against the Soviet Union.[20] That, certainly, was how Gromyko saw it. In his book *Memories*, published in 1988, he wrote, "I stated that the treaty resulting from the San Francisco Peace Conference *contradicted* agreed Allied decisions. . . . The United States and Britain, *despite* their obligations from the Yalta Conference and the weight of historical justice, in the San Francisco Peace Treaty, did not recognize these islands as the inherent territory of the Soviet Union" (italics added).[21]

Whether his indignation was appropriate, what is indicated here is that he had clearly recognized that the San Francisco Peace Treaty was not designed to implement the Yalta Agreement, and that the Soviet Union was now at a disadvantage with regard to claims of sovereignty over the Northern Territories.

To recapitulate:

1. The Yalta Agreement was a secret wartime arrangement among the leaders of the United States, Britain, and the USSR, about postwar apportionment of territory to the Soviet Union.

2. Stalin's delegates at the San Francisco Peace Conference refused to sign the treaty when they failed to secure confirmation of that secret arrangement from a U.S. government that had by then changed its stance.

Gromyko therefore concluded his speech at the conference by proposing that the article concerning Japan's relinquishment of title over Southern Sakhalin and the Kurile Islands (Article 2, clause C) be amended to read, "Japan recognizes full sovereignty of the Union of Soviet Socialist Republics over the southern part of Sakhalin, and over the Kurile Islands and renounces all right, title, and claim to these territories."[22] This statement was fatal to the Soviet case because it showed Soviet awareness that, although Japan had relinquished the territory, in international law the Soviet Union could not legitimately acquire the sovereignty over it without Japanese acquiescence.[23]

With the sole objective of the San Francisco Peace Conference being to have the delegates sign the U.S.-UK–drafted peace treaty, Gromyko's proposed amendments were, of course, neither debated nor put to a vote. Therefore, for the Soviet Union the conference did not provide a satisfactory resolution to the Northern Territories issue with Japan. The stern reality of this issue is something clearly acknowledged by subsequent Russian commentators. For example, the following comment can be found in *A History of International Relations in the Far-East (1945–1977)* (published in 1987), compiled under the supervision of Mikhail Kapitsa (former Soviet vice-minister of foreign affairs and director of the Institute of Oriental Studies, Russian Academy of Sciences): "If the Soviet proposed amendments had been accepted [at the San Francisco Peace Conference] this *would have meant the final and complete resolution of the territorial problem*" (italics added).[24] This obviously means that as the Soviet amendments were not adopted, the territorial issue was not resolved. No other interpretation is possible.

Big Mistakes in Soviet Diplomacy

Of course, we should not discuss the whys and wherefores of Soviet diplomacy with regard to the San Francisco Peace Conference and the resulting treaty solely from the viewpoint of the Kurile Islands issue. However, bearing in mind that—with the passage of time—most other issues have been resolved (for example, Okinawa and the Ogasawara Islands have been returned, and the People's Republic of China participates fully in the international community), it is meaningful to question the reasoning and wisdom of Soviet policies regarding that conference.

At that time no one could have imagined that in the second half of the twentieth century Japan would grow as much as she did, to become a major political and economic power in the Asia–Pacific region, nor, perhaps, that Japanese national feeling on the Northern Territories issue would be strong enough to prevent conclusion of a peace treaty with Russia and to hamstring Russo-Japanese relations for more than sixty years. That does not mean, however, that we should turn a blind eye to the inflexibility and shortsightedness shown by the Soviet leaders, or to their inability to adapt their policies in response to changing circumstances.[25]

Whatever its reasons for not signing the San Francisco Peace Treaty, the Soviet Union's refusal to do so was, at least in terms of policy toward Japan, particularly with regard to the Northern Territories dispute, a "great blunder,"[26] in Russian *krupnyi proschët* (a big mistake).[27] Some Soviet commentators also judged it the *main* failure of "Gromyko Diplomacy." For example, in his many pre-perestroika works on Russo-Japanese relations, Soviet Japanologist Dmitrii Petrov (then head of the Japanese Section, Institute of Far Eastern Studies, Soviet Academy of Sciences) went to great lengths to avoid mentioning Gromyko's name in connection with the San Francisco Peace Conference, instead using such abstract expressions as "the Soviet Union," "the Soviet delegation," "Soviet representative," or, "he," thereby separating Gromyko from the peace treaty issue, in order not to harm his reputation.[28]

Khrushchev wrote in his memoirs that not signing the San Francisco Peace Treaty was a diplomatic error on Stalin's part. Although the following citation is a little long, it is an important statement by a key Soviet figure:

> However, we have to give the Americans some credit. When the protocol of the peace treaty with Japan was drafted, there was a place reserved for our signature. Our interests were totally taken care of there. All we had to do was sign, and everything would have fallen into place; we would have gotten everything we were promised. We would also have restored peaceful relations with Japan and been able to send representatives of our diplomatic service to Tokyo.
>
> We should have signed. I don't know why we didn't. Perhaps it was vanity or pride. But primarily it was that Stalin had an exaggerated idea of what he could do and what his influence was on the United States. He took the bit in his mouth and refused to sign the treaty. . . . Still, we should have taken a more sober view of events. . . .
>
> When we refused to sign the Japanese surrender, forces in the West probably thought it was to their advantage. And it later turned out they were right. Just look at who benefited from the situation: it was our own fault because if we had signed we would have had an embassy there. We would have had access to Japanese public opinion and influential circles. We would have established trade relations with Japanese firms.
>
> We missed all that. That's just what the Americans wanted; it was in their interest. . . . They wanted to isolate us. . . . Now we ourselves swallowed this very bait and ended up pleasing aggressive, anti-Soviet forces in the United States, all because of our shortsightedness.
>
> Since we had absolutely no contacts with Japan, our economy and our policy suffered.[29]

Legal Title to the Kurile Islands

For many years the Soviet Union would routinely claim that the sovereignty over the four Northern Territories islands had been legally transferred from Japan to it through "a series of international treaties, agreements, and arrangements." When asked what exactly these were, they mainly cited the "Yalta Agreement and San Francisco Peace Treaty." However, at the risk of being repetitive, the Yalta Agreement was no more than a secret understanding between the Big Three, to which Japan was not a party, and the San Francisco treaty is one that the Soviet Union did not sign. Therefore Soviet/Russian claims of sovereignty over the Northern Territories lacked an adequate foundation in international law. The transfer of territory can only take place by a treaty accepted and entered into by both parties. No such treaty was ever concluded between Japan and the Soviet Union or Russia.[30]

But Japan was also remiss, both during and for some time after the San Francisco Peace Conference. That is to say, in Article 2, clause C of the peace treaty, Japan "renounces all right, title and claim to the 'Kurile Islands'" (see the Joint Compendium, Item 27). This can be interpreted to mean that the islands relinquished included part or all of the Northern Territories. As the Kurile Islands were not defined at the peace conference—and it is possible to assert Dulles deliberately left this vague—dispute arises as to whether Habomai, Shikotan, Kunashiri, and Etorofu are included, in whole or in part, in the "Kurile Islands" relinquished by Japan. The Soviet Union, and now Russia, insists that these islands are part of the Kurile chain, and that this is evidenced by the fact that Japan sometimes refers to separate parts of the chain as the Northern Kuriles, Central Kuriles, and Southern Kuriles. After examining the original texts of the Treaties of Shimoda and St. Petersburg, academics such as Professors Shichirō Murayama[31] and Haruki Wada[32] conclude that the Japanese Ministry of Foreign Affairs' interpretation—that the Kurile Islands equates to the eighteen islands from Uruppu north—has no academic foundation.[33] Moreover, authorities on international law such as Yūichi Takano, professor emeritus, University of Tokyo,[34] and Takane Sugihara, professor of international law, Kyoto University, have no doubt that, as Dulles also subsequently stated, the Kurile Islands that Japan relinquished do not include Habomai and Shikotan, which are seen as part of Hokkaido, but are of the opinion that there is little legal basis for interpreting the "Kurile Islands" as not including Kunashiri and Etorofu. This does not necessarily mean, however, that these scholars acknowledge that there *is* a legal basis for Russia, which did not sign the peace treaty, to claim the Northern Territories.[35]

The answer given by Kumao Nishimura (then director of the Department of International Treaties, Japanese Ministry of Foreign Affairs) to a question asked in the Diet undoubtedly weakened Japan's position. During a meeting of the House of Representatives Special Committee on Peace on October 19, 1951, he was asked, "What exactly is meant by the 'Kurile Islands'?" He replied, "I consider that the Kurile Islands referred to in the . . . peace treaty include both the Northern Kuriles and Southern Kuriles."[36] That someone in such a senior diplomatic position would make such a statement reflects the confusion that reigned in Japan at the time. Nevertheless, this was a statement made for domestic consumption and has no significance in international law. Also, Nishimura immediately qualified himself, saying, "However, as our delegate Mr. Yoshida has already made clear in his speech at the Peace Conference, in historical terms the situation regarding the Northern Kuriles and the Southern Kuriles is completely different. As the prime minister has frequently stated in this House, our government will continue to hold fast to this opinion."[37]

In the years before perestroika, the Soviet Union sought to use Nishimura's statement as a defense against Japan's demands to have the four islands returned. In the process of compiling the Joint Compendium the teams from the two Ministries of Foreign Affairs agreed to mention the Nishimura statement in the introduction, but not include it in the main collection of materials. On April 18, 1992, the *Hokkaido Shimbun* explained the reason why the Nishimura statement, previously seen as "Japan's biggest point of weakness" had been excluded from the main body of the Joint Compendium. The explanation given was that, according to Japanese Ministry of Foreign Affairs sources, their Russian counterparts probably judged it not necessary to include the statement for the following reasons:

1. There was no clear basis for proving Russian sovereignty over the four islands. To take the debate to radical extremes would not necessarily be advantageous for Russia;

2. To secure economic assistance from Japan, it would not be advisable to completely rule out the return of Kunashiri and Etorofu; and

3. It was a display of a more realistic position, in response to the Japanese government suggestion in April 1992 of willingness to accept a two-phase formula, with Kunashiri and Etorofu returned later than Habomai and Shikotan.

Provoked by the *Hokkaido Shimbun* article, Nikolai Tsvetkov, Tokyo correspondent of the newspaper *Komsomol'skaia Pravda*, wrote a feature for its April 28, 1992, issue, with the sarcastic title, "Shall We Leave Parliamentary

Records Out?" He wrote, "The *Hokkaido Shimbun* is reporting the situation as though Russia agreed to leave out (of the Joint Compendium) the materials that were most disadvantageous for the Japanese position. Specifically, the 1952 parliamentary records pertaining to Japan formally renouncing title over Kunashiri and Etorofu. According to the *Hokkaido Shimbun*, the Japanese Ministry of Foreign Affairs interprets this absence as an indication that their Russian counterparts were "prepared to make concessions."

At the same time, there are of course those who interpret the extent of the "Kurile Islands" differently from Professors Wada and Murayama. The Japanese Ministry of Foreign Affairs and a number of scholars see what is now referred to as the Northern Territories as not belonging to the "Kurile Islands" over which Japan renounced sovereignty. First, they note that in accepting the San Francisco Peace Treaty, on September 7, 1951, Japanese delegate Yoshida Shigeru added the proviso that the four islands are not included in the Kurile Islands relinquished by Japan. Yoshida stated, "With respect to the Kuriles and Southern Sakhalin, I cannot yield to the claim of the Soviet Delegate that Japan had grabbed them by aggression. . . . The islands of Habomai and Shikotan, constituting part of Hokkaido, one of Japan's four main islands . . . and Japan's . . . ownership of the two islands of Etorofu and Kunashiri of the South Kuriles was not questioned at all by the tsarist government" (see the Joint Compendium, Item 26). However, there are doubts whether this statement could be judged to have the legal effect of excluding Etorofu and Kunashiri from the definition of the Kurile Islands relinquished by Japan.

Also, the Japanese Ministry of Foreign Affairs, among others, responded as follows to the question of who should give the definition and extent of the Kurile Islands as mentioned in Article 2, clause C of the peace treaty. It stated that if no clear definition was provided from either the conference or the treaty, the only proper way to acquire one was to ask the signatory nations. In such a case, the judgment of the United States, as the country that drafted the treaty, assumes particular importance. American announcements on the extent of the Kurile Islands have not necessarily been consistent, but the following examples are important. First of all, in the *aide-mémoire*, titled "United States Government Memorandum on Soviet-Japanese Negotiations," handed to Ambassador Masayuki Tani by Secretary of State Dulles on September 7, 1956 (made public on September 12), it states that by clearly recognizing Japan's sovereignty over the four islands, the United States officially announced that they were not included in the "Kurile Islands." To be exact: "After careful examination of the historical facts, the United States has reached the conclusion that the islands of Etorofu and Kunashiri (along with the Habomai Islands and Shikotan, which are part of Hokkaido) have always been a part of Japan proper and should in justice be acknowledged as under Japanese sovereignty."[38]

Professor Sugihara commented that the meaning of the words "should *in justice* be acknowledged as under Japanese sovereignty" is unclear (italics added).[39] He outlined two meanings: first, that when interpreting the peace treaty, "both Kunashiri and Etorofu must be seen as Japanese territory"; or second, that the disputed areas must be acknowledged as under Japanese sovereignty in "a political ideal." If the former, we could say this represented the American interpretation of the law, but if the latter, it is a policy statement. Professor Sugihara continued, "In either case, it has some meaning. If Japan makes legal requests for the return of Kunashiri and Etorofu, it would be necessary to confirm that the United States is assuming the former interpretation, as the country that drafted the peace treaty. It would be also necessary to confirm that that stance was understood, or at least was not opposed, by the other signatory nations."[40]

While I consider Professor Sugihara's question legitimate, I think that so long as we cannot judge which interpretation was intended, should we, considering both the legal and political aspects, interpret this statement to mean that, at least at this stage, the United States intends to recognize that Japan has sovereignty over the four islands, including both Kunashiri and Etorofu? Boris Slavinsky stated that "politics and geography should not be confused. *In terms of geography*, the 'Northern Territories' might fall within the parameters of the 'Kurile Islands,' *but from a political perspective*, as was decided at the San Francisco Peace Conference, the 'Kurile Islands' mean the Northern and Central Kuriles that were (until 1875) formerly part of tsarist Russia" (italics added).[41]

As the country that accepted the terms of the peace treaty, the stance and interpretation of the Japanese government also carries weight. At a meeting of the House of Representatives Foreign Affairs Committee, on February 11, 1956, Parliamentary Vice-Minister of Foreign Affairs Kunio Morishita gave this explanation of the Japanese government's position:

Just to make sure that there will be no misunderstandings on the issue of the Southern Kuriles, I would like to make one clear statement: The Southern Kuriles, that means the two islands, Kunashiri (Kunashir) and Etorofu (Iturup), have always been Japan's territories, and there has been no doubt whatsoever about this point, and the return of these islands is only natural. The Soviet Union did not participate in the San Francisco Peace Treaty, but it is our government's view that even in that treaty, the two islands are not included in the Kurile Islands stipulated therein.[42]

Furthermore, not one of the forty-eight signatory nations voiced a word of objection against the previously mentioned U.S. interpretation of the "Kurile Islands."[43] In light of this, at least so far as this particular treaty is concerned, we are obliged to accept the American interpretation that the Northern Territories are not included in the "Kurile Islands" as indeed the most authoritative and appropriate interpretation. There is no good reason why the Russian interpretation, which runs contrary to this, should be accepted, when the Soviet Union did not sign the treaty.

Khrushchev and Hatoyama

The first opportunity to improve Soviet–Japanese relations came not long after Stalin's death in 1953. When Nikita Khrushchev solidified his position as Soviet Party leader in 1955–56, he started to change Soviet foreign relations from a Cold War track toward peaceful coexistence. In his secret speech to the Twentieth Congress of the Soviet Communist Party (CPSU) in February 1956, he strongly criticized the "personality cult" that had developed around Stalin, and he rejected the doctrine of "inevitability of war," instead promoting a new doctrine of peaceful coexistence. This dramatic change in Soviet foreign policy can be traced to the development of nuclear weapons, rather than a mere change of leader. Khrushchev was concerned that if the Cold War continued, it might eventually lead to nuclear war and possibly the destruction of mankind. He thus came to realize that peaceful coexistence was the only choice.

Just as criticism of Stalin was not something that suddenly occurred at the Twentieth Congress of the CPSU, the thesis of "peaceful coexistence" had already started to appear before 1956. We could even go so far as to say that the change from Stalin's Cold War approach to Khrushchev's peaceful coexistence was in 1955 rather than in 1956 when it was officially unveiled. In 1955 the following incidents occurred that point to a change of direction in Soviet diplomacy.[44] In March to May of that year, the Soviet Union concluded a state treaty with Austria and withdrew its occupation forces. In May–June, Khrushchev traveled to Yugoslavia for conciliatory talks with President Josip Tito. In July Khrushchev traveled with Bulganin to Geneva for a summit meeting (with the United States, Britain, and France), which gave rise to what was lauded as the "Spirit of Geneva," the most friendly atmosphere between East and West since the end of World War Two. In September 1955 the Soviet Union established relations with West Germany and returned its Porkkala Naval Base to Finland, as a condition for renewing their Treaty of Friendship, Cooperation, and Mutual Assistance.

Khrushchev's approaches to Japan from 1955, aimed at normalizing relations, were also part of this historical transformation in Soviet foreign relations. More specifically, it reflected Khrushchev's realization that the Soviet Union had nothing to gain by prolonging the deadlock with Japan. On January 25, 1955, Andrei Domnitskii, Soviet deputy head trade representative, wrote a note stating, "If Japan so desires, the Soviet Union is prepared to commence [Soviet-Japanese] negotiations at any time."[45] On February 16 he handed a letter from Prime Minister Bulganin to his Japanese counterpart Hatoyama, stating "Either in Moscow or Tokyo, whichever Japan prefers, let's start talks straight away."[46]

For Japan, too, circumstances at that time made these Soviet approaches acceptable. At the end of 1954 Ichiro Hatoyama replaced Shigeru Yoshida as prime minister, and by opening diplomatic channels with the communist bloc sought to move to some degree away from Yoshida's guiding principle of toeing the American line, and to adapt to trends in the U.S.–Soviet relationship. It is also likely that Hatoyama wanted to make his mark by adopting a different foreign policy orientation from that of Yoshida.[47] On January 22, 1955, in his first policy speech after becoming prime minister, Hatoyama declared, "We intend to coordinate our policies to allow us to establish relations with countries with whom we have thus far been unable to share diplomatic ties."[48] At this stage Hatoyama saw relations with the Soviet Union and China in the same light and had not necessarily given priority to one over the other. The Soviet Union, itself in process of changing its diplomatic strategies, jumped at the opportunity, and from then on normalization of relations with the Soviet Union became the main and only real feature of foreign relations of Hatoyama's administration.

Two or Four Islands?

Soviet–Japanese normalization talks commenced in London in June 1955 between Ambassadors Shunichi Matsumoto and Yakov Malik, who had been Soviet ambassador to Japan in 1942–45 (the "first round" of London talks). Not surprisingly, the talks soon stalled over the territorial issue. On August 5, when the two representatives had adjourned to the garden for a cup of tea after the official meeting, Malik is recorded as having delighted Matsumoto by saying the Soviet Union "is prepared to hand over Habomai and Shikotan to Japan."[49] Malik effectively repeated this statement at the official talks on August 9.[50] When Matsumoto requested guidance from Tokyo as to how he should respond to such an important Soviet proposal, he was instructed to tell Malik that "the territorial problem will not be solved by the return of Habomai and Shikotan alone," that "the two islands of Kunashiri and Etorofu . . . represent inherently Japanese territory," and he should do his utmost to ensure their return.[51] At an unofficial session on February 10, 1956, during the "second round" of London talks, Malik again proposed the return of only Habomai and Shikotan, but Matsumoto responded by requesting Kunashiri and Etorofu in addition.[52]

When it was decided to suspend negotiations after the failure of the two rounds of London talks, the Soviet Union suddenly notified Japan that "until a Fisheries Agreement can be put in place, fishing zones and access periods to those zones will be set." The North Pacific salmon- and trout-fishing season was fast approaching, and this move represented a subtle tactic to place the Japanese fishing industry in a difficult position. Matsumoto suggested that the Soviet linkage of the fisheries negotiations with the normalization talks (and the peace treaty issue) was "apparent" from the fact that the negotiating deadlines for the normalization talks were set at the fisheries talks.[53] However, Nicolai Adyrkhaev, who acted as interpreter at the Kōno–Bulganin talks, claimed that the one who proposed this linkage so that "the fisheries treaty would come into effect on condition that Soviet–Japanese normalization talks be recommenced" was Ichiro Kōno, Japanese minister of agriculture and fisheries.[54] Adyrkhaev suggested that for this to become known in Japan would jeopardize Kōno's political career, so he asked to disguise it to appear that he had reluctantly given in to Soviet pressure.[55]

Normalization talks recommenced in Moscow in July 1956. The negotiations between Foreign Minister Mamoru Shigemitsu and his Soviet counterpart Dmitrii T. Shepilov soon threatened to break down, when the standpoints of the two representatives conflicted once again over Kunashiri and Etorofu. Shigemitsu judged that he had done all he could, and he telegrammed Tokyo stating that there was nothing left but to accept the Soviet proposal as it stood. The Hatoyama cabinet did not agree to this. In his diary Shigemitsu wrote, "Although I myself was ready to take all the responsibility, I was prevented by Tokyo from making a decision."[56]

The talks were suspended, and Shigemitsu left for London to attend an international conference on the Suez Crisis. While there, on August 19, he explained to American Secretary of State Dulles the situation in the Soviet–Japanese negotiations. Dulles responded with the "threat" that if Japan were to conclude a peace treaty with the Soviet Union seeing only Habomai and Shikotan returned and renouncing rights to Kunashiri and Etorofu, the United States would reconsider its plans for returning the Ryukyus (Okinawa) to Japanese sovereignty.[57] Expressly, "If Japan gave better terms to Russia we could demand the same terms for ourselves. That would mean that if Japan recognized that the Soviet Union was entitled to full sovereignty over the Kuriles, we would assume we were equally entitled to full sovereignty over the Ryukyus."[58] Article 26 of the San Francisco Peace Treaty specifies, "Should Japan make a peace settlement or war claims settlement with any State granting that State greater advantages than those provided by the present treaty, those same advantages shall be extended to the parties to the present treaty."[59] During the Cold War, the United States preferred Japan not to resolve its differences with the Soviet Union. In this respect, it is likely that Dulles judged it in American national interests to allow the Northern Territories issue to remain a bone in the craw of Soviet–Japanese relations. At least in terms of results, it could be said that all Soviet leaders from Stalin to Brezhnev were taken in by this American stratagem.

Faced with such a situation, Hatoyama judged that, unless he himself went to Moscow, his long-cherished hope of normalizing relations with the Soviet Union would not come to fruition. So he decided to go to Moscow himself. To ensure it would be worth staking his political career on this issue, some hope of success was required. In that respect, Hatoyama worked with Shunichi Matsumoto to compose "five conditions" for the visit and sent Matsumoto ahead to Moscow to secure Soviet agreement to them beforehand.[60] After repeated negotiations, on September 29, Matsumoto and First Deputy Foreign Minister Gromyko traded letters that both included the sentence, "The Japanese government assumes that negotiations on the conclusion of a peace treaty including the territorial issue will continue after the reestablishment of normal diplomatic relations between the two countries" (see the Joint Compendium, Items 28 and 29).

During the years before the dissolution of the Soviet Union, there was some discrepancy between Japanese and Soviet views of the legal value of these so-called Matsumoto–Gromyko letters. The Japanese Foreign Ministry, amongst others, interprets them as forming a single set of documents together with the Soviet–Japan Joint Declaration, concluded twenty days later but made public at the same time. For example, Matsumoto emphasizes that the Gromkyo letter and joint declaration were released simultaneously, and interprets them as one. Shinsaku Hōgen, who was in charge of the arrangements for the negotiations (and later served as vice-minister of foreign affairs) has steadfastly held that no other interpretation is possible, stating, "I want to make it clear, as one of the people directly involved in the Soviet–Japanese negotiations, that the joint declaration was announced *on the basis of* the content of the letters exchanged by Gromkyo and Matsumoto" (italics added).[61] The practical significance of this Japanese interpretation was that since the letters promised continued negotiations on the conclusion of a peace treaty, "the territorial negotiations" would revolve around return of Kunashiri and Etorofu, as the transfer of Habomai and Shikotan was already promised.

In contrast to this interpretation, Soviet and some Japanese commentators suggested that the legal standing of the letters is lower than that of the joint declaration. For example, while Professor Akio Kimura (Aoyama Gakuin University) is second-to-none in enthusiastic support of Japan's claims for return of the Northern Territories, for that very reason he has strongly advocated that we should be prepared to view the issue from the other side of the fence and to try to envisage the Russian way of thinking about it. He stated, "The Soviet Union agreed to Japanese wishes in publicly announcing the 'letters,' but they see this as nothing more than a part of the process of reaching the subsequent Japanese–Soviet Joint Declaration, and not as one with the declaration itself, and therefore that the 'letters' became null and void upon the signing of the declaration."[62] Furthermore, while the former were merely letters, the latter was a document ratified by the parliaments of Japan and the Soviet Union, and therefore it was of far greater legal weight. Although the "letters" may have promised negotiations on Etorofu and Kunashiri, it could be interpreted that the promise was not necessarily confirmed by the joint declaration, or indeed was actually cancelled by it.

Japanese-Soviet Joint Declaration, 1956

In fact, during Hatoyama's negotiations in Moscow, there was fierce debate over whether to remove the clause "including the territorial question." As though to demonstrate a typically Soviet negotiating technique of seeking a major concession from the other party at the very last moment, just when the talks had reached a critical point, Khrushchev demanded removal of the words "including the territorial question" from the text of the joint declaration.[63] Hatoyama and the Japanese delegation judged that so long as the joint declaration clearly stated that the two countries would continue negotiations toward a peace treaty, by definition involving negotiation on territorial issues and border delimitation, the territorial question would be covered by default even if those words were removed. With that, and on condition it be made public on the same day as the Matsumoto-Gromyko "letters," the Japanese side agreed to the removal of the words from the joint declaration. It goes without saying that the removal of these words did not help the Japanese case. Until Gorbachev did an about-face on the issue, Soviet governments thereafter insisted that there was no territorial problem. If the words "which includes the territorial question" had been clearly stated in the joint declaration, Soviet governments through the years might not have been able to be so insistent on this point.

Be that as it may, on October 19, 1956, the Soviet–Japanese Joint Declaration was signed in Moscow, Ichiro Hatoyama, Ichirō Kōno, and Shunichi Matsumoto representing Japan, Nikolai Bulganin and Dimitrii Shepilov the Soviet Union. It was ratified by the Japanese Diet and the Presidium of the Supreme Soviet, and it represents the highest-level legal document entered into between the two nations. Soviet legal scholars have unanimously acknowledged that its lack of provisions on territorial delimitation rules it out from becoming a peace treaty. It is therefore clear that after the normalization of relations, both countries were to continue negotiations for a peace treaty, as stated in Article 9 of the joint declaration, and equally clear that those negotiations would include the territorial question.

The second paragraph of Article 9 states, "The Union of Soviet Socialist Republics, desiring to meet the wishes of Japan and taking into consideration the interests of the Japanese State, agrees to hand over to Japan the Habomai Islands and the island of Shikotan. However, the actual handing over of these islands to Japan shall take place after the conclusion of a peace treaty between Japan and the Union of Soviet Socialist Republics" (see the Joint Compendium, Item 30). This paragraph requires some explanation.

First of all, the Soviet Union agreed to "transfer" (*peredat*) Shikotan and Habomai to Japan rather than "return" them. They avoided the word "return" with its nuance of restoring territory to its previous possessors, preferring the more neutral word "transfer." Furthermore, the wording was chosen to suggest that the Soviet Union was making a special gesture to meet Japanese wishes, despite there being no real reason why they should hand these islands over. Next, as of 1956 the Soviet Union clearly agreed to transfer Habomai and Shikotan to Japan. That being so, the subject of Japanese–Soviet territorial negotiations since the joint declaration has been Kunashiri and Etorofu. Third, the timing of the actual transfer of Habomai and Shikotan is set to occur after the conclusion of a peace treaty. One interpretation of this is that only those two islands would be returned to Japan when a peace treaty is concluded. This would only be the case if Japan were to abandon its claims to Etorofu and Kunashiri. But as this is highly unlikely, it should be understood as representing no more than a statement of the timing for the transfer of Habomai and Shikotan. Following the 1956 Joint Declaration, the Soviet government judged the return of Shikotan and Habomai to Japan as already decided and completed the preparation to do so, evacuating all Soviet residents from the islands and leaving only a few dozen border guards behind. This was indicated by Hiroshi Satō in March 1993, in an interview featured in the *Hokkaido Shimbun*.[64] Sato had acted as interpreter for many years in Soviet–Japanese fisheries negotiations and became aware of this in December 1959, when he became the first Japanese to visit the Northern Territories in the postwar period. Most of the specialists asked by the *Hokkaido Shimbun* to comment said they had heard rumors to that effect, and that Sato's remarks were highly plausible. For example, Konstantin Sarkisov, the head of the Center for Japanese Studies attached to the Institute of Oriental Studies, said, "After the signing of the joint declaration, as it was thought that the reversion of two islands [Habomai and Shikotan] would go ahead, it is true that preparation for evacuation of residents was carried out."[65] Kyoji Komachi, head of the Russian Section of the Japanese Ministry of Foreign Affairs also stated, "It is likely that the evacuation [of Soviet residents] from the island was actually carried out once."[66]

The Japan-U.S. Security Treaty

The 1956 Joint Declaration was a milestone in the history of postwar Soviet–Japanese relations. Although it may not have led to the conclusion of a peace treaty, it marked the official end to hostilities and paved the way for normal diplomatic relations through the establishment of embassies and consulates in each country. Soviet–Japanese relations during the fifteen-year period between Hatoyama's visit to Moscow and the late 1960s–early 1970s had their ups and downs, but in general can be described as a period of stagnation in relations between the two nations. Let me discuss two or three incidents that occurred during that period.

One of the most important incidents affecting the Northern Territories problem was the incomprehensible, or rather, outrageous, behavior of the Soviet Union when in 1960 the Japanese government revised the security treaty it had first signed with the United States in 1951 directly after the San Francisco Peace Treaty, and which the Soviet Union had reviled. Nine years later a revised U.S.-Japan Treaty of Cooperation and Security included a system of "prior consultation" lacking in its predecessor and was altered to make it less one-sided than previously. In January 1960, the Soviet Union, under Nikita Khrushchev, sent the Japanese government a "memorandum" declaring its discontent with the new security treaty (see the Joint Compendium, Item 31). The Japanese government was astounded to read that this memorandum was delivered as notification of a unilateral revision of the clause in the 1956 Joint Declaration about Soviet agreement to transfer Habomai and Shikotan to Japan after the conclusion of a peace treaty. The memorandum stated, "Habomai and Shikotan will be handed over to Japan, only if all foreign [read American: Kimura] troops are withdrawn from Japan, and a Soviet-Japanese peace treaty is signed." Needless to say, the Japanese government responded immediately with a memorandum countering the Soviet statement (see the Joint Compendium, Item 32).

In terms of international law, Khrushchev's memorandum was preposterous, for three reasons. First of all, legal documents or acts of diplomacy only apply from the time when they are issued. Therefore, Khrushchev's behavior violates the principle that laws cannot be applied retrospectively. Second, this represented one party to an agreement unilaterally delivering an amendment to the other party. If legal agreements that have been earnestly deliberated over and signed by all parties, then ratified by their governing bodies, could be invalidated unilaterally, the world of law would be plunged into darkness, and no country would want to enter into treaties and agreements with nations such as the Soviet Union. Third, Khrushchev did not seek to invalidate the entire Joint Declaration, but only Article 9. Almost all treaties, agreements, and contracts are packages, representing some give-and-take bargaining, and they are only meaningful when observed in their entirety. Selective application, by seeking later to reject only those parts that do not meet one's satisfaction, is worse than rejecting the whole.[67] It is like plucking only raisins out of a cake.

Even before the appearance of Gorbachev, some Soviet-Japan specialists were already stating that Khrushchev's preposterous stance was a mistake, linked to overreaction to the revision of the U.S.–Japanese Security Treaty. After many years both the Gorbachev and Yeltsin administrations changed their stance to one of approval for that treaty. During the Gorbachev years academic criticism grew in strength, and some Soviet politicians and advisors publicly concurred, suggesting that Khrushchev's "Memorandum" was a product of the Cold War and that it had lost its effect when the Cold War ended, thus meaning that the 1956 Joint Declaration is valid in its entirety.

The next most important developments during this period of stagnation were the two visits to Japan by Anastas Mikoyan, in August 1961 and May 1964. Until Gorbachev came in 1991, Mikoyan, then first deputy chairman of the Council of Ministers, was the highest-ranking Soviet official to visit Japan.

Mikoyan observed that the Japanese economy had developed far beyond what the Soviet Union had imagined, and by all accounts, he rued the lack of Soviet-Japanese economic cooperation. His experiences were reported to Khrushchev and must have had no small influence on the Soviet leader's thinking. Former Japanese ambassador to Moscow Kinya Niizeki wrote, "Khrushchev was forever saying that all there was in Japan was volcanoes and earthquakes, but after hearing the reports from Mikoyan's visits to Japan he started to appreciate Japanese economic strength."[68] In general it would seem that Soviet leaders were much less knowledgeable about Japan than people would imagine. The Japanese have tended to think the KGB provided the Kremlin's top leaders with a plethora of intelligence information about Japan, but that would not seem to be the case. In fact we cannot rule out the possibility that Soviet decision-makers knew very little about the realities of the outside world. Perhaps a lesson can be found here, that it is in Japan's best interests to have high-ranking Russian officials visit as often as possible, to see the country with their own eyes.

However, during his stays in Japan Mikoyan was as unyielding as ever on the crucial issue of the Northern Territories. The following comments were recorded during his stay. To Prime Minister Hayato Ikeda he said, "Most of the Soviet Union is frozen, so each acre of Japanese land is worth one hundred acres of Soviet soil. . . . Etorofu and Kunashiri may only be small islands, but they are the gateway to Kamchatka and cannot be abandoned."[69] Also, to Aiichirō Fujiyama, chairman of the General Council of the Liberal

Democratic Party, and Takeo Miki, chairman of the Policy Affairs Research Council, he said, "The islands might only be small, but their location is important.... I cannot imagine that Kunashiri and Etorofu would be any great value to Japan. For the Soviet Union they are necessary as a link with Kamchatka and so long as Japan and the United States have a military alliance we cannot ever consider returning them."[70]

CHAPTER 5

Years of the Aging Soviet Leaders

ON OCTOBER 14, 1964, Leonid Brezhnev replaced Nikita Khrushchev as leader of the Soviet Union. What effect, we may ask, did the ebb and flow of Soviet administrations and the changing of the guard in the Kremlin have on Soviet-Japanese relations, particularly on the Northern Territories issue? At least for the organized Japanese movement for return of the territories, it was preferable that the Soviet leadership had a strong and stable political base. During the Khrushchev and Brezhnev years, the Soviet stance toward Japan was most flexible when both leaders were at the peak of their powers, and it hardened as their authority waned, especially on the territorial issue. In other words, if we view the Khrushchev and Brezhnev administrations (approximately ten and eighteen years, respectively) as having first and second halves, the Soviet stance toward Japan can be described as relatively flexible in the first and unyielding in the second halves.

One notable event during the Brezhnev years was the meeting between Japanese Minister of Foreign Affairs Takeo Miki and Soviet Premier Alexei Kosygin during the former's visit to Moscow in July 1967. This meeting is particularly noteworthy because Kosygin apparently suggested concluding an "interim document," on the grounds that neither side was currently willing to sign a peace treaty on terms acceptable to the other. It is not clear what he had in mind, but the most likely theory is a compromise, involving the return to Japan of Habomai and Shikotan. Miki judged the proposal not in Japan's interests, and neither pursued it nor made it public.

What is interesting here is that just after Miki became prime minister, in December 1974, his foreign policy advisor, Kazushige Hirasawa, had an article published in the influential American journal *Foreign Affairs*, advocating the return of Habomai and Shikotan in 1975 in conjunction with a peace treaty and putting the question of the other two islands on hold for the remainder of the twentieth century.[1] However, this proposal did not win the support of the Japanese Ministry of Foreign Affairs or people, and before long Hirasawa died.

Sino-American Détente

The next opportunity to improve postwar Japanese–Soviet relations came in the late 1960s–early 1970s. In some respects it was an even better opportunity than that of 1955–56, because it involved shifts of such magnitude as to have profound effects on the bipolar U.S.–Soviet international political system that had been in place since the end of World War Two. The honeymoon period between the two communist powers of China and the Soviet Union had already ended in 1956, about the time of Khrushchev's criticisms of Stalin, but into the mid-1960s the Sino–Soviet conflict had gone no further than oral and written exchanges of opposing views, mainly regarding matters of socialist ideology, and did not become fully public until July 1963, when the Soviet Union signed the Test Ban Treaty with the other nuclear powers, at a time when China was still some time away from its first nuclear test. In August 1968 the Warsaw Pact invasion of Czechoslovakia, conducted under the banner of "limited sovereignty" subsequently elucidated as the Brezhnev Doctrine, was followed in March 1969 by armed clashes between Soviet and Chinese forces over Damansky (Chenpao) Island in the Ussuri River on the Sino–Soviet border. Then in June 1969, at an international meeting of Communist Parties in Moscow, Brezhnev delivered a speech that both condemned China and advocated creation of an Asian collective security scheme. He did not say against what countries it would be directed, but its anti-Chinese implications were obvious. This sequence of events had a profound effect on China, with its 7,500 kilometers of border with the Soviet Union, causing Mao Tse-tung not only to suspend the Cultural Revolution, but also to decide that he must take steps to improve relations with the United States.

The United States correctly read the signals indicating China's fear of the Soviet Union and resulting desire for rapprochement with the West. President Nixon's national security advisor, Henry Kissinger, held that U.S.-Soviet relations above all provided the foundation for world peace and stability, viewed relations with all other nations in terms of their effects on them, and in that context saw Sino-U.S. reconciliation as a useful way of strengthening America's position vis-à-vis the Soviet Union. Nixon gave the green light for initiatives to seek a rapprochement with China.

Brezhnev's Asian collective security scheme attracted little support, and his advocacy of it was sporadic, his main effort to revive it coming in March 1972, just after Nixon's visit to China in February. Judging at least from these circumstances, it is possible to interpret this plan as a Soviet defensive measure to establish a counterbloc, in order to avoid becoming isolated by improving Sino–American relations. Regardless of whether the Asian collective security scheme was of an offensive or defensive nature, there is no doubt that Japan was of vital importance to Brezhnev's plan.

Until that time the Soviets tended to underestimate Japan. It was viewed somewhat disdainfully for its "lack of military power," as sheltering under the American nuclear umbrella, incapable of defending itself without the security treaty with the United States, and so firmly within the American sphere of influence that no propaganda campaigns or attempts at influencing it would bring any major improvement in bilateral relations. Thus, during much of the postwar period, Soviet efforts had gone into negative activities, such as advocating violent revolution or neutralism with an anti-American tinge and denigrating alleged revivals of militarism.

However, changed times obliged Soviet leaders to amend their views, particularly through witnessing Japan's spectacular economic growth. Minor structural adjustments were proving ineffective in lifting the Soviet economy out of stagnation, and the nation was now at a point where relentlessly persisting with the same approach might endanger the very foundations of the Soviet-style socialist system. For Brezhnev, economic exchange with the advanced capitalist nations of the world was the preferable option. This being the case, the Soviet Union was desperate to acquire Japanese capital, technology, and know-how. At the same time, it appeared to Soviet leaders as though—in the wake of the second of the Nixon Shocks in the early 1970s—Japan was searching for a more self-directed path forward, reevaluating its previous complete reliance on the United States in diplomatic, economic, and intellectual arenas. Therefore, as well as reeling from the structural changes in power configurations on the international scene, the Kremlin was keenly aware that Japan might be about to undergo changes of its own and thus attempted to influence it in that direction.

Gromyko's Diplomacy

The Soviet Union could not use a stick on Japan, so instead it tried a carrot. The Kremlin dispatched Foreign Minister Andrei Gromyko to Tokyo early in 1972. It was Gromyko's first visit to Japan for six years, and that he came there, instead of attending the Warsaw Pact Summit Meeting held in Prague at the same time, was testimony to the visit's importance. During his stay Gromyko was all smiles, showing no signs of the manner that had previously earned him the nickname "Mr. Nyet," and before returning to Moscow he agreed that negotiations toward a Japan–Soviet peace treaty should begin before the end of the year.

His uncharacteristic affability during his visit can be viewed in two ways. One interpretation is that there was a possibility of concluding a peace treaty that included concessions on the return of the Northern Territories. The second is that his priority was to assess the effect on Japan of the second Nixon Shock (the Sino-American rapprochement). The first was exemplified by an article in *Le Monde* by French journalist Robert Guillan. Under the headline, "The U.S.S.R. Considers the Return of the Four Southern Kurile Islands," he wrote:

Recent changes on the international scene have created a situation from which both Japan and the Soviet Union can accrue joint benefit in the Pacific region. In particular, for Moscow, improving relations with Japan has become an important issue in order to offset Sino–U.S. rapprochement. Gromyko is no longer in a position to be able to say an unqualified "nyet" to the return of these islands. Tokyo's being able to provide a balance to the relationship between the two communist superpowers puts Japan in an advantageous but delicate position. The next round of negotiations will probably decide the fate of Habomai, Shikotan, Kunashiri, and Etorofu. The Soviet Union will likely reach a compromise allowing Japan to secure these four islands.[2]

In introducing this article, Professor William E. Griffiths of Massachusetts Institute of Technology suggested that it was almost certain that at that stage in 1972 "the Soviets saw improvement of their relations with Japan as the most obvious and rapid countermove to the Sino–American rapprochement."[3]

The second, conflicting, view holds that, while the Kremlin probably did consider using Japan in this way, it is difficult to imagine this including return of the Northern Territories. Proponents of this view suggest that Gromyko's visit to Japan in 1972 was little more than a reconnaissance mission, and it was unlikely that the Soviet Union had already decided to make concessions on the Northern Territories issue.

Which of these interpretations is correct? In terms of outcomes, the first view's optimistic predictions were significantly wide of the mark, which might suggest the second view be seen automatically as correct. As it happens, however, the following points, throwing new light on the matter, were reported in summer 1992, just before Yeltsin's scheduled visit to Japan. In an interview conducted by Kenro Nagoshi, Moscow correspondent of *Jiji Press*, Mikhail Kapitsa (former deputy foreign minister, and director of the Institute of Oriental Studies, Russian Academy of Sciences), stated that during the visit Gromyko secretly proposed the return of Habomai and Shikotan to his Japanese counterpart. Even more specifically, Kapitsa said that on January 28, 1972, at the prime minister's residence, Gromyko said to Prime Minister Eisaku Satō, "I want to present a proposal to the Politburo that we return Habomai and Shikotan and conclude a Japanese–Soviet peace treaty. The Politburo will no doubt agree with me, so I want to get peace treaty negotiations moving along these lines."[4]

Foreign Minister Takeo Fukuda was not present, and the only others said to be there were Kapitsa, then director of the Far Eastern Division of the Soviet Foreign Ministry, accompanying Gromyko as an advisor, and Gromyko's interpreter Liudvig Chizhov (subsequently Soviet/Russian ambassador to Japan). According to Kapitsa, Prime Minister Satō was quiet for some time before replying, "I'll think about it."[5] This conversation was never made public, and there was no known response from Japan. In 1992, Fukuda and Ministry of Foreign Affairs Russia Section Chief Kyōji Komachi both denied that Gromyko made any such offer, asserted that no such meeting was held on January 28, and alleged that at one held on the previous day Kapitsa was not even present.[6]

Although Kapitsa's credibility is therefore in question, it was not unthinkable that the Soviet Union would suggest the return of the two islands, provided, of course, that Japan would renounce all future claim to the two larger islands. Such "departure-time decisions," delivering the most important proposal just before boarding the aircraft for home, were a feature of Soviet negotiating style.[7] But more importantly, if we opt for the other interpretation, why was Gromyko sent to Tokyo at all? The visit was undertaken hastily, out of a deepening Soviet sense of isolation in Asia due to the Sino–American rapprochement and the specter of normalization of Sino-Japanese relations. Therefore, Gromyko's mission would not have been merely to present a smiling face in Tokyo and to gather information about trends there, information that he had an embassy to provide. The 1956 Joint Declaration indicated that at that time the Soviet Union was prepared to hand over Habomai and Shikotan, although it subsequently withdrew the commitment in a fit of pique at the renewal of the U.S.–Japanese Security Treaty. If a peace treaty with Japan could be concluded by returning these two islands, it would be a satisfactory solution for the Soviet Union. But, at least since the 1955–56 period, Japan had consistently demanded the return of all four, so even if Kapitsa's account is accurate, the outcome remained unchanged.[8]

Tanaka's Visit to Moscow

In October 1973 Japanese Prime Minister Kakuei Tanaka traveled to Moscow for talks with Brezhnev, taking with him four trump cards. First, major changes were afoot on the world stage, with Japan rapidly assuming an important position. Second, Japan was in a diplomatically advantageous position, with both China and the Soviet Union vying for its attention. Third, the Kremlin had expectations of Tanaka, as apparently the first Japanese political leader many years to possess a good mix of strength and popularity. Last, there was the invaluable bargaining chip of cooperation in the economic development of Siberia.

However, Tanaka met his political demise without effectively playing any of these cards. The Oil Shock following the Israeli–Arab War of October 1973 saw the first fade away, at least in Soviet eyes. The second had already been squandered by Tanaka's persistence in rushing the process of normalization of relations with China, in September 1972, and the third was then negated by his involvement in the Lockheed Scandal, which led to his resignation in December 1974.

He also failed to make effective use of the matter of the joint economic development of Siberia because he measured everything in terms of economic merit and was blind to the politico-strategic value of such cooperation. He gave in to pressure from some sectors of the financial world and initiated a policy of "de-coupling" economics from politics. Kissinger would have lamented this waste of a golden opportunity and criticized Tanaka for his failure to make such strategic linkages. In a letter to Brezhnev in March 1973, Tanaka wrote that plans for Soviet–Japanese joint development of Siberia should be carried out independently of political issues such as the Northern Territories problem.[9] He stressed that "rather than being merely neighboring countries, the economic relationship between Japan and the Soviet Union was unique in that it was mutually complementary." Keisuke Suzuki, an expert on Japanese–Soviet economic matters (then employed by Keidanren, Federation of Economic Organizations, and later a professor at Kyushu University) saw this as a truly groundbreaking statement, since linkage between economics and politics had been one of the few effective bargaining cards Japan had vis-à-vis the Soviet Union.[10]

Tanaka is recorded as having harangued Brezhnev about the Northern Territories issue on a number of occasions during his visit. However, he is said to have done so in such an overbearing and vehement tone as to have annoyed Brezhnev, thereby producing the opposite effect to what he intended.[11] All that remained was the text of the Soviet–Japan Joint Communiqué: "Recognizing that the settlement of unresolved problems left over from WWII and conclusion of a peace treaty would contribute to the establishment of truly good-neighborly and friendly relations between the two countries, both sides held negotiations on issues pertaining to the contents of a peace treaty" (see the Joint Compendium, Item 33).

The wording "unresolved problems left over from WWII" represented a Japanese attempt to get around the stubborn Soviet refusal to mention the territorial issue in the communiqué. As Brezhnev had used the similar expression "problems left over from WWII" in an important speech in December 1972, the Soviet side could not easily refuse to use these words.[12] Their choice was the work of Hirokazu Arai, Russia section chief in the Ministry of Foreign Affairs, who had arranged Tanaka's visit,[13] though others had also grasped their potential and made informal approaches to officials of the Soviet

Ministry of Fisheries to ensure their use in the joint communiqué.[14] There being no other "unresolved problems," to the Japanese the wording could only mean the "territorial problem."

The Japanese had first proposed this wording in the singular form, but agreed to amend this to the plural, as "unresolved problems," in response to a request from Kosygin at the final meeting, another good example of the aforementioned Soviet negotiating technique of looking to make crucial changes at the very final stages of talks. About a year later, in an interview with Northern Territories Issue Association President Kyûhei Suzuki, Tanaka commented, "Just to be sure, I then said to Brezhnev that I'd like to confirm that the most important of these 'unresolved problems' is the matter of the four islands of Habomai, Shikotan, Kunashiri, and Etorofu. He replied 'That's right, I confirm that, that's right.' The reply was clearly stated twice."[15] According to Japanese Foreign Ministry staff present at this meeting, Brezhnev said "Ia znaiu" (I know) and "Da" (Yes). Hirokazu Arai, who attended this meeting to take notes, confirmed this.[16]

However, the Soviet Union later officially took the line that the territorial question was not included in the "unresolved problems." For example, at the fifth Japanese–Soviet Symposium sponsored by the *Sankei Shimbun* in 1980, Igor Latyshev (then head of the Japan Division, Institute of Oriental Studies, Russian Academy of Sciences) said, "There is no foundation to claims that in his talks with Prime Minister Tanaka, Brezhnev acknowledged that the territorial question was included among 'unresolved problems.' Neither are there any official documents to support these claims."[17] Latyshev was merely reiterating the Soviet official line, since in 1975 Gromyko wrote of "groundless demands regarding the so-called 'Northern Territories,'" in an article in the journal *Kommunist*.[18] In 1977, in response to questions posed by Shōryu Hata, editor-in-chief of the *Asahi Shimbun*, Brezhnev wrote, "Statements to the effect that there are 'unresolved problems in relations between our two countries with regard to territorial issues' are one-sided and inaccurate."[19]

The Japan-China Peace and Friendship Treaty

Even into the late 1970s the Soviet Union was still doing its utmost to strengthen its military forces relative to those of the United States. The Watergate Scandal in 1974 and the fall of South Vietnam in the following year were great blows to American confidence. At this stage, it would seem that the United States believed it no longer had the ability to stand up to the Soviet Union by itself, so while seeking greater cooperation and burden sharing from allies such as the NATO countries and Japan, it adopted a strategy whereby China would be used to counter the Soviet Union. This approach had already been employed by the Nixon-Kissinger team (1969–74) and then by the Ford administration (1974–76) before appearing as the "China card" in the hands of the Carter–Brzezinski team (1977–80). As though to fit this strategy, Chinese leader Deng Xiaoping's Machiavellian tendencies led him to eventually reinterpret his original view of the world, consisting of "three worlds" (capitalist, communist, and nonaligned), and to seek rapprochement with the United States, leader of the First World Nations, against the Soviet Union, presumed leader of the Second World, but in Chinese eyes a traitor to that position. Japanese foreign policy was also affected by the American and Chinese strategic shifts. Foreign Minister Sunao Sonoda, known for his loquacity, even went so far as to say in January 1979, "I see the Japan-China Peace and Friendship Treaty as consistent with American global strategy."[20]

At that time, the late 1970s, the Soviet Union was fully committed to increasing its military capabilities, and in no mood to initiate diplomatic overtures toward Japan. On the contrary, it seemed to see threats as the most effective approach, and exasperated the Japanese by its high-handed attitude during negotiations over the MiG-25 incident in 1976 and the two-hundred-mile fishing zone in 1977. Japanese public feeling toward the Soviet Union was dominated by distrust and a sense of hopelessness regarding the prospect of any improvement in relations with it.

The flexibility and modesty of the Chinese approach, even if but a façade, was fast gathering appeal for most Japanese people. However, Chinese demands for inclusion of an "antihegemony clause" in a Sino-Japanese peace treaty led Japan to hesitate for almost six years after the 1973 normalization of relations, for fear of Soviet antagonism and retaliation. However, in that period the Soviet Union offered no real alternatives and went no further than alluding to unspecified "retaliatory measures" if Japan concluded a peace treaty with China that included such a clause. During Sonoda's visit to Moscow in early 1978, a Soviet draft of the Treaty of Good-Neighborliness and Cooperation was announced and presented suddenly, with a request for his signature. This had no appeal whatsoever to Japan, the draft apparently attempting to define Japan as a Soviet satellite state, or even ally. Furthermore, in a breach of diplomatic protocol and manners, the draft was published beforehand in *Izvestiia* on February 23, 1978.[21]

Against this background negotiations between China and Japan turned a corner. A compromise was reached by including both the "antihegemony" clause and one that stated, "The present treaty shall not affect the positions of either contracting party regarding its relations with third countries," and in August 1978, the Fukuda cabinet agreed to conclude the Japan–China

Peace and Friendship Treaty. Following this improvement in Sino-Japanese relations, Japan turned again toward the Soviets, to maintain "equidistance-diplomacy" toward the two communist powers. For example, there are rumors that in 1978 Japan attempted to achieve a breakthrough in Japanese-Soviet relations by secretly using the president of Tokai University, Shigeyoshi Matsumae, as an intermediary. However, this initiative faded away before it could get off the ground, when Masayoshi Ōhira defeated Fukuda in the LDP primaries in autumn of that year.[22]

Whether this can be interpreted as a direct response to the China–Japan Peace and Friendship Treaty is another matter, but in 1978–79 the Soviet Union redeployed troops on Kunashiri, Etorofu, and Shikotan. We can assume that this deployment was carried out with the following objectives in mind: (1) to improve the Soviet Union's strategic position vis-à-vis the United States; (2) as retaliation for Japan concluding the Peace and Friendship Treaty with China; (3) to send a message to Japan that the Northern Territories would not be returned; and (4) to raise the level of Soviet threat toward Japan. Among them the first objective was the primary one because the deployment of troops in the Northern Islands in 1978–79 was a complement to the stationing of Soviet nuclear submarines (SSBN) in the Sea of Okhotsk. From 1963 to 1978 the Sea of Okhotsk had been so strategically unimportant that there had been no soldiers or sailors on any of the Northern Islands. From 1978, however, the situation radically changed, when Soviet SSBNs began to be deployed in the Sea of Okhotsk from a base at Petropavlovsk-Kamchatskii. These Soviet SSBNs were carrying ballistic missiles targeted on North America west of the Great Lakes. For protection of this SSBN "sanctuary" or "bastion" against penetration by American attack submarines the facilities (sonar, radars, airfields, stocks of mines, stationing of antisubmarine ships, and personnel to operate them) were installed east of the islands. These measures were entirely a matter of Soviet-U.S. relations, not prompted by anything Japan did.[23]

In conjunction with the general buildup of Soviet military forces in Northeast Asia and the region around Japan, the deployment of Soviet troops in the Northern Territories engendered in the Japanese public the greatest sense of a "Soviet threat" in the postwar period. An incident involving the leaking of secret information by members of the Japanese Ground Self-Defense Forces and Soviet detention of Japanese fishing boats allegedly engaged in espionage contributed to a further heightening of anti-Soviet feeling. But more than anything else, the development that took Japanese wariness of the Soviet Union to an unprecedented level was the Soviet military intervention in Afghanistan in December 1979.

Soviet Action in Afghanistan

When judged in the context of international politics, the Soviet sending of troops into Afghanistan was a momentous event that drew a line between the 1970s and the 1980s. To be sure, the Afghan government was communist, and its head, Hafizullah Amin, invited Soviet troops in. Nevertheless, the outside world, including Japan, perceived the Soviet action as expansionist, especially after the Soviets killed Amin and replaced him with Babrak Karmal. This act was evidence that the Kremlin was prepared to directly use military force to intervene in the affairs of countries that were outside "its own" East European empire. Some commentators even described this as the "end of détente," "a return to the Cold War," and the "beginning of a new Cold War era." It served as a kind of litmus test for the Western nations, forcing them to make a choice as to whether they were prepared to tolerate such an action.

Because Japan's only means of survival was as a trading state in an open and free system, the Ōhira cabinet followed the U.S. lead in imposing sanctions on and suspending official exchanges with the Soviet Union, and boycotting the 1980 Moscow Olympics. For Ōhira, a prime minister known for his often-puzzling approach to domestic politics, this was an exceptionally clear-cut, almost Yoshida-like example of diplomacy toeing the American line. As well as serving to heighten a sense of vigilance toward the Soviet Union, it created a feeling within Japan that it was absurd to expect relations with it to improve so soon after normalization of relations with China.

Of course, even without the Afghanistan crisis, it can be assumed that sooner or later Soviet-Japanese relations would have run into difficulties. Whichever way we look at it, the Soviet and Japanese policy tracks showed absolutely no signs of converging. The Soviet Union continued to seek a Soviet-Japanese Treaty of Good-Neighborliness and Cooperation that made no mention of territorial issues, while Japan was insisting that negotiations must start from the premise that they would culminate in the conclusion of a "peace treaty" that included return of the four islands. Neither side gave any indication of willingness to close this gap. The Soviet-Afghan Treaty of Friendship, Good-Neighborliness, and Cooperation had not exempted Afghanistan from Soviet military intervention, and that contributed to ruling out a similar Soviet-Japanese treaty, nor did it create an atmosphere conducive to the Ōhira administration's making any positive moves to improve Japanese-Soviet relations. In the context of the feeling of relief at having cleared a debt through the Treaty of Peace and Friendship with China, the Soviet action in Afghanistan served as a "divine wind" for the Japanese government. If the Kremlin hoped for Japan, after improving relations with China, to turn its attention to improving Japanese-Soviet relations, it had better stay out of Afghanistan, as for the time being its action there closed all doors.

However, it can also be said that even before the Soviet intervention in Afghanistan, Ōhira had already showed signs of departing from Fukuda's "omnidirectional" and "equidistance" diplomacy toward the Soviet Union and China. For example, the Pacific Basin Cooperation Concept that he and Foreign Minister Saburō Ōkita promulgated apparently excluded the Soviet Union. Although described as an open system with, as Ōhira remarked, "no reason to refuse the participation of any nation that wishes to join the [Pacific] community," it certainly held out no expectations for the Soviet Union.[24] In the final report of the prime minister's personal policy research group, the Pacific Basin Cooperation Group (chaired by Saburō Ōkita until he was appointed foreign minister) the words "Soviet Union" appeared only once, and in passing, reminiscent of President Ford's New Pacific Doctrine speech of 1975, which mentioned the Soviet Union only once.[25] The Ford administration's opting to play down or ignore the Soviet Union's significance was a clear indication of the new U.S. strategy of containing it in Asia through a combination of Japan, the United States, and China. It was even suggested by Soviet spokesmen that Ōhira's Pacific Basin Cooperation Concept was designed not merely to "exclude the Soviet Union, but to encircle it." In this view, the involvement of the Japanese Maritime Self-Defense Force in the Rimpac-80 Joint Exercises program of naval maneuvers held in the Pacific Ocean in January 1980 together with the ANZUS Alliance members (Australia, New Zealand, and the United States) could not be seen in any other light.[26] However, as Ōhira, the chief protagonist of this stance, died suddenly in June 1980, the real motives behind his Concept never became clear.

Suzuki and Nakasone Versus the Soviet Gerontocracy

The Suzuki cabinet (July 1980–November 1982) that provided some short relief after Ōhira's sudden death, and the Nakasone cabinet, which went on to become the third-longest postwar administration (November 1982–November 1987), were similar in that both generally adhered to the foreign policy courses established by previous Liberal Democratic Party cabinets. If we were to highlight a difference between the two, it might be summarized that the Suzuki administration lacked the will to promote a completely cooperative course of action vis-à-vis the United States, but did make a strong statement about return of the disputed islands from the USSR, whereas the Nakasone government first stressed the strength of its relationship with the United States, but then employed a series of sophisticated tactics to try to lure the Soviet Union toward Japan.

During Prime Minister Suzuki's first visit to the United States in May 1981, he announced that Japan was prepared to assume the responsibility for defending both the seas around its own shores and the sea-lanes as far as one thousand nautical miles south.[27] In an interview that same day at the National Press Club in Washington, he acknowledged that the U.S.-Japanese relationship constituted an "alliance," but on his return to Japan he became embroiled in a debate over whether this signified a military alliance. His inarticulate and ambiguous attempts to back away from his comment led to a crisis of credibility in U.S.–Japan relations.

By contrast, his government did initiate a range of measures to demonstrate its commitment on the Northern Territories issue. It created a Northern Territories Day; allocated fiscal revenue for three of the four islands now under Soviet rule, treating them as parts of Japanese territory; instituted a number of measures to promote industry in the Nemuro area; appointed an ambassador in charge for the Northern Territories, to be stationed in Hokkaido; and sent Suzuki himself on an inspection tour to Nemuro (September 1981). The designation of February 7, the date the Treaty of Shimoda was signed, as "Northern Territories Day," and the newly stated determination to continue holding special events on that day until the territories were returned, invited a fierce reaction from the Soviet Union. At the same time, it led to the establishment in every Japanese prefecture of a Citizens' Council for the Return of the Northern Territories, which since then has played an important role as a nucleus for the campaign for their return. Suzuki's decision to visit Nemuro—something that even a leader as powerful as his successor Nakasone did not do—was a bold one, considering that to avoid needlessly provoking the Soviet Union it had previously been customary for such visits to be made by the foreign minister or the director-general of the prime minister's office. Why did Suzuki, generally seen as a dove among the ranks of the Liberal Democratic Party, approach the Northern Territories issue with such enthusiasm? Some suggest that Suzuki's previous humiliating experiences at Soviet hands when minister of agriculture, forestry, and fisheries may have influenced his attitude toward the Soviet Union. At the negotiations over fishing rights in Moscow in spring of 1977, the Soviet side suddenly declared an exclusive two hundred nautical-mile fishing zone and kept Suzuki waiting day after day in the Japanese embassy for an appointment with his Soviet counterpart, Aleksandr A. Ishkov. However, this is mere speculation.

On November 10, 1982, Brezhnev died, and on the 26th the Suzuki cabinet was succeeded by that of Yasuhiro Nakasone. While visiting the United States, in January 1983, Nakasone confirmed that the notion of "alliance," over which Suzuki had vacillated, included a military alliance.[28] He also made such sensational comments as that Japan should become "an unsinkable aircraft carrier" and also be able to "control the Sea of Japan straits."[29] Although he chose to overstate the matter, he did make it completely clear that he placed great importance on solidarity between Japan and the United States. At the Williamsburg Summit in May 1983, and from the viewpoint that the security of the two nations was "indivisible," Nakasone gave full support to the Western stance of demanding the "zero option" from the Soviet Union in the INF (Intermediate-range Nuclear Forces) negotiations.[30] By contrast, he indicated that he was willing, to the greatest degree possible, to try to pull the Soviet Union, the "bear that was about to hibernate," to the negotiating table.[31]

The Andropov (November 1982–February 1984) and Chernenko (February 1984–March 1985) governments were both short-lived, and in general terms they can be seen as transitional regimes, effectively no more than an interval between the Brezhnev and Gorbachev administrations.

The incident that had the greatest impact on Soviet–Japanese relations during Yuri Andropov's fifteen-month tenure was undoubtedly the shooting down of Korean Airlines (KAL) 007 on September 1, 1983. Of the 269 people who lost their lives that day, 28 were Japanese, the largest number from any one foreign country. Moreover, as KAL 007 was shot down over Sakhalin, near Japan, this served to further heighten the mood of the "threat from the North" to levels unprecedented since 1979. As with the MiG 25 incident of 1976, the Soviet response was both arrogant and shameless. Good examples of this were Marshal Nikolai Ogarkov, chief of the Soviet General Staff, who candidly acknowledged that Kamchatka and Southern Sakhalin is the location of "a major base of the Soviet Union's strategic nuclear forces" and "important military installations."[32] Therefore, Ogarkov flatly stated in a press conference on the KAL incident held in Moscow on September 9, 1983, "In the future, if need be, the Soviet military forces will also perform their combat tasks."[33] Foreign Minister Andrei Gromyko stated, "In time the incident will be forgotten."[34] All these statements dramatically intensified the anti-Soviet mood among the people of Japan.

The death of General Secretary Andropov (February 9, 1984) saw Konstantin Chernenko assume the top political position in the Soviet government, but he too died before he could do anything about relations with Japan. Chernenko's policy is clear in the section of his *Collection of Speeches and Papers*, titled "To Readers in Japan." First of all, he recommended that Japan conclude either a Soviet-Japanese Treaty of Good-Neighborliness and Cooperation, or institute Confidence-Building Measures (CBMs) in the Far East, in other words a substitute for a peace treaty. Second, he called for expansion of mutually beneficial exchanges, particularly economic, between the Soviet Union and Japan. Third, he proposed that cultural exchanges be expanded.[35] There was nothing new here. Chernenko repeated, and even strengthened, the anti-Japanese slogans of the Brezhnev era about the formation of an alleged "Tripartite Alliance involving Washington, Tokyo, and Seoul," "rebirth of Japanese militarism," and "revanchist territorial demands."

There were several other indications that the Chernenko administration had hardened its stance toward Japan. The Soviet Union increased its deployment of SS-20s (intermediate-range ballistic missiles) in the Far East and further strengthened the Soviet Pacific Fleet through deployment of one more aircraft carrier, the *Novorossiisk*, in addition to the *Minsk*. Also, at the end of April 1984, the content of a speech by Japanese Ambassador Masuo Takashima, due to be broadcast on Soviet national television, was judged unacceptable and was therefore cancelled by the Soviet authorities, even though the speech was almost identical to the one he delivered on the emperor's birthday in the previous year, when Andropov was in power. Furthermore, political maneuvering by the Chernenko government was one reason why the salmon–trout fisheries negotiations of 1984 took much longer than on previous occasions.

To summarize, policy orientation toward Japan under Andropov and Chernenko changed very little from that of the Brezhnev years, as demonstrated by the following four points: first of all, policy toward Japan was consistent with the basic tenets of Soviet diplomacy determined by its global strategy. In an attempt to halt the deployment of Pershing-II and cruise missiles in Europe, Andropov said at the end of 1983 that Soviet "SS-20 missiles removed from Europe would be destroyed, and not redeployed in Asia." Nakasone greeted this as a "welcome concession," but it also indicated that Andropov's global strategy was centered on the United States and Europe.[36] Second, there were continued efforts to strengthen the Soviet military forces in the Far East and regions adjacent to Japan. Third were the persistent requests to conclude a Soviet-Japanese Treaty of Good-Neighborliness and Cooperation or any form of "substitute treaty" instead of a peace treaty.[37] Fourth was the Soviet attitude toward the Northern Territories. Both statements and speeches displayed the attitudes of the Andropov and Chernenko administrations toward the disputed islands as unchanged from the Brezhnev era, often using exactly the same rhetoric and again describing Japanese territorial demands as "unfounded and illegal."[38]

CHAPTER 6

The Gorbachev Years

ON MARCH II, 1985, Mikhail Sergeyevich Gorbachev became general secretary of the Communist Party of the Soviet Union (CPSU). Gorbachev's
fresh, bold appearance on the scene after three old and fragile leaders such
as Brezhnev, Andropov, and Chernenko was welcomed not only by the Soviet people but by the whole world. As well as introducing a number of
revolutionary reforms on the domestic scene under the catch-cry of perestroika, he lived up to expectations on the diplomatic front by striking out
in brave innovative directions.[1] Discarding the old Marxist-Leninist ideology based on class struggle, he advocated a diplomatic doctrine designated
"new political thinking" (*novoe politicheskoe myshlenie*), and he indicated a willingness to deal with those problems of common concern to all mankind.[2]
In order to put this new doctrine into practice, Gorbachev appointed Eduard
Shevardnadze as foreign minister in place of Andrei Gromyko,[3] whose twenty-
eight years of experience in the post had earned him the sobriquets of "living witness to postwar diplomacy" and "Mr. Nyet."[4]

Changing Perceptions of Japan

Gorbachev's reputation for being more skilled at external than internal affairs was the result of many achievements in the field of diplomacy. First of
all, he withdrew Soviet troops from Afghanistan; then, through summit meetings with Presidents Reagan and Bush Sr., he concluded the INF Treaty,
eliminating the class of missiles known as Intermediate Range Nuclear Forces,
and succeeded in putting in place further agreements under the START
(Strategic Arms Reduction Talks) process, heralding an improvement in U.S.-
Soviet relations. Also, partially by design and partially by chance, through the
liberation of Eastern Europe and the unification of East and West Germany,

Gorbachev dramatically improved relations with Western Europe. Although his visit to China was overshadowed by the Tian'anmen Square Incident, it did help move Sino-Soviet relations from the realms of ideological conflict toward normality. Gorbachev completely changed Soviet policy toward the Korean Peninsula, effectively abandoning North Korea and normalizing relations with South Korea, which in economic power and other respects was playing a far more important role in the world. In recognition of his achievements, Gorbachev was awarded the Nobel Peace Prize in 1990.

If we are to find fault with Gorbachev's otherwise spectacular record in international relations, it would be with his diplomacy toward Japan. For all his diplomatic skills, this was one area of international relations where even he could not achieve success. This failure can be attributed almost entirely to the deep rift over the Northern Territories dispute. That said, the Gorbachev years (March 11, 1985, to December 25, 1991) did bring about some improvements. Although there was no major breakthrough, there were some other positive developments.

First, Gorbachev's administration valued Soviet-Japanese relations more highly than its predecessors, a result of Japan's increasing economic power, but simultaneously reflecting the new thinking that had brought about major changes in Soviet views of international politics. The Soviet Union had undergone a "conceptual revolution," replacing the old yardstick of judging a nation by its military might with one that assessed its economic, scientific, and technological strength.[5] According to Gorbachev, postwar West Germany and Japan were examples of nations that refuted a basic tenet of Lenin's *Imperialism: The Highest Stage of Capitalism* (1916), by proving it possible to establish a thriving capitalist economy without taking extra steps to imperialism and militarism. Some Soviet academics and politicians even went so far as suggesting that late-comer Japan, by utilizing the power of science and technology, had, in a relatively short period, succeeded in transforming its economy into something capable not only of weathering shocks and crises but even of overtaking the most advanced capitalist nations. On this basis they advocated that the "Japanese miracle" (*iaponskoe chudo*) and the "Japanese phenomenon" (*iaponskii fenomen*) provided the best possible model for the kind of perestroika Gorbachev was promoting.[6]

However, perceptions are only *one of* the important factors involved in a nation's foreign policy decision-making process, and changed perceptions did not automatically bring changes in Soviet policy toward Japan, which was therefore a mixture of change and continuity during the Gorbachev years. The greatest change was in mutual perception of each nation by the other. Before Gorbachev's advent, two issues in particular had made the Soviet Union extremely unpopular with the Japanese. The first was, of course, the illegal occupation of the Northern Territories. The second was the disdainful superpower arrogance manifested by Soviet behavior in the MiG 25 incident, the unilateral proclamation of an exclusive 200–nautical-mile fishing zone, and behavior after shooting down KAL 007. Apart from North Korea in some postwar years, and China during the Cultural Revolution, the Soviet Union was consistently the country most disliked in Japanese public opinion.

During the Gorbachev period, reflecting the changed Soviet perceptions of Japan, Soviet politicians and bureaucrats adopted more benign and less arrogant attitudes and behavior toward Japan. As though in response, Japanese perceptions of the Soviet Union also changed. In June 1985, shortly after Gorbachev came to power, a public opinion survey conducted for the Japanese prime minister's Office, showed 83.7 percent of respondents "not favorably disposed toward the Soviet Union," versus only 8.6 percent "favorably disposed." But another survey, in October 1991, gave figures of 69.5 percent and 25.4 percent, respectively, a significant change, though still indicating that only one-quarter of Japanese looked favorably on the Soviet Union, a mere two months before the USSR ceased to exist.[7]

Dialogue Commences

These adjustments in perception and attitude were accompanied by some tangible changes. First, regular foreign ministerial consultations resumed. When Shevardnadze visited Japan, on January 15–19, 1986, it was eight years since Sonoda had been to Moscow and ten years since Gromyko had come to Tokyo. Shevardnadze did not go so far as acknowledging that a "territorial issue does exist," but he did listen carefully to Foreign Minister Shintarō Abe's three-hour explanation of Japan's position on the disputed islands. Just five months later, at the end of May, Abe went to Moscow. As a result of these reciprocal visits, former Japanese residents were again permitted to visit graves on the islands, and agreements were reached on issues such as taxation, trade and payments, cultural exchanges, and reactivation of the Japan–Soviet Commission on Scientific and Technological Cooperation.

The failure of the U.S. and Soviet leaders to achieve a tangible outcome at the Reykjavik Summit in October 1986 saw Soviet-American relations become somewhat strained for a period.[8] A visit by Gorbachev to Japan had appeared possible, but was postponed. A series of events and incidents with national security implications, which took place in April–May 1987, helped render any improvement in the bilateral relationship impossible. The Toshiba Machine Company was accused of selling to the Soviet Union sensitive, high-technology equipment that could be used to make quieter propellers for Soviet submarines, in violation of the regulations of the Coordinating Committee on Multilateral Export Control (COCOM). Soviet-Japanese relations were further eroded by a series of "spy" incidents. Two former officials of the Japanese Self-Defense Forces (SDF) were arrested on charges of selling to Soviet agents intelligence information on fighter aircraft based at Yokota U.S. Air Force Base. Mutual expulsion of diplomats and officials from the Japanese and Soviet embassies followed. These events and incidents created an atmosphere that dashed the last hope of reviving the idea of Gorbachev's visit to Japan. However, from winter 1987 onward, the two countries' efforts to maintain a positive momentum began to bear fruit. In December 1988 Shevardnadze made his second visit to Japan, followed four months later by Japanese Foreign Minister Sōsuke Uno's visit to Moscow. Shevardnadze came again in September 1990, and in January 1991 Foreign Minister Tarō Nakayama went to Moscow.

In addition to these regular consultations, the foreign ministers also met annually at September sessions of the United Nations General Assembly. Regular meetings of deputy-ministers led in December 1988 to formation of a permanent working group at that level, to further promote negotiations about a peace treaty.

All this promoted dialogue between the two countries, in a less rigid and limited, more unconstrained and generous spirit, than previous discussions, on which the Soviets had imposed unilateral limits. Former Foreign Minister Gromyko, for example, had excluded the territorial problem from talks by stating, "If territorial issues are raised, we will not be able to continue discussions with Japan." During the Brezhnev–Gromyko years the Soviet Union had completely ignored the principle of equality and reciprocity in talks, while top Soviet leaders never, and their foreign ministers rarely, visited Japan. But in the Gorbachev years, while not displaying any intent to relinquish territory to Japan, they did concede that they could not prevent it raising the territorial issue. Also, toward the end of Gorbachev's tenure, the Soviet government conceded that if Japan insisted there was a territorial issue, then they must recognize its existence.

The next change worth mentioning is that the Gorbachev administration realistically accepted as a fait accompli the Treaty of Mutual Cooperation and Security between Japan and the United States of America. This was a huge change, if we consider that in 1960, when the treaty was revised, Khrushchev was so incensed that he unilaterally added to Article 9 of the 1956 Soviet-Japanese Joint Declaration on transfer of Habomai and Shikotan the new condition, "on withdrawal of all foreign troops from Japanese territory." Even before Gorbachev's advent, some Soviet Japan specialists had already begun to argue that excessive emphasis on the existence of the Japanese-American security treaty was unproductive, it was unrealistic to press Japan to abrogate the cornerstone of its alliance with the United States and nonsensical to formulate policy toward Japan based on such an unfeasible expectation. That is to say, if the security treaty continued to be the focus of

Soviet attention, then there was no room to improve Soviet-Japanese relations; it would be more realistic to acknowledge the treaty's existence and work toward improving relations within that context.

Slowly but surely, proponents of this line of thinking started to make their way into the upper levels of the Soviet policy decision-making process, and during the Gorbachev years his government began claiming that it "did not want Japan in any way to sacrifice its relationship with any other country as a result of improved Soviet–Japanese relations."[9] At the 9th Foreign Ministerial Consultation, in Moscow in May 1989, Shevardnadze said, "The Soviet Union considers it possible to start negotiations on a Soviet-Japanese peace treaty and conclude the treaty, *even under such circumstances that the Japanese-American security treaty exists*" (italics added).[10] That was the first official acknowledgment of the treaty by a top-ranking Soviet foreign policy decision-maker, "indirectly suggesting that the Soviet Union was thereby canceling Khrushchev's 1960 'memorandum.'"[11]

Some Soviet commentators were bold enough to suggest that, compared to a scenario whereby Japan was released from the bounds of the U.S.–Japanese security framework, emerged as an independent force and possibly developed into a militarily strong regional power, it was for the Soviet Union a lesser evil if Japan stayed passively within her security arrangement with the United States. Some even suggested that the Japanese-American security treaty was a factor for stability in the Asia-Pacific Region.[12]

In permitting resumption of gravesite visits by former Japanese inhabitants of the disputed islands, Gorbachev's administration assumed a humanitarian perspective and waived visa requirements, allowing the visits to be divorced from the sovereignty issue, and thus reversing a ban Brezhnev had suddenly imposed in the 1970s. Brezhnev had promised to reconsider this issue in the joint communiqué issued at the end of Tanaka's 1973 visit, but the former CPSU general secretary never did so.[13] Gorbachev gave the green light for such visits beginning in the summer of 1986.

The Soviet government under Gorbachev also looked to apply glasnost to the issue of the prolonged detention of more than six hundred thousand Japanese prisoners of war in Siberia, where about 10 percent of them died. For the first time ever the Soviet authorities indicated willingness to cooperate regarding information on names of POWs, location of graves, and return of ashes. On Gorbachev's way to visit Japan in 1991, he stopped at Khabarovsk, where he paid his respects at graves outside the city of Japanese who had died there. In his speech at the Imperial Palace in Tokyo, he expressed *soboleznovanie* (sympathy or condolence) for the deaths and agreed to a brief meeting with representatives of three groups of former POWs.

During the Gorbachev years, mutual exchanges became more and more frequent, due to initiatives such as the Agreement on Cultural Exchange.

Initiatives such as the humanitarian medical aid offered by Japan in 1990 to Konstantin Skoropyshnyi, a three-year-old burn victim from Sakhalin, produced a friendly mood between the Soviet Union and Japan unimaginable just a few years before. According to a public opinion survey carried out in 1989 by Moscow's All-Soviet Center for Public Opinion Studies (VTsIOM), headed by Tatiana Zaslavskaia, Japan was the most popular foreign country for the respondents. There were twenty-four applicants for every place among students seeking to major in Japanese at Moscow State University (MGU).[14]

There was also a resurgence in Soviet-Japanese economic exchanges, which took Japan to positions as a trading partner of the Soviet Union varying from year to year between third and fifth among advanced industrial countries (along with West Germany, Finland, Italy, and France) and by a long way its top trading partner in Asia (between five and six billion U.S. dollars a year, compared to $800 million-worth of Soviet trade in 1990 with second-placed South Korea).

In short, in a range of fields, other than the territorial issue, Gorbachev took some very progressive measures to improve relations with Japan, and as a result the Japanese view of the Soviet Union improved dramatically. Nevertheless, Japan was never as caught up by "Gorbymania" as were the United States and West European countries. Most public opinion surveys indicated that Japan's level of enthusiasm toward Gorbachev and perestroika was the lowest among advanced nations, and that this somehow manifested an element of disillusionment.

Why was this? The reason was that most Japanese judged Gorbachev's "new political thinking" as totally oriented toward the West and did not apply in any clear form toward Japan. To be even more frank, we could say it was because Gorbachev basically maintained his predecessors'-stance toward the main reason for Soviet unpopularity with the Japanese people, the Northern Territories issue. To what extent, if at all, had the Soviet attitude toward the disputed islands actually changed? In considering this question, let us focus on Gorbachev's visit to Japan in April 1991.

Gorbachev's Visit to Japan

Mikhail Gorbachev visited Japan on April 16–19, 1991. A visit by the top Soviet political leader was unprecedented in the history of Japanese-Soviet relations, and, coincidentally, this visit by Gorbachev, who eight months later found himself the last president of the Soviet Union, took place almost exactly one hundred years after the attack at Otsu, on May 11, 1891, on Crown Prince Nikolay Alexandrovich, who became the last tsar of Russia.

During his three-day visit Gorbachev had six (according to Soviet records, eight) meetings, totaling twelve hours, with Prime Minister Toshiki Kaifu, signed the Japan-Soviet Joint Communiqué (see the Joint Compendium, Item 34), and went sightseeing in Kyoto and Nagasaki.[15]

The joint communiqué included this vague sentence:

As well as emphasizing the primary importance of accelerating work to conclude the preparations for a peace treaty, the prime minister and the president expressed their firm resolve to make constructive and vigorous efforts to this end, taking advantage of all **positive elements** that have been built up in bilateral negotiations in the years since *Japan and the Union of Soviet Socialist Republics jointly proclaimed an end to the state of war and the restoration of diplomatic relations in 1956.* (bold type and italics added)

First of all, the italicized reference to events of 1956 did not specifically mention the joint declaration, nor did it refer to its undertaking to conclude a peace treaty that would result in the return of Habomai and Shikotan to Japan. Next, the expression "positive elements" (*pozitiv*) highlighted in bold type is ambiguous.[16] Since the Soviet and Japanese positions on the Northern Territories issue were diametrically opposed, any element the Japanese considered positive the Soviets would consider negative, and vice versa.

As expected, Gorbachev indicated that he did not see Article 9 of the 1956 Joint Declaration, that promised Habomai and Shikotan would be handed over to Japan, as a "positive element." At the press conference following signing of the joint statement, Gorbachev, unasked, said, "Let me say straightaway, so that you do not ask the question and I do not wait for it: Why is there no mention of the [1956] Declaration?" He replied to his own question saying, "We took from this document those elements that have not only become part of history but also acquired legal force and had consequences in international law. But, as for those things that did not take place—because chances were missed and history took a different course—we were unable to revive the second part of the document more than thirty years later."[17]

Gorbachev also mentioned this issue in his postvisit report to the Supreme Soviet. It pertains to an extremely important point.

Prime Minister Kaifu pressed persistently to have the 1956 Joint Declaration referred to in the joint statement. We did not agree to this proposal. The reason for this is that his insistence was not because the joint declaration refers to the termination of the state of war or the restoration of diplomatic relations, but that it promises the handover of two islands to Japan when a peace treaty is concluded. . . . We consider that we should depend only on those parts of the joint statement that are in keeping with the consequences of the international, legal, and physical realities of history. What did not take place and what subsequent history has, as it were, "erased" cannot thirty years later *simply* be revived in this way. The chance has gone. A new reality has been born, and we must press forward on that basis.[18] (italics added)

Gorbachev's addition of "simply" (*prosto tak*) to the expression, "cannot thirty years later be revived" he used at the Tokyo press conference on April 19 invites the interpretation that there is still a chance to realize "the handover of two islands."[19]

Be that is it may, these statements indicate that Gorbachev adopted a similar position to that of Khrushchev's 1960 memorandum, a selective approach, acknowledging the parts of the 1956 Joint Declaration that were advantageous to the Soviet Union, but claiming those parts that were not advantageous to be invalidated. As I have said many times before, this violates international law. I could only conclude that the same Gorbachev who was telling the world that perestroika aimed to make the Soviet state a *Rechtsstaat* (a state ruled by law) was as guilty as Khrushchev of treating an international agreement selectively. Unfortunately, my interpretation was proved correct. Kazuhiko Tōgō, who was busy behind the scenes during Gorbachev's visit, also frankly acknowledged this point. He wrote of Gorbachev's statement, "We could not confirm whether the expression 'positive element' was meant to include the 1956 Joint Declaration in its *entirety* or more specifically, its Article 9 was included" (italics added).[20]

In conclusion, at least in regard to policy toward Japan, we have no choice but to judge that Gorbachev backed away from his "new political thinking." Many Japanese had noted, even before Gorbachev's visit, that he had already shown signs of assuming a slightly more conservative stance in domestic politics, but had seen this as the unavoidable result of pressure from conservative factions. No Japanese had ever expected that he would bring to Japan an approach effectively the same as the "old political thinking" of Khrushchev's days. So in the end, Gorbachev applied more or less the same tactics as Stalin, Khrushchev, Brezhnev, and Gromyko. The Japanese people may have been far too naive in their assumptions about him.

The 1991 Japan-Soviet Joint Communiqué

I began my explanation of this communiqué by focusing on the points that were not to Japan's advantage, but of course not all of its content can be so described. Had there been no advantageous points, Japan of course would not have signed it. Let us now turn our attention to those points.

First, the Soviet Union acknowledged that a territorial dispute existed. We can interpret the use in Article 4 of the communiqué of expression such as "the issue of territorial demarcation" and "territorial issue" as the Soviet government finally *officially* acknowledging the existence of a territorial dispute. Gorbachev, as top political leader, officially abandoned the stance of the Brezhnev-Gromyko years that "the territorial issue has been resolved once and for all and no longer exists." Before the Japanese–Soviet Summit in April 1991, Foreign Minister Shevardnadze had all but recognized that the territorial problem did exist, but because he subsequently resigned, it would have

been problematic to rely on him. In Gorbachev's report to the Supreme Soviet, he said:

For a long time we pretended that no such (territorial) problem exists. However, the
problem did not go away. This has become clearer and clearer as long as we became
objectively familiar with the problem, studying the problem's history, its legal, political, psychological aspects. Through recent contacts with Japanese representatives we
cannot help but feel, how deeply this problem has been rooted in national con-
science. It is impossible to resolve this problem in a unilateral way.[21]

This remark was therefore seen as particularly important as acknowledging,
even if in a roundabout way, that a territorial issue clearly existed.

The second reason for Japan's signing of a joint communiqué, and a considerable plus for Japan, was that it clearly mentioned negotiations as concerning the *four* islands, allowing Japan to reassert its position that the "territorial
issue" concerned all four.

Third, it was also agreeable to Japan that the Soviet Union undertook to
take measures in the near future to establish a simplified visa-free framework
for visits by Japanese to the four disputed islands. This framework for exchange greatly contributed to improving the atmosphere between the two
countries.

Fourth, Gorbachev's proposal in the joint communiqué to take steps in
the near future to reduce Soviet military forces on the disputed islands was
a welcome development for Japan. In 1978–79, around the time the Sino-
Japanese Peace and Friendship Treaty was signed, the Soviet deployment of
one division (about ten thousand troops) to these islands that Japan considered to be her own territory had rankled with many Japanese, and it encouraged those who adhered to the "Soviet Threat Theory." From a strategic
point of view, the return of the islands to Japan, or for that matter, reductions
in military forces stationed there, was not something that came easily for the
Soviet Union because since 1978 it had employed a "bastion strategy" of
transforming the Sea of Okhotsk into a "sanctuary" for ballistic-missile firing
nuclear submarines (SSBNs) of the Soviet Pacific Fleet.[22] At that time, Soviet submarine-launched missiles could reach targets in North America west
of the Great Lakes only from launch points in the Sea of Okhotsk. To protect the submarines against U.S. naval attack, maintain the Sea of Okhotsk
as a sanctuary, and turn its enclosed nature from disadvantage to asset, the
Kurile Islands were militarized after 1978, with a sonar barrier, radars, ships,
aircraft, and stocks of mines and depth charges. The Northern Territories
thus became strategically important, and military demands for their reten-
tion decisive.

However, by the start of the 1990s submarine-launched missiles, able to
reach any target in North America from the Barents Sea, off Russia's north

coast, were coming into service, reducing the need for a Far East "sanctuary," and hence of its protective barrier in the Kuriles.[23] The official announcement, during Gorbachev's visit to Japan in April 1991, of a partial withdrawal of Soviet military forces from the islands signified their reduced strategic value. This was indeed a positive development in terms of Japan's demand for return of the islands.

Next, if we expand discussion to include issues other than the disputed islands, we note that the joint communiqué also acknowledges, "Cooperation should take place in trade-economic, scientific-technological, and political spheres."[24] Gorbachev was most insistent on having this sentence included in the joint communiqué. However, they would mean little unless Japan decided to act positively on them. Japan could tighten or loosen her purse strings in response to Soviet moves, and at a time when turmoil in the Soviet economy was holding Japanese private corporations back from doing business with it, there was effectively no chance of expanding economic ties, unless the Japanese government decided to invest public funds. If Gorbachev couldn't even go so far as acknowledging a previous promise to return two of the four islands, the Japanese government could hardly say anything other than "without taxpayers' agreement the Export-Import Bank of Japan cannot make large loans available on a long-term, low-interest basis to a high-risk country such as the Soviet Union."

In short, at the time of his visit to Japan in April 1991, Gorbachev was successful on the negative point of not giving up the islands to Japan, but on the positive side was unable to secure any economic cooperation or aid from Japan. This is one reason why Gorbachev himself used the words "drawn fight" (*boevaia nich'ia*) in his report to the Supreme Soviet.[25] Maybe he should have put his political career on the line during his time in Japan and afterward persuaded the Soviet people of the logic behind his decisions. Perhaps he should have said, "Relations with Japan are extremely important for the Soviet Union. Without an improvement in relations between our two countries the Soviet Union cannot be a nation of the Asia-Pacific region. Not only is the Soviet economy in decline, every aspect of our society is in crisis. I will return the four islands to Japan, and in return secure long-term, large-scale, low-interest loans to revive the faltering process of perestroika." Had Gorbachev approached the Soviet people boldly and earnestly with this line of logic, he just might have been able to win them over. At least, this was the kind of innovative leadership the Japanese expected of him. However, by April 1991 the nature of his leadership had already changed from "innovative" to "representative," and he made it clear to all that his prime concern was his own political survival.

Granted this view may be based on hindsight; it might have been better had Gorbachev visited Japan before the shift in political priorities changed his approach to leadership. As it was, the procrastination over his visit served to heighten Japanese expectations of the outcome of the summit meeting and had the effect of focusing world attention on the territorial issue. I would say Gorbachev squandered at least six chances to visit Japan. (1) If he had come soon after taking office, he could have paid a protocol visit to Tokyo and got away with taking a relatively small "souvenir" with him. (2) Gorbachev lost another opportunity, due to hesitancy, before the Toshiba Machine Tool incident of April 1987 caused Soviet-Japanese relations to deteriorate. (3) Another missed opportunity was the funeral of the Showa emperor in 1989, when he could have come without bringing any gifts. (4) As an executive member of the Central Committee of the Soviet Communist Party privately commented to me, Gorbachev should have visited Japan during the Nakasone years when the administration was both strong and stable. (5) In the meantime, "All sorts of ethnic issues and domestic problems emerged, so dealing with matters such as the territorial dispute with Japan was out of the question" (Georgii Arbatov, director of the Institute of the USA and Canada, Soviet Academy of Sciences).[26] (6) Gorbachev should have visited Japan before May 29, 1990, when his arch-rival, Boris Yeltsin, was elected chairman of the RSFSR (Russian Soviet Federated Socialist Republic) Supreme Soviet. That day signaled the end of Gorbachev's domination of Soviet politics and the start of what was effectively a dual power structure, meaning that it became difficult for Gorbachev to decide policy toward Japan without considering a possible "Nyet" from Yeltsin.

Gorbachev had let it be known that he wanted to visit Japan in spring, when the cherry blossoms were in bloom, but by the time he arrived in Tokyo, on April 16, 1991, the cherry blossom season was over. This was indeed symbolic of the fact that Gorbachev's visit to Japan did not involve the best timing.[27] He would have been well-advised to pay greater attention to Lenin's famous saying, "All things come to those who use time wisely."[28]

CHAPTER 7

The Yeltsin Years

Rising Expectations Among the Japanese

Boris Yeltsin's attitude toward the Northern Territories issue is somewhat unclear. During his unofficial visit to Japan in January 1990, when he was a Supreme Soviet deputy from the RSFSR, he attracted attention by announcing a "five-stage proposal for solution of the territorial issue between Russia and Japan."[1] The gist of it was that the Soviet Union first of all "officially declare that it acknowledges the existence of a territorial dispute" in Soviet-Japanese relations. The second step was to designate the disputed territory as a Soviet-Japanese "joint free-enterprise zone." The third and fourth steps involved "demilitarizing the islands" and then "signing a peace treaty." On the basis of these steps being carried out during a fifteen- to twenty-year period, the fifth and last step would leave the final solution to "the discretion of a new generation," that would choose between joint administration, independent, free status, and reversion to Japan.[2]

This proposal by Yeltsin was a step forward, as the first public acknowledgment by a senior Soviet politician of the territorial dispute.[3] At least that is how it was viewed in Japan, as Soviet President Gorbachev had not even acknowledged the existence of a territorial issue by the time of Yeltsin's announcement. At the same time, the fourth stage advocated concluding a peace treaty without any delineation of the border between the Soviet Union and Japan.[4] A peace treaty is the diplomatic document that ultimately determines territorial borders. Was Yeltsin unaware of this? Yeltsin seemed to be aiming to conclude a peace treaty without returning any of the islands, though his real intentions were not confirmed. Be that as it may, it was true that Japan did not judge his proposal to warrant genuine consideration.

During Gorbachev's visit to Japan in April 1991, Yeltsin actively pressured him to make no concessions on the territorial issue. He extracted a promise to that effect beforehand and added a representative from the RSFSR to the delegation to ensure it was kept. *Komsomol'skaia Pravda* reported that on the night before Gorbachev's departure for Tokyo: "Professionals from ministries of [both] the USSR and the Russian Republic jointly worked out the Soviet side's position at the negotiations and reached a consensus on all points: to officially acknowledge that the problem of a territorial dispute exists; not to give back the islands; and to swiftly create a mechanism for negotiations on this problem. Yeltsin agreed with the USSR's position, which he had been informed of in advance."[5] While Gorbachev was in Japan, Yeltsin also made numerous comments from Paris and Strasbourg, specifically aimed at holding the Soviet President in check during his negotiations with the Japanese government.

However, after the failed coup d'état of August 1991, Yeltsin, by then president of the RSFSR, found himself de facto leader of the USSR's government, rather than its opponent, and immediately sensed the need for approaches to Japan as an economic superpower. In September 1991 he sent Ruslan Khasbulatov, deputy chairman of the Russian Supreme Soviet, to Japan to hand a letter to Prime Minister Toshiki Kaifu. The gist of it was: (1) judging international politics in terms of victors and vanquished is an anachronism; (2) conclusion of a peace treaty is a matter of urgency; (3) the "five-stage proposal" should be implemented as quickly as possible; and (4) the territorial dispute should be settled on the basis of "law and justice."[6]

So what did the Yeltsin letter mean? It signified no less than a revolutionary shift in Russian leadership thinking on the Northern Territories issue. One might even go so far as to say that successive Soviet leaders had adhered to the famous axiom of Karl Haushofer, the German proponent of geopolitics, whose views provided a theoretical bedrock of Nazi Germany: "Boundaries are places for fights rather than legal decisions."[7] Successive Soviet governments claimed that changing national boundaries determined as results of World War Two amounted to destroying the peace and stability of the postwar international order. This position is based on theories of "irreversible results of war,"[8] or "recognition of current possession."[9]

In his letter, Yeltsin advocated that the territorial issue be decided not according to who was the victor (*pobeditel'*) or vanquished (*pobezhdennyi*) in war, but rather according to "law and justice" (*zakonnost' i spravedlivost'*). "Law and justice" refers to international law and historical justice. More specifically, "law" should refer to the return to Japan of Habomai and Shikotan as promised in the 1956 Soviet–Japanese Joint Declaration, and "justice" ("fairness" is another possible translation) to discussions regarding sovereignty over Kunashiri and Etorofu. Therefore "law and justice" represents a proposal for "two islands plus alpha."[10] That Yeltsin proposed a solution based on "law and justice" was a momentous development, a "conceptual revolution"[11] on the Russian side about the criteria governing the territorial dispute.[12]

On November 16, 1991, less than two months after Khasbulatov's visit to Japan, Yeltsin issued a "Letter to the Russian People" (see the Joint Compendium, Item 35), in which he wrote:

It would be unforgivable to continue to endure a situation where relations with Japan remain practically frozen because of the absence of a peace treaty between the two countries. . . . In the end, the future of a new democratic Russia as a member of the international community, and its international authority depends on how fast we manage to overcome the difficult heritage of the past, accept the norms of the international community, and thus make legality, justice and strict adherence to the principles of international law the criteria of its policy.

Furthermore, he said that the approach to demarcation of borders between Russia and Japan would be guided by "principles of justice and humanism," a significant addition to the criteria of "law and justice" mentioned in his letter to Kaifu. This can be interpreted to mean that any settlement of the territorial dispute must benefit current Russian residents on the islands.

Flexibility on Tokyo's Side

The Japanese government had already begun to modify its traditional Soviet policy. In May 1989 Prime Minister Noboru Takeshita had sent his foreign minister, Sōsuke Uno, to Moscow to propose a policy of "balanced expansion or expanded equilibrium [*kakudai kinkō*]" to replace the previously rigid adherence to the principle of "inseparability of economics and politics [*seikei fukabun*]." "Balanced expansion" did not require that progress on economic cooperation be delayed until steps were taken toward resolving the territorial dispute. In other words, although there was an unbreakable link between these two factors, "political" and "economic" matters could be expanded in a carefully balanced and concurrent manner. Now, in response to the shifts in Russian policy indicated by Yeltsin's letters, the governments of Toshiki Kaifu and Kiichi Miyazawa began to adopt an even more flexible stance toward Russia.

While visiting Moscow in October 1991, Tarō Nakayama, foreign minister in Kaifu's government, modified the Japanese government's post-1956 insistence that all four islands must be returned immediately in their entirety (*yonto ikkatsu sokuji henkan*). He informed the Russian government that if it recognized Japanese sovereignty over the islands, Tokyo was prepared to be flexible about the timing, manner, and conditions of their reversion. Subsequently Michio Watanabe, foreign minister in Miyazawa's government, declared that Japan was prepared to take account of the concerns of the Russian residents of the islands. If Russia recognized Japanese sovereignty and returned the islands, Japan would not require the Russian residents to leave immediately.[13] The Miyazawa government also suggested that Russian residents of the disputed islands could be given the opportunity to leave or stay, and those who stayed would be eligible for Japanese citizenship. These statements indicate that the Japanese side accepted and was willing to apply the "humanitarian criteria" mentioned in Yeltsin's "Letter to the Russian People" to finding solutions for the territorial dispute.

The Cancellation of Yeltsin's Visit to Japan

People often talk about the "Gorbachevization" of Yeltsin. It may be that such a transformation is the fate of all those who become rulers. Even if a ruler consciously decides to adopt different policies and style of rule and policies, he may, if the environment or issues in question are largely unchanged, end up mostly following his predecessor's line. Yeltsin's "Gorbachevization" was particularly evident in policy toward Japan. As Gorbachev had been, so too was Yeltsin hamstrung by the Northern Territories issue, and ultimately he was obliged to step down without having effected any significant improvement in relations with Japan.

An example of this was the timing of his visit to Japan, where he made the same mistake as his predecessor. Gorbachev visited Japan in April 1991, during his last months in power, when his power base was becoming increasingly fragile, and he was in no position to make significant concessions on the Northern Territories issue. Correspondingly, Yeltsin should have boldly visited Japan after the failed coup d'état of August 1991, or the dissolution of the Soviet Union, when his power and popularity were at their peak, and authority of conservative forces at its weakest. At that time few would have dared to offer objections to any decisions he might have chosen to make during a visit. Instead he sent Khasbulatov and made no effort to go himself.

Yeltsin also postponed his visit planned for June 1992, thereby missing another chance to improve relations with Japan. Comments such as, "We hope the visit to Japan can be realized before the rainy season, when it gets humid" (Deputy Foreign Minister Georgii Kunadze), contributed to building a degree of expectation that the Russian president would visit Japan in June.[14] But then in late January 1992, while attending a United Nations meeting in New York, he suddenly proposed, during his first meeting with Prime Minister Miyazawa, that he visit Japan in September of that year. In discussion with the author, Konstantin Sarkisov (head of the Center for Japanese Studies at the Institute of Oriental Studies, Russian Academy of Sciences) referred to this change of plans as a "bolt from the blue."

From that point on, the Russian domestic situation developed in ways that eroded Yeltsin's political power base. The radical economic reforms he had implemented by acting Prime Minister Yegor Gaidar caused great confusion in the Russian economy. In particular, the price liberalization policies (the so-called shock therapy) effective from January 2, 1992, led to inflation soaring to 2,500 percent per annum.[15] Gaidar's financial reforms did stimulate the distribution sector, but as the privatization of state property and enterprises was not carried out before or at the same time as them, they did not result in increased production in the crucial manufacturing sector. Yeltsin managed to stave off attacks on his reforms during the sixth Russian Congress of People's Deputies in April 1992, but later appeased conservatives and the Civic Union by appointing spokesmen of the military-industrial complex and state enterprises to senior posts in Gaidar's cabinet. Toward the end of summer 1992 the old guard and conservative forces, typified by former Communist Party leaders and prominent nationalists, began their resurgence.

On the evening of September 9, 1992, only four days before Yeltsin's visit was due to begin, he telephoned Prime Minister Miyazawa to tell him he was canceling his trip. This dashed the hopes of those Japanese who had thought a new era was about to dawn after the long chill in Russo-Japanese relations. How did this come about? What caused it? Who was responsible?

Broadly speaking, three primary factors were behind the cancellation, namely, the resurgence of conservative forces in Russia, the eruption of nationalism, and the weakening of Yeltsin's leadership. However, these are all indirect, background factors. We must distinguish between them and the more direct cause of the cancellation, which was, of course, the standoff over the disputed islands. Without satisfying Japan's demands on the territorial issue, Yeltsin would have returned from Japan with no more assurance of economic aid than had Gorbachev in the previous year. I suspect this thought was intolerable for Yeltsin, and it was probably enough to sway him to cancel his visit, despite the negative impact the cancellation would have on Russo-Japanese relations.

Another reason why the cancellation ruffled Japanese feathers was the way Yeltsin did it. The Japanese side had done everything possible to make the visit a success, and cancellation at such short notice was a serious breach of protocol, highly unusual if not unprecedented. That was not all. In Yeltsin's telephone conversation with Miyazawa, and in a speech he made two days later in Cheboksary, a provincial town near the Volga, he cited "Japan's attitude and posture" among his reasons for canceling the visit.[16] It is unfair in the extreme to blame another party for a decision one has taken for one's own reasons. Such feelings among Japanese saw the popularity of Yeltsin and his nascent Russian state plummet.

Generally speaking, Japanese anti-Soviet/Russian feeling can traditionally be traced back to two issues. One is the issue of the disputed islands, and the other the arrogance Soviet governments have displayed by their disdainful attitudes and behavior toward Japan. The MiG 25 incident (1975), negotiations over declaration of an exclusive 200–nautical-mile fishing zone (1976–77), and the shooting-down of KAL 007 (1983) are examples of heavy-handed Soviet attitudes and behavior. Gorbachev's advent led to remarkable alleviation of the second of the two causes, but the Yeltsin leadership's behavior before and after cancellation of his planned visit in September 1992 took us back to the days of Brezhnev and Gromyko, and sparked a resurgence of anti-Russian feeling among Japanese. Let us cite the result of public opinion polls commissioned by the Japanese prime minister's office on "Feelings Toward the Soviet Union/Russia." In a poll taken in June 1985, shortly after Gorbachev came to power, only 8.6 percent of respondents were favorably disposed toward the Soviet Union, but in a poll taken in October 1991, shortly before the end of his tenure, 25.4 percent of respondents were so disposed, while unfavorably disposed respondents decreased during the same period from 83.7 to 69.5 percent. However, in a poll carried out in October-November 1992, after Yeltsin cancelled his visit, favorably disposed respondents had dropped to 15.2 percent, and those who "felt no affinity toward Russia" had increased to 79.6 percent.[17]

The Tokyo Declaration

Yeltsin finally visited Japan on October 11–13, 1993. Let us consider exactly what Japan gained at the Yeltsin-Hosokawa Summit meeting. Compared to Gorbachev's visit, Yeltsin's resulted in two steps forward for Japan.

First, Yeltsin officially apologized for the long detention of Japanese prisoners of war in Siberia after World War Two.[18] During his visit in April 1991, Gorbachev had gone no further than to express *soboleznovanie* (sympathy or condolence) in referring to the detainees. By contrast, Yeltsin used *izvinenie* (apology) no less than five times.[19] Yeltsin's words laid to rest the concept of infallibility of communist dictatorship, and with it the argument that the Soviet Union could do no wrong. The apology for "inhuman" treatment of Japanese detainees after World War Two and the occupation of the Northern Territories are closely related, in that both were "crimes committed by totalitarianism" around the end of World War Two. If the Yeltsin government could apologize for the detention of Japanese POWs, it could rectify another mistake committed by the same dictator, Josef Stalin, that is, the illegal seizure of the Northern Territories. Many Japanese, including this author, had such expectations.

Progress on the territorial issue was what I see as the second step forward. This was because, compared to the joint communiqué signed in 1991 by Gorbachev and Kaifu, there were six aspects of the Tokyo Declaration on Russo-Japanese Relations signed by Yeltsin and Hosokawa (see the Joint Compendium, Item 36), which were advantageous to Japan.

First, Yeltsin reiterated that a territorial problem existed. This, of course, was not particularly new; he had already officially acknowledged this in his five-stage proposal of January 1990, as had Gorbachev in April 1991. Nevertheless, this reiteration remained important. The reason, of course, was that political standpoints can change with changes of leaders, political status, and other circumstances. In that respect, a new president's confirmation of a predecessor's standpoint is of no little significance.

Second, the order in which the disputed islands were listed in the 1993 Tokyo Declaration was of greater benefit to Japan than that used in the 1991 Joint Communiqué. In the 1991 document, the four islands were listed as "Habomai, Shikotan, Kunashiri, and Etorofu," starting with the one nearest to Hokkaido, but in the 1993 Tokyo Declaration, they were listed in exactly the opposite order, as "Etorofu, Kunashiri, Shikotan, and Habomai."[20]

Third, that Yeltsin did not seek to just cherry-pick in his interpretation of the 1956 Joint Declaration of Japan and the USSR was another beneficial point for Japan. Gorbachev had insisted that only elements of the joint declaration found positive to the USSR were valid, that the article referring to "the handover of two islands" had "lost its validity with the passage of time," and therefore that this portion of the declaration was no longer in effect. Yeltsin differed from his predecessor by not inserting the words "positive elements" in the Tokyo Declaration.

Fourth, the Tokyo Declaration also differed from the 1991 Joint Communiqué in that, while the communiqué referred to "taking advantage of all positive elements that have been built up in bilateral negotiations in the years *since* Japan and the Union of Soviet Socialist Republics jointly proclaimed an end to the state of war and the restoration of diplomatic relations in l956" (italics added), the 1993 declaration stated that "*all* treaties and international agreements" between Japan and the Soviet Union would continue to be applied (italics added). Specifically, the 1993 declaration stated that the Joint Compendium of Documents on the History of Territorial Issues between Japan and Russia would be used as a basis for bilateral negotiations toward a peace treaty.

Fifth, Yeltsin referred, albeit indirectly, to the validity of the 1956 Soviet–Japanese Joint Declaration. At his joint press conference with Hosokawa he said, "We will not shirk any of the obligations that require us to implement all of the agreements and treaties that have been concluded between Japan and the former Soviet Union. This, of course, includes that [1956 Soviet–Japanese Joint] Declaration."[21]

Sixth, another important point as I see it is that Yeltsin acknowledged the validity of the letters exchanged on September 29, 1956, between Matsumoto, then Japanese chief negotiator, and Gromyko, then Soviet first deputy foreign minister.

During the Soviet years the legal standing of these "letters" was, as previously mentioned, a bone of contention between Tokyo and Moscow. Japan's Foreign Ministry stressed that because they were released together with the Soviet–Japanese Joint Declaration they shared the same legal foundation as that declaration. The Soviet Union, however, contended that they did not constitute an integral part of the declaration, which, they insisted, took precedence in terms of international law because it had been signed by the leaders of both nations and ratified by the highest organs of both countries, whereas the "letters" were nothing more than an exchange between two officials. They also argued that by being agreed after the "letters" were written, the joint declaration superseded them, so any point from the "letters" not included in the joint declaration had no legal standing.

This difference in interpretation between the two countries would lead to an important disagreement. The Soviets held that while the words, "[The USSR] announces its agreement to continue negotiations on the conclusion of a peace treaty, which would also *include the territorial issue*" (italics added), appear in the Matsumoto-Gromyko letters, omission of the italicized words from the joint declaration, that read simply "[The USSR will] agree to continue . . . negotiations for the conclusion of a peace treaty," meant that any subsequent peace treaty negotiations would not necessarily "include the territorial issue." In other words, the Soviet Union, having agreed in the joint declaration to hand over Shikotan and Habomai on conclusion of a treaty, was not required to enter into any negotiations about Kunashiri and Etorofu. However, since the Japanese interpreted the Matsumoto-Gromyko letters and the joint declaration as one, their position is that there was "agreement to continue negotiations on the conclusion of a peace treaty, which would also *include the territorial issue*." As the return to Japan of Shikotan and Habomai was already agreed, subsequent negotiations on the territorial issue must therefore be about Kunashiri and Etorofu.

This discrepancy in the interpretations was ended with the 1993 Tokyo Declaration. My interpretation is that the declaration specifically mentions all four islands, so negotiations toward a peace treaty hinge on the issue of sovereignty over all four, and the Tokyo Declaration is in line with the Japanese interpretation of the 1956 documents.

This assessment is confirmed by the wording of the declaration. Firstly, it states that both governments "confirm that . . . *all treaties and other international agreements* between Japan and the Soviet Union continue to be applied between Japan and the Russian Federation" (italics added). It is natural, therefore, to interpret this as meaning that the Matsumoto-Gromyko letters are included in such "international agreements." The following points further support this. The Tokyo Declaration states that both governments agree that "negotiations toward an early conclusion of a peace treaty through the solution of this issue . . . [will be sought] . . . on the basis of historical and legal facts and based on the documents produced with the two countries' agreement." This of course refers to the forty-two historical documents contained in the Joint Compendium, which include the Matsumoto-Gromyko letters. In addition, while I may be repeating myself, as in the 1991 communiqué, all four islands are named in the declaration, and it is stated that negotiations should continue regarding all of them. This meant that, as agreement had already been reached on returning Habomai and Shikotan to Japan, subsequent negotiations would focus on the other two.

To summarize, we can conclude that Yeltsin's state visit to Tokyo in autumn 1993 was an important development in Russo-Japanese relations. Firstly, it confirmed Gorbachev's acknowledgment of the existence of a dispute over the islands, and secondly, it determined the criteria or formula for resolving the issue. According to William Zartman, who categorized the process by which agreement is reached in negotiations as comprising three stages, this signifies that the negotiations had passed through the first stage, diagnosis, and entered the second stage of thrashing out a formula for reaching the third stage, a solution.[22]

However, there is a problem here. It is unclear just how seriously Yeltsin was committed to solving the territorial problem. The Japanese side could not rid itself of the suspicion that his statements in Tokyo were designed merely as lip service. During his time in Tokyo, he said "a territorial problem does exist and does need to be solved *at some stage*" (italics added), but mentioned no specific time frame for solving it.[23] Two other comments he made in Tokyo had an ominous ring about them. One was that "a solution to the territorial dispute will be reached by developing relations between our two countries and bringing the peoples of both countries [psychologically] closer together."[24] A double barrier was skillfully worked in here. One involved preparing the environment, the other closing the gap in thinking between the people of the two countries. Yeltsin therefore hinted that there could be no return of territory until both criteria were met, thereby implying that Japan was not doing enough to improve relations between the two countries, and that even if it were, the Russian people were still far from mentally prepared to hand over the islands. In short, Yeltsin's strategy toward Japan was basically the same as Gorbachev's, namely, that facilitating an appropriate environment should come first, and it would be Russia that would decide when and whether it was achieved, thereby postponing solution of the island issue as much as possible.

Yeltsin made a second ominous statement in Tokyo, "It is not possible to resolve this [territorial] dispute *all at once*" (italics added).[25] Territorial disputes, because they involve issues of sovereignty, eventually manifest themselves as zero-sum games, requiring decisive actions by political leaders to resolve them once and for all. However, at least in October 1993, there was no indication that Yeltsin would take any such action. His inability or unwillingness to act decisively in October 1993 meant that the best possible chance to cut the Gordian knot was lost. That, perhaps, is how future historians will view this stage of developments.

Hashimoto's Initiatives

From around 1997 Japan reconsidered her Russia policy and began to display a slightly more relaxed approach toward Moscow. This was necessitated by the recognition of the dramatic changes in the international scene and domestic trends in Russia, and it perhaps also reflected recognition that previous policy had failed to secure the return of the disputed islands, so some adjustment in the stance toward Russia was needed.

The section of Prime Minister Ryutaro Hashimoto's 1997 policy speech concerning Russia is an example of this change. Comparison of it with the unvarying content of previous prime ministerial speeches, including his own speech of the previous year, shows clearly that a new perspective on Russia was emerging. In his annual policy address to the Diet in January 1996, he had followed precedent by saying, "I will continue my efforts for settlement of the northern territorial dispute based on the Tokyo Declaration and for complete normalization of relations by concluding a peace treaty."[26] In his policy speech in January 1997, he used these same words, but he prefaced them with "as for relations with Russia, I will further promote dialogue and cooperation with the country *in various fields*" (italics added).[27]

The new Russia policy was described as "multilayered."[28] The thrust of it was that, although a solution to the Northern Territories issue would remain an objective, at the same time efforts would also be put into a broad range of areas in Russo-Japanese relations. To some extent this approach had begun to be applied in 1992–93, but a good example of its more intensive application was the accelerated progress in the security dialogue and defense cooperation that occurred in 1996–97. The agreement that the two governments concluded in February 1998 (see the Joint Compendium, Item 37), covering safe operation of Japanese fishing vessels in the seas around the four islands, can also be seen as a product of this approach. Further progress was made in September 1998, when Japan decided to give Russian residents of the islands entry on a visa-free basis to receive emergency humanitarian assistance (see the Joint Compendium, Item 38). Similarly, in September 1999 Russia agreed to allow Japanese former residents and members of their families to make visa-free visits to the islands (see the Joint Compendium, Item 40).

In a speech delivered on July 24, 1997, to the Japanese Association of Corporate Executives (Keizai Doyukai), Hashimoto announced a new diplomatic policy toward Russia.[29] Let me summarize its key aspects. First of all, Hashimoto clarified his own perception of Russo-Japanese relations. "The interrelationships linking the United States, China, Japan, and Russia provide peace and stability to the Asia-Pacific region," but among the relationships between these countries, "Russo-Japanese relations lag furthest behind."[30] Based on this view of the realities, Hashimoto advocated that the key elements of a new Japanese policy toward Russia should be: first, the need to promote "Eurasian or Silk Road Diplomacy." Hashimoto recognized that Russia had been developing a "Eurasian diplomacy viewed from the Atlantic," so Japan intended to pursue a "Eurasian diplomacy viewed from the Pacific," thereby keeping in step with Russian diplomacy.[31]

Second, Hashimoto emphasized that Russo-Japanese relations should be governed by three guiding principles, "trust, mutual benefit, and a long-term perspective." Third, he made concrete proposals designed to strengthen Russo-Japanese relations. One was a call for cooperation in Russia's energy development projects in Siberia and the Russian Far East. Another was that the Japanese government provide business-training programs for young Russians. In essence, his speech illustrated a remarkable degree of sensitivity to Russia's aspirations.

Predictably, Yeltsin and his foreign policy advisors warmly welcomed Hashimoto's overtures. However, one important point that cannot be overlooked is that while they welcomed Hashimoto's speech, they somewhat misrepresented the true intent of his new policy and interpreted it in a way that suited Russia. Specifically, Russian leaders and mass-media outlets tried to present the speech as a sign that Japan's giving precedence to economic exchanges and cooperation meant it had abandoned its traditional policy of linking the Northern Territories problem with other bilateral issues.

Hashimoto's July 1997 address paved the way for three successive summit meetings (informal and formal) between the two countries' top leaders in less than eighteen months. The two informal Yeltsin-Hashimoto summits in 1997 and 1998 were, in a sense, epoch-making. On both occasions they achieved remarkable breakthroughs that were expected to end the four-year stalemate that followed the signing of the Tokyo Declaration in 1993.

Two important agreements were reached at the informal "no-necktie" summit held on November 1–2, 1997, at Krasnoyarsk in Siberia. The first was an agreement to make every effort to conclude a peace treaty by the year 2000. It was a pleasant surprise for the Japanese that Yeltsin took the initiative in proposing this deadline. Why did Yeltsin take it upon himself to make this proposal, so pleasing to Japan, and not indicate any disagreement with Hashimoto's attempts to confirm this commitment? His motives remain a mystery. Some Russian experts considered that it was merely one of his typical improvisations: that the idea for such a deadline, which had not been discussed in either the Russian Ministry of Foreign Affairs or the president's office, probably just came into his head during the flight to Krasnoyarsk.[32] Be that as it may, other Russian experts suggest his comments can be interpreted as representing his true intentions. They state that he was giving serious consideration to a plan to combine a possible solution of the territorial issue with a dramatic expansion of economic cooperation.[33] However, as Yeltsin's physical and mental condition deteriorated from then on, he was unable to follow through on any such intentions.

The other significant agreement reached at Krasnoyarsk was the so-called Hashimoto-Yeltsin Plan.[34] This included a commitment by the Japan Export-Import Bank (now the Japan Bank for International Cooperation) to provide approximately 1.5 billion U.S. dollars in untied loans to Russia. As with the resolve to conclude a peace treaty by 2000, the Hashimoto-Yeltsin Plan promised economic assistance for Russia continuing beyond 2000. So in that sense the two were clearly bundled together.

The second informal Hashimoto-Yeltsin Summit took place on April 18–19, 1998, in the seaside resort town of Kawana in Shizuoka Prefecture. Few expected any breakthroughs because the two leaders had already made so much headway at Krasnoyarsk. Probably the most noteworthy aspect of the Kawana Summit was Hashimoto's unofficial proposal to Yeltsin regarding resolution of the territorial issue. The content of this Kawana Proposal has still not been made public, but media sources suggest it involved the following points:[35]

1. The boundary between Russia and Japan would be drawn north of the four disputed islands, namely, between Uruppu and Etorofu. That would be tantamount to recognizing Japanese sovereignty over them all.

2. In return, Japan would not immediately seek the return of the islands and would acknowledge that Russia should exercise transitional administrative rights over them for a specified time.

3. The actual timing of transfer of the islands should be decided by the next generation.

Yeltsin said that Hashimoto's proposal "is worthy of serious consideration from our side," adding that he had an "optimistic feeling" about it.[36] Seen from the Russian side, the Kawana Summit was also a success.

1. The Japanese accepted the Russian proposal that a peace treaty should be made more comprehensive, to cover not only the settlement of the territorial dispute but also a broader range of issues, such as economic and cultural cooperation. As a result, the peace treaty could be called a treaty of peace, friendship, and cooperation.

2. The proposal for joint economic activities on the four disputed islands, put forward enthusiastically by Yeltsin and Foreign Minister Evgenii Primakov, received de facto acceptance from Hashimoto with the caveat that development of joint economic activities should create a favorable environment for advancement of negotiations on a peace treaty (see the Joint Compendium, Item 41). As examples of such possible joint activities, Yeltsin mentioned construction of facilities for processing marine resources, infrastructure, roads, ports, and airports.

3. Yeltsin had obtained Hashimoto's assurance of more active fulfillment of the Hashimoto-Yeltsin Plan, including the release of $600 million of the 1.5 billion-dollar untied credit in commercial loans in 1998.

The Moscow Summit

On November 12, 1998, an official summit was held in Moscow between Yeltsin and Keizo Obuchi, Hashimoto's successor.[37] Obuchi was the first Japanese prime minister to make an official visit to Moscow since Tanaka in 1973. Both signed a document, titled the Moscow Declaration to Build a Creative Partnership Between Japan and Russia (abbreviated as the Moscow Declaration), which included official reaffirmation of the informal agreements Yeltsin and Hashimoto had reached at Krasnoyarsk and Kawana (see the Joint Compendium, Item 39).

It goes without saying that the Japanese government viewed the Moscow Declaration as an important step forward. Strictly speaking, the pledges made by Hashimoto and Yeltsin at Krasnoyarsk and Kawana were simply oral agreements. Moreover, after the Kawana Summit, Hashimoto was obliged to take responsibility for his Liberal Democratic Party's defeat in the Upper House election and resign. The ailing Yeltsin remained in power, but he was losing his political authority and becoming a lame duck. In this context Tokyo considered it crucial that the friendly relationship, hitherto cultivated on a man-to-man basis, now be transformed into a formal one on a state-to-state basis. Fortunately, the Moscow Declaration signed by Obuchi and Yeltsin reaffirmed the Hashimoto-Yeltsin agreements on conclusion of a peace treaty by 2000 and on the Hashimoto-Yeltsin Plan. The declaration also included an agreement to create two new subcommittees, one to draw a demarcation line around the four disputed islands, and the other to study the possibility of joint economic activities on them (see the Joint Compendium, Item 39).

However, apart from these points, the November 1998 Moscow Summit was disappointing for Japan. Yeltsin's reply to Hashimoto's unpublished Kawana proposal ran counter to Japanese expectations. Due to Yeltsin's failing health he did not give the reply himself, but had Foreign Minister Primakov deliver it in writing to Obuchi.[38] The gist of the reply was that a peace treaty should be concluded first, and the border then demarcated under a separate treaty. Yeltsin's inconsistency may be ascribable in part to his deteriorating physical and mental state, but also to Primakov's desire to exploit this to reverse previous statements and proposals. In February 1999, during his first visit to Japan as Russian foreign minister, Igor Ivanov, previously Primakov's deputy and then his successor, made the November 1998 proposal public and officially rejected not only Hashimoto's secret proposal but also the Hashimoto-Yeltsin agreement to make every effort to sign a peace treaty including resolution of the territorial dispute by the year 2000.[39]

To summarize, by spring 1999, the diplomatic euphoria stirred by the "no-necktie" summits of November 1997 and April 1998 appeared to have evaporated. Hashimoto's and Yeltsin's diametrically opposed proposals illustrated all too clearly the vast gap between their two nations when it came to settling the dispute over the islands.

CHAPTER 8

The Putin Years

VLADIMIR PUTIN was elected president on March 26, 2000, and officially in-augurated on May 8 of that year. The first twelve months of his administra-tion more or less match the prime ministership of Yoshiro Mori, who was chosen as president of the Liberal Democratic Party (LDP) on April 5, 2000, and stepped down, handing the reins to Junichiro Koizumi in April 2001.

The choice of Mori did not appear to be the result of a transparent de-mocratic process. When Prime Minister Keizo Obuchi was incapacitated by a stroke on April 1, five members of the LDP executive, including Hiromu Nonaka (the secretary general), hurriedly convened a meeting behind closed doors and chose Mori as Obuchi's successor. No objections were raised at the time to these five men's entitlement to select the next prime minister, but the undemocratic nature of the selection would cast a shadow on that administration's Russia policy. For example, on April 4 (the day Mori was "selected"), the incumbent LDP president's schedule of diplomatic visits to Russia had already been discussed between President-elect Putin and Mu-neo Suzuki, a Diet member, sent to Moscow as Obuchi's special emissary.

Putin's Official Visit to Japan

President Putin made his first official visit to Japan on September 3–5, 2000. During his stay he showed very little interest in concluding a peace treaty to resolve the territorial problem, nor did he acknowledge that he had inher-ited any legal obligations to "do his utmost to conclude a peace treaty by 2000," in accordance with the Yeltsin-Hashimoto Plan.

Given Putin's caustic statement "I am a lawyer" (*ia iurist*), there is one is-sue that cannot be denied. That is, the irrevocable legal validity of the 1956 Japan-Soviet Joint Declaration, signed by the top leaders of both countries and ratified by their highest legislative organs. In international law, no document relating to the territorial issue has greater legal standing than the declaration. In fact, at his meeting with Mori on the morning of September 5, Putin did orally acknowledge the declaration's validity. This was made public by Kazuhiko Tōgō, then director-general of the European Affairs Bureau of the Japanese Ministry of Foreign Affairs, during a media briefing held that same afternoon. However, the Russians indicated that they would prefer not to have this acknowledgment mentioned in the joint statement from the Mori-Putin Summit (see the Joint Compendium, Item 42), so the Japanese side chose not to pursue the issue further on this occasion.[1]

The "Phased-Return" Proposal

On July 27, 2000, just over five weeks before Putin's visit, LDP Secretary-General Hiromu Nonaka stated in a speech in Tokyo that the territorial dispute should not stand in the way of a peace treaty with Russia. This invited a wave of opposition within Japan, the ferocity of which was abated only by Nonaka's issuing a statement that his stance matched that of the LDP government. However, Muneo Suzuki, who was considered Nonaka's advisor on foreign policy issues, made no attempt whatsoever to amend his own pet theory that there should be a "phased-return" of the Northern Territories.

The media referred to Suzuki's "phased-return" as "a return of two islands first approach" for resolving the dispute, namely, return of Habomai and Shikotan initially, and of the other two at a later date. Suzuki said that this equation did not accurately reflect his stance, but essentially his approach focused on the difference in status in the 1956 Joint Declaration between Habomai and Shikotan, return of which was specified, and Kunashiri and Etorofu, return of which was not so specified. Based on this difference, Suzuki maintained that a realistic approach would be to seek first the return of the two small islands specified in 1956 and of the remaining two later.

It seems that Tōgō of the Foreign Ministry in principle more or less agreed to this step-by-step approach. However, the official position of both the LDP government and Ministry of Foreign Affairs remained "return of all four islands in their entirety." That is to say, agreement to conclude a peace treaty with Russia would only be forthcoming once all four islands reverted to Japanese sovereignty. Although the "phased-return" approach of the Suzuki-Tōgō proposal might not necessarily contradict the traditional stance, it did represent the appearance of a new, alternative approach.

After Nonaka's statement in July 2000, the debate in Japan became divided. If a peace treaty were to be concluded in 2000, it would obviously have to happen before December. Possibly for that reason, the debate over "phased-return" or "simultaneous return of all four islands in a batch" reached its peak in that month. On December 25, 2000, Muneo Suzuki met Putin's closest confidant, Sergei Ivanov, then secretary of Russia's Security Council and later minister of defense. This meeting was significant in two ways. First, it established a separate diplomatic channel alongside the official route between Foreign Ministers Yohei Kōno and Igor' Ivanov. It is possible that Suzuki in fact took a message from Mori for Putin and therefore acted as the prime minister's special envoy. Nevertheless, by going outside the normal Ministry of Foreign Affairs channel, this development risked being seen as an example of "dual diplomacy." Secondly, and this is related to the first point, Suzuki put forward his "phased-return" proposal to Ivanov. At the press conference after the talks, Suzuki explained his thoughts: "The territorial problem is reaching a stage at which we need to look at the issue realistically, and not be restricted by suggestions that all four islands should be returned at once. We need to consider the possibilities offered by a phased return of the islands."[2]

The Irkutsk Statement

On March 25, 2001, Mori and Putin held an unofficial summit in the Siberian city of Irkutsk. In the Irkutsk Joint Statement, issued following their talks, both for the first time formally confirmed the 1956 Japan–Soviet Joint Declaration as the starting point for the negotiation process.

Why then did Putin decide to acknowledge the validity of the 1956 declaration? His Leningrad University degree in law is not sufficient explanation. Gorbachev had a Moscow University law degree, but during his official visit to Japan in April 1991 he denied the declaration's legal validity. Putin's reasoning was probably that skillful use of Suzuki's "phased-return" proposal might see the long-standing territorial dispute brought to an end at the cost of only two islands. Even in 1956, when Japan's national strength was low compared to the Soviet Union's, Khrushchev was prepared to return Shikotan and Habomai to Japan. So if Putin could resolve the problem by returning just those two islands (which are only 7 percent of the disputed territories' land area), it would indeed be a cheap price for current Russia to pay. Japan would of course request ongoing negotiations for return of the remaining two islands, but Russia would have no real need to worry about that. It could simply revert to tried-and-true delaying tactics and go through the motions of continuing talks, during which time it could use Etorofu and Kunashiri as "hostages" to extract economic and other assistance from Japan.[3]

Opinions on the significance of the Irkutsk Joint Statement are divided according to how necessary one thinks it was for Japan to have the 1956 Joint Declaration's validity confirmed. Kazuhiko Tōgō viewed the confirmation

as an essential step toward securing the return of all four islands and therefore saw the Irkutsk Statement as an important step forward. But the likes of
Sumio Edamura, a former Japanese ambassador to the Soviet Union, advance a quite different opinion, contending that the 1956 Joint Declaration
remains the highest relevant instrument in international law unless Japan
and Russia specifically agree to deny its validity. They have not done so, and
there is therefore no need to seek confirmation of its validity. Furthermore,
placing the brightest spotlight on it risks inviting relative downgrading of
the importance of other documents issued jointly by Japan and Russia. By
"other documents" Edamura is, of course, referring to the joint communiqué issued during Gorbachev's visit to Japan in 1991, and the 1993 Tokyo
and Moscow declarations, that resulted from Yeltsin's and Obuchi's visits in
that year.

Edamura asserted that the following extract from the Irkutsk Joint Statement, the 1956 Joint Declaration "*is a basic legal document that established the
starting point in the negotiation process* for conclusion of a peace treaty, subsequent to the restoration of diplomatic relations between both countries"
(italics added), attributes too great significance to the declaration. He considers that the clauses of the declaration that refer to the territorial dispute
"merely confirm the results of the negotiations thus far," and "do not set the
formula for future negotiations." Nonetheless, the highlighted section of the
Irkutsk Joint Statement describes the 1956 Joint Declaration as a "basic legal
document" that established the "starting point" in the negotiation process
for the conclusion of a peace treaty. In so doing, the Irkutsk Joint Statement
indeed attributes too much significance to the declaration, and one may be
forgiven for thinking that was its deliberate intent.[4]

Edamura put greater weight on the 1993 Tokyo Declaration than on that
of 1956. His reasoning was that the later one specified the formula for future
negotiations, whereas the earlier one did not. He cited a leading textbook
on negotiation studies, *The Practical Negotiator*, by I. William Zartman and
Maureen R. Berman, that emphasizes the second of the three stages that
comprise negotiations, that of setting the "formula for negotiations."[5] The
1993 Tokyo Declaration allowed negotiations to progress to this second
stage by setting the three formulas, "historical and legal facts," "the documents produced with the two countries' agreement," and "the principles of
law and justice." As this is an important point, I quote Article 2 of the 1993
declaration in its entirety: "They [Japan and Russia] agree that negotiations
toward an early conclusion of a peace treaty through the solution of this issue
*on the basis of historical and legal facts and based on the documents produced with the
two countries' agreement* as well as *on the principles of law and justice* should continue, and that the relations between the two countries should thus be fully
normalized" (italics added).

Edamura contended that Tōgō went back to the 1956 Joint Declaration without paying due attention to the Tokyo Declaration's setting of "the formula for negotiation," and was therefore guilty of either not knowing, or ignoring, the "ABCs of negotiating."[6]

The "Two-Track" Approach

The Irkutsk Summit's problematic nature is further underlined by the fact that Mori unofficially told Putin that talks about Habomai and Shikotan could be separate from those about Kunashiri and Etorofu. It is a fact that the 1956 Joint Declaration had already decided Habomai and Shikotan would be handed over to Japan, whereas sovereignty over Kunashiri and Etorofu was undetermined, so discussions over the former should revolve around the method of transfer of the islands and be separate from those concerning the latter, which would be about determination of sovereignty. Mori proposed that the separate sets of talks be conducted simultaneously. At first glance, this would seem an innocuous proposal, but the problem with a "two-track" approach is that it has inherently risky aspects difficult for either side to accept easily.

First of all, from the Russian side, agreement to simultaneous separate talks would be tantamount to recognizing the return of Habomai and Shikotan as a matter of course and to having to negotiate the actual details of their reversion to Japanese sovereignty, while simultaneously conducting negotiations concerning sovereignty over Kunashiri and Etorofu. By contrast, in the minds of at least some Japanese, the "two-track" approach could negate the possibility of having all four islands returned simultaneously. Although the Russians might be prepared to return the two small islands, no doubt they would procrastinate as much as possible over the remaining two, and as a result Japan might recover only the two smaller islands.

The Advent of the Koizumi Administration

In April 2001 Yoshiro Mori stood down, and Junichiro Koizumi took over as prime minister. Soon after taking office Koizumi rejected the idea of "phased-return" that had appeared during Mori's tenure and reinstated the primacy of the "return of all four islands in a batch" approach. Statements he made soon after inauguration certainly suggest as much. For example, on April 27, in his first press conference as prime minister, he declared that "if two islands are returned first, this will not mean, in our view, that the territorial problem is therefore solved."[7] Then in his first policy speech, on May 7, 2001, he said, "I intend to press forward with negotiations, based on the unswerving conviction that a peace treaty should be concluded by resolving the issue of attribution of the four islands."[8]

This policy change impacted negatively on the Russian side. The vice-ministerial talks held on March 13, 2002, produced no results. Deputy Foreign Minister Alexander Losyukov, in charge of Asia-Pacific affairs, rejected "two-track negotiations." A few days later, on March 18, a public debate on The Southern Kuriles Issue in the State Duma (the lower house of the Russian Parliament) was dominated by hard-liners, including a representative of the Sakhalin provincial administration.

In April 2001, Foreign Minister Yoriko Kawaguchi attempted to put an end to the meanderings Suzuki had introduced into Japan's Russia policy. On April 2 it was announced that a number of Foreign Ministry staff, including Kazuhiko Tōgō and Masaru Satō, who had favored Suzuki's "phased-return" approach, were to be removed from their posts, for meddling inappropriately in policymaking, especially over matters concerning Russia on the Northern Territories issue. Needless to say, the Russians reacted strongly, with a spokesman for their embassy in Tokyo stating that the "Suzuki Group" had been "marvellous authorities on Russia."[9] Russian media criticized the dismissals as "an act of suppression by the Japanese government in keeping with the best traditions of McCarthyism."[10] The Russian side even went so far as suggesting that Prime Minister Mikhail Kasyanov's visit to Japan, planned for the first half of 2002, might be in jeopardy, and visits to Russia by Foreign Minister Kawaguchi and Prime Minister Koizumi, scheduled to follow it, would then have to be postponed.

Repairing the Situation

Difficulties aside, Japanese–Russian relations are of such significance in international affairs that neither country can allow them to be compromised by emotional reactions to developments. For Russia Japan is of no little significance. First, there is no guarantee that the "honeymoon" in relations with the United States and Europe following the 9/11 attacks will continue indefinitely.[11] In such times Russia's relations with Asian countries, including Japan, play a crucial role as a counterbalance and insurance policy with respect to the United States and Europe. Secondly, maintaining good relations with Japan will be essential for Russia in the context of China's rise in the twenty-first century. Thirdly, so long as Russia is incapable of developing Siberia and the Russian Far East by herself, sooner or later she will need financial, scientific-technological, managerial, and other types of cooperative assistance from Japan. If Vladimir Putin were a pragmatist, the strategic, geographic, and economic importance of relations with Japan would rule out the possibility of allowing any chill in relations between the two countries and certainly would make any posturing toward the Japanese unthinkable. It goes without saying that after the commotion involving Muneo Suzuki,

Putin would before too long want to start wheels turning to reconstitute Russian policy toward Japan.

The greatest impediment to Japanese–Russian relations is of course the Northern Territories issue. The failure to resolve it has also meant that a peace treaty is yet to be concluded. Without one, a relationship based on genuine neighbourly cooperation cannot be constructed. Russia is well aware of this. Gorbachev acknowledged the existence of the territorial problem in April 1991, and since then the Russian position has remained unchanged. In fact, the Putin administration has made it very clear that it considers it regrettable that there is no agreed-upon border between the two countries. For example, during Question Time in the State Duma on March 13, 2002, then Foreign Minister Igor' Ivanov said, "As you are aware, we do not have a border that has been set by an internationally recognized treaty. With Tokyo we do not have a peace treaty, either. Therefore, these questions naturally constitute important parts of our negotiations with Japan. . . . We must acknowledge that the so-called problem of border demarcation is and will be an existing hindrance to development of full-blooded cooperation between Russia and Japan."[12] In October of that year, in talks with Foreign Minister Kawaguchi, Putin brought up the Northern Territories issue, borrowing his foreign minister's words, "That problems remain from the past, and that we do not have a peace treaty, is truly sad and loathsome, indeed painful and regrettable. It is something that both countries need to work together to resolve."[13]

With this, Japan and Russia set about improving relations from around May 2002. First of all, at the end of May Yasuo Saitō, then director-general of the European Affairs Bureau of the Japanese Foreign Ministry, visited Russia, and had administrative-level talks with Mikhail Bely, director of the Russian Foreign Ministry's Second Asian Department. Talks at the G-8 Summit in Canada in June, between Koizumi and Putin and their foreign ministers, represented an attempt by both parties to lift relations from the depths they had plumbed since spring of the preceding year. Foreign Minister Ivanov commented that Russia was aware of the importance of Japanese–Russian relations, and Putin agreed with Koizumi's statement that he wanted to "take an overall view on progress in a wide range of areas." Putin also agreed that Koizumi should soon visit Russia to formulate the Japan–Russia Action Plan.

From Europe to Asia

The Japanese initiatives to repair relations between the two countries fortunately met a favorable response. Why did this happen? Apart from the various reasons mentioned above, it is probable that the policies of rapprochement toward the United States and Europe, which Putin adopted after 9/11 through to the spring of 2002, had paid off to a certain extent and needed less attention. On May 24, 2002, in Moscow, Russia and the United States concluded the Strategic Offensive Reductions Treaty, and four days later, in Rome, establishment of the Russia–NATO Council was approved, giving Russia quasi membership of NATO. On June 26 Russia was admitted to the G-7 and attended the G-8 Summit in Kananaskis, Canada. By this stage it was clear that Russia had reaped the maximum benefits possible on this front. That being the case, Russia now needed to put her efforts into relations with countries she had neglected since 9/11. This would also be useful in influencing or restraining the United States and Europe.

From the end of July 2002 through January 2003, the focus of Russian diplomacy turned again to Moscow's more traditional clients, as well as countries of Asia. To start with, from late July into August, there were moves to strengthen relations with Iran, Iraq, and North Korea, the three countries of President George W. Bush's "axis of evil." A contract was concluded with Tehran to provide five more reactors for the Bushehr nuclear-power plant. An agreement was concluded with Iraq to provide long-term economic aid, to the tune of five billion dollars. North Korean leader Kim Jung Il visited Russia's Far East and was escorted around it by Konstantin Pulikovskii, presidential envoy to the Far Eastern administrative district.[14]

In August Putin himself undertook a one-week observation tour of Russia's Far East. Seeing evidence of problems such as severe economic hardship, crime, and mafia influence, and noting the increasing presence of Chinese immigrants, no doubt he keenly sensed the need for economic cooperation from Japan. Not only did he go to great lengths to stress the need to connect the Trans-Korean and Trans-Siberian Railroads, but he made specific mention of China when sounding a warning of what was at stake, saying, "If Russia does not push this project ahead, the economy of the Russian Far East will probably lose potential profits from transit services for South Korean freight. Instead, that freight will be transported through China."[15] In early December he visited China, India, and Kyrgyzstan, and in early January 2003 he received Koizumi in Moscow.

The Japan–Russia Action Plan

Let us turn our attention back to Japan. What approach did the Koizumi government assume toward Russia after the "Suzuki scandal" died down? What are its characteristics? First of all, there was the rejection of Suzuki's "phased-return" proposal and a clear reversion to the "return of all four islands in a batch." Secondly, Koizumi's cabinet considered a "comprehensive package approach" would be most effective for resolving the territorial problem and should be facilitated by joint formulation of the Japan–Russia Action Plan.

Agreement on this plan was reached during Koizumi's first official visit to Moscow of January 9–12, 2003. The plan committed both countries to cooperate closely in six fields: (1) political dialogue; (2) peace treaty negotiations; (3) the international arena; (4) trade and economic matters; (5) defense and security; and (6) culture and interpersonal exchange. The action plan differs from the previous "balanced expansion" and "multilayered approach" in that it is not merely a unilateral declaration of Japanese policy, but a document signed by both sides.[16]

Almost without exception, Russian commentators praised Koizumi's January 2003 visit, hailing it as "epoch-making" (*epokhal'nyi*), heralding a new stage in Japanese–Russian relations.[17] The Russian media unanimously depicted Koizumi as more interested in securing energy sources than in getting the islands back, and he applauded the January summit meeting accordingly.[18] However, this is an old trick that the Russian media often use. And because it is easily digestible, Western media, in turn, sometimes tend to follow.[19] It is natural for Japan, which has hardly any natural resources of her own, to be interested in development of energy sources in Siberia and the Russian Far East, to reduce her excessive dependence on the Middle East. However, it is incorrect to assume, on the basis of this truism, that during Koizumi's visit to Russia, Japan "softened" her stance on return of the islands.[20] In fact, a more accurate interpretation would be that both countries adopted a more sophisticated long-range view for their mutual benefit. This at least is how I interpret Koizumi's visit. Let me explain.

Shared Potential Threat: China

What was it about the events of September 11, 2001 that brought the United States and Russia closer together? In simple terms, it was the recognition that international terrorism is a "shared enemy." In the same way, might the existence of such a "shared enemy" bring Japan and Russia together? The specter of North Korea's possession of nuclear missiles might do so. So might Chinese expansionist tendencies. At some time in the twenty-first century, China may become a potential threat for both Japan and Russia, but particularly for the latter. If this comes to pass, Russia and Japan would need to prepare for such a scenario. Was this not the hidden agenda of the January 2003 Koizumi-Putin Summit? Put another way, could we not even say that China was a hidden participant in the Japan–Russia summit meeting?

First, the words "strategic and geopolitical interests," employed by both leaders in the Moscow Summit, can be interpreted mainly as a euphemism meaning "to deal with the threat of China." The joint communiqué issued after the Moscow Summit also mirrored the Moscow Declaration of 1998, in aiming to "build a creative partnership that is consistent with their *strategic and geopolitical interests*" (italics added).[21] Also, Putin himself expressly told Koizumi, "We need each other, not in the short term, but in the strategic sense" (italics added).[22] Why did he choose specifically to include the words "not in the short term"? If he were referring to North Korean nuclear weapons, that country's *Nodong* and *Taepodong* missiles already represent a clear and present danger to Japan. From a longer-term perspective, the statement that "we need each other, not in the short term, but in the strategic sense" can only logically refer to the latent threat posed by China.

In this respect, the sections of the Japan–Russia Action Plan that refer specifically to cooperation in the international arena and in defense and security are noteworthy. Japan and Russia are not facing off against one another, so these categories can only refer to their assuming a combined position vis-à-vis a clearly actual or potential enemy. What might this enemy be? International terrorism? Smuggling? Organized crime syndicates? North Korean nuclear threats? Is it inappropriate to include a scenario whereby escalating Chinese expansionism becomes a threat to countries of the region?

There is no doubt that China is a country with which Russia has a strategic partnership. But why does Russia need such relationships with China in the first place? Could the reason be that Russia sees China as such a potential threat? Russia has grown increasingly uneasy over China's rapid economic growth, and particularly her rising expansionist tendencies in recent years. A potential threat might, in the course of time, become very real. At such a time, Japan would be a strong candidate for Russia to align herself with. Might it be that current Russian leaders have come to view Japan in this way? Which country will Russia choose, Japan or China? This may not be the right way to pose the question—the answer to which is probably both, rather than one or the other.[23] Both Japan and China are important to Russia in their own way. For this reason, for the time being at least, Russia will adopt a friendly and balanced line of diplomacy, courting both at the same time. But if Japan and China should be in competition over any issue, it will be difficult for Russia to satisfy both.

For example, to where would the oil from East Siberia's Angarsk be pumped? Selection of a route for the pipeline brought China and Japan into serious competition.[24] There were two possibilities.[25] One would be the "China route" from Taishet in the East Siberian region of Irkutsk, via the Amur region town of Skovorodino near the Chinese border, to Daqing in the Chinese province of Heilongjiang. The alternative, the "Pacific route," would run from Taishet via Skorovodino to Kozmino Bay near the port of Nakhodka on the Sea of Japan. There was not enough capacity or profitability to justify both routes.

The pipeline options were complicated by conflict within Russia over the route.[26] The "China route" was promoted by Russia's second-largest oil company, Yukos. Its president, Mikhail Khodorkovsky, was one of the oligarchs close to Yeltsin's family.[27] He opposed state monopoly control over the pipeline. By contrast, the Pacific route is of great interest to Transneft, which, owned by the State, has monopoly control over all Russia's pipelines.[28] It seems Putin would like to use state control of pipelines to prevent newly risen oligarchs from becoming involved in politics.[29] In October 2003 Khodorkovsky was arrested on charges of fraud and tax evasion, jailed, and sentenced to eight years' imprisonment. In the meantime his company, Yukos, was virtually broken up and confiscated by State-run companies.

Also there is a three-way conflict among Japan, China, and Russia. First, on the economic front, the China route for the pipeline would be shorter and cheaper to construct, but choice of it would enable the Chinese to exert some influence over the price of the oil and who purchases it. The Pacific route would cost considerably more, but piping the oil to Kozmino would mean that Russia would retain complete control and would have the great benefit of exporting the oil to Japan, South Korea, Southeast Asia, the U.S. West Coast, and even China at international market rates. Next is the political aspect. Oil is a commodity of strategic value, and economic security is indivisible from political and military security. Russia's choice of route will involve giving either Japan's or China's interests preference over the other's, so the decision will not necessarily be made solely on economic grounds. Some in the Japanese Foreign Ministry predict that Russian appreciation of "geopolitical necessities" will, in the end, see them opt for the Pacific route.[30] For exactly the same reasons, it can be suggested that Russia should in fact choose the route through China. In other words, Russia must avoid needless hostility with China, directly connected as they are as neighbors.

As of this writing in November 2006, the Kremlin appeared to decide that the pipeline project to Asia proceed in the two phases: phase 1 of the project is scheduled to build a pipeline from Taishet to Skovorodino; and phase 2 foresees construction of an offshoot pipeline from Skovorodino across the Chinese border to Daqing, and/or construction of a second leg from Skovorodino to Pacific coast. In fact, the construction of the first leg of its pipeline to Asia has already begun. What it comes to phase 2, however, the Kremlin leaders have not yet made their final decision. First of all, they cannot be sure whether there are sufficient oil reserves in East Siberian oilfields before their feasibility studies are complete. In the meantime they appear to consider it not a bad idea to let Japan and energy-hungry China compete against each other in providing them better conditions.

Why Go to Khabarovsk?

In January 2003, on his way home from Moscow, Koizumi visited Khabarovsk. His main objective was ostensibly to meet Putin's presidential envoy to the Far Eastern administrative district, Konstantin Pulikovskii, to exchange information on problems concerning North Korea, such as the abduction of Japanese nationals. This interpretation of Koizumi's motives is somewhat superficial. Japan's top leader would not visit the Russian Far East for talks that could easily be arranged by quietly inviting Pulikovskii to Japan. There is little doubt that Koizumi's visit was staged to lift the Japanese presence in Russia's Far East and to suggest that Japanese cooperation is essential to develop that region. Also, the visit would allow him to make the acquaintance of Viktor Ishaev, governor of Khabarovskii *krai* (region), who might serve as a "powerful ally" (*moshchnii soiuznik*) to Japan in her bid to resolve the Northern Territories issue.[31]

What sort of region is the Russian Far East? Under the Soviet regime, it prospered thanks to huge central government subsidies paid to support its military-industrial complex. It has gone into decline with the end of the Cold War and dissolution of the Soviet Union. Much of its population has drifted south and west, while at the same time it has become the focus of "quiet expansion" by its Chinese neighbor.[32] According to the *New York Times*, the people of the Russian Far East "will admit that, while Japan was their paranoia of the past, China is their paranoia of the future."[33]

Viktor Ishaev is not just governor of Khabarovskii krai (a post he has held for eleven years). He is also chairman of the Association for International Cooperation of the People of Russia's Far East and Transbaikalia, made up of representatives from the Far East and East Siberia. He is also known for his strongly anti-Chinese position in the negotiations with China over the territorial issue about Bol'shoi-Ussuriisk and Tarabarov Islands on the Amur River and Bol'shoi Island on the Argun River.[34] He maintains that to be prepared for the threat of Chinese expansionism, Russia has no alternative but to promote economic cooperation with Japan in order to boost the economy of her Far Eastern region.

It would seem that this logic has somehow made Ishaev an advocate of returning the Northern Territories to Japan.[35] At a meeting of the Presidium of the Russian Academy of Sciences, on May 14, 2001, Ishaev was quoted as saying, "It is obvious from an historical point of view that these islands should be handed over [to Japan]. There is nothing we can do about this."[36] And, "Japan is a major investor in the world, with its investment of US$620 billion overseas in the past twenty-six years, 42 percent of which was invested in the United States and 7 percent in China, but only a mere 0.054 percent in Russia and 0.025 percent in the Russian Far East."[37] Then he said, "Once Japan finds a diplomatic solution to the territorial dispute over the four islands she will consider boosting investment in Russia. It will not happen the other way round. So in order to induce Japan to increase her investment in Russia, the territorial dispute needs to be resolved."[38] He concluded by urging the Russian administration to make a political decision on the matter, saying, "The solution to the issue will depend entirely on the wisdom of the Russian leadership."[39]

So while Khabarovskii krai fears the prospect of Chinese expansion, it is desperate for Japanese economic assistance, even at the expense of returning the islands to Japan. It was no coincidence (*ne sluchaino*) that Koizumi chose not to spend the second half of his official visit to Russia in this region.[40] The aim of the visit was to convey to the Russian people the message that shared "strategic and geopolitical interests" should make both countries overcome small differences and cooperate.

Putin's Reelection

Putin was reelected president on March 14, 2004, with an overwhelming 71 percent of votes. There were two views regarding the policy he would employ toward Japan in his second term. The optimistic view was that he now had immense power because his reelection followed a landslide victory by his supporters in the parliamentary elections of December 2003. Such omnipotence would suggest that now nothing was impossible for him, and he could resolve the territorial problem if he chose, an ideal scenario for Japan.

The pessimistic view was that this was just Japanese wishful thinking. If we asked ourselves, "Why was Putin reelected in the first place?" we found developments not necessarily to Japan's advantage. There were several reasons behind Putin's success. Russian voters preferred stability rather than change, and they opted for a "strong leader." In addition, Putin's almost complete control over the media meant that other candidates did not have equal opportunities to conduct their electoral campaigns. However, if we narrow it down to just one reason, it would be the emergence of the *siloviki* in Russia's corridors of power.

Siloviki are people who use "force" (*sila*) to affect decisions. They are a formerly or currently employed official in the "power ministries" that deal in the use of "force," such as the armed services, law enforcement bodies, and intelligence agencies. The emergence of the siloviki under Putin is evident from research conducted by Olga Kryshtanovskaya of the Institute of Sociology, Russian Academy of Sciences.[41] The siloviki accounted for 3.7 percent of the Russian political elite in the Gorbachev era, growing to 11.2 percent in the first years of Yeltsin's presidency, 17.4 percent in its later years, and no less than 25.1 percent during Putin's first term. Russia is divided into seven federal administrative districts, each overseen by a president's envoy. Five of the seven envoys (70 percent) have siloviki backgrounds. So do 58 percent of the staff members of Russia's Security Council and 35 percent of the deputy ministers.[42]

Putin himself is a silovik. But the real point of interest during his second term of office will be his power relationship with the siloviki. If he can control them, he will become a president with unsurpassed power, in which case no one would venture to object if he decided to return the islands to

Japan; the optimistic predictions mentioned above may come true. However, it also is quite plausible that he would be unable to control them. In the worst-case scenario he would become their puppet, the pessimistic forecasts would be borne out, and he would be unable to make any decisions that would lead to the return of the four islands. Why is this?

The siloviki are not a single, monolithic group, but one common political outlook they all share is that they are nationalists. Many siloviki are proponents of the strong state (*gosudarstvenniki*), or advocates (*derzhavniki*) of "great power" (*velikaia derzhava*) whose aim is to rebuild a "strong Russia." They regret the Soviet Union's dissolution and eagerly await the opportunity to reunite with such former Soviet republics as Belarus and Kazakhstan. They openly advocate protection of Russia's "territorial integrity" and oppose it becoming any smaller than it already is. We could even define the siloviki as opponents of the reversion of the disputed islands. It is difficult to imagine Putin taking it on himself to override them and return the islands to Japan.

Putin's own character and the nature of his leadership have a significant bearing on this issue. Is he an "innovator," a "dictator" type of leader, or a "manager/balancer" type of leader who considers the views of those around him? At least judging from his first term, he adopted the latter style. This is hardly surprising; as a mere KGB colonel, tapped on the shoulder by Yeltsin to become his prime minister, then to succeed him as president, he did not necessarily possess the ability or the credentials to justify occupying the top position in Russian politics. During his first term in office he did his utmost to minimize unnecessary risk.[43] However, the question was whether this "balancing-act" style of leadership would continue into his second term. If this approach reflected Putin's own character, he would beware of opposition from the siloviki and would avoid making any decisions that might lead to return of the disputed islands. However, the reverse was also possible. His cautious first-term stance might have only been an expedient to solidify his political power base, and not a reflection of his real character. If this was so, then Japan could expect Putin to reveal his true colors in his second term.

"The Return of Two Islands"

Scarcely was he reelected in 2004 when President Putin had proved to be an authoritarian, even a quasi-dictatorian type of leader. Putin began to take a tough policy toward Japan with nationalistic tone. In mid-November 2004, the Putin government stated its intention to return two of the four Northern Islands. On November 14 and 15, Foreign Minister Sergei Lavrov and President Putin made statements to the effect that in keeping with the 1956 Soviet–Japanese Joint Declaration Russia would hand over Habomai and Shikotan. However, it would do so only on condition that a peace treaty was signed, thereby settling the territorial issue between Japan and Russia once and for all.

The Putin government's advocacy of the return of two islands is nothing new.[44] Putin made statements to this effect during his first official visit to Japan in September 2000, then again in March 2002, first in an NHK interview and then in talks with Prime Minister Mori. Why, then, choose this period to repeat these statements? An explanation of the background and timing is needed.

The year 2004 was a very bad one for Putin's diplomacy. Intimidation then breakup of the oil giant Yukos, the school massacre in Beslan, North Ossetia, and the presidential election in Ukraine demonstrated that Russia and the Western nations were of different worlds. Russian-Western relations chilled as a result, and Russia had no choice but to promote diplomacy toward Asia. Putin himself traveled to Central Asia, China, India, and Turkey. Having succeeded in border demarcation with China and Kazakhstan during October 2004 to January 2005, Russia may hope to settle its border problems with Japan and show the Western nations what it can do.

There were at least three hidden objectives behind the November 2004 statements about returning two of the four islands. First was the objective of testing the Russian general public's reaction and at the same time educating them about the issue. Putin visited Beijing just one month earlier, on October 14, 2004, and reached agreement with his Chinese counterpart, Hu Jintao, over border demarcation. Those negotiations were settled under a "50–50 formula" (thus called by Foreign Minister Lavrov), whereby the disputed territory was equally divided.[45] Some Russians opposed this as an unnecessary concession. So how would the Russian people react if the Kremlin followed this with another "50–50 concession," by returning two of the four disputed islands to Japan? The Russian leaders wanted to test Russian public opinion, but the statements also served the purpose of educating the Russian people about the issue. Japan is not only Russia's important eastern neighbor but also a country with economic and science-technological capabilities second only to the United States. To add vigor to exchange and cooperation with such a power, Russia needs to honor its legal obligations and promises already made to Japan. The statements represented an effort to educate the Russian people to understand these necessities.[46]

The second function of these statements was that of a "trial-balloon" designed to test Japan's response, as well as to put the brakes on Tokyo's demands and to push for concessions by informing Japan that there will be strong Russian opposition to the idea of returning even two islands, so that this represents the greatest concession Russia can make.[47]

The third objective was to shift the burden of responsibility for resolving the problem onto Japan. Putin's planned visit to Japan in 2005 would occur five years after his first official visit in September 2000. Similarly, it would be more than two years since Koizumi's official visit to Russia in January 2003. Expectations surrounding Putin's visit were rising in Japan. What then would happen if he returned to Moscow without even mentioning the territorial issue? The result could only be great disappointment in Japan and a serious worsening of feelings toward Russia. With that in mind, clarifying beforehand that Russia was prepared to return two of the four islands served to put a damper on Japanese expectations. Hitting the ball into Japan's court put responsibility for the next move on Japan.[48] Moscow was perhaps laying grounds for an excuse that Tokyo's continued unyielding stance on the territorial issue ruled out a compromise agreement.

Something New

In terms of the logic explained above, Putin's and Lavrov's statements in 2004 were no more than a rehash of their standard line that Russia was prepared to return only two of the four islands. In fact, the Russian Foreign Ministry's chief spokesman Alexander Yakovenko said, "There has been no change of Russia's position."[49] Be that as it may, I do think there is something worthy of attention here. We need to read carefully the entire text of Lavrov's statement, made on NTV television on November 14, 2004. Most Japanese tended to concentrate only on the part that referred to relations with Japan. But that paragraph was linked to the previous section, about border demarcation with China, so it should be read in that context.

But how did the Kremlin attempt to link Sino-Russian territorial demarcation with that between Japan and Russia? The answer is quite straightforward: Russia makes linkages as it sees fit. Where it thinks a gain can be made, it will link two sets of negotiations. Similarly, where it judges such linkage not advantageous, it will not make it. This is a continuation of Soviet-era practice. Let me explain.

First of all, the Kremlin emphasized the unique nature of the Sino-Russian border negotiations. The reason for this was concern lest other countries take the outcome as setting a precedent. Indeed, after October 14, 2004, when demarcation of the Sino-Russian border was completed, Putin and other high-ranking Russian officials went to great lengths to emphasize that the issue of territorial demarcation between Russia and China differs from that between Russia and Japan. Putin stated, "Russia and China, as opposed to Russia and Japan—there are no grounds for seeking common, analogous approaches of resolution to the respective territorial problems."[50] Indeed he may be right. However, he may have gone too far in saying these two sets of negotiations had absolutely nothing in common. The current Russian government was involved in both, and both were bilateral negotiations about territorial demarcation. Thus they have at least these two points in common, so there is nothing strange in thinking the approach used in one may be relevant to the other. However, such logic is not at all welcome to the Russian side. What aspect of the Sino-Russian formula does Russia least want applied to the negotiations with Japan? I believe it is that the issue of the three islands so fiercely disputed between Russia and China was settled by dividing their land areas equally. No doubt this is why the Kremlin decided not to link the two sets of negotiations.

But the Kremlin then did an about-face and sought to link the two sets of negotiations. The reason for this lies in the stance assumed by both Russia and China in successfully negotiating their border. Why were they able to achieve what they did? Above all, they worked hard to produce closer mutual relations and have become essential to each other, created a fully fledged strategic partnership, and as a result have resolved their territorial problems. Viewed from a slightly different angle, the first thing required is a general improvement in mutual relations. Then, and only then, could a territorial issue be resolved. The inherent truth in the Russian logic cannot be understated. Be that as it may, Japan should learn from developments between Russia and China and make the same efforts. The Kremlin certainly suggests as much.

The Russian side resorts to this selective way of linking. With this in mind, let us take a close look at the section about Russia and China in Foreign Minister Lavrov's televised statement of November 14, 2004. As I see it, there are five important points.

Lavrov's Statement

First, he stressed the need to resolve territorial disputes. Let me quote him directly. He commented that through the October 2004 Sino-Russian agreement Russia had "removed a significant source of irritation in relations with China. This is something that cannot be overlooked. Any unresolved territorial problems are always a source of *razdrazhitel'* [irritant]."[51] The Russian expression "razdrazhitel'" has no close equivalent in English, but if we change it to "thorn" or "nettle," we can easily understand its meaning. The unresolved border problem is a "thorn" in Japanese-Russian relations, a "thorn" that must be removed. That is to say, the territorial dispute that plagues relations with Japan should be resolved as was that with China. Lavrov's statement can be interpreted to mean just that.

Second, Lavrov recommended that the Sino-Russian formula be applied to relations with Japan. "It became possible to settle the territorial dispute with China in full when we reached the level of a real, fully-fledged strategic partnership."[52] "We are confident that . . . *the same approach* toward Russo-Japanese relations is the right way to create an atmosphere necessary for starting talks on the peace treaty" (italics added).[53] Russian political commentator Andrei Baranov offered the following bold interpretation of Lavrov's statement: "We are prepared to approach the matter of peace with the Japanese according to the 'China formula.' The 'China formula' is essentially that Russia will de facto cede its (disputed) territory to its neighboring country. However, in a legal sense de jure this will be done so as to remove sources of irritation that exist between Russia and its neighbor."[54]

Third is the proposal of a comprehensive package. Lavrov advocated producing some concessions by combining the territorial problem with other issues. In other words, if the approach used with China is applied with Japan, not only will conclusion of a peace treaty become possible, but also "there will be huge benefits for Russia and Japan through the development of trade and economic, scientific and technical cooperation."[55] This statement can be interpreted to mean that the Kremlin is trying to persuade the Russian people along the following lines. If Russia makes concessions to Japan on the territorial issue, in exchange it will reap "huge benefits" from Japan. Although Il'ia Barabanov excused himself for dealing with it in a "slightly simplistic manner," he gave his opinion on the possibility of "such dealings" in the internet newspaper *Gazeta.Ru*.[56] "In his TV interview, Foreign Minister Lavrov clearly indicates there would be financial conditions of such dealings. . . . Russia is completely at liberty to set its own price for the Southern Kuriles, and Moscow expects to receive from Tokyo whatever price it sets."[57] Barabanov went on boldly to conclude, "'Give them the islands, but under certain conditions.' This is the first time the Russian position has been stated so precisely."[58]

Fourth, the Kremlin contended that Japan needed to compromise. Although Lavrov did not say so in so many words, his position can certainly be interpreted in that way. Russia's latest position is that compromises are part and parcel of negotiations, so it is crucial that Japanese-Russian territorial negotiations include "mutually acceptable compromises." But just what did they mean by compromises as a means to reach a settlement? Russians use bazaar-style negotiating technique.

The word "bazaar," meaning "market," is taken from Persian. It indicates a commercial transaction in which no fixed price or other condition is set in advance, and a satisfactory price and other conditions are attained through a bargaining process. It also indicates a technique of starting negotiations by asking an exorbitant price or making other demands, so as to be able to make an acceptable profit even after substantial concessions. The "bazaar" tactic is not confined to Levantine merchants; all nations use it to varying degrees. Russians, who have a strong tendency to test their opponents' strength, and not to worry unduly about inconsistency, are fond of the bazaar technique.[59] Faced with strong refusals of their high initial demands, they cut their "prices" gradually and, in the end, propose "*popolam*" (meet you half-way). Russian-style compromise refers to dividing down the middle issues that remain unresolved at the end of negotiation.

Fifth is that Lavrov disclosed just how the Sino-Russian border demarcation negotiations were settled. This is an extremely important point for Japanese-Russian border demarcation, so let me give the historical background and some explanation.

The curtain went up on Sino-Russian border demarcation with Gorbachev's famous Vladivostok speech in 1986, in which he said, "The border runs through the center of the main channel in a navigable river and through the center of any river or center of its main course in a nonnavigable river."[60] This was the first time the Soviet Union declared acceptance of this general principle of international law. In keeping with this principle, in May 1991, near the end of the Gorbachev era, an agreement on the Sino-Soviet eastern border was signed. In November 1997 Yeltsin signed an agreement on the Sino-Soviet western border with President Jiang Zemin. As a result, the Sino-Russian border forced on China by the "unequal" Aigun (1858) and then Beijing (1860) treaties by tsarist imperialism was adjusted, and "many of Russia's hundreds of islands" were handed to China.[61] Three islands, however, were not covered by the agreements: Bol'shoi Island in the Aigun River; and the Bol'shoi Ussuriiskii and Tarabarov islands at the confluence of the Amur and Ussuri rivers (in Chinese: Abagaitui, Heixiazi, and Yinshe). During a visit to Beijing, Putin and his Chinese counterpart, President Hu Jintao, reached agreement on these three on October 14, 2004.

Lavrov's televised statement, exactly one month later, was the first public mention of the content of the border demarcation agreement with China. Tarabarov Island was given to China, Bol'shoi and Bol'shoi Ussuriiskii islands divided equally. What is significant for Japan here is that the land area of these three islands, for so long objects of dispute, was "in the end divided approximately 50–50" (Lavrov).[62]

Is Russia Prepared to Return Part of Etorofu?

How then do the five above-mentioned points relate to the negotiations over the four islands disputed by Japan and Russia? First, the proposal to return to Japan only two of the four Russian-held islands is a trial balloon launched to gauge reactions in both Russia and Japan. The Kremlin does not think Japan so naïve as to be taken in straightaway by this tactic. There is no way the Russian leaders would expect Japan to accept Russia's first offer to return only two islands. The day after Lavrov's televised statement, Sergei Strokan of the newspaper *Kommersant'* commented, "We are just as likely to see pigs fly as Japan accept this."[63]

Next, Lavrov's statement can be interpreted as suggesting a "50–50 compromise formula," as was adopted in the border negotiations with China and Kazakhstan (January 18, 2005).[64] If this is so, however much Russia might protest that the two cases are different, it will find it difficult to reject the 50–50 formula in dealings with Japan. Considering that Japan has been unbending in its demand for return of all four islands, Russia may even be happy if it were to accept this formula.

Regardless of whether or not Tokyo accepts this approach, the application of the 50–50 formula to Japan means the following. The approach of taking the number between two and four islands, namely, the return of three islands, means deciding the attribution of the islands by their number. Habomai, Shikotan, and Kunashiri make up only 37 percent of the total land area, Etorofu 63 percent.

So what if the islands' land area is divided into halves? The results differ according to which of two approaches is used. It had already been decided in the 1956 Japan-Soviet Joint Declaration that Habomai and Shikotan would be handed over to Japan, so the disputed territory is Kunashiri and Etorofu. If we follow this logic, as advocated by Japan, we produce a figure of 2,341 square kilometers, half the combined land area of Kunashiri and Etorofu. This equals 73.5 percent of the area of Etorofu, and using this formula approximately three-quarters of Etorofu would remain Russian, the other quarter becoming Japanese. The other approach, as advocated by Russia, is based on the view that all four islands are still disputed. If we divide the land area of all four in half, 79 percent of Etorofu would remain Russian, and 21 percent would revert to Japan. So the 50–50 formula would give Japan the Habomais, Shikotan, and Kunashiri, plus either 26.5 or 21 percent of Etorofu.

Whichever approach is used, part of Etorofu would become Japanese territory. However, with Tokyo continuing to insist that all four islands in their entirety should be returned, this solution is not acceptable to Japan. On November 16, 2004, directly after Putin's and Lavrov's statements, Koizumi reiterated Japan's position, saying, "A peace treaty cannot be concluded until after it is made clear to whom the four islands belong."[65]

Putin's Televised Statement

In a television program on September 27, 2005, President Putin made an extraordinary statement about the Northern Territories. In response to a question he stated, "Regarding the negotiation process with Japan over the four Kurile Islands, they are Russian sovereign territory and this is fixed in international law. This is one of the results of World War Two. We have nothing to discuss on this particular point."[66] He repeated the statement later, on

November 21, during his official visit to Tokyo. Running completely contrary to Putin's previous statements and to those of prominent members of his administration, it came as a great surprise to the Japanese if this is how Putin really felt about the issue. Three points lead us to this conclusion.

First, his September 27 statement ignores international law, which does not recognize the four islands as Russian territory. No international treaties or agreements give credibility to Russia's claims to the islands. The Yalta Agreement was merely a secret arrangement among the leaders of the United States, Britain, and Soviet Union about postwar policy directions. Since Japan neither participated in, nor consented to, those arrangements, the Yalta Agreement is not binding on Japan. Similarly, while the Soviet Union was represented at the San Francisco Peace Conference, it did not sign the resulting peace treaty.

Second, the Putin statement emphasizes victory and defeat in World War Two. He states, "The four islands are Russian sovereign territory" as "one of the results of World War Two." This contradicts the position of the Allies in World War Two and the spirit and methods of the Yeltsin administration. The Atlantic Charter (1941), Cairo Declaration (1943), and Potsdam Declaration (1945) all championed "the principle of no territorial expansion," and as one of the Allied nations, the Soviet Union agreed to the provisions of all three. Nevertheless, under Stalin the Soviet Union saw fit to ignore this "principle of no territorial expansion," seizing more than 670,000 square kilometers of territory from a total of eleven countries, including Japan. When rejecting demands for return of these territories, the Soviet Union/Russia has consistently maintained the spurious logic that changing national borders resulting from World War Two would upset the peace and stability of the postwar international order. This approach is based on what is known as "the theory of irreversible results of war."

During the Soviet period, in particular under Brezhnev, those in charge of Soviet foreign policy were steadfast in their advocacy of "the theory of the irreversible results of war." For example, in an interview with Shōryū Hata, then editor-in-chief of the *Asahi Shimbun*, CPSU Secretary Leonid Brezhnev said, "Only if Japan takes more seriously *the realities born from the result of World War Two* will the Soviet Union and Japan be able to resolve the question [of concluding a peace treaty between them], and probably resolve it quickly" (italics added).[67] A similar comment appeared in *Pravda* in response to an open letter from the Japanese Communist Party about the Northern Territories issue. "The rationale behind the request from the executive of the Japanese Communist Party for the return of Kurile Islands is neither correct nor objective; they are attempting to change *the outcome of World War Two*" (italics added).[68] The Yeltsin administration moved in a bold new direction, declaring that international relations in the postwar era must not be framed in terms of victorious and defeated nations. However, in his statement of September 27, 2005, President Putin rejected Yeltsin's view, thereby returning to the logic of the Brezhnev years that justifies victors taking territory from the vanquished.

Russian use of the claim that "this is one of the results of World War Two" to justify retaining the Northern Territories runs against Stalin's claim in his "victory" speech on September 2, 1945, in which the Soviet leader boasted of having reversed the result of the Russo-Japanese War of 1904–5. Furthermore, in Europe the majority of "results of World War Two" have already been changed. Division of Germany, reannexation of the Baltic States, and establishment of communist rule in Central and East European countries provide such examples.

The third notable point of Putin's September 27 statement is that he brooked no argument, abruptly dismissing the issue. Let me quote him again: "They [the disputed islands] are Russian sovereign territory. . . . This is one of the results of World War Two. We have nothing to discuss [*myi nichego ne sobiraemsia obsuzhdat'*] on this particular point." This response is reminiscent of Soviet Foreign Minister Gromyko, whom, we should remember, Gorbachev, on coming to power, replaced with Shevardnadze because he knew that unless the Soviet Union abandoned the Gromyko model of "nyet diplomacy" it would become increasingly difficult to interact with other countries.[69] This change had an immediate impact on Soviet diplomacy toward Japan, since Shevardnadze chose it as the destination for his first official visit and took the position there that no matter how uncomfortable an issue might be for the Soviet Union, he must listen if Japan wished to discuss it.

When asked to explain the intention behind his September 27 statement, Putin replied that he wanted people to listen carefully to the second half of his statement, which he repeated.

The issue raised is, of course, a very sensitive matter both for Japan and for Russia. I hope and am really convinced that if we show *good will* [*dobraia volia*], and Russia does have this *good will*, we will always be able to find a solution that suits both parties, a solution that will benefit the people living on these islands and benefit the peoples of Russia and Japan. If we show that we are willing to accommodate each other, we can find a solution.[70] (italics added)

It is not difficult to read between the lines of this. He is suggesting that if Japan acknowledges Russia's sovereignty over the four islands and agrees to conclude a peace treaty, the Russian side will show "good will," that is, it will hand back the two islands mentioned in the 1956 Joint Declaration.

Putin's Second Official Visit to Japan

President Putin made his second official visit to Japan during November 20–22, 2005. In the summit meeting, held for more than two and a half hours on November 21, Prime Minister Koizumi made an impassioned plea to him to return the four disputed islands. However, despite Koizumi's fervent appeals, no other official summit meeting took place during Putin's stay, and contrary to normal practice, when joint declarations or communiqués are issued following such meetings, no such statement was issued on this occasion—no doubt because the gap between the two leaders' positions on the Northern Territories issue was too great. The Russian side did not even agree to a joint communiqué to confirm what the two countries had agreed to in the past, namely, that all four islands were within the scope of negotiations, and that there was consensus on the three formulas for pressing ahead with territorial negotiations. By all accounts Putin was not prepared to confirm either point, even though both are clearly mentioned not only in the 1993 Tokyo Declaration but also in the 2001 Irkutsk Statement and the 2003 Japan-Russia Action Plan signed by Putin himself. It seems the Russian side was looking to employ a strategy that saw the 1956 Joint Declaration as the only relevant legal document because it mentions handover of only two islands, and that ignored the Tokyo Declaration, which lists all four islands as subjects of negotiations.

Another surprising development after the meeting in Tokyo in November 2005 was that, instead of a joint statement, twelve documents were adopted, covering areas other than "conclusion of a peace treaty resolving the territorial problem." Specifically, they cover areas for cooperation, such as economics, antiterrorism, and culture. The Japanese Ministry of Foreign Affairs stated that their adoption aimed "to expand the cooperation based on this [Japan-Russia] Action Plan," compiled by Japan and taken to Moscow by Koizumi in January 2003. It lists six areas of close cooperation for Japan and Russia: (1) deepening political dialogue; (2) peace treaty negotiations; (3) cooperation in the international arena; (4) cooperation in trade and economic areas; (5) development of relations in defense and security; and (6) advancements in cultural and interpersonal exchange. However closely we examine the action plan we find no reference to an order of priority for these six areas, nor any explanation of how they relate to each other. This is the action plan's greatest failing.

Does this mean, therefore, that Russia is likely to adhere only to those parts of the action plan that suit it? This may indeed be so. The first piece of evidence that Russia has in effect adopted just such a stance is in a book, titled *Thunder then Blue Skies*, by Alexander Panov, formerly Russian ambassador to Japan. He had this to say: "Metaphorically speaking, the Japan-Russia Action

Plan is like a smorgasbord. Sitting on the table is a range of dishes prepared by top Russian and Japanese chefs. Needless to say, the 'hottest and most spicy' dish is the issue of a peace treaty."[71] Panov does not need to elaborate on the nature of a smorgasbord. The individual can make his own choice, selecting what appeals and ignoring what does not. It is not a package; on the contrary, it facilitates and even encourages cherry-picking.

When viewed in isolation, there is no doubt that the territorial issue is extremely difficult to resolve. That is probably why Koizumi looked to resolve it by bundling it into a package with the other five areas in a comprehensive approach. This idea itself is not bad; in fact, because negotiations over territory tend to become zero-sum games it may even be the only way to resolve them. There is, however, a risk in adopting the comprehensive approach, namely, that the other party may avoid the territorial issue and opt instead to pick the cherries. Provisions to prevent this are essential, but unfortunately Koizumi's Japan-Russia Action Plan included no such wording, and this is the gravest error committed by the Japanese side.

Regrettably, our concerns were borne out by Putin's visit to Japan; the twelve documents referred to everything except the action plan's second issue, the peace treaty. In hindsight, when Prime Minister Koizumi proposed the action plan, he should have ensured that it included some mechanism to avoid such a scenario. His failure to do so meant that the November 2005 summit meeting saw no progress whatsoever for Japan on the territorial issue. Ambassador Panov is, I dare to say, smiling to himself back in his office in the Russian Ministry of Foreign Affairs in Moscow.

Conclusions

THAT JAPAN AND RUSSIA have been unable, in more than sixty years since World War Two ended, to resolve the territorial problem, or conclude a peace treaty, is one of the great mysteries of modern international affairs. I would like to conclude this volume by putting forward what I consider to be the five reasons for this abnormal situation, and under what circumstances I think this problem will be finally solved.

Let me discuss, first, why this dispute between Russia and Japan has not been solved for such a long time.

Low Priority

The first is that of low priority. Japan and the Soviet Union/Russia have rarely seen each other as a high foreign-policy priority. After 1945, the United States was obviously the fulcrum of Japan's world. Even the confirmed Anglophile Shigeru Yoshida considered that reconstruction and prosperity for Japan would be impossible without an alliance with America. The world was divided into Eastern and Western blocs during the Cold War years, and most leading countries belonged to one bloc or the other. Japan naturally belonged to the noncommunist world, led by the United States, and that naturally constrained its relations with the Soviet Union. To be honest, Japan had very little interest at all in the Soviet Union.

For the Soviet Union, Japan's position on the diplomatic scale of importance was so low as to barely register. During the Cold War years the Kremlin's perception of the world was based on bipolar U.S.-Soviet rivalry. Soviet leader Nikita Khrushchev was recorded as saying, "The case of international tension is like a cabbage. If you tear off the leaves one by one, you come to the heart. And the heart of this matter is U.S.-Soviet relations."[1] Andrei Gromyko,

Soviet foreign minister for twenty-eight years, expressed a similar bipolar perception in his statement, "International situations depend largely on Soviet-United States relations."[2] If we look at international politics solely in terms of the bipolar U.S.-Soviet conflict, Japanese-Soviet and Japanese-Russian relations are merely a subset of U.S.-Soviet and U.S.-Russian relations. Some Western analysts even went so far as to say, "Soviet policy toward Japan is merely a spin-off from Soviet global strategy toward the United States."[3]

The U.S.-Japanese Treaty of Mutual Cooperation and Security gave Japan an alliance with the leader of the Western camp, and Japan dutifully toed the line as its faithful disciple. What could the Soviet Union expect from Japan? Hostility, contempt? The Soviet Union had very little to gain by seeking to manipulate Japan, and the chances of enticing it toward the Eastern bloc were almost nonexistent. Even if the Soviet Union returned the disputed territory, Japan was extremely unlikely to match such a show of goodwill by offering something in return. Besides, Soviet perception was that once sovereignty reverted to Japan, it might even permit the United States to establish military installations on the islands. In short, Japan hastened to seek the leader of the Western camp's protection, then demanded the return of the four islands from the leader of the Eastern camp. No doubt the Kremlin must have wondered just whom Japan was trying to fool with such a self-seeking demand.

The situation has of course changed with the end of the Cold War. The East-West conflict and discord between Washington and Moscow have mostly disappeared. Russia can no longer unilaterally judge Japan as America's faithful subordinate, so it can no longer simply reject its demands for the return of the islands as self-seeking. This is most probably why Gorbachev, Yeltsin, and Putin acknowledged that a territorial dispute exists between Russia and Japan and ceased refusing to negotiate.

However, one point remains unchanged. Neither country rates the other as of high foreign policy or trading priority. For example, at its peak the volume of trade between Japan and Russia was US$ 10 billion, but Japan's trade with China and with the United States was twenty times as large. Every year sixteen million Japanese travel overseas, but only eighty-six thousand, just over half of one percent of them, visit Russia; forty times as many go to the United States, and thirty times as many to China. One might even say that each country could get by without any contact with the other. Their low level of mutual dependence means that they rate each other as of low diplomatic priority.

The Value of the Four Small Islands

What is the value of the four disputed islands? The Soviet Union/Russia and Japan do not see eye to eye on this. Not only do their views differ, but also they change with the times. Herein lies another point of difficulty in resolving the problem.

First, there is Japan's view of the value of the four Northern Islands. This may seem obvious, but the importance of the four small islands is far less than that of the four large islands (Hokkaido, Honshu, Shikoku, and Kyushu.) This is clear in terms of comparative land area alone. Also, no Japanese live on the four small islands. Stalin forcibly repatriated all of the 17,291 residents immediately after the war.

Why do I restate the obvious? I would like to emphasize that the former Soviet Union never thought to totally oppose returning the four Northern Islands to Japan. Had the terms been right, no doubt even the former Soviet Union would have been prepared to return them. What would those terms be? For example, that Japan renounce its security treaty with the United States, become a neutral state, and maybe from there join the Soviet camp. Had that happened, no doubt Moscow would have gladly returned those four small islands. The benefits of Japan becoming neutral, or joining the Soviet camp, far outweighed the cost of losing them.

I have put forward an extreme scenario here to emphasize my point. Let me give two or three specific examples. In 1980 Prime Minister Zenkō Suzuki stated, "So long as the Soviet Union remains unchanged in its policy with regard to Afghanistan and the Northern Territories, any improvement in Japanese-Soviet relations will be impossible."[4] Until then, Tokyo had always put the "return of the Northern Territories" as the first prerequisite for any improvement in Japanese-Soviet relations. However, in 1980, not only did the Suzuki government add the requirement of "Soviet withdrawal from Afghanistan," but Suzuki placed this before the "return of the Northern Territories."

In 1982, the same Suzuki government demanded revocation of the Soviet decision to move its SS-20s (mobile intermediate-range ballistic missiles) from the European to the Asia theater and their removal from the Russian Far East.[5] Again the demand concerning these missiles came before that for return of the Northern Territories, indicating that for Japanese national interests, the security of the four large islands was more important than return of the four small ones. Postwar Japanese diplomacy emphasized relations with the United States, so security of Japan's four large islands was seen as a greater priority than the return of four small ones. In this respect, there was nothing unusual about the Suzuki government's statements, which were similar to those of Prime Ministers Masayoshi Ōhira and Yasuhiro Nakasone.

Every nation considers national security of prime importance. But there is no straightforward answer to the question whether Japan should give priority to pursuing economic gain in terms of *energy* or *fish*, or acquiring sovereignty over four small *islands*. Opinions vary as to how necessary energy and fish are to Japan. In the Soviet-Japanese negotiations following the Soviet declaration of a 200–nautical-mile exclusive fishing zone in late 1976, there is no doubt that the question of *islands* or *fish* was a hidden topic on the agenda. More recently the issue has evolved to one of *energy* or *islands*. Prime Minister Ryutaro Hashimoto's speech at the Japanese Association of Corporate Executives (Keizai Doyukai) on July 24, 1997, was interpreted as signaling something quite different from his intended meaning. Russia, as well as several Western nations, interpreted Hashimoto's speech as reflecting a totally new perspective, one that separated the issue of the *islands* from that of overarching Japanese-Russian relations, including *energy*. Also, during his visit to Russia in January 2003, and on subsequent occasions, Koizumi asked Putin to have Russia construct a pipeline from the East Siberian oilfields to the Pacific coast. As a result, Russia and the rest of the world judged that Tokyo saw *energy* as more important than *islands*.

By contrast, what value does Russia place on the four islands? The waters around them are among the world's best fisheries resources. Nevertheless, it is difficult to see economic reasons as the main driving force behind the former Soviet Union's stubborn refusal to return the islands to Japan. Had that been the case, Japan's willingness to provide economic benefit to the Soviet Union would have led to some form of compromise. To be sure, one time the military-strategic value of the four islands was one of the greatest reasons why the Soviet Union was so firm in its refusal to return the islands to Japan:[6] when during the 1970s Soviet submarines carrying missiles targeted on the United States west of the Great Lakes began to be deployed at Petropavlovsk–Kamchatskii. Initially they could do so only from launch-points well out in the Pacific, but development of longer-range missiles enabled them to operate from the Sea of Okhotsk. Its enclosed nature made it a "sanctuary" provided incursions by the U.S. Navy could be monitored in peacetime and prevented in war.[7] The Kurile Islands, hitherto so strategically unimportant that no military were stationed there between 1963 and 1978, were militarized after 1978, with a sonar barrier along their east coasts, radars, stockpiled mines and depth-charges, a naval base, and, on Etorofu, reactivation of a Japanese wartime airfield.

However, even before the end of the Cold War all of North America could become targeted by longer-range Soviet SLBMs launched from the Barents Sea by Soviet Northern Fleet boats. Due to this development of military technology the importance of the Soviet Pacific Fleet's deployment of SLBMs in the Sea of Okhotsk was reduced. Increased missile ranges have made the "second sanctuary/bastion" superfluous. The Sea of Okhotsk has thus reverted to its pre-1978 low strategic status. Furthermore, the SSBNs deployed in the Sea of Okhotsk are aging. In 1989 the Soviet Pacific Fleet had twenty-six missile-firing submarines, seventeen of which were SSBNs, but by the end of 2004 only four were left, all elderly and likely to be life-expired by 2012 at the latest.[8] Under the Strategic Offensive Reductions Treaty (Moscow Treaty), signed with the United States in 2002, the post-2012 seaborne component of Russia's strategic nuclear forces will require only about fifteen submarines, all probably based with the Northern Fleet.[9]

These three recent developments invalidate traditional military assertions that the four Northern Islands are of crucial strategic value for Russia. When President Gorbachev visited Japan in 1991 he spoke of reducing the level of Soviet deployment on the islands, and President Yeltsin stated that their demilitarization was the third stage of his "five-stage proposal."[10] The number of Russian troops on the islands has been reduced from ten thousand to less than thirty-five hundred. However, the mind-set of Russian nationalists, communists, and officers of the armed forces cannot change overnight, and such groups remain prisoners to the attitudes of the past. In their minds, "the four islands became Russian territory after a bloody struggle and have now assumed the status of sacred territory" (in the words of Dmitrii Rogozin, leader of the Motherland Party).[11] Such people cling firmly to the principle of "territorial integrity" and insist that the islands can never be ceded to Japan.

Domestic Politics Dominate

Japan and Russia both lack comprehensive, long-term strategies and policies toward each other. I have already alluded to the reason behind this, namely, that the priority in both countries' foreign policy is focused on relations with the United States. As a result, each places low priority on relations with the other, leading to makeshift, muddling-through measures. Add to this the emphasis on domestic politics. That is to say, both Japan and Russia tend to frame their diplomacy toward each other mainly in the context of what is happening on their own domestic political scene. As a result, Japan's Russia policy and Russia's Japan policy lack consistency, and the position and importance of the territorial issue varies within that policy. Let us now examine this tendency, first of all for Japan and then for Russia.

The tenure of most Japanese prime ministers has been extremely short. The president of the Liberal Democratic Party can serve only two two-year terms, a total of four years. The governments of Sōsuke Uno (69 days), Tsutomu Hata (64 days), and Morihiro Hosokawa (263 days) lasted under one year, and those led by Takeo Fukuda, Masayoshi Ōhira, and Zenkō Suzuki all lasted only two years. That Yasuhiro Nakasone and Junichiro Koizumi stayed in power for five and five and a half years respectively was quite exceptional. No other country in the G-8 member states except Italy changes its leader so often. The same applies to Japanese ministers of foreign affairs and heads of the Defense Agency, who change so frequently that it is hardly worth the bother of remembering their names. In this respect, Prime Minister Koizumi's advocacy that cabinets should be staffed by ministers who stay in their position for the full term is only a statement of the obvious.

Also, while Japanese prime ministers and foreign ministers call vociferously for return of the four Northern Islands, just how serious are they? For example, only rarely do they ever visit the Nemuro area, where the movement for the return of the Northern Territories originated. One reason for this is that local people harbor excessive expectations. The local fishing community and other residents fervently petition visitors to put policies in place or commit to spending to support regional development. Wary of this, powerful politicians have opted to stay away, leading to a vicious cycle in terms of expectations.

Furthermore, the organizations involved with the issue are typical examples of compartmentalized administrative systems. The Northern Territories Issue Association comes under the auspices of the Management and Coordination Agency. The Japan League for the Return of the Northern Territories is under the Ministry of Foreign Affairs. Organizations such as the League of Residents of Chishima and Habomai Islands and the Cabinet Office's Northern Territories Affairs Administration also exist. Although the reasons for their establishment and the nature of their activities vary slightly, they are all united in their desire to promote the swift return of the Northern Territories. These organizations are now independent administrative institutions, and their budgets are being dramatically reduced. That being so, one would think they would look to join forces, but they are not doing so.

Similarly, there is no coherent Japan policy on the Russian side. The Kremlin does not seem to have any long-term strategy or plan based on Japan's status as an economic superpower. For Russia's leaders, Japan seems to exist merely as a card to play in order to restrain the United States, Europe, or China when there is an impasse in relations. Only when relations with the West settled down or stagnated did President Gorbachev turn his attention toward Japan and attempt to improve relations. However, by then it was already too late. His domestic power base had weakened, and conservative forces strengthened, so that he was no longer strong enough to resolve the islands issue, the key to improving relations with Japan.

President Yeltsin followed basically the same path as Gorbachev. He should have visited Japan when he was at the peak of his power, directly after quelling the coup d'état of August 1991. If he had done so, few in Russia would have ventured to voice serious opposition to his making concessions on the territorial issue. Instead he went on extended leave to recover from the stress of defeating the attempted coup d'état and sent Ruslan Khazbulatov (deputy chairman of the Russian Supreme Soviet) in his place.[12] In the meantime, discontent and dissatisfaction with his unpredictable leadership style grew, and in the fall of 1992 he committed the great diplomatic blunder of canceling his scheduled visit to Japan on very short notice.

After reelection by a slim margin in 1996, Yeltsin repeated his pattern of capricious, off-the-cuff diplomacy. At this stage his external policy was heavily influenced by developments not only on the internal political scene but maybe also in his internal organs. At the unofficial "No-neckties" summit at Krasnoyarsk in November 1997, he had Prime Minister Ryutaro Hashimoto jumping for joy when, quite unsolicited, he proposed a specific deadline of the year 2000 for concluding a peace treaty, on the basis of the Tokyo Declaration. However, this proved to be just another flippant, off-the-cuff statement. The Krasnoyarsk Summit was held with only interpreters present, and Evgenii Primakov, foreign minister at the time, and high-ranking officials of his ministry, were completely ignored. Their reaction to this was to lie in wait for a chance to revise Yeltsin's unilateral statements. The deterioration in his health and the waning of his political power at the time of Prime Minister Obuchi's visit in 1998 provided the perfect opportunity. When Yeltsin was unable to meet Obuchi, Primakov took his place, and he handed Obuchi a reply to the unpublished proposal Hashimoto had made at Kawana in the previous April. It completely negated the Yeltsin-Hashimoto agreement "to strive to conclude a peace treaty by the year 2000."[13] In his memoirs, *Prezidentskii Maraton*, published in 2000, Yeltsin wrote, "Unfortunately I was not successful in realizing my promise with Prime Minister Hashimoto."[14]

Mismatch of Approaches

The national characters of Japan and Russia could not be more different. One is meticulous, sensitive, and impatient, the other happy-go-lucky toward everything, broad-minded and patient. It would be hard to find a more contrasting pair of countries anywhere in the world. If they have an aspect of national character in common, it would be the fact that each uses its own benchmarks to judge the other, and each therefore tends to assume the other is actually thinking along the same lines as itself. Let me give an example.

In its negotiations with Russia, Japan employs a "no-bargaining approach." At a very early stage, the Japanese government ceased to demand return of the eighteen islands north of Etorofu and of Southern Sakhalin, which it acknowledged to be Russian territory by establishing a consulate in Iuzhno-Sakhalinsk (formerly Toyohara). Japan thereafter put forward a "fixed price" tag and does not look to bargain, stating from the outset that it wants all four islands back—nothing more, nothing less.

However, the Russian side considers that negotiations always involve bargaining, and that this entails concessions, so that Tokyo's initial demand for four islands implies that ultimately Japan will accept less than four. Let me explain again the bazaar-style negotiating technique that the Russians use.[15]

Basically it is an approach whereby exorbitant prices are demanded at the outset to test the other side's reactions. Faced with strong refusals, they gradually reduce the price and, in the end, propose a compromise by *popolam* (meet you halfway). This bazaar-style negotiating approach raises the question whether Japan's "no-bargaining" approach is actually appropriate when dealing with Russia. I doubt that it is. Russia does not look beyond bazaar-style negotiation and makes no attempt to understand that Japan's "no-bargaining" approach is the only stance Japan will take. This mismatch of negotiating approach hinders progress in resolving the territorial dispute.

Lack of Urgency

If Japan and Russia resolve the territorial problem and conclude a peace treaty, they would enjoy "enormous benefits" (*kolossal'nye vygody*), in the words of Russian Foreign Minister Lavrov.[16] Despite this, neither country appears willing to compromise, which suggests that international relations cannot always be satisfactorily explained by the "rational actor model."[17] It also suggests that material interests are not always at the root of patterns of human behavior, and that even dramatic changes in the international environment, such as the end of the Cold War, do not necessarily induce changes in foreign policy. In other words, policymakers have the same human frailties as anyone else. They too have emotions, emphasize "face," and are affected by inertia.

One reason why neither Japanese nor Russian governments have taken positive steps to resolve the territorial problem is that they are not pressed by any sense of urgency to make decisions on the matter. Of course, it is true that the Soviet Union's demise has changed the situation somewhat to Japan's advantage. The three Baltic States are again independent and any future claims by Poland, Romania, or Slovakia would be against Belarus, Moldova, and Ukraine, not Russia. That leaves only Finland, Kaliningrad, and the Northern Territories. There is no apparent pressure in Finland or Germany for return of the lost territories, so any Russian concessions to Japan would no longer set a dangerous precedent of territorial concessions that could possibly be used against Russia by other nations.

The conservatives, including the military, who succeeded in obstructing Yeltsin's visit to Japan in September 1992, used to exploit, among other things, the line of argument with emphasis of setting a precedent, namely, the so-called Pandora's box effect of a chain reaction Russia could not possibly endure.[18] But the validity of Pandora's box or domino theory was lost further by recent developments between Russia and China, Ukraine, and Kazakhstan. In 1954 Nikita Khrushchev half-jokingly made a statement that he would give the Crimean Peninsula to the Ukrainian Republic, which was then a part of the USSR. In 1997 Boris Yeltsin formally acknowledged

Ukraine's claim of sovereignty over Crimea.[19] Gorbachev and Yeltsin handed over many of its hundreds of islands to China.[20] Putin agreed in 2004 to use the 50–50 formula for demarcating the remaining three disputed islands on the Russo-Chinese border.[21] Border demarcation with Kazakhstan in 2005 is also reported resolved by the 50–50 formula.[22]

These territorial issues had their own "policy imperatives."[23] First, these countries all share a land border with Russia, so it was in Moscow's best interests to deal with potential causes of conflict before they escalate. The border between Russia and China stretches for 4,250 kilometers and is a great psychological threat because of the potential for Chinese immigration and economic encroachment. For this reason, Russia needs China to be a friendly, neutral power. At 6,846 kilometers, the border between Russia and Kazakhstan is quite long, only second to the border between Canada and the United States, that is, 8,900 kilometers. That in October 2004 and January 2005 the Putin government hurried to set its national borders with China and Kazakhstan by dividing disputed areas in half clearly indicates that the matter was perceived as urgent.

The situation with Japan is quite different. If Russia establishes and deepens a friendly cooperative relationship with Japan, the benefits are probably not only greater than in the case of Kazakhstan, but, depending on how one looks at it, greater than those to be accrued with China. There is no question that "enormous benefits" would be forthcoming, but the cost is the return of the Northern Islands. Pros and cons aside, no particular urgency is required. Japan does not represent a military menace to Russia's national security. It can be said so safely, judging from the changed nature of the Japanese state, which can be expressed in its constitution, the restricted size of its Self-Defense Forces, deliberately not equipped with long-range offensive weapons, and not becoming a nuclear power even though Japan could easily do so if it chose to. Moreover, Japan has a security treaty with the United States and sits firmly under the American nuclear umbrella. This effectively rules out Russian military action against Japan, but it also means that Japan cannot embark on any acts of adventurism without U.S. approval. So although it is certainly preferable for Russia to maintain friendly relations with Japan, there is no immediate need to pay a price for that friendship. The status quo suffices, and a breakthrough in relations with Japan is not justified if there is a substantial cost involved.

Changes on the international or domestic scene may render the status quo unworkable. Then, when "policy imperatives" come into play, Russia will realize that it must improve relations with Japan, despite the "cost" of returning four islands. This also applies basically to Japan. That is, only when faced with the need to develop closer ties with Russia will Tokyo seek to improve relations irrespective of the territorial dispute.

"A Full-Blooded and Dynamic" Relationship

There will be no peace treaty between Japan and Russia without resolution of the territorial problem. Some will ask if that really matters, and indeed these days territorial conflict does not necessarily lead to war as often as in the past. But however we look at it, there is nothing normal about the existence of this territorial problem more than sixty years after the end of World War Two. Not only it is abnormal, but it is also a major obstacle to further dynamic development of relations between Japan and Russia.

In years gone by, when Gorbachev was asked what kind of relationship he would like to see between Japan and the Soviet Union, he replied, "One that is *polnokrovnoe*," which translates as "full-blooded" or "dynamic."[24] So how can we create a full-blooded and dynamic relationship between Japan and Russia? First we must remove the obstacle to free circulation, which in the simplest of terms means resolving the territorial dispute. Konstantin Sarkisov (currently a professor at Yamanashi Gakuin University) perceptively described it as "like a fishbone stuck in the throat . . . uncomfortable, at times painful, and above all, as time passes it may even lead to quite an undesirable outcome."[25]

Undoubtedly excessive sensitivity toward past events is both retrogressive and unproductive, but the present and future are both extensions of the past. If we move into the future without having properly settled the past, in all probability we will end up wasting both time and energy when those same problems come back to haunt us. Japanese are no freer than other humans from emotional baggage or hard feelings, and they have the same need to know that past troubles have been expunged. Merely saying the future must include Russia will not excite them, nor secure their heartfelt cooperation.

Japan could even be seen as testing Russia, which many Japanese still view as an ominous presence. The Soviet Union unilaterally violated the Japanese-Soviet Neutrality Pact, and Soviet troops occupied the four Northern Islands after Japan had accepted the Potsdam Declaration. President Yeltsin apologized for the detention of Japanese POWs in Siberia, but Russia has shown no remorse for its occupation of the Northern Territories. Japanese see the detention of the POWs in Siberia and the Soviet occupation of the islands as violations of international law. Many Japanese thus consider that Russia should return the islands as a tangible display of remorse. Japanese attribute this kind of symbolic meaning to these four small islands.[26] Russia's return of the four Northern Islands seized under Generalissimo Stalin's orders would surely prove that Russians are normal human beings and worthy to relate to as neighbors. Anything less will leave the impression that Japan has again been duped, and a sense of dissatisfaction that negates any feelings of obligation or gratitude engenders no desire to work toward a cooperative relationship, leaving Japanese-Russian relations neither "full-blooded" nor "dynamic."

With a peace treaty under which the four Northern Islands are returned, the territorial dispute would then be resolved in a way in which Russia also benefits. Recognizing Japan's sovereignty over the islands may be difficult for the Russians to stomach, but they stand to gain a great deal by doing so. Let me explain. Currently no border exists between Japan and Russia that is recognized in terms of international law. By drawing a line between Uruppu and Etorofu not only does Russia legally regain the territory previously given to Japan in the Treaty for Exchange of Sakhalin for the Kurile Islands (1875) and the Treaty of Portsmouth (1905), but it could also create a "full-blooded and dynamic" relationship with Japan. Considering the "enormous benefits" (Foreign Minister Lavrov) that Russia would reap from this, drawing the border north of Etorofu would not be a large price to pay.

The next questions are: What circumstances are needed to enable a peace treaty to be concluded that sees the four islands returned to Japan? What are the conditions that would make this happen? I will bring this book to a close with answers to these questions.

Changes on the International Scene

The first prerequisite for realizing Japan's demand for the return of all four islands is the creation of an international climate in which the Putin administration is obliged to agree with it. Let us turn the chessboard around and look at things from Moscow's perspective. At present Moscow does not have to respond urgently to Japanese demands for the return of the islands, but it is quite possible that at some stage changes in the international environment will create such a policy imperative.

Sudden changes required the Soviet Union to dramatically revise its foreign policy. A typical example was when rapprochement between the United States and China transformed the international political scene during the 1970s. Another was at the end of the Cold War from 1989 to 1991, when skillfully taking advantage of that opportunity, Germany succeeded in achieving reunification. Japan, by contrast, was unable to make anything of either opportunity. What is the case since Putin came to power? The terrorist attacks of September 11, 2001, brought about a transformation in Putin's diplomacy toward the United States, from "balance-of-power diplomacy," in which Russia sought to form a coalition against the United States, to "bandwagon diplomacy," stressing harmony with the United States. Then the Iraq crisis, with us since spring of 2003, caused the pendulum of Putin's policy toward the United States to swing at least partially from "bandwagon" to "balance-of-power" diplomacy.

If the international environment again undergoes the kind of upheaval described above, some kind of change in Putin's diplomacy toward Japan will occur. This is within the realms of possibility, and Japan should now start preparing, so as to be able to deal appropriately with each possible scenario.

Not only has Russian diplomacy during Putin's second term been light in terms of results, it could even be described as little more than a series of blunders. Three major incidents, the break-up of the oil giant Yukos, the school massacre in Beslan, North Ossetia, and the political crisis in Ukraine, strained Russia's relations with the West.

The series of "color revolutions" that occurred in Georgia, Ukraine, Moldova, and Kyrgyzstan were all subtly different in nature. Some involved the kind of systemic change befitting the term "revolution," while others were simply changes of regime or policy. However, they all possessed one clear common denominator, namely, signs of leaning toward the West and loosening ties between CIS members. It seems to be only a matter of time before other CIS countries begin to lean the same way. Under the banner of "Expansion of Freedom and Democracy" the Bush government supports such movements behind the scenes. The Organization for Security and Co-operation in Europe (OSCE) is also interested in these trends and is applying pressure on Russia to affect an early withdrawal of its troops from CIS countries. It also is keeping a close eye on these countries' presidential and parliamentary elections to ensure that they are held in a fair manner. Such moves by the West, which could result in an eastward expansion of NATO or the EU, antagonize Russia.

Partly out of a desire to counter such Western nations, the Putin government will probably attempt to move closer to China or India, or other countries. In May 2005, the government of Uzbekistan, led by Islam Karimov, did not hesitate to use force to quell antigovernment riots in Andijan. Moscow and Beijing both support the Karimov regime, and in August of the same year Russia and China carried out large-scale joint military exercises. However, Russia, China, and India are obliged to pay due consideration to their relations with the United States, Europe, and Japan, and there is a limit to the effectiveness of this kind of diversionary card.

Dissatisfaction of the Russian People

The second prerequisite that will determine whether Japan's desire to re-solve the problem through return of all four islands will come to fruition is Russia's domestic situation. As on the international scene, there appears to be an awesome array of problems ahead on Russia's domestic horizon, and these may oblige President Putin to actively seek improved relations with Japan. With this the case, let us take a brief look at Russian domestic affairs, in terms of the economy, society, and national security.

First, let us look at the economy. Russia's robust growth is precarious, based on high prices for oil and gas that may not last and may not prove sustainable. Undoubtedly, the rise in the international price of crude oil is a positive factor for Russia, gaining an extra two billion dollars in income every time the price per barrel goes up by one dollar. Instability in the Middle East, manifested by such developments as the Iraq War, saw the price of oil exceed US$70 per barrel on the New York Mercantile Exchange. As the world's second-largest oil producer after Saudi Arabia, Russia is smiling all the way to the bank. However, international oil prices that have increased because of particular factors can just as easily drop because of other factors. Depending on such developments as the calming down of the situation in the Middle East, or expansion of production by the Organization of Petroleum Exporting Countries (OPEC), sooner or later the price of oil that increased so swiftly may come down again. The Russian Finance Ministry forecasts that the price of Russian crude oil may end up at US$50 per barrel in 2009–10.[27] Moreover, energy reserves in Russia, of course, are not unlimited. Yegor Gaidar, former deputy premier during the Yeltsin government and now head of the Transition Economy Institute, predicts, "By the most optimistic estimates, oil production (in Russia) will start falling in the 2020s, and gas production will start falling in the 2030s."[28] In fact, Putin's Russia has already begun to face an energy decline at home.

The above would not be an issue if Russia had pursued economic reform in the past. Carelessness is a very human trait. During the 1970s, the former Soviet Union sat back, content to enjoy the fruits of its newfound status as a major energy supplier. It neglected the kind of structural reforms to its economy that Japan and other countries carried out. History repeats itself, and there are concerns that that may happen here too. The major power cuts that hit Moscow on May 25, 2005, could not have been more ironic or symbolic. Russia, a major exporter of oil, gas, and nuclear energy, failed to reform its power industry and took no bold steps to renew its aging infrastructure; as a consequence, the residents of its capital city suffered power outages.

Being fully aware of such a danger of "oil euphoria," some Russian elite people have began to make some proposals. For example, Russian Finance Minister Alexei Kudrin wrote the following in his article on the *Vremia Novosti* in early December 2006: (1) in the last few years a euphoria of high oil prices has strengthened. But this euphoria is dangerous; if global energy prices fall it could spark social tensions and even protests in Russia; (2) because global prices of oil and gas are likely to decrease, the Russian budget cannot continue to rely on oil and gas revenues in the long-term; in fact, the federal budget is already feeling significant macroeconomic risks; (3) (in the meantime) the entire sectors of the Russian economy are becoming uncompetitive; (4) in order to resolve all these problems, what Russia should do is find alternative sources for financing spending, to boost market institutions, to increase taxes, and to develop a high-tech economy.[29]

"Greatly concerned by the fact that Russian economy was too dependent on exports of raw materials," President Putin himself urged to diversify the economy by changing its focus more on high-value-added industries.[30] In his meeting with representatives from the Russian Union of Industrialists and Entrepreneurs in the Kremlin on February 6, 2006, the Russian president announced a new economic policy course, saying, "We must take qualitative steps to change from simply exploiting natural resources to fully processing these resources."[31] First, Putin warns, "The Russian economy relied too much upon raw materials and low amount of processing, which has even increased recently."[32] This is neither an appropriate nor a healthy trend for Russia in his view, particularly because it means that "Russian economy subjects to the fluctuation of world (energy) prices."[33] Instead, President Putin emphasizes that "we need to develop our system for processing raw materials."[34] To do so, he continued, "We need to significantly increase the share of high-value-added processing industries within Russia."[35] "In other words," he continues, "we need to maximize profits from each tone of ore, other hydrocarbons and raw materials extracted in Russia."[36] President Putin concludes, "One extremely important aspect is that thus more jobs will be created in Russia."[37]

For Russia to do the above-mentioned efforts advocated by Kudrin and Putin it is advisable and even inevitable for Russia to seek cooperation from Japan. Japan has been a leading country in the world in the field of high-tech industries. Particularly, in terms of its efforts in utilizing energy resources in the most efficient and effective fashion Japan occupies the top place in the world. Compared with Japan, the primary energy consumption per one GDP unit in Russia is twenty times larger, and ten times larger in China or India.[38]

Why will the government face social tensions and protest in Russia? To be sure, the Russian national coffers will benefit from increases in the price of energy, which is good, and yet profits will not be distributed evenly to all the citizens of Russia. Inequality is perilously wide. According to *Forbes* (2007) Russia's total number of billionaires (fifty-three) has now surpassed that of Japan (twenty-four), ranking third behind the United States and Germany. However, despite significant reductions in the number of Russian people with incomes below the substance minimum (in 2004, 2,451 rubles a month, or about US$92) from about 42 million (29 percent of the population in 2000), they still numbered 25.5 million (17.8 percent of the population at the end of 2004).[39] The rich-poor gap, as represented by the gap in income between the poorest 20 percent and the wealthiest 20 percent of the population is high compared to most Western nations. On the GINI index that measures income inequality, Russia in 2004 registered 40.7, almost exactly the same as the United States (40.8 percent), showing much greater inequality than Japan (24.9 percent), or Western Europe, where the range was from 24.7 (Denmark) to 36.8 (United Kingdom).[40]

To placate the disgruntled Russian public, President Putin has set out a plan to double the gross domestic product (GDP) in the next eight years. Russia's per head GDP at purchasing power parity (PPP) (2005) is eighty-second in the world. Russia's GDP (2005) is 763.7 billion, while Russia ranks sixty-fifth (as equivalent to US$11,041) in the world as a "place to live," according to the UN Human Development indicators, taking into account education, health, welfare, and so on, as well as GDP. If Russia's GDP is to double in the next eight years, it would need to grow at an annual rate of 9.3 percent. However, almost all research agencies predict Russia's GDP growth rate for 2005 to be between 6 and 7 percent, a level far short of what the Russian government needs to be able to fulfill their commitment to double GDP in eight years. On the other side of the coin, there is an inflation rate that is advancing much faster than in the advanced Western nations.

The Putin administration is also implementing economic and social policies that infuriate a portion of the Russian public. The social welfare system of benefits that previously covered housing, heating, transport, and medical costs free or very cheaply has switched to charging services at full cost, notionally covered on average by a cash benefit. This may be a necessary part of the move toward a market economy, but welfare beneficiaries are dissatisfied because the change was introduced without much explanation, does not take regional governments' ability to pay into account, and, most importantly, because inflation erodes the value of the cash benefit. About 30 million beneficiaries—approximately 20 percent of the population—have voiced vehement opposition to the changes. Since summer 2004 pensioners, veterans, disabled people, and students have turned out in droves at street rallies and demonstrations in Russia's main cities. These are the first such protests since Putin came to power, though they have subsided now.

Other Serious Problems in Russia

The most serious social problem faced by Putin's Russia is declining population. Its population has been shrinking fast, even before the full impact of a gathering AIDS/HIV epidemic will be felt. Russia's current population in 2006 is 142.3 million people—the seventh largest in the world. The population of Russia has been declining ever since 1960. The first reason is the dwindling number of children, a problem it shares with the other advanced nations of the world, such as Japan. However, Russia's birthrate of 1.17 per family is even lower than Japan's 1.29. Next is its high mortality rate, which is vastly different from that of other advanced nations, such as Japan. In the background are issues such as the loss of a justification for existence that has followed the collapse of the socialist system, unemployment, poverty, alcoholism, drug dependence, expansion of the AID/HIV pandemic, inadequate health services, and rampant crime, among other things. For these reasons, the adult mortality rate in Russia increases, and the average lifespan shrinks to an extent unthinkable in other civilized nations. The average life expectancy for a Russian male is 59.63 years (134th in the world), almost 20 years shorter than that of a Japanese male, at 78.58 years (2005). Russian women live an average of 71.9 years (100th in the world), which is more than 13 years less than Japanese women, 85.52 years (2005).

The decrease in population is particularly marked in the Far East Region. The Russian Far East economic region comprises 36.4 percent of Russia's territory, but in 2004 it had only 4.6 percent of its population and 4.9 percent of its workforce. It had 5.7 percent of the country's stock of resources, received 6.2 percent of all capital investment, including 12.5 percent of all foreign investment, but contributed only 5.2 percent to the GDP, 4.2 percent to industrial and 3.4 percent to agricultural output, 4.2 percent to tax revenues, 2.6 percent to the federal budget, and only 3.5 percent of Russia's exports, versus 3.8 percent of its imports. Among Russia's seven economic regions the Far Eastern economic region was second highest for capital investment per head, incomes of the employed, and crime rates, third highest for average incomes and GDP per head, but last for industrial and agricultural production and contribution per head to state revenues. It had the highest infant mortality, lowest life expectation, and highest divorce rate (708 per 1,000 marriages).[41]

In 1990–91 just slightly more than eight million people lived in the Far East, but by 2005 their numbers fell down even faster than that of the country as a whole, to 6.59 million, that is, a rate of decline almost six times the national average.[42] But what is the situation on the Chinese side of the Amur and Ussuri rivers that mark the border? Each year China's entire population grows by between eight and ten million, which in just two years equates to the population of Australia.[43] On the other side of the border approximately 109 million people live in China's three northeastern provinces (Heilongiang, Jilin, and Liaoning). Considering Russia's nightmare of China's "quiet expansion," final settlement in 2004 of a dispute over the Sino-Russian border (one of the world's longest and the cause of a war in 1969) may have been timely.

The most pressing issue for the Putin government is a separatist insurgency in Chechnya. Six years have passed since Putin (then prime minister) gave the orders that started the Second Chechen War. This war undoubtedly helped Putin rise to presidential stardom, but now it represents his greatest Achilles heel. The fortunes of war in Chechnya sway one way then the other, and it is now a quagmire just as the Vietnam War was for the United

States. The cost of the war is putting pressure on the national coffers, and the number of Russians who agree with those, including former President Gorbachev, who advocate that peace negotiations be commenced, has increased considerably. The Kremlin has dealt with a separatist insurgency in Chechnya by fostering rule by a thuggish strongman, whose men terrorize and kill opponents not only in the region but also in Moscow. The army is crippled by graft. The North Caucasus is combustible. These problems all impact negatively on Putin's popularity ratings.[44]

President Putin's Resolve

What is the third condition that has to be satisfied before Russia accepts Japan's demands for the return of all four islands and concludes a peace treaty on that basis? The answer is the will of the Russian leader. Needless to say, the international and domestic environments play critical roles in determining foreign policy, and no leader can afford to ignore them for long. However, both are only reflected in, and determinant of, policy when the foreign-policy decision-makers acknowledge and evaluate them. Such people perceive these factors through a lens or filter consisting of their own beliefs, ideologies, sense of values, even personal likes and dislikes. The policy-determining factors are selected, interpreted, and at times modified through this lens or filter.[45] In this respect, leaders play a very large role in policymaking.

At present Russia's highest-ranking policymaker is President Putin, whose role is defined by the statement in Article 86 of the Russian Constitution, "The President of the Russian Federation shall supervise the conduct of the Russian Federation's foreign policy." The fact is that President Putin has almost exclusive control over the fundamentals of Russian foreign policy. This has certainly been the case at least in the years following the terrorist attacks of September 11, 2001. Since then he has chosen a line of cooperation with the United States, even giving tacit approval to American military bases in Central Asia. None of his closest advisors voiced any opposition to these decisions. Minister of Defense Sergei Ivanov and then Minister of Foreign Affairs Igor Ivanov did voice conflicting views immediately before Putin announced his decision, but once it was taken they fell obediently into line. In addition, in October 2004, the Russian Parliament rubber-stamped the agreement on Sino-Russian border demarcation reached under the 50–50 formula by Putin and his Chinese counterpart, Hu Jintao.

Putin possesses a complex character, philosophy, and view of life, aspects of which would seem to be quite contradictory. For instance, on the one hand, his ideological standpoint is nationalistic or patriotic, emphasizing the maintenance of territorial integrity. At least in this respect, it is unthinkable that he would easily agree to Japan's demand for the return of all four islands. On the other hand, he is a pragmatist, with a keen eye for a deal, and a shameless opportunist who, depending on the needs of the moment, will quite happily change his positions and policies. His adoption of a cooperative approach toward the United States after 9/11 was a perfect example of both pragmatism and opportunism.

Between autumn 2004 and early 2005 Putin brought an end to territorial disputes with China and Kazakhstan by dividing the disputed territories equally. He could have taken the easy way out and left such bothersome problems to the next generation of leaders, but instead he took it upon himself to find a solution. If we apply this interpretation, it is quite possible that he has what it takes to end the territorial problem between Japan and Russia.

Putin's second term in office will end in May 2008, when he will be only fifty-five years old. Even if he wants to retire, there is no way that the siloviki will agree without resistance. They owe their power and wealth to the fact that their former KGB colleague became the Kremlin's top leader, so are likely to do all they can to keep him in power beyond 2008. There are two possible ways to do this: (1) amend the Russian Constitution to legitimize Putin seeking a third consecutive term in office. Given the fact that the pro-Putin's ruling party, United Russia, occupies two-third of the Duma, it is not hard to amend the constitution. If Putin amended the constitution, however, the West would surely criticize him bitterly, regarding him as similar to dictators in the Central Asia and Belarus. Most probably Russia under such a dictator will be expelled from the G-8. (2) Putin stands down as president, but resumes the post of chairman of the United Russia and/or prime minister, under a faithful figurehead president, or speaker of the upper or lower house, then in 2012 or even before this period standing for reelection to the presidency. Candidates for the role of puppet president in 2008–12 may, for example, include two first deputy prime ministers, Dmitrii Medvedev and Sergei Ivanov, president of the Russian Railways Co. Vladimir Yakunin, head of the presidential administration, Sergei Sobianin, and speaker of the Duma, Boris Gryzlov. But whoever happens to be the next Russian president, he or she will take foreign policies toward Japan differently from his or her predecessor. First of all, he or she is a different person, who, whether he or she likes it, cannot take one and the same policy. Besides, a successor is usually tempted to be different from his or her predecessors. Putin is a case in point, since he was appointed by Yeltsin and yet what he has been doing turns out to be exactly the denial of Yeltsin's policies.

Japan's Approach

Japanese-Russian relations concerning the territorial problem can be likened to a four-dimensional equation. The four variables are the "international scene" (let us call it "X"), Russia's "internal situation" ("Y"), the "leader" ("Z")—all three variables have been discussed above—and "Japan's approach" ("J").

The J-variable is made up of three factors. First is the resolute "desire" to see the Northern Islands returned. The islands have been under Russian control for more than half a century, and no Japanese live there. In such circumstances, regaining sovereignty will be a task of "Mission Impossible" proportions. To achieve it, Japan must be prepared to endure every hardship and make whatever sacrifices are required. This goal will probably not be achieved without such firm resolve.

The next factor is "strength." Some kind of strength is necessary to make a formidable negotiating power like Russia accept Japan's demands. Japan's approach must be that the four Northern Islands are inherent, inalienable Japanese territory. However, this in itself is not enough to make Russia agree. The reason of course is that negotiations in international politics are not "an inter-collegiate debate—an exercise in histrionics and logic, with the decision going to the side that scores the best in presentation."[46]

Japan's economic, scientific-technological, and managerial powers are useful in supplementing law, justice, and morality. For example, if Russia leaves Siberia and especially the Far East as they are now, the population drain will continue, and as a result, the region will either be ruined, or risk falling under the Chinese sphere of influence. As Fiona Hill and Clifford Gaddy pointed out, "The problem is not that Siberia is underpopulated, but that it is now overpopulated."[47] Now that military-related industries in Siberia and the Far East have gone into decline, there are insufficient job opportunities to support the local population, who are forced to consider moving. Natalya Alyakrinskaya also writes in the March 9, 2007, issue of *Moscow News*, "Although the authorities in Russia's Far East encouraged resettlement there, they failed to create more jobs."[48] Unemployment there—according to her—remains very high."[49] This is the core of the problem.

If Hill's and Gaddy's observations are correct, merely attracting labor from China or Central Asia will not solve the problem facing Siberia and the Far East. President Putin himself seems to be aware of this. In his opening remark at the Security Council session on December 20, 2006, he drew attention to the fact that the large inflow of illegal immigration from China in Russia's Far East, whose population is dwindling, has aroused serious concerns.[50] Then the Russian President Putin made a proposal as his way of offering a solution to this concern, stating, "The task of attracting and preserving able bodies population in the Far East should be primarily resolved in the context of *realizing huge economic projects and creating new jobs in the region*" (italics added).[51] New huge projects would create new job opportunities, but such projects cannot be created and run without injections of money, infrastructure, technological know-how, and management skill. The country most capable of carrying this out on a huge scale and in a speedy manner in Northeast Asia is only Japan. Dmitrii Trenin, deputy director of the Carnegie Moscow Center, wrote:

In my opinion Russia ought to rely on Japan as its main partner in modernizing Siberia and the [Russian] Far East. Japan would be capable of playing the same kind of role in these regions as Germany and the EU played in Russia's western regions. Japan's financial capabilities, technological leadership, and geopolitical location all make it an ideal "partner for modernization for Russia in the East." If Russia develops this sort of partnership with Japan, it would similarly enhance Russia's position in Asia in general.[52]

The third factor of the J-variable is the "strategy" that links "desire" and "strength." One of Japan's mistakes in relation to Russia is that all goals have been pursued simultaneously, with no order of priority. For example, Tokyo has demanded return of the islands at the same time as asking for energy and fishing rights. Of course, cooperation and links in areas not related to the islands may contribute to preparing the way for resolving the islands issue, but the islands and energy or fishing rights are sometimes in an antinomy or trade-off situation, where one can only be gained by sacrificing the other. The goals should be prioritized, taking into account trade-offs of one against another. Herein lies the key to success in Japan's strategy toward Russia.

Japan wants the islands returned. However, to achieve this it must commit itself to a course of action that enhances rather than reduces the chances of success. Japan should place the islands issue at the top of its list of priorities in its Russia policy and see other goals as of secondary importance, or even abandon them. For example, the Japanese should bite the bullet, strive to use less energy, and redouble their efforts to develop nuclear power or other alternative sources of energy. This will not only stop Japan from casting longing glances at Russia's energy resources but also reduce or negate the need to rely on them. Similarly Japan should stop casting hungry looks at the marine resources in the Russian-controlled seas around the Northern Territories. In simple terms, Japan wants to have its cake (more precisely, its crab and sea urchin) and eat it too, if it aspires to load its tables with delicacies as well as get back the islands. If Japan genuinely wants the islands returned, then its people must be prepared to make some kind of sacrifice. Only when it does so will Tokyo be able to negotiate on an equal footing with Moscow. Then, if other circumstances also fall into place, getting the islands back will no longer be Mission Impossible.

In the sixty years since the end of World War Two, the people of Japan have succeeded in restoring almost everything to their satisfaction, but at least one aspect of overcoming the past (*Vergangenheitsbewältigung*) has eluded them—the complete normalization of relations with its neighbor, Russia. The payback for Japan's reckless war against the United States and its allies will indeed be expensive. Regaining something lost among the spoils of war requires not only an incredible degree of commitment and inexhaustible patience but also a great deal of sacrifice. The Northern Territories problem serves to remind the people of Japan of this cold fact.

Reference Matter

Joint Compendium of Documents on the History of Territorial Issue between Japan and Russia

---

MINISTRY OF FOREIGN AFFAIRS OF JAPAN
MINISTRY OF FOREIGN AFFAIRS OF THE RUSSIAN FEDERATION

Preface

This compendium has been jointly prepared by the Ministries of Foreign Affairs of Japan and of the Russian Federation with the aim of helping the people of Japan and Russia to obtain an objective view of the "territorial issue" between Japan and Russia.

As a result of the Japanese advance from the South onto the Kurile Islands and the Russian advance from the North by the middle of the 19th century, a Japanese-Russian border emerged between the islands of Etorofu and Uruppu. This border was legally established by the Treaty of Commerce, Navigation and Delimitation between Japan and Russia of February 7, 1855. The treaty peacefully established that the islands of Etorofu, Kunashiri, Shikotan and Habomai were Japanese territory, and that the islands from Uruppu northwards were Russian territory.

According to the Treaty for the Exchange of Sakhalin for the Kurile Islands of May, 1875, the islands from Uruppu to Shumshu were peacefully ceded by Russia to Japan in exchange for the concession of Japanese rights to the island of Sakhalin.

With the signing of the Treaty of Commerce and Navigation between Japan and Russia on June 18, 1895, the Treaty of 1855 became invalid, but at the same time, the validity of the Treaty of 1875 was reaffirmed.

According to the Portsmouth Peace Treaty between Japan and Russia of September 5, 1905, Russia ceded that part of the island of Sakhalin south of the 50th parallel North to Japan. In light of Japanese and Russian documents from this period, it is obvious that from the time that Japanese-Russian diplomatic relations were established in 1855, Japan's title to Etorofu, Kunashiri, Shikotan and Habomai was never held in doubt by Russia.

In the Convention on Fundamental Principles for Relations between Japan and the USSR of January 20, 1925, that announced the establishment of diplomatic relations between Japan and the Soviet Union, the Soviet Union agreed that the Portsmouth Treaty of 1905 would remain in force.

The Joint Declaration of the US and the UK of August 14, 1941 (the Atlantic Charter), which the Soviet Union acceded to on September 24, 1941, stated that "they desire to see no territorial changes that do not accord with the freely expressed wishes of the peoples concerned."

The Cairo Declaration of the US, the UK and China of November 27, 1943, which the Soviet Union acceded to on August 8, 1945, stated that the "Allies covet no gains for themselves and have no thought of territorial expansion." At the same time the Declaration stated that the Allies' goal was particularly to drive Japan from "the territories which she has taken by violence and greed."

The Yalta Agreement of the Three Great Powers (the USSR, the US and the UK) of February 11, 1945 stipulated as one of the conditions for the USSR's entry into the war against Japan: "the Kurile Islands shall be handed over to the Soviet Union." The Soviet Union maintained that the Yalta Agreement provided legal confirmation of the transfer of the Kurile Islands to the USSR, including the islands of Etorofu, Kunashiri, Shikotan and Habomai. Japan's position is that the Yalta Agreement is not the final determination on the territorial issue and that Japan, which is not party to this Agreement, is neither legally nor politically bound by its provisions.

The Potsdam Declaration of July 26, 1945, which the Soviet Union acceded to on August 8, 1945, stated that "the terms of the Cairo Declaration be carried out" and that "Japanese sovereignty be limited to the islands of Honshu, Hokkaido, Kyushu, Shikoku and such minor islands as the Allies would determine." On August 15, 1945 Japan accepted the terms of the Potsdam Declaration and surrendered.

In the Neutrality Pact between Japan and the USSR of April 13, 1941, the parties had an obligation to mutually respect each other's territorial integrity and inviolability. The Pact also stated that it would remain in force for five years and that if neither of the contracting parties denounced it a year before its date of expiration, it be considered to be automatically extended for the next five years.

After the Soviet Union announced its intention to denounce the Japanese-Soviet Neutrality Pact on April 5, 1945, the Pact was to have become invalid on April 25, 1946. The Soviet Union declared war on Japan on August 9, 1945.

From late August to early September 1945, the Soviet Union occupied the islands of Etorofu, Kunashiri, Shikotan and Habomai. After that, by Decree of the Presidium of the USSR Supreme Soviet of February 2, 1946, these islands were incorporated into the then Russian Soviet Federal Socialist Republic.

The San Francisco Peace Treaty with Japan of September 8, 1951 provides for Japan's renunciation of rights, titles and claims to the Kurile Islands and South Sakhalin. However, the Treaty did not determine to which state these territories were to belong. The Soviet Union did not sign this treaty.

The question of the limits of the Kurile Islands that were renounced by Japan in the San Francisco Peace Treaty, was mentioned, for example, in a statement by K. Nishimura, Director of the Treaties Bureau of the Ministry of Foreign Affairs of Japan, in the Japanese Parliament on October 19, 1951, and in a statement by Mr. K. Morishita, Parliamentary Vice-Minister for Foreign Affairs of Japan, in the Japanese Parliament on February 11, 1956, as well as in an Aide-Memoire from the Department of State of the USA, which was one of the drafters of the Treaty, to the Government of Japan, dated September 7, 1956.

As the Soviet Union did not sign the San Francisco Peace Treaty, separate negotiations on the conclusion of a peace treaty were conducted between Japan and the Soviet Union. However, because of differences in the positions of the two sides over the territorial clause of the treaty, an agreement was not reached.

An exchange of letters between Mr. S. Matsumoto, Plenipotentiary Representative of the Government of Japan, and Mr. A. A. Gromyko, USSR First Deputy Minister of Foreign Affairs, on September 29, 1956, showed that the two sides agreed to continue negotiations on the conclusion of a peace treaty, which would also include the territorial issue, after the reestablishment of diplomatic relations between the two countries. This exchange of letters also paved the way for reestablishment of Japanese-Soviet diplomatic relations and the signing of a Joint Declaration by Japan and the USSR.

The Joint Declaration by Japan and the USSR of October 19, 1956, ended the state of war and reestablished diplomatic and consular relations between the two countries. In the Joint Declaration Japan and the USSR agreed to continue negotiations on the conclusion of a peace treaty after the reestablishment of normal diplomatic relations, and the USSR also agreed to hand over the islands of Habomai and Shikotan to Japan after the signing of a peace treaty. The Joint Declaration by Japan and the USSR was ratified by the Japanese Parliament on December 5, 1956, and by the Presidium of the Supreme Soviet of the USSR on December 8, 1956. Instruments of ratification were exchanged in Tokyo on December 12, 1956.

In 1960, in connection with the conclusion of the new Japanese-US Security Treaty, the Soviet Union stated that the return of the islands of Habomai and Shikotan to Japan would be conditional upon the withdrawal of all foreign troops from Japanese territory. In response, the Government of Japan raised the objection that the terms of the Joint Declaration between

Japan and the USSR could not be changed unilaterally, because it was an international agreement that had been ratified by the Parliaments of both countries.

The Soviet side later asserted that the territorial issue in Japanese-Soviet relations had been resolved as a result of World War II, and such an issue did not exist.

The Japanese-Soviet Joint Communiqué of October 10, 1973, issued at the conclusion of the summit in Moscow, noted that "the settlement of unresolved problems left over since World War II and the conclusion of a peace treaty will contribute to the establishment of truly good-neighborly and friendly relations between the two countries."

The Japanese-Soviet Joint Communiqué of April 18, 1991, issued at the conclusion of the summit in Tokyo, stated that both sides had conducted negotiations "on a whole range of issues pertaining to the preparation and the signing of a peace treaty between Japan and the USSR, including the problem of territorial demarcation, taking into consideration the positions of both sides on the issue as to where the islands of Habomai, Shikotan, Kunashiri and Etorofu belong." The Communiqué also stressed the importance of accelerating the work on the conclusion of a peace treaty.

After the creation of the Commonwealth of Independent States in December 1991 and Japan's recognition of the Russian Federation as the state with the continuity from the USSR, the negotiations on a peace treaty which were conducted between Japan and the USSR, have been continuing between Japan and the Russian Federation.

Both sides are firmly committed to a common understanding of the need to resolve the territorial issue on the basis of "law and justice."

In November 1991 Mr. B. N. Yeltsin, President of the Russian Federation, in his letter to the Russian people, indicated the need to reach a final postwar settlement in relations with Japan, and noted that attention would be paid to the interests of the inhabitants of the said islands. The Government of Japan has also declared its intention to respect fully the human rights, interests and wishes of the Russians who now live on the islands, in the course of the resolution of the territorial issue.

This compendium, offered to readers of Japan and Russia, contains principal Japanese-Russian and Japanese-Soviet documents pertaining to the territorial demarcation between the two countries as well as a series of other documents and materials relevant to the given issue.

September 1992

Ministry of Foreign Affairs   Ministry of Foreign Affairs
of Japan   of the Russian Federation

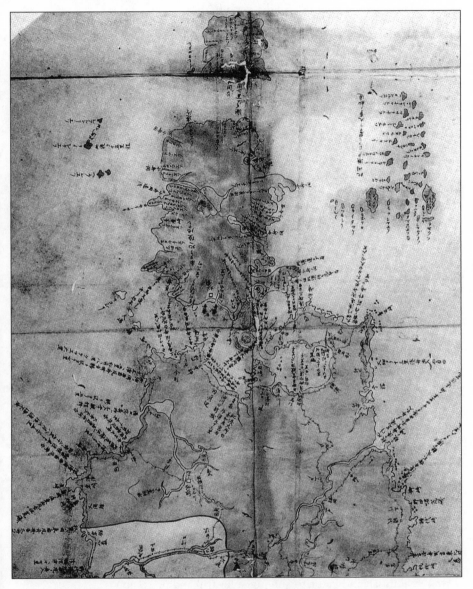

MAP 3. Map of Japan from the Shoho period, dated 1644.

SOURCE: Reprinted from the pamphlet "Our Northern Territories" by the Japanese Ministry of Foreign Affairs' Bureau of Public Relations.

1. Map of Japan from the Shoho period (1944)

An official publication of the Tokugawa Shogunate (ruler of Japan), based on the map from which the principality of Matsumae defines its territory. It is the oldest map in the world that marks the islands of Kunashiri, Etorofu, Habomai and Shikotan. Handmade on Japanese paper, measurements: 227.5cm by 253.7cm. Belongs to Mt. T. Akioka.

2. "Sketches of the Sea Islands," I. Kozyrevsky (1713)

The island of Kunashir. It is inhabited by the same foreigners as Iturup and Urup; the same religion is observed there; I did not find out whether they speak the same language or have their own; they travel to the island of Matsumae, on which the castle of Matsumae is located, and people from the island of Matsumae come to Kunashir every year to trade their goods. This island is larger than Iturup and Urup and more populous. I did not find out whether the inhabitants of Kunashir are subjects of Matsumae or not. But, the inhabitants of Iturup and Urup are living their own lives, not subject to anyone and engage in free trade.

(*The Russian Pacific Epic. Khabarovsk*, 1979, p. 453.)

3. Instruction from the collegium of the Admiralty to G.I. Mulovsky (1787)

Excerpt from the Instruction from the collegium of the Admiralty to G.I Mulovsky. Captain of the First Rank, leader of the first Russian expedition around the world, on the tasks of the expedition (April 1787)

> 12. As noted above, when appointing a senior captain, to provide a description of the Kurile Islands, instruct him to do the following:
>
> 1) Sail around and describe all the small and large Kurile Islands from Japan to Cape Lopatka of the Kamchatka peninsula, identify them on the map as precisely as possible, and formally include all the islands from the island of Matsumae to the Cape Lopatka under the possession of the Russian state by erecting symbols of the state and burying medallions in the ground in appropriate places with inscriptions in Russian and Latin, to announce his trip and possession . . .

(*Expeditions in Russia to study the northern part of the Pacific Ocean in the second half of the 18th century*, Moscow, 1989, p. 236.)

4. Effective Japanese administration of the four Northern Islands in the late 18th–early 19th centuries

On the 11th year of the Kansei era (1799) the central Government of Japan sent an order to the principalities of Nanbu and Tsugaru regarding the administration of the land of Ezo. It said that in consideration of the strategic importance of the land of Ezo, the principalities, if the necessity arose, should send their garrisons to the land of Ezo. To begin with, for this year, the principality of Tsugaru was ordered to send 3 officers and 50 infantrymen from garrisons in Hakodate and the principality of Nanbu to send officers and 20 infantrymen. These troops would subsequently be separated into three parts and be put under the command of Shinanokami Matsudaira. Some time later, on November 2 of that same year, the two principalities were ordered again to send 3 commanders and 500 infantrymen to the land of Ezo for the period for which it remained under direct administration of the central government. They were to arm each 10 infantrymen with three rifles and to quarter the soldiers of the principality of Tsugaru to the East of Sunahara and he soldiers of the principality of Nanbu to the East of Urakawa. This method of defense was employed following the practice of the defense of Nagasaki by forces from the Kurodas and Nabeshimas.

After this, the principalities of Tsugaru and Nanbu established military camps in Hakodate, and the principality of Nanbu founded outposts in Nemuro, on Kunashiri and Etorofu, and the principality of Tsugaru in Sunahara and Furuibetsu on Etorofu. The two principalities were responsible for the defense of those territories. In April of the 1st year of the Bunka era (1804) the two principalities were ordered to ensure the defense of these territories on a permanent basis. In the 2nd year of this era (1805). Yasuchika Tsugaru was awarded a salary increase from 40 thousand to 70 thousand koku of rice for his successes in many years of service in the land of Ezo. In February of the 4th year of the Bunka era (1807) the central Government of Japan also began to control the western land of Ezo and made the principality of Nanbu responsible for the defense of the eastern land of Ezo, and the principality of Tsugaru responsible for the defense of the western land of Ezo. In the same year a Russian invasion took place, as a result of which both principalities increased the number of their troops and also accepted help from other principalities of the Ou region, which sent their troops. We will go into more detail later. In December of that same year the central Government of Japan sent financial assistance of 7 thousand ryo to the principality of Nanbu and 5 thousand ryo to the principality of Tsugaru. In December of the 5th year of the Bunka era (1808) Toshitaka Nanbu's salary was raised to 100 thousand koku of rice and he was appointed to the post of chamberlain. Yasuchika Tsugaru's salary was also raised to 100 thousand koku, and he was promoted to the rank of Junior Fourth Class and was invited to demonstrate further zeal in state service.

(*A New History of Hokkaido*, published by the Governorship of Hokkaido, 1937, Vol. 2, pp. 416–17.)

5. Decree by Emperor Alexander I (1821)

1. The commerce, whaling, fishing and different kinds of industries along the coast of America, extending from the Bering Strait to 51° North, as well as along the Aleutian islands, the east coast of Siberia and the Kurile Islands, extending from the Bering Straits down to the southern cape of the island of Uruppu, that is as far as 45° 50' north, is the exclusive province of Russian subjects.

2. Thus, all foreign ships are forbidden not only to moor at the coasts and islands under Russian authority which are mentioned above, but also to sail within 100 Italian miles of them. All cargoes are confiscated from those who violate this provision.

(*Complete Code of Laws of the Russian Empire*, vol. 37, 1821, p. 904.)

6. Instruction from Emperor Nicholas I to Putiatin (1853)

This is in regard to the letters to the Governor of Nagasaki island and to the Supreme Council of Japan, which were dispatched to Your Honor in sealed packages with Dutch translations included. The Ministry of Foreign Affairs considers it is duty to explain as follows about the contents of the letter to the Supreme Council, which is more important to them:

This letter, which is accompanied by an exact copy (as is the case with the letter to the Governor). In addition to proposing that Japan establish trade relations with us and that Japan allow our trading vessels which will be later allocated (and also, if the necessity arises—our military vessels) to moor in Japanese ports, requests that a border be established between the Russian and Japanese domains. The idea of dealing with the border issue as soon as possible seems highly sound to us: to do so, we can compel the Japanese to enter into negotiations with us by necessity. Otherwise they could, as is their usual fashion, immediately take evasive action and give a negative response. But our desire to clarify the border is the kind of demand they will find difficult to refuse. By posing this question we might provoke the Japanese government to show more compliance.

On the border issue, it is our wish to be as indulgent as possible (without compromising our interests), bearing in mind that the achievement of the other goal—trade benefits is of vital importance to us. The southernmost island of the Kurile Islands that belongs to Russia is Uruppu, which could identify as the last point of Russian authority in the south—so that from our side, the southern tip of this island would be (as it actually is today) the border with Japan, and from the Japanese side, the northern tip of the island of Etorofu would be considered to be their border. If, contrary to expectation, the Japanese Government starts to lay claim to the island of Uruppu, the fact that the island of Uruppu is shown on all of our maps as the territory of Russia, and that the Russian-American Company, which manages Russian property in America and in the various seas there, not only governs Uruppu in the same way as it does all our other Kurile Islands, but even has a settlement there, is the best evidence of its attribution, and such facts allow us to prove that this island is usually regarded as the border of our territory in the Kurile Islands.

7. Article 2 of the Treaty of Commerce, Navigation and Delimitation between Japan and Russia (1855)

ARTICLE 2

Henceforth the boundary between Russia and Japan will pass between the islands of Etorofu and Uruppu. The whole island of Etorofu belongs to Japan and the whole island of Uruppu and the Kurile Islands to the north of the island of Uruppu constitute possessions of Russia. As regards the island Karafuto (Sakhalin), it remains unpartitioned between Russia and Japan, as has been the case up to this time.

Signed in Shimoda, Japan

8. Article 2 of the Treaty for the Exchange of Sakhalin for the Kurile Islands (1875)

ARTICLE 2

In exchange for the cession to Russia of the rights on the island of Karafuto (Sakhalin) stipulated in the first article, His Majesty the Emperor of All the Russias, for Himself and His descendants, cedes to His Majesty the Emperor of Japan the group of islands, called Kurile which He possesses at present, together with all the rights of sovereignty appertaining to this possession, so that henceforth all the Kurile Islands shall belong to the Empire of Japan and the boundary between the Empires of Japan and Russia in these areas shall pass through the Strait between Cape Lopatka of the peninsular of Kamchatka and the island of Shumushu. This group comprises the following eighteen islands: 1) Shumushu, 2) Araido, 3) Paramushiru, 4) Makanrushi, 5) Onekotan, 6) Harimukotan, 7) Ekaruma, 8) Shasukotan, 9) Mushiru, 10) Raikoke, 11) Matsua, 12) Rasutsua, 13) the islets of Suredonekawa and Ushishiru, 14) Ketoi, 15) Shimushiru, 16) Buroton, 17) the islets of Cherupoi and Brat Cherupoefu, 18) Uruppu.

(Signed in Saint Petersburg on May 7, 1875. Ratified on August 22, 1875. Instruments of ratification were exchanged on August 22, 1875 in Tokyo.)

9. Article 18 of the Treaty on Commerce and Navigation between Japan and Russia, and Declaration (1895)

ARTICLE 18

This treaty, from the day it goes into effect, replaces the following documents: the treaty signed on the 21st day of 12th moon of the first year of Ansei, which coincides with January 26, 1855; the treaty on trade and friendship, signed on the 11th day of the seventh moon of the fifth year of Ansei, which coincides with December 11, 1867 and all additional agreements and conventions, signed or existing between the High negotiating Parties; and from that same day the noted contracts, agreements and conventions become invalid. As a result of that, the jurisdiction which Russian courts exercised in Japan and all the special privileges, exceptions and advantages, which Russians used to enjoy until then as part of this jurisdiction, are terminated and abolished completely without special notice, the rights under this jurisdiction will be from that moment transferred to the Japanese judiciary and will be exercised by it.

Signed in St. Petersburg

DECLARATION

The parties, who have signed below, declare that Article 18 of the treaty signed on this date does not relate either to the treaty signed on April 25 (May 7), 1875 between His Majesty the Russian Emperor and His Majesty the Japanese Emperor, or to the additional article, signed in Tokyo on August 10 (22) of that same year, whereas the treaty and the article remain in effect.

St. Petersburg, May 27 (June 8) 1895

10. Article 9 of the Treaty of Portsmouth (1905)

ARTICLE 9

The Imperial Russian Government cedes to the Imperial Government of Japan in perpetuity and full sovereignty the southern portion of the Island of Sakhalin and all the islands adjacent thereto and the public works and properties thereon. The fiftieth degree of north latitude is adopted as the northern boundary of the ceded territory.

(Signed at Portsmouth (USA) on September 5, 1905. Ratified on October 14, 1905. The exchange of instruments of ratification took place in Washington on November 25, 1905.)

11. *Article 2 of Convention Embodying Basic Rules of the Relations Between Japan and the Union of Soviet Socialist Republics, and Declaration (1925)*

ARTICLE 2

The Union of Soviet Socialist Republics agrees that the treaty concluded in Portsmouth on September 5, 1905 shall remain in full force.

It is agreed that the Treaties, Conventions and Agreements, other than the said Treaty of Portsmouth which were concluded between Russia and Japan prior to November 7, 1917, shall be re-examined at a Conference to be subsequently held between the Governments of the High Contracting Parties, and are liable to revision or annulment as altered circumstances may require.

DECLARATION

On the occasion of signing the Convention on the Fundamental Principles for relations between Japan and the Union of Soviet Socialist Republics and Japan, today, the Plenipotentiary Representative of the Union of Soviet Socialist Republics, who has signed below, has the honor to declare that his government's recognition of the Portsmouth Treaty of September 5, 1905 in no way means that the Soviet government shares the political responsibility with the former Tsarist government for signing the said Treaty.

Peking, January 20, 1925

(The Convention was ratified on February 25, 1925. The exchange of instruments of ratification took place in Peking on April 15, 1925.)

12. *Neutrality Pact between Japan and the USSR (1941)*

His Majesty the Emperor of Japan and the Presidium of the Supreme Soviet of the Union of Soviet Socialist Republics, guided by a desire to strengthen peaceful and friendly relations between the two countries, have decided to conclude a neutrality pact, and have agreed on the following:

ARTICLE 1

Both Contracting Parties undertake to maintain peaceful and friendly relations between them and mutually respect the territorial integrity and inviolability of the other Contracting Party.

ARTICLE 2

In the event that one of the Contracting Parties becomes subject to military action on the part of one or more third countries, the other Contracting Party will remain neutral throughout the WHOLE period of the conflict.

ARTICLE 3

This pact shall enter force from the date of its ratification by both Contracting Parties and shall remain in force for a period of five years. If denounced by either Contracting Party a year before the expiration of that period, it shall be considered to be automatically extended for the next period of five years.

ARTICLE 4

This pact shall be ratified as soon as possible. In addition, the exchange of instruments of ratification shall take place at Tokyo as soon as possible.

Yosuke Matsuoka
Yoshitsugu Tatekawa
V. Molotov

(Signed in Moscow on April 13, 1941. Ratified on April 25, 1941.)

13. Atlantic Charter (1941)

The President of the United States of America and the Prime Minister, Mr. Churchill, representing His Majesty's Government in the United Kingdom, being met together, deem it right to make known certain common principles in the national policies of their respective countries on which they base their hopes for a better future for the world.

First, their countries seek no aggrandizement, territorial or other;

Second, they desire to see no territorial changes that do not accord with the freely expressed wishes of the peoples concerned;

14. Declaration of the Soviet Government regarding participation in the Atlantic Charter (1941)

The Soviet Union has always followed and intends to follow the principles of respecting the sovereign rights of nations. In its foreign policy, the Soviet Union was and is guided by the principle of the right of nations to self-determination. Through its entire national policy, which forms the basis of the state structure of the Soviet Union, the Soviet Union is guided by that principle, the basis of which is formed by the recognition of the sovereignty and equal rights of all nations. According to this principle, the Soviet Union defends the right of every people to state independence and territorial inviolability of its country, the right to establish a state structure and to choose a form of government that it considers necessary in order to ensure the economic and cultural prosperity of the whole country.

Guided by these principles in all of its policies and in all of its relations with other nations, the Soviet Union has always been consistently and decisively against all the violations of the sovereign rights of nations, against aggression and aggressors, against all and all kinds of attempts of aggressive countries to impose their will on other peoples and lead them into war. The Soviet Union was and is tirelessly and decisively asserting that collective action against the aggressors is one of the effective means of struggling for the victory of the principles and for the peace and security of nations.

Striving for a radical resolution of the problem of protecting freedom-loving peoples from all dangers presented by the aggressors, the Soviet Union has simultaneously launched a struggle for total and complete disarmament. Being ready to respond to any blow by an aggressor, the Soviet Union has at the same time always based and will base its foreign policy on the idea of striving towards peaceful and good-neighborly relations with all countries that respect the integrity and inviolability of its borders. It has always been ready to support wholly those nations who have fallen victim to aggression and who are fighting for the independence of their motherland.

In accordance with the policy that the Soviet Union steadfastly conducts, based on the principles mentioned above and expressed in numerous acts and documents, the Soviet government expresses its agreement with the basic principles of the declaration of the President of the United States Mr. Roosevelt and the Prime Minister of Great Britain Mr. Churchill, and main principles that are of great importance in the current international situation.

15. Cairo Declaration (1943)

Statement Issued Following the Conference of President Roosevelt, Generalissimo Chiang Kai-shek, and Prime Minister Winston Churchill

The several military missions have agreed upon future military operations against Japan. The Three Great Allies expressed their resolve to bring unrelenting pressure against their brutal enemies by sea, land, and air. This pressure is already mounting.

The Three Great Allies are fighting this war to restrain and punish the aggression of Japan. They covet no gain for themselves and have no thought of territorial expansion. It is their purpose that Japan shall be stripped of all the islands in the Pacific which she has seized or occupied since the beginning of the First World War in 1914, and that all the territories Japan has stolen from the Chinese, such as Manchuria, Formosa, and the Pescadores, shall be restored to the Republic of China. Japan will also be expelled from all other territories which she has taken by violence and greed. The aforesaid three great powers, mindful of the enslavement of the people of Korea, are determined that in due course Korea shall become free and independent.

With these objects in view the three Allies, in harmony with those of the United Nations at war with Japan, will continue to persevere in the serious and prolonged operations necessary to procure the unconditional surrender of Japan.

16. Roosevelt–Stalin meeting during the Yalta Conference (1945)

... Marshal Stalin said that he would like to discuss the political conditions under which the USSR would enter the war against Japan. He said he had already had a conversation on this subject with Ambassador Harriman.

The President said that he had received a report of this conversation, and he felt that there would be no difficulty whatsoever in regard to the southern half of Sakhalin and the Kurile Islands going to Russia at the end of the war ...

... Marshal Stalin said that it is clear that if these conditions are not met it would be difficult for him and Molotov to explain to the Soviet people why Russia was entering a war against Japan. They understood clearly the war against Germany was one which had threatened the very existence of the Soviet Union, but they would not understand why Russia would enter a war against a country with which they had no great trouble. He said, however, if these political conditions were met, the people would understand the national interest involved and it would be very much easier to explain the decision to the Supreme Soviet. (*Foreign Relations of the United States: The Conferences of Malta and Yalta*, Volume 4, Washington D.C., 1955, pp. 765–769.)

Stalin said that he would like to know the status of the political conditions under which the USSR would enter the war against Japan. An exchange took place regarding the political questions which he, Stalin, had already discussed with Harriman in Moscow.

Roosevelt answered that the southern part of Sakhalin and the Kurile Islands would be handed over to the Soviet Union.

(*Crimean Conference Between the Leaders of the Three Allied Powers*, Moscow: Publishing House of Political Literature, 1984, page 129.)

17. Yalta Agreement (1945)

The leaders of the three great powers—the Soviet Union, the United States of America and Great Britain—have agreed that in two or three months after Germany has surrendered and the war in Europe is terminated, the Soviet Union shall enter into war against Japan on the side of the Allies on condition that:

1. The status quo in Outer Mongolia (the Mongolian People's Republic) shall be preserved.

2. The former rights of Russia violated by the treacherous attack of Japan in 1904 shall be restored, viz.:

   (a) The southern part of Sakhalin as well as the islands adjacent to it shall be returned to the Soviet Union;

   (b) The commercial port of Dairen shall be internationalized, the pre-eminent interests of the Soviet Union in this port being safeguarded, and the lease of Port Arthur as a naval base of the U.S.S.R. restored;

   (c) The Chinese-Eastern Railroad and the South Manchurian Railroad, which provide an outlet to Dairen, shall be jointly operated by the establishment of a joint Soviet-Chinese company, it being understood that the pre-eminent interests of the Soviet Union shall be safeguarded and that China shall retain full sovereignty in Manchuria;

3. The Kurile Islands shall be handed over to the Soviet Union.

It is understood that the agreement concerning Outer Mongolia and the ports and railroads referred to above will require concurrence of Generalissimo Chiang Kai-Shek. The President will take measures in order to maintain this concurrence on advice from Marshal Stalin.

The Heads of the three Great Powers have agreed that these claims of the Soviet Union shall be unquestionably fulfilled after Japan has been defeated.

For its part, the Soviet Union expresses its readiness to conclude with the National Government of China a pact of friendship and alliance between the U.S.S.R. and China in order to render assistance to China with its armed forces for the purpose of liberating China from the Japanese yoke.

I. Stalin
Franklin D. Roosevelt
Winston S. Churchill

18. Announcement from the Soviet Government on the denunciation of the Neutrality Pact (1945)

The Neutrality Pact between Japan and the Soviet Union was signed on April 13, 1941, that is before the German attack on the USSR and before the war between Japan on the one hand and Great Britain and the United States of America on the other.

The situation has drastically changed since then. Japan, ally of Germany, helps Germany in its war against the USSR. Moreover, Japan is at war with the USA and Great Britain who are allies of the Soviet Union.

Under these circumstances, the Neutrality Pact between Japan and the USSR has lost its significance, and the extension of that Pact has become impossible.

As a result, according to Article 3 of the said pact, that provides for the right of denunciation one year before the end of the five year period of validity of the Pact, the Soviet Government hereby announces to the Government of Japan its desire not to extend the Pact from April next year.

19. Announcement from the Soviet Government to the Government of Japan on the Declaration of War (1945)

After the defeat and capitulation of Hitler's Germany, Japan remains the only great power still continuing the war.

The demand of the three powers, the United States, Great Britain and China, dated July 26 of this year, demanding an unconditional capitulation of the Japanese military forces has been rejected by Japan. Thus the suggestion of the Japanese Government to the Soviet Union to mediate in the war in the Far East loses all grounds. Considering Japan's refusal to capitulate, the Allied forces approached the Soviet Government with a proposition to join in the war against Japanese aggression in order to bring the end of the war closer, to decrease the number of victims and to promote the soonest possible reestablishment of peace in the world.

Being faithful to its duty as an ally, the Soviet Government decided to accept the proposition of the Allies and joined the declaration of the Allied Powers of July 26 of this year.

The Soviet Government thinks that such a policy would be the only means to advance peace, to free people from further casualties and suffering and give the Japanese people an opportunity of avoiding the dangers and destruction which Germany had to endure after her refusal of unconditional capitulation.

As a result of everything mentioned above, the Soviet Government declares that from tomorrow, August 9, the Soviet Union considers itself to be at war with Japan.

20. *Potsdam Declaration (1945)*

1. We-The President of the United States, the President of the National Government of the Republic of China, and the Prime Minister of Great Britain, representing the hundreds of millions of our countrymen, have conferred and agree that Japan shall be given an opportunity to end this war.

2. The prodigious land, sea and air forces of the United States, the British Empire and of China, many times reinforced by their armies and air fleets from the west, are poised to strike the final blows upon Japan. This military power is sustained and inspired by the determination of all the Allied Nations to prosecute the war against Japan until she ceases to resist.

3. The result of the futile and senseless German resistance to the might of the aroused free peoples of the world stands forth in awful clarity as an example to the people of Japan. The might that now converges on Japan is immeasurably greater than that which, when applied to the resisting Nazis, necessarily laid waste to the lands, the industry and the method of life of the whole German people. The full application of our military power, backed by our resolve, all mean the inevitable and complete destruction of the Japanese armed forces and just as inevitably the utter devastation of the Japanese homeland.

4. The time has come for Japan to decide whether she will continue to be controlled by those self-willed militaristic advisers whose unintelligent calculations have brought the Empire of Japan to the threshold of annihilation, or whether she will follow the path of reason.

5. Following are our terms. We will not deviate from them. There are no alternatives. We shall brook no delay.

6. There must be eliminated for all time the authority and influence of those who have deceived and misled the people of Japan into embarking on world conquest, for we insist that a new order of peace security and justice will be impossible until irresponsible militarism is driven from the world.

7. Until such a new order is established and until there is convincing proof that Japan's war-making power is destroyed, points in Japanese territory to be designated by the Allies shall be occupied to secure the achievement of the basic objectives we are here setting forth.

8. The terms of the Cairo Declaration shall be carried out and Japanese sovereignty shall be limited to the islands of Honshu, Hokkaido, Kyushu, Shikoku and such minor islands as we determine.

9. The Japanese military forces, after being completely disarmed, shall be permitted to return to their homes with the opportunity to lead peaceful and productive lives.

10. We do not intend that the Japanese shall be enslaved as a race or destroyed as a nation, but stern justice shall be meted out to all war criminals, including those who have visited cruelties upon our prisoners. The Japanese Government shall remove all obstacles to the revival and strengthening of democratic tendencies among the Japanese people. Freedom of speech, of religion, and of thought, as well as respect for the fundamental human rights shall be established.

11. Japan shall be permitted to maintain such industries as will sustain her economy and permit the exaction of just reparations in kind, but not those [industries] which would enable her to re-arm for war. To this end, access to, as distinguished from control of, raw materials shall be permitted. Eventual Japanese participation in world trade relations shall be permitted.

12. The occupying forces of the Allies shall be withdrawn from Japan as soon as these objectives have been accomplished and there has been established in accordance with the freely expressed will of the Japanese people a peacefully inclined and responsible government.

13. We call upon the government of Japan to proclaim now the unconditional surrender of all Japanese armed forces, and to provide proper and adequate assurances of their good faith in such action. The alternative for Japan is prompt and utter destruction.

21. *Announcement from Japanese Government (1945)*

With reference to the Japanese Government's note of August 10 regarding their acceptance of the provisions of the Potsdam declaration and the reply of the Governments of the United States, Great Britain, the Soviet Union, and China sent by American Secretary of State Byrnes under the date of August 11, the Japanese Government have the honor to communicate to the Governments of the four powers as follows:

1. His Majesty the Emperor has issued an Imperial rescript regarding Japan's acceptance of the provisions of the Potsdam declaration.

2. His Majesty the Emperor is prepared to authorize and ensure the signature by his Government and the Imperial General Head-quarters of the necessary terms for carrying out the provisions of the Potsdam declaration. His Majesty is also prepared to issue his commands to all the military, naval, and air authorities of Japan and all the forces under their control wherever located to cease active operations, to surrender arms and to issue such other orders as may be required by the Supreme Commander of the Allied Forces for the execution of the above-mentioned terms.

22. *Memorandum from the Commander-in-Chief of the Allied Forces to the Japanese Imperial Government (1946)*

3. For the purpose of the directive, Japan is defined to include the four main islands of Japan (Hokkaido, Honshu, Kyushu and Shikoku) and the approximately 1,000 small adjacent islands, including the Tsushima islands and the Ryukyu (Nansei) islands north of 30° North Latitude (excluding Kuchinoshima island), and excluding (a) Utsryo (Ullung) Island, Liancourt Rocks (Take Island) and Quelpart (Saishu or Cheju Island), (b) the Ryukyu Islands south of 30° North Latitude (including Kuchinoshima Island), the Izu, Nanpo, Bonin (Ogasawara) and Volcano (Kazan or Iwo) Groups, and all outlying Pacific Islands including the Daito (Ohigashi or Oagari) island Group, and Parece Vela (Okinotori), Marcus (Minami-tori) and Ganges (Nakno-tori) Islands, and (c) the Kurile (Chishima) Islands, the Habomai (Hapomaze) Island Group (including Suisho, Yuri, Akiyuri, Shibotsu and Taraku Islands) and Shikotan Island.

6. Nothing in this directive shall be construed as an indication of Allied policy relating to the ultimate determination of the minor islands referred to in Article 8 of the Potsdam Declaration.

23. Decree of the Presidium of the USSR Supreme Soviet on the Creation of the South-Sakhalin Province in the Khabarovsk Region (1946)

Create on the territory of South Sakhalin and the Kurile Islands the South Sakhalin province (oblast) with its center in the city of Toyohara and include it in the RSFSR Khabarovsk region (krai).

Chairman of the Presidium   M. Kalinin
of the Supreme Soviet

Secretary of the Presidium   A. Gorkin
of the USSR Supreme Soviet

Moscow, the Kremlin, February 2, 1946

24. Statement of the Delegate of the USA, John Foster Dulles at the San Francisco Peace Conference in San Francisco (1951)

Chapter I ends the state of war, with consequent recognition of the full sovereignty of the Japanese people. Let us note that the sovereignty recognized is the "sovereignty of the Japanese people."

What is the territory of Japanese sovereignty? Chapter II deals with that. Japan formally ratifies the territorial provisions of the Potsdam Surrender Terms, provisions which, so far as Japan is concerned, were actually carried into effect six years ago.

The Potsdam Surrender Terms constitute the only definition of peace terms to which, and by which, Japan and the Allied Powers as a whole are bound. There have been some private understandings between some Allied Governments; but by these Japan was not bound, nor were other Allies bound. Therefore, the treaty embodies article eight of the Surrender Terms which provided that Japanese sovereignty should be limited to Honshu, Hokkaido Kyushu, Shikoku and some minor islands. The renunciation contained in article 2 of chapter II strictly and scrupulously conform to that surrender term.

Some question has been raised as to whether the geographical name "Kurile Islands" mentioned in article 2(c) includes the Habomai Islands. It is the view of the United States that it does not.

25. Statement of the First Deputy Minister of Foreign Affairs of the USSR, A.A. Gromyko, at the Conference in San Francisco (1951)

...The peace treaty with Japan should, naturally, resolve a number of territorial questions connected with the peace settlement with Japan. It is known that in this respect as well the United States, Great Britain, China and the Soviet Union undertook specific obligations. These obligations are outlined in the Cairo Declaration, in the Potsdam Declaration, and in the Yalta Agreement.

These agreements recognize the absolutely indisputable rights of China, now the Chinese People's Republic, to territories severed from it, such as Taiwan (Formosa), the Pescadores, the Paracel Islands and other Chinese territories, should be returned to the Chinese People's Republic.

The rights of the Soviet Union to the southern part of the Sakhalin Island and all the islands adjacent to it, as well as to the Kurile Islands, which are at present under the sovereignty of the Soviet Union, are equally indisputable.

Thus, while resolving the territorial questions in connection with the preparation of a peace treaty with Japan, there should not be any lack of clarity if we are to proceed from the indisputable rights of states to territories which Japan got hold of by the force of arms.

... As regards the American—British draft peace treaty with Japan in the part pertaining to territorial questions, the Delegation of the USSR considers it necessary to state that this draft grossly violates the indisputable rights of China to the return of integral parts of Chinese territory: Taiwan, the Pescadores, the Paracel and other islands severed from it by the Japanese militarists. The draft contains only a reference to the renunciation by Japan of its right to these territories but intentionally omits any mention of the further fate of these territories. In reality, however, Taiwan and the said islands have been captured by the United States of America and the United States wants to legalize these aggressive actions in the draft peace treaty under discussion. Meanwhile the fate of these territories should be absolutely clear—they must be returned to the Chinese people, the master of their land.

Similarly, by attempting to violate grossly the sovereign rights of the Soviet Union regarding Southern Sakhalin and the islands adjacent to it, as well as the Kurile Islands already under the sovereignty of the Soviet Union, the draft also confines itself to a mere mention of the renunciation by Japan of rights, title and claims to these territories and makes no mention of the historic appurtenance of these territories and the indisputable obligation on the part of Japan to recognize the sovereignty of the Soviet Union over these parts of the territory of the USSR.

We do not speak of the fact that by introducing such proposals on territorial questions the United States and Great Britain, who at an appropriate time signed the Cairo and Potsdam Declarations, as well as the Yalta Agreement, have taken the path of flagrant violation of obligations undertaken by them under these international agreements.

. . . To sum up, the following conclusions regarding the American—British draft peace treaty can be drawn:

1. The draft does not contain any guarantees against the re-establishment of Japanese militarism, the transformation of Japan into an aggressive state. The draft does not contain any guarantees ensuring the security of countries which have suffered from aggression on the part of militarist Japan. The draft creates conditions for the re-establishment of Japanese militarism, creates a danger of a new Japanese aggression.

2. The draft treaty actually does not provide for the withdrawal of foreign occupation forces. On the contrary, it ensures the presence of foreign armed forces on the territory of Japan and the maintenance of foreign military bases in Japan even after the signing of a peace treaty. Under the pretext of self-defense of Japan, the draft provides for the participation of Japan in an aggressive military alliance with the United States.

3. The draft treaty not only fails to provide for obligations that Japan should not join any coalitions directed against any of the states which participated in the war against militarist Japan, but on the contrary is clearing the path for Japan's participation in aggressive blocs in the Far East created under the aegis of the United States.

4. The draft treaty does not contain any provisions on the democratization of Japan, on the ensurance of democratic rights to the Japanese people, which creates a direct threat of the rebirth in Japan of the prewar Fascist order.

5. The draft treaty is flagrantly violating the legitimate rights of the Chinese people to the integral part of China–Taiwan (Formosa), the Pescadores and the Paracel Islands and other territories severed from China as a result of Japanese aggression.

6. The draft treaty is in contradiction to the obligations undertaken by the United States and Great Britain under the Yalta Agreement regarding the return of Sakhalin and the transfer of the Kurile Islands to the Soviet Union.

7. The numerous economic clauses are designed to ensure for foreign, in the first place American, monopolies the privileges which

they have obtained during the period of occupation, Japanese economy is being placed in a slavery-like dependence from these foreign monopolies.

8. The draft actually ignores the legitimate claims of states that have suffered from Japanese occupation regarding the redemption by Japan for the damage they have suffered. At the same time, providing for the redemption of losses direct by the labor of the Japanese population it imposes on Japan a slavery-like form of reparations.

9. The American–British draft is a not a treaty of peace but a treaty for the preparation of a new war in the Far East.

26. Statement of the Prime Minister of Japan, S. Yoshida at the Conference in San Francisco (1951)

The peace treaty before the Conference contains no punitive or retaliatory clauses; nor does it impose upon Japan any permanent restrictions or disabilities. It will restore the Japanese people to full sovereignty, equality, and freedom, and reinstate us as a free and equal member in the community of nations. It is not a treaty of vengeance, but an instrument of reconciliation. The Japanese Delegation gladly accepts this fair and generous treaty.

On the other hand, during these past few days in this very conference hall criticisms and complaints have been voiced by some delegations against this treaty. It is impossible that anyone can be completely satisfied with a multilateral peace settlement of this kind. Even we Japanese, who are happy to accept the treaty, find in it certain points which cause us pain and anxiety. I speak of this with diffidence, bearing in mind the treaty's fairness and magnanimity unparalleled in history and the position of Japan. But I would be remiss in my obligation to my own people if I failed to call your attention to these points.

In the first place, there is the matter of territorial disposition.

. . . With respect to the Kuriles and South Sakhalin, I cannot yield to the claim of the Soviet Delegate that Japan had grabbed them by aggression.

At the time of the opening of Japan, her ownership of two islands of Etoroff and Kunashiri of the South Kuriles was not questioned at all by the Czarist government. But the North Kuriles north of Uruppu and the southern half of Sakhalin were areas open to both Japanese and Russian settlers. On May 7, 1875 the Japanese and Russian Governments effected through peaceful negotiations an arrangement under which South Sakhalin was made Russian territory, and the North Kuriles were in exchange made Japanese territory. But really, under the name of "exchange" Japan simply ceded South Sakhalin to Russia in order to settle the territorial dispute. It was under the Treaty of Portsmouth of 1905 concluded through the intermediary of President Theodore Roosevelt of the United States that South Sakhalin became also Japanese territory.

Both Sakhalin and the North and South Kuriles were taken unilaterally by Russia as of September 20, 1945, shortly after Japan's surrender.

Even the islands of Habomai and Shikotan, constituting part of Hokkaido, one of Japan's four main islands, are still being occupied by Soviet forces simply because they happened to be garrisoned by Japanese troops at the time when the war ended.

27. Article 2 and Article 25 of the San Francisco Peace Treaty (1951)

ARTICLE 2

(a) Japan, recognizing the independence of Korea, renounces all right, title and claim to Korea, including the islands of Quelpart, Port Hamilton and Dagelet.

(b) Japan renounces all right, title and claim to Formosa and the Pescadores.

(c) Japan renounces all right, title and claim to the Kurile Islands, and to that portion of Sakhalin and the islands adjacent to it over which Japan acquired sovereignty as a consequence of the Treaty of Portsmouth of September 5, 1905.

(d) Japan renounces all right, title and claim in connection with the League of Nations Mandate System, and accepts the action of the United Nations Security Council of April 2, 1947 extending the trusteeship system to the Pacific Islands formerly under mandate to Japan.

(e) Japan renounces all claim to any right or title to or interest in connection with any part of the Antarctic area, whether deriving from the activities of Japanese nationals or otherwise.

(f) Japan renounces all right, title and claim to the Spratly Islands and to the Paracel Islands.

ARTICLE 25

For the purposes of the present Treaty the Allied Powers shall be the States at war with Japan, or any State which previously formed a part of the territory of a State named in Article 23 provided that in each case the State concerned has signed and ratified the Treaty. Subject to the provisions of Article 21, the present Treaty shall not confer any rights, titles or benefits on any State which is not an Allied Power as herein defined; nor shall any right title or interest of Japan be deemed to be diminished or prejudiced by any provision of the Treaty in favor of a State which is not an Allied Power as so defined.

28. Letter from the Plenipotentiary Representative of the Japanese Government, S. Matsumoto, to the USSR First Deputy of Foreign Affairs, A.A. Gromyko (1956)

Excellency,

I have the honor to refer to the letter of Prime Minister Hatoyama of September 11, 1956 and the reply of the Chairman of the Council of Ministers of the USSR of September 13, 1956, and to announce the following:

The Government of Japan is ready to enter into negotiations in Moscow on the normalization of Japanese–Soviet relations without the conclusion of a peace treaty at this time, as it was noted in the letter of Prime Minister Hatoyama as referred to above. At the same time the Japanese Government thinks that after the reestablishment of diplomatic relations as a result of these negotiations, it is quite desirable that Japanese–Soviet relations develop even further on the basis of a formal peace treaty, which would include the territorial issue.

With regard to this, the Japanese Government assumes that negotiations on the conclusion of a peace treaty including the territorial issue will continue after the reestablishment of normal diplomatic relations between the two countries.

In entering into negotiations according to the letter of Prime Minister Hatoyama, I should be grateful if the Soviet Government would also confirm beforehand that it shares the same intention.

I avail myself of this opportunity to extend to Your Excellency the assurance of my highest consideration.

S. Matsumoto
Plenipotentiary Representative of
the Japanese Government

His Excellency
Mr. A. A. Gromyko
First Deputy Minister of Foreign Affairs of
the Union of Soviet Socialist Republics

29. Letter from the USSR First Deputy Minister of Foreign Affairs, A.A. Gromyko, to the Plenipotentiary Representative of the Government of Japan, S. Matsumoto (1956)

Excellency,

I have the honor to acknowledge the receipt of Your Excellency's letter of September 29, 1956, which reads as follows:

[Japanese note Item 28 above]

I have further the honor to inform you on behalf of the Government of the Union of Soviet Socialist Republics that the Soviet Government accepts the view of the Japanese Government referred to above and announces its agreement to continue negotiations on the conclusion of a peace treaty, which would also include the territorial issue, after the reestablishment of normal diplomatic relations.

I avail myself of this opportunity to extend to Your Excellency the assurance of my highest consideration.

A.A. Gromyko
First Deputy Minister of Foreign Affairs of
the Union of Soviet Socialist Republics

His Excellency
Mr. S. Matsumoto
Plenipotentiary Representative of
the Japanese Government

30. Paragraph 9 of the Joint Declaration of Japan and the USSR (1956)

> 9. Japan and the Union of Soviet Socialist Republics and Japan agree to continue, after the restoration of normal diplomatic relations between the Union of Soviet Socialist Republics and Japan, negotiations for the conclusion of a peace treaty.
>
> The Union of Soviet Socialist Republics, desiring to meet the wishes of Japan and taking into consideration the interests of Japan, agrees to hand over to Japan the Habomai Islands and the island of Shikotan. However, the actual handing over of these islands to Japan shall take place after the conclusion of a peace treaty between Japan and the Union of Soviet Socialist Republics.

(Signed on October 19, 1956 in Moscow. Ratified on December 7, 1956. The exchange of instruments of ratification took place on December 12, 1956, in Tokyo.)

31. Memorandum from the Soviet Government to the Government of Japan (1960)

But the Soviet Union certainly cannot ignore such a step as Japan's conclusion of a new military treaty which undermines the basis for peace in the Far East and creates obstacles to the development of Soviet-Japanese relations. A new situation has formed in relation to the fact that this treaty actually deprives Japan of independence and that foreign troops stationed in Japan as a result of Japan's surrender remain on Japanese territory. This situation makes it impossible for the Soviet Government to fulfill its promises to return the islands of Habomai and Shikotan to Japan.

It is because the Soviet Government met Japan's wishes and took into consideration the interests of Japan and the peace-loving intentions expressed by the Japanese Government during the Soviet-Japanese negotiations that it agreed to hand over such islands to Japan after the signing of a peace treaty.

But since the new military treaty signed by the Japanese Government is directed against the Soviet Union and the People's Republic of China, the Soviet Government cannot contribute to extending the territory available to foreign troops by handing over such islands to Japan.

Thus, the Soviet Government finds it necessary to declare that the islands of Habomai and Shikotan will be handed over to Japan, as was stated in the Soviet-Japanese Joint Declaration of October 19, 1956, only if all foreign troops are withdrawn from Japan and a Soviet-Japanese peace treaty is signed.

32. Memorandum from the Japanese Government to the Soviet Government (1960)

The Government of Japan considers it necessary to lay out the position of Japan with regard to the memorandum which was handed to Japanese Ambassador to the USSR Kadowaki by USSR Minister of Foreign Affairs Gromyko on January 27 and which refers to the Treaty of Mutual Cooperation and Security between Japan and the United States of America which was been recently signed.

... It is extremely incomprehensible that in its latest memorandum, the Soviet Government is connecting the issue of the revised Japan-US Security Treaty with the issue of handing over the islands of Habomai and Shikotan. As regards the islands of Habomai and Shikotan, the Joint Declaration by

Japan and the Soviet Union states the following clearly: "The Union of Soviet Socialist Republics, desiring to meet the wishes of Japan and taking into consideration the interests of Japan, agrees to hand over to Japan the Habomai Islands and the island of Shikotan. However, the actual handing over of these islands to Japan shall take place after the conclusion of a peace treaty between Japan and the Union of Soviet Socialist Republics."

This Joint Declaration is an international agreement regulating the foundations of the relationship between Japan and the Soviet Union. It is an official document which has been ratified by the highest organs of both countries. It is needless to say that the contents of this solemn international undertaking cannot be changed unilaterally. Moreover, since the current Japan-U.S. Security Treaty which is valid indefinitely already existed and foreign troops were present in Japan when the Joint Declaration by Japan and the Soviet Union was signed, it must be said that the Declaration was signed on the basis of these facts. Consequently, there is no reason that the agreements in the Joint Declaration should be affected in any way.

The Government of Japan cannot approve of the Soviet attempt to attach new conditions for the provisions of the Joint Declaration on the territorial issue and thereby to change the contents of the Declaration. Our country will keep insisting on the reversion not only of the islands of Habomai and Shikotan but also of the other islands which are inherent parts of Japanese territory.

33. Japanese–Soviet Joint Communiqué (1973)

1. Recognizing that the settlement of unresolved problems left over from WWII and conclusion of a peace treaty would contribute to establishment of truly god-neighborly and friendly relations between the two countries, both sides held negotiations on issues pertaining to the contents of a peace treaty. Both sides agreed to continue negotiations on the conclusion of a peace treaty between the two countries at an appropriate time in 1974.

34. Japanese–Soviet Joint Communiqué (1991)

1. President M.S. Gorbachev of the Union of Soviet Socialist Republics paid an Official Visit to Japan from April 16 through April 19, 1991, at the invitation of the Government of Japan. President M.S. Gorbachev of the Union of Soviet Socialist Republics was accompanied by Minister of Foreign Affairs A.A. Bessmertnykh of the Union of Soviet Socialist Republics and other government officials.

2. President M.S. Gorbachev of the Union of Soviet Socialist Republics and Mrs. Gorbachev had an audience with Their Imperial Highnesses The Emperor and The Empress of Japan in the Imperial Palace on April 16.

3. President M.S. Gorbachev of the Union of Soviet Socialist Republics had frank and constructive discussions with Prime Minister Toshiki Kaifu of Japan on issues between Japan and the Union of Soviet Socialist Republics, including the negotiations for the conclusion of a peace treaty, and on major international issues of mutual interest. President M.S. Gorbachev of the Union of Soviet Socialist Republics invited Prime Minister Toshiki Kaifu of Japan to pay an Official visit to the Union of Soviet Socialist Republics. This invitation was gratefully accepted. The details of the visit are to be arranged through diplomatic channels.

4. Prime Minister Toshiki Kaifu of Japan and President M.S. Gorbachev of the Union of Soviet Socialist Republics held in-depth and thorough negotiations on a whole range of issues relating to the preparation and conclusion of a peace treaty between Japan and the Union of Soviet Socialist Republics, including the issue of territorial demarcation, taking into consideration the positions of both sides on the attribution of the islands of Habomai, Shikotan, Kunashiri, and Etorofu.

The joint work done previously—particularly the negotiations at the highest level—has made it possible to confirm a series of conceptual understandings: that the peace treaty should be the document marking the final resolution of war-related issues, including the territorial, that it should pave the way for long-term Japan-USSR relations on the basis of friendship, and that it should not infringe upon either side's security.

The Soviet side proposed that measures be taken in the near future to expand exchanges between residents of Japan and residents of the aforementioned islands, to establish a simplified visa-free framework for visits by Japanese to these islands, to initiate joint, mutually beneficial economic activities in that region, and to reduce the Soviet military forces stationed on these islands. The Japanese side stated its intention to consult on these questions in the future.

As well as emphasizing the primary importance of accelerating work to conclude the preparations for a peace treaty, the Prime Minister and the President expressed their firm resolve to make constructive and vigorous efforts to this end taking advantage of all positive elements that have been built up in bilateral negotiations in the years since Japan and the Union of Soviet Socialist Republics jointly proclaimed an end to the state of war and the restoration of diplomatic relations in 1956.

At the same time, they recognized that the development of constructive cooperation between Japan and the Union of Soviet Socialist Republics, including the adjacent Russian Soviet Federal Socialist Republic, is advisable in an atmosphere of good-neighborliness, mutual benefit, and trust. Cooperation should take place in trade-economic, scientific-technological, and political spheres as well as in social, cultural, educational, tourism, and sports realms through free and wide-ranging exchanges between the citizens of the two countries.

35. Letter from the President of the Russian Federation, B. N. Yeltsin, to the Russian People (1991)

Dear compatriots!

Having received your appeal in which you express your concern about the destiny of the Southern Kuriles, I consider it my duty to clarify the position of the Government of the Russian Federation.

I fully agree with you in that the current generation of Russians is not responsible for the political "adventurism" of the former leaders of our country. At the same time an obvious obligation of the new Russian leadership is to look for way of resolving problems which we inherited from the policies of previous eras, and which stand in the way of developing normal relations between Russia and the international community today. In the end, the future of a new democratic Russia as a member of the international community, and its international authority depends on how fast we manage to overcome the difficult heritage of the past, accept the norms of the international community, and thus make legality, justice and strict adherence to the principles of international law the criteria of it policy.

One of the problems we will have to resolve in the near future is reaching a final post-War settlement in our relations with Japan. I am convinced that from the Russian point of view, it would be unforgivable to continue to endure a situation where relations with Japan remain practically frozen because of the absence of a peace treaty between the two countries.

It is well-known that the main obstacle to the conclusion of this treaty is the issue of the demarcation of borders between Russia and Japan. This problem has a long history, and it has lately attracted broad attention and provoked diverse feelings among the citizens of Russia. In approaching this issue, we will be guided by the principles of justice and humanism, and we will firmly defend the interests and dignity of Russians including those of the inhabitants of the Southern Kuriles. I assure you that no inhabitant of the Southern Kuriles will see their future ruined. Their socio-economic and property interests will be fully provided for taking into account the emerging historical realities.

The initial principle for any agreement with Japan will be to ensure the well-being of our one and indivisible Fatherland. Being the first democratically elected President of Russia history, I assure you that the Russian pubic will be fully informed of the intentions and plans of its government in a timely manner.

I sincerely hope for your understanding and support.

B. Yeltsin

Preface
to the New Edition of the
Joint Compendium of Documents
on the History of Territorial Issue
between Japan and Russia

The formation of the Russian Federation and its emergence on the international stage as a nation retaining continuity with the Soviet Union has enabled Japan-Russia relations to achieve new progress. The policy to advance democratic and market economy reforms was pursued by leaders of Russia, and Japan's support for such policy in its bilateral relations with Russia has resulted in the erasure of political competition, ideological and military confrontation, and in the engenderment of a completely different set of conditions in which both nations stand upon the common platform of universal values of democratic society. Such qualitatively new conditions have opened up far-reaching possibilities of radically improving and activating all areas of Japan-Russia relations.

One of the most important tasks in such a context is overcoming past legacies of the bilateral relations, namely the conclusion of a peace treaty through the solution of the issue of where the islands of Etorofu, Kunashiri, Shikotan and Habomai belong, which means the accomplishment of the complete normalization of Japan-Russia relations in the post-war period.

After 1993, a series of important documents concerning this issue was newly adopted by both countries.

On 13 October 1993, Prime Minister Morihiro Hosokawa of Japan and President Boris N. Yeltsin of the Russian Federation signed the Tokyo Declaration on Japan-Russia Relations. This was the first comprehensive document signed between Japan and the Russian Federation establishing the principal direction of progress for bilateral relations. The Tokyo Declaration stipulates the necessity for the early conclusion of a peace treaty through the solution of the issue of where the aforementioned islands belong, on the basis of historical and legal facts and based on the documents produced subject to the consent between both countries as well as on the principles of law and justice. Consequently, the Tokyo Declaration is especially important.

The Tokyo Declaration forms a cornerstone of the Japan-Russia relations concerning the conclusion of a peace treaty.

At the Krasnoyarsk Informal summit Meeting in 1997, Prime Minister Ryutaro Hashimoto of Japan and President Boris N. Yeltsin of the Russian Federation agreed to make all the efforts to conclude a peace treaty by 2000 based on the Tokyo Declaration.

The positive momentum brought about by the Krasnoyarsk Summit Meeting made an extremely significant contribution to the Japan-Russia relations first and foremost in terms of activating dialogue concerning the issue of a peace treaty.

The Japanese-Russian Joint Committee on the Conclusion of a Peace Treaty was established, which is chaired by the Foreign Ministers of both countries.

A proposal for the solution of the above-mentioned issue was presented by Japan at the talks between Prime Minister Ryutaro Hashimoto of Japan and President Boris N. Yeltsin of the Russian Federation in Kawana in April 1998. Russia's response to this was conveyed to Prime Minister Keizo Obuchi of Japan at the summit meeting in Moscow in November 1998. This contributed to deepening mutual understanding regarding each other's positions, and to facilitating the continuation of the pursuit of a mutually acceptable method of resolving the above-mentioned issue.

Since the Krasnoyarsk Summit Meeting, bilateral exchange and contact in the region of the islands have been rapidly boosted, forming a crucially positive element to the Japan-Russia relations and have substantially improved the atmosphere surrounding the peace treaty negotiations.

In the early half of the 1990s, mutual visits without visas enabling Japanese nationals to visit the islands and Russian residents in the islands to visit Japan were initiated based on the exchange of letters between the Minister for Foreign Affairs of Japan and the Minister for Foreign Affairs of the Russian Federation on 14 October 1991. Moreover, humanitarian assistance to island residents has been provided by the Government of Japan, especially after the earthquake in 1994.

On 21 February 1998, the Agreement between the Government of Japan and the Government of the Russia Federation on some matters of cooperation in the field of fishing operations for marine living resources was signed, ensuring that Japanese fishermen are able to operate in the waters around the islands.

On 18 September 1998, the exchange of Notes Verbale took place between the Embassy of Japan in the Russian Federation and the Ministry of Foreign Affairs of the Russian Federation regarding visits without visas aimed at providing emergency humanitarian assistance.

The Moscow Declaration on Establishing a Creative Partnership between Japan and the Russian Federation was signed on the Russian Federation on 13 November 1998. The Declaration, for the first time in the history of the Japan-Russia bilateral relations, pointed out the task of building a partnership between the two countries. In accordance with the Declaration, for the purpose of activating the peace treaty negotiations, two sub-committees were established within the framework of the Japanese-Russian Joint Committee on the Conclusion of a Peace Treaty, namely the sub-committee on border demarcation and the sub-committee on joint economic activities in islands.

Furthermore, in order to implement the relevant provision of the Declaration, on 2 September 1999, both countries set up a framework, streamlined to the maximum extent possible, for visits to the islands of former Japanese residents and members of their families.

In the talks between Prime Minister Yoshiro Mori of Japan and Vladimir V. Putin of the Russian Federation in St. Petersburg on 29 April 2000, a common understanding was confirmed regarding the strategic importance of the Japan-Russia relations in the modern world, and the main direction for the development of the relations in the modern world, and the main direction for the development of the relations in the future was set up, namely strategic coordination in international issues, cooperation in the areas of trade and economy as well as the conclusion of a peace treaty.

From 3 to 5 September 2000, President Vladimir V. Putin of the Russian Federation made an official visit to Japan. As an outcome of the visit, both countries were able to advance notably the bilateral relationship towards a genuine partnership.

As a result of this summit meeting, Prime Minister Yoshiro Mori of Japan and President Vladimir V. Putin of the Russian Federation signed a statement on the issue of a peace treaty, conforming to the direction of improving the efficiency of the negotiating process. Improving the efficiency of the negotiating process mentioned above means drawing up new measures to accelerate the work carried out by the Japanese-Russian Joint Committee on the Conclusion of a Peace Treaty and the sub-committee on border demarcation, preparing a new edition of the Joint Compendium of Documents on the History of Territorial Issue between Japan and Russia, and striving to explain to the citizens of both countries the importance of concluding a peace treaty.

In accordance with the decision made by Prime Minister Yoshiro Mori of Japan and President Vladimir V. Putin of the Russian Federation, readers are provided with a new edition of the Joint Compendium of Documents on the History of Territorial Issue between both countries produced by the Ministry of Foreign Affairs of Japan and the Ministry of Foreign Affairs of the Russian Federation. This reference material was published as an expanded edition of "the Joint Compendium of Documents on the History of Territorial Issue between Japan and Russia" in September 1992. This expand edition includes documents produced subsequent to 1993.

We hope that reference to this material will contribute to forming an objective understanding with regard to the issues touched upon in the document.

16 January 2001
Ministry of Foreign Affairs of Japan
Ministry of Foreign Affairs of the Russian Federation

36. TOKYO DECLARATION
on Japan-Russia Relations (October 1993)

The Prime Minister of Japan and the President of the Russian Federation,

Based upon the recognition that, with the end of the Cold War, the world is moving away from the structure of confrontation towards cooperation which will open new vistas for advances in international cooperation on both global and regional levels as well as in bilateral relations between different countries, and that this is creating favorable conditions for the full normalization of the Japan-Russia bilateral relations,

Declaring that Japan and the Russian Federation share the universal values of freedom, democracy, the rule of law and the respect for fundamental human rights,

Recalling that the promotion of market economy and free trade contributes to the prosperity of the economies of both countries and to the sound development of the global economy,

Believing firmly that the success of the reforms under way in the Russian Federation is of decisive importance for building a new world political and economic order,

Affirming the importance of building the relations between the two countries in accordance with the objectives and principles of the United Nations Charter,

Determined that Japan and the Russian Federation should work together on the basis of the spirit of international cooperation, overcoming the legacy of totalitarianism, to build a new international order and to normalize their bilateral relations fully,

Declare the following:

1. The Prime Minister of Japan and the President of the Russian Federation share the recognition that the democratic and economic reforms under way in the Russian Federation are of tremendous significance not only for the people of the Russian Federation but also for the entire world. They are also of the view that the Russian Federation's successful transition to a true market economy and its smooth integration into the democratic international community are indispensable factors for increasing stability in the world and making the process of forming a new international order irreversible.

   In this regard, the Prime Minister of Japan conveyed to the President of the Russian Federation the following message from the leaders of the G7 countries and the representatives of the European Community:

   "We regret that the armed clash in Moscow which was provoked by the supporters of the former parliament resulted in many victims. We nevertheless welcome the fact that the situation has ended and law and order is being restored including respect of human rights.

   We reconfirm that our support remains unchanged for democratic reform and economic reform pursued by President Yeltsin. We strongly hope that a truly democratic society which reflects the will of the people will be born through free and fair election of the new parliament with broad participation of the people and that reform will be further promoted."

2. The Prime Minister of Japan and the President of the Russian Federation, sharing the recognition that the difficult legacies of the past in the relations between the two countries must be overcome, have undertaken serious negotiations on the issue of where the islands of Etorofu, Kunashiri, Shikotan and Habomai belong. Both sides agree that negotiations towards an early conclusion of a peace treaty through the solution of this issue on the basis of historical and legal facts and based on the documents produced with the two countries' agreement as well as on the principles of law and justice should continue, and that the relations between the two countries should thus be fully normalized. In this regard, the Government of Japan and the Government of the Russian Federation confirm that the Russian Federation is the State retaining continuing identity with the Soviet Union and that all treaties and other international agreements between Japan and the Soviet Union continue to be applied between Japan and the Russian Federation.

The Government of Japan and the Government of the Russian Federation recall that a constructive dialogue has taken place in the Peace Treaty Working Group between the two countries, and that one of the fruits thereof has been the joint publication in September 1992 of the Joint Compendium of Documents on the History of Territorial Issue between Japan and Russia.

The Government of Japan and the Government of the Russian Federation agree to take a series of measures aimed at increased mutual understanding, including further facilitation of mutual visits between the current residents of the aforementioned islands and the residents of Japan that have been conducted within the framework agreed upon between the two countries.

3. The Prime Minister of Japan and the President of the Russian Federation, convinced that expanded political dialogue is a beneficial and effective means to promote Japan-Russia relations, agree to continue, deepen, and develop political dialogue through regular mutual visits at the levels of the Heads of State and Government, the Ministers and the Vice-Ministers for Foreign Affairs.

4. The Prime Minister of Japan and the President of the Russian Federation, based on the common principles of freedom and openness, share the recognition on the potential for remarkable development which the Asia-Pacific region may demonstrate in the world in the 21st century. Both sides confirm the significance of the Russian Federation's becoming an active and constructive partner in the region by implementing the principles of law and justice to further contribute to the development of political and economic relations among the countries in this region. They also share the recognition that the full normalization of the relations between Japan and the Russian Federation, both of which play important roles in the Asia-Pacific region, is of essential importance, in the context of making this region a region of peace and stability as well as a place for developing economic cooperation based on free trading system open to all countries and regions, including the Russian Federation.

The Prime Minister of Japan and the President of the Russian Federation, based on their shared recognition of the need for promoting peace and stability in the Asia-Pacific region, confirm the importance of dialogue between the authorities of their two governments on a wide range of issues including security, and agree to further activate such exchanges.

5. The Prime Minister of Japan and the President of the Russian Federation welcome the progress thus far achieved in the area of arms control and disarmament, confirm the need for faithful implementation thereof, and share the recognition that it is important to further promote such a process and to make it irreversible.

Both sides share the recognition that the dismantling of nuclear weapons and the ensuing storage, control and disposal of fissile materials have an important bearing on the security of the entire world, and confirm their intention to cooperate in these areas. Furthermore, both sides confirm that the ocean dumping of radioactive wastes raises a grave concern on a global scale, particularly due to its effects on the environment of the neighboring countries, and agree to consult closely through the Japan-Russia Joint Working Group to consider this problem further.

Both sides welcome the signing of the Convention on the Prohibition of Chemical Weapons in Paris in January 1993, and express their expectation for as many countries as possible joining the Convention and thereby contributing to peace and stability of the world. Both sides also agree to cooperate closely for effectively securing non-proliferation of weapons of mass destruction, their delivery systems, related material and components, and technologies and knowledge, as well as for promoting increased transparency in transfers of conventional weapons.

6. The Prime Minister of Japan and the President of the Russian Federation note the ongoing deliberations at the United Nations on such issues as how the United Nations should function and be structured, so that it can play a central role in maintaining and creating a new world peace while adapting itself to the changing international circumstances, and agree to engage in common efforts to enhance the authority of the United Nations by further activating the contributions by both countries to the United Nations' efforts for solving global and regional problems.

In Tokyo, 13 October 1993

Prime Minister of Japan   Morihiro Hosokawa

President of the Russian Federation   B. N. Yeltsin

37. AGREEMENT
between the Government of Japan
and the Government of the Russian Federation
on some matters of cooperation
in the field of fishing operations for marine living resources
(February 1998)

The Government of Japan and the Government of the Russian Federation (hereinafter referred to as "the Parties"),

Hoping to promote the development and enhancement of good neighborliness between Japan and the Russian Federation,

Aiming to further develop and enhance the traditional and mutually beneficial relations between both countries in the field of fisheries, including relations based on the Agreement on Mutual Relations in the Field of Fisheries off the coast of Both Countries between the Government of Japan and the Government of the Union of Soviet Socialist Republics, signed at Tokyo on 7 December 1984, and the Agreement between the Government of Japan and the Government of the Union of Soviet Socialist Republics Concerning Cooperation in the Field of Fisheries, signed in Moscow on 12 May 1985,

Based on the principles stipulated in the Tokyo Declaration on Japan-Russia Relations signed on 13 October 1993, and the Declaration on the Future Prospects of Relations in the Fields of Trade and Economy as well as Science and Technology between Japan and the Russian Federation,

Attaching importance to further promotion of cooperation for the conservation, rational utilization and reproduction of living resources (including cooperation for the protection of the marine environment),

Hoping to establish the patterns of the operations of a temporary nature carried out on a commercial basis by Japanese fishing vessels in the waters stipulated in this Agreement, and the conservation, rational utilization and reproduction of living resources in the said waters,

Have agreed as follows:

ARTICLE I

In accordance with the provisions of this Agreement, the Parties shall cooperate so that operations for living resources carried out by Japanese fishing vessels will be conducted in waters delineated by the geodetic connecting the points of latitude and longitude in the sequence, indicated in the annexed table, around the islands of Etorofu, Kunashiri, Shikotan and Habomai, and shall also cooperate for the conservation, rational utilization and reproduction of living resources in the said waters.

ARTICLE 2

1. Operations for living resources carried out by Japanese fishing vessels in the waters stipulated in Article 1 above shall be implemented in accordance with a memorandum of understanding agreed each year between organizations from respective countries and confirmed through mutual notification by the Parties via the diplomatic channels.

2. Through the exchange of official diplomatic documents, the Parties shall mutually notify their recognition of arrangements between organizations from respective countries referred to in paragraph 1 above as the memorandum of understanding referred to in Paragraph 1 above.

3. The Government of Japan, in conjunction with fishing operations, preservation and reproduction of living resources, shall take measures within the scope of laws and regulations of Japan to ensure that payment is made in accordance with this Agreement and the memorandum of understanding referred to in paragraph 1 above by the Japanese organizations referred to in paragraph 1 above.

ARTICLE 3

Where a mutual interest exists, the Parties shall endeavor to develop cooperation in the field of fisheries in general between the two countries, including exchange of information concerning trends in the market price of fishing products, and fishing product processing.

The Parties, where appropriate, shall encourage the development of mutual cooperation between organizations and corporations of both countries in the field of fisheries within the scope of their respective relevant laws and regulations of the respective countries.

ARTICLE 4

The Parties shall hold consultations, at a time to be mutually agreed upon, in principle, once a year, on issues related to the implementation of this Agreement.

ARTICLE 5

The Parties, where appropriate, shall promote contact between their relevant organizations, including the Fisheries Agency of the Ministry of Agriculture, Forestry and Fisheries of Japan, the Maritime Safety Agency of the Ministry of Transport of Japan, the Ministry of Agriculture and Food of the Russian Federation, and the National Border Guard Agency of the Russian Federation.

ARTICLE 6

Nothing in this Agreement, nor any activities conducted in accordance with this Agreement, nor any measures taken to implement this Agreement nor any activities or measures related there to shall be deemed as to prejudice the positions or views of any Party with respect to any issues of their mutual relations.

ARTICLE 7

1. This Agreement shall enter into force on the date on which the Parties mutually notify via the diplomatic channels that they have completed their respective necessary domestic legal procedures for the Agreement's entry into force, and shall remain in force for a period of three years unless either Party notifies in writing to the other Party at least six months before the date on which it intends to terminate this Agreement.

2. This Agreement shall be automatically extended for further year unless, after a period of three years, from the date of its entry into force, either Party notifies in writing to the other Party of its intention to terminate this Agreement at least six months before the expiration of this Agreement.

   Done in duplicate in the Japanese and Russian languages, both equally authentic, 21 February 1998 in Moscow.

For the Government of Japan
For the Government of the Russian Federation

38. NOTE VERBALE
presented by the Embassy of Japan in the Russian Federation
regarding visits without visas to the islands of
Etorofu, Kunashiri, Shikotan and Habomai aimed at
providing emergency humanitarian assistance
(18 September 1998)

The Embassy of Japan in the Russian Federation presents its compliments to the Ministry of Foreign Affairs of the Russian Federation and has the honor to refer to the Tokyo Declaration on Japan-Russia Relations of 13 October 1993, which states the agreement between the Government of Japan and the Government of the Russian Federation to take a series of measures aimed at increasing mutual understanding, including further facilitating mutual visits between Japanese citizens and the residents of the islands of Etorofu, Kunashiri, Shikotan and Habomai (hereafter referred to as "the Islands"); the exchange of letters of 14 October 1991 between the Minister for Foreign Affairs of Japan and the Minister for Foreign Affairs of the Union of Soviet Socialist Republics regarding visits to the Islands by Japanese citizens and visits to regions of Japan by the residents of the Islands; and the Note Verbale of 20 April 1993 exchanged between the Embassy of Japan in the Russian Federation and the Ministry of Foreign Affairs of the Russian Federation regarding partial revision and addition of procedures for the above-mentioned visits; and to inform that visits to the Islands by Japanese citizens and visits to regions of Japan by the residents of the Islands with the aim of implementing emergency humanitarian assistance including that in emergency situations such as occurrences of threats to the lives and health of people, and technical cooperation related to such assistance, will be implemented by the procedures provided in the above-mentioned exchange of letters and the Note Verbale.

Visits and cooperation carried out in accordance with these procedures must not be deemed as to prejudice the legal positions of either side regarding any issue pertaining to such visits and cooperation.

The Embassy avails itself of this opportunity to renew to the Ministry of Foreign Affairs of the Russian Federation the assurances of its highest consideration.

39. MOSCOW DECLARATION
on Establishing a Creative Partnership
between Japan and the Russian Federation
(November 1998)

The Prime Minister of Japan and the President of the Russian Federation,

Sharing the recognition that, on the eve of the twenty-first century, as the democratization process advances and new forms of relations between States develop in the international community against a background of the realities of the present-day world, the roles and responsibilities of Japan and the Russian Federation are increasing and closer cooperation between the two countries is needed,

Convinced that Japan and the Russian Federation, which are now jointly sharing the universal values of freedom, democracy, the rule of law and the respect for fundamental human rights, should build a creative partnership consistent with their strategic and geopolitical interests by, inter alia, fully normalizing their bilateral relations based on the Tokyo Declaration of 13 October 1993, and on this Declaration,

Appreciating the development of relations between Japan and the Russian Federation based on the Tokyo Declaration, which formed the foundation for the construction of this creative partnership, and determined to further develop the bilateral relationship in all areas,

Confirming their common recognition that their bilateral relations are currently developing rapidly as a result of the constructive dialogue between the leaders of the two countries, at the informal summit meetings in Krasnoyarsk and Kawana and on other occasions, and that the time is approaching to overcome the difficult legacies of the past mentioned in the Tokyo Declaration,

Pointing out the need to realize the potential for economic cooperation between the two countries in a broader and more effective manner, and that this is possible in many areas through continued economic reform in the Russian Federation and support from Japan,

Recognizing that a substantive improvement in Japanese/Russian relations will have a favorable influence on the international situation, particularly on the situation in the Asia-Pacific region, whose political and economic significance is continuously growing,

Affirming the importance of activating their common efforts to strengthen international peace and security based on the purposes and principles of the Charter of the United Nations and to solve global issues which require an immediate response,

Declare the following:

I. BILATERAL RELATIONS

1. The Prime Minister of Japan and the President of the Russian Federation State that the relations between their countries occupy an important place in their respective foreign policies. The Prime Minister of Japan and the President of the Russian Federation recognize that the most important task for their countries is to build a long-term creative partnership founded on the principles of trust, mutual benefit, a long-term perspective and close economic cooperation.

   Under this partnership, both leaders are determined not only to solve various bilateral issues jointly but to contribute to the peace and stability of the Asia-Pacific region and the international community through cooperation in international forums, to cooperate more actively for the solution of various global issues and to usher the bilateral relationship into an era of "agreement" by strengthening "trust."

2. The Prime Minister of Japan and the President of the Russian Federation, taking into consideration the fact that the Russian side communicated its reply to the proposal regarding a solution to the issue of the attribution of the islands of Etorofu, Kunashiri, Shikotan and Habomai made by the Japanese side at the Summit Meeting in Kawana held in April this year, instruct their Governments to

accelerate negotiations on the conclusion of a peace treaty on the basis of the Tokyo Declaration as well as on the agreements reached at the summit meetings in Krasnoyarsk and Kawana.

The two leaders reaffirm their resolve to make their utmost efforts to conclude a peace treaty by the year 2000. Towards that end, both leaders instruct their Governments to establish a sub-committee on border demarcation within the framework of the existing Japanese-Russian Joint Committee on the Conclusion of a Peace Treaty.

The two leaders also instruct their Governments to establish a subcommittee on joint economic activities on the above-mentioned islands, which would conduct its activities in parallel with those of the subcommittee on border demarcation and define what kinds of joint economic activities could be implemented in the above-mentioned islands without prejudice to the legal positions of both sides.

The two leaders agree in principle, from a humanitarian perspective, on implementing so-called free visits to the above-mentioned islands, which would be streamlined to the maximum extent possible, by Japanese nationals who are former residents of those islands or their family members. They also instruct their Governments to examine legal and practical aspects of the procedures for such visits.

3. The Prime Minister of Japan and the President of the Russian Federation recognize the importance of cooperation regarding the islands of Etorofu, Kunashiri, Shikotan and Habomai aiming at deepening mutual understanding among the residents of neighboring regions in Japan and the Russian Federation and further developing multifaceted and mutually beneficial cooperation, thereby fostering an environment conducive to the early conclusion of a peace treaty.

In this regard, both leaders welcome the expansion of the framework for cooperation between the two countries in situations where, for humanitarian reasons, an urgent response is required.

Furthermore, both leaders highly value the conclusion of the agreement between the Government of Japan and the Government of the Russian Federation on some matters in the field of fishing operations for living marine resources, as well as the smooth implementation of operations under that agreement, and confirm that this is greatly contributing to strengthening the relations of trust between the two countries.

4. The Prime Minister of Japan and the President of the Russian Federation firmly intend to deepen and strengthen political dialogue between the two countries. The two leaders express their intention to have formal contacts at the leaders' level each year and to continue to utilize actively practice of holding informal summit meetings.

5. The Prime Minister of Japan and the President of the Russian Federation evaluate positively the recently expanding exchanges between Japan and the Russian Federation in the fields of security and defence. They affirm that they are prepared to continue and deepen such exchanges, since they not only enhance trust and mutual understanding in the bilateral relationship, but also advance the positive process of improving confidence-building measures and securing transparency in the field of Asia-Pacific security.

6. The Prime Minister of Japan and the President of the Russian Federation will promote more exchanges among the law enforcement authorities of the two countries, in view of the importance of co-operation in the prevention of organized crime and smuggling.

7. The Prime Minister of Japan and the President of the Russian Federation agree that wide-ranging exchanges at the grass-roots level play an extremely important role in maintaining an environment conductive to the further steady development of Japanese-Russian relations. For that purpose, the two leaders welcome the establishment of the Russian Committee of the Twenty-first Century in the Russian Federation and of the Japanese-Russian Friendship Forum 21 in Japan, and intend to provide all possible assistance to their activities.

   Furthermore, the two leaders note the importance of broad exchanges between Japan and the Russian Federation at the State and regional levels.

8. The Prime Minister of Japan and the President of the Russian Federation note that the cultures, traditions and world outlook of their peoples have much in common and note the importance of cooperating for the mutual enrichment of the cultures of the peoples of Japan and the Russian Federation. The two leaders intend to promote diverse relations further between their countries in the areas of culture and information exchange.

9. The Prime Minister of Japan and the President of the Russian Federation recognize the particular significance of youth exchanges between the two countries, considering that the accuracy and objectiveness of their understanding of the importance of Japanese-

Russian relations and the formation of their sense of responsibility for the future will be enhanced through more active exchanges between the youth of both countries.

10. The Prime Minister of Japan and the President of the Russian Federation affirm that further enhancement of cooperation by both countries in the areas of trade and economics is to their mutual benefit, and state their determination to develop cooperation further in these areas from a long-term perspective. In this regard, both leaders note the important role of the Hashimoto-Yeltsin Plan, which is a comprehensive programme for economic cooperation between Japan and the Russian Federation prepared by the leaders of the two countries, and will continue to implement steadily the plan and discuss possible ways of further expanding it.

    Based on the common recognition that there is ample potential for cooperation by the two countries in the economic field, including the development of the abundant natural resources in Siberia and the Russian Far East, the two leaders state their intention to further promote such cooperation. The two leaders share the view that cooperation by the two countries in this direction will contribute to the prosperity of both countries as well as the entire Asia-Pacific region in the twenty-first century.

    The two leaders affirm that their countries will continue working to accomplish the above tasks and to improve the environment for trade and investment between the two countries. For this purpose, the two countries will hold annually meetings of the Japanese-Russian Intergovernmental Committee on Trade and Economic Affairs.

    Both leaders welcome the signing of the Agreement between the Government of Japan and the Government of the Russian Federation, on the Promotion and Protection of Investments, aimed at the establishment of the Japanese-Russian Investment Company.

11. The Prime Minister of Japan and the President of the Russian Federation share the view that economic development in the Russian Federation and the integration of the Russian Federation into the international community will contribute not only to the development of bilateral relations, but also to the prosperity of the Asia-Pacific region and of the world as a whole. The Russian Federation will continue reforms towards the establishment of a stable economic infrastructure as well as the earliest possible integration into the international economic system, and the Government of Japan will provide every support for these reform efforts

by the Russian Federation and will work in close coordination with the international community to achieve these objectives.

12. The Prime Minister of Japan and the President of the Russian Federation recognize that the potential for cooperation in the fields of science and technology between both countries is great. They support exchanges and cooperation, including joint projects, in basic and applied scientific research as well as in areas of research and development with potential for the development of modern society and sustainable economic growth in the future.

II. COOPERATION ON INTERNATIONAL ISSUES

The Prime Minister of Japan and the President of the Russian Federation state their intention to expand and deepen coordinated action by Japan and the Russian Federation on international issues, as follows:

Global issues

1. Japan and the Russian Federation will strengthen their coordinated action within the framework of the Group of Eight (G-8).

2. Japan and the Russian Federation will continue their dialogue on various issues concerning United Nations reform, including reform of the Security Council. The Russian Federation understands Japan's intention to become a permanent member of the Security Council, supports that intention and states its recognition that Japan is a strong candidate for obtaining this status.

3. Japan and the Russian Federation will expand cooperation on the strengthening of the Treaty on the Non-Proliferation of Nuclear Weapons, the early entry into force of the Comprehensive Nuclear-Test-Ban Treaty and the negotiation of a treaty on the prohibition of the production of fissile material for nuclear weapons or other nuclear explosive devices. They will also expand their collaborative relations within the international export control regimes in which both participate, continue their dialogue on domestic export control issues and take coordinated action to secure the effective implementation of the Chemical Weapons Convention and the Biological Weapons Convention.

4. Japan and the Russian Federation will promote information exchanges on peacekeeping operations. Both countries will cooperate with efforts by the international community to prevent conflicts and normalize the situation in conflict areas around the world. Japan and the Russian Federation will strengthen their coordinated action in various forums, particularly within the G-8 framework, in the fight against terrorism.

5. Japan and the Russian Federation will coordinate their various efforts with regard to environmental issues, particularly on climate change.

The Asia-Pacific region

6. Maintaining close bilateral contact and in cooperation with other countries, Japan and the Russian Federation will participate actively in efforts to build confidence and ensure peace and security in the Asia-Pacific region.

7. Japan and the Russian Federation will continue coordinated action with the Association of South-East Asian Nations (ASEAN) and work to continue making constructive contributions to the activities of the ASEAN Regional Forum (ARF) on security issues.

8. Japan and the Russian Federation will hold consultations and co-operate with a view to easing tensions and assisting the development of dialogue and cooperative relations on the Korean Peninsula. They will also continue collaborative action in addressing the issue of Cambodia.

9. Japan and the Russian Federation express their expectations for progress in the four-party talks on peace on the Korean Peninsula.
    Furthermore, the two countries share the view that, in the future, the creation of a forum for discussing security and confidence-building in North-East Asia among the concerned countries, including Japan and the Russian Federation, will be important in contributing to the peace and stability of North-East Asia.

10. Japan supports the constructive participation of the Russian Federation in the activities of Asia-Pacific Economic Cooperation (APEC). Japan and the Russian Federation will strive to deepen dialogue on stable economic development in the Asia-Pacific region.
    Japan and the Russian Federation will cooperate in the development of international cooperation in the area of energy in the Asia-Pacific region, in the belief that it will promote energy security as well as contribute to the solution of global warming issues and, in turn, to the stability and socio-economic development of the region.

11. Japan and the Russian Federation will continue their cooperative efforts to counter ocean pollution, acid rain and other environmental problems in the Asia-Pacific region.

Regional issues

12. Japan and the Russian Federation will continue their cooperation to promote the progress of peace in the Middle East.

13. Japan and the Russian Federation will develop cooperative relations to foster an environment for stable and multidimensional cooperation with the Central Asia and the Trans-Caucasus regions.

Consultations on international issues

14. Japan and the Russian Federation will actively conduct regular bilateral consultations and information exchanges on international issues relating to various regions and fields with a view to strengthening and making more effective their bilateral cooperation on such issues.

Moscow, 13 November 1998

Prime Minister of Japan   Keizo Obuchi

President of the Russian Federation   B.N.Yeltsin

40. NOTE VERBALE
presented by the Ministry of Foreign Affairs of Japan
regarding the framework, streamlined to the maximum extent possible,
for visits to the islands of Etorofu, Kunashiri, Shikotan and Habomai
by Japanese nationals who are former residents
and members of their families
(2 September 1999)

The Ministry of Foreign Affairs of Japan presents its compliments to the Embassy of the Russian Federation in Japan and has the honor to confirm that it has received from the said Embassy the Note Verbale No. 138 of 2 September 1999, which states the following:

"The Embassy of the Russian Federation in Japan presents its compliments to the Ministry of Foreign Affairs of Japan, and has the honor to inform that the Russian Federation, referring to Part I, Clause 2 of the Moscow Declaration on Establishing a Creative Partnership between the Russian Federation and Japan, signed by President of the Russian Federation B.N.Yeltsin and Prime Minister of Japan Keizo Obuchi on 13 November 1998, in regarding to the agreement in principle, stipulated in the said clause, concerning the implementation of the so-called free visits, streamlined to the maximum extent possible, to the islands of Etorofu, Kunashiri, Shikotan and Habomai (hereinafter referred to as "the Islands") by Japanese nationals who are former residents and members of their families, and noting the existing system and procedures for visits to the Islands by Japanese citizens and visits by the residents of the Islands to regions of Japan provided in the Correspondence of 14 October 1991 between the Minister for Foreign Affairs of Japan and the Minister for Foreign Affairs of the Union of Soviet Socialist Republics (hereinafter referred to as "the Correspondence"), and the Note Verbale of 20 April 1993 exchanged between the Embassy of Japan in the Russian Federation and the Ministry of Foreign Affairs of the Russian Federation (hereinafter referred to as "the exchanged Note Verbale"), is prepared to take necessary measures in accordance with the procedures attached to this Note Verbale to ensure that visits to the Islands by Japanese nationals who are former residents and members of their families, are implemented by framework of visits, streamlined to the maximum extent possible.

1. (1) Visits to the Islands will be carried out by groups without passports or visas, based on identification materials and inserts for multiple visits (hereinafter referred to as "IDs" and "inserts"), and the required attachments (visiting group name list and visit itinerary). Visiting groups may be accompanied by central or local authorities (no more than two people) and doctors and interpreters.

   (2) The program that stipulates the basic provision regarding group visits will be adjusted annually at the conference stipulated in Part 2. Clause (2) of the Correspondence.
   The program that stipulates details regarding individual visits will be determined in accordance with Part 2. Clause (2) of the Correspondence.

2. This framework will be implemented in accordance with the following conditions:

   (1) This framework does not in any way exert influence on the framework of visits to the Islands provided in the Correspondence and the exchanged Note Verbale, and the framework of visits to gravesites provided in the mutually appropriate Note Verbale of 2 July 1986.

   (2) Visits within this framework should not be deemed as to prejudice the legal positions of either side regarding any issue pertaining to such visits.

3. The Government of the Russian Federation states that it is prepared to hold discussion with the Government of Japan regarding any issue arising in regard to the application of this framework, including the circumstance of implementing this framework and possibility for its improvement.

Should the Ministry of Foreign Affairs of Japan, representing the Government of Japan, affirm its consent to the above-mentioned contents, this Note Verbale and a reply to this Note Verbale from the Ministry of Foreign Affairs of Japan with contents identical to those of this Note Verbale will constitute a mutual understanding between the Government of the Russian Federation and the Government of Japan regarding the implementation of cooperation under the conditions described in this Note Verbale.

The Embassy of the Russian Federation avails itself of this opportunity to renew to the Ministry of Foreign Affairs of Japan the assurances of its highest consideration."

The Ministry of Foreign Affairs of Japan, representing the Government of Japan, has the honor to inform its consent through this Note Verbale to the taking of the necessary measures described in the Note Verbale from the Embassy of the Russian Federation in Japan.

Procedures Attached to the Note Verbale No. 138 of 2 September 1999 from the Embassy of the Russian Federation in Japan

Procedures for visits to the Islands by Japanese nationals who are former residents and members of their families

I. GENERAL PROVISIONS

1. Japanese nationals who are former residents and members of their families means Japanese nationals and their spouses and children, who resided on the Islands during the period until the end of 1945.

2. The Japanese side will submit to the Russian side each year through diplomatic channels a list of the names (including former domiciles on the Islands) of Japanese nationals who are former residents and members of their families.

3. Visits will be carried out, based on IDs, inserts and the required attachments (visiting group name list and visit itinerary).

4. The Government of Japan will prepare IDs. The form and the items to be included on them will be agreed upon with the Russian side separately.

5. Inserts for multiple visits will be issued by the appropriate organization in Japan, after printing the items provided in Clause 3. of the exchanged Note Verbale.

II. ADVANCE PROCEDURES

1. The Ministry of Foreign Affairs of Japan will inform the Embassy of the Russian Federation in Japan via a Note Verbale no less than, in principle, two weeks prior to the scheduled visit start date, regarding the items provided in Part 1., Clause (1) of the exchanged Note Verbale and the pass point for entry and exit procedures.

2. The Embassy of the Russian Federation in Japan will inform the Ministry of Foreign Affairs of Japan via a Note Verbale, regarding the advisability of reception of participants in the visiting groups indicated in the Note Verbale.

III. ENTRY AND EXIT PROCEDURES.

1. The leader of the visiting group will carry the list of names of the members comprising the visiting group, and will hand it to the Russian side upon the visiting group's arrival at the pass point.

   The members comprising the visiting group will carry IDs and inserts.

2. The Russian side will make an appropriate entry on the inserts attached to the IDs at the items of entry into and exit from the pass point by the visiting group.

   IDs valid for multiple visits will be returned along with their inserts to those carrying such IDs.

41. JAPAN-RUSSIA COOPERATION PROGRAM
on the Development of Joint Economic Activities
in the islands of Etorofu, Kunashiri, Shikotan and Habomai
(September 2000)

Deputy Minister for Foreign Affairs of Japan, Ryozo Kato, and Deputy Minister for foreign Affairs of the Russian Federation, A. P. Losyukov, served as joint Chairs in a subcommittee on Joint Economic Activities in the islands of Etorofu, Kunashiri, Shikotan and Habomai, established in accordance with Clause 2 of the Moscow Declaration of 13 November 1998 on Establishing a Creative Partnership between Japan and the Russian Federation, with the aim of elucidating what Joint Economic Activities could be implemented on the above-mentioned islands, based on the work conducted within the framework of the said subcommittee, confirm the following:

1. The gradual development of Joint Economic Activities in the islands will be advanced to strengthen mutual understanding and trust between Japan and the Russian Federation in this region, to

create a favorable environment for the advancement of the negotiations between the two countries on a peace treaty, and to improve the overall atmosphere in the Japan-Russia relations.

2. Both sides consider as a possible form of future Joint Economic
Activities cooperation in areas of mutual interest, including the reproduction and aquaculture of marine living resources, and fishery
operations processing.

3. As a means of putting Joint Economic Activities on track, based
on the Agreement between the Government of Japan and the
Government of the Russian Federation on some matters of cooperation in the filed of fishing operations for marine living resources,
signed on 21 February 1998 (hereinafter referred to as "the Agreement"), it is appropriate for purpose to realize cooperation in the
areas relating to the reproduction of marine living resources in the
islands. Currently, this joint work may encompass, as a possible
form, the cultivation of sea urchin roe and shellfish.

4. Japan-Russia cooperation in the area of reproduction of marine
living resources will be implemented in accordance with Article 1
of the Agreement.

    Joint Economic Activities in the areas of reproduction of ma-
rine living resources will be implemented in the sea areas, specified in the annex of the Agreement.

    The progress of this cooperation will be reviewed in the meet-
ings of a subcommittee on Joint Economic Activities. With regard
to the issue of the swift formulation of a document pertaining to
the cultivation of sea urchin roe and shellfish, active study will be
continued in working groups within the framework of this sub-
committee.

5. Cooperation in the areas of reproduction of marine living resources
within the framework of this program should not be deemed as to
prejudice the legal positions of either side in any related issues.

4 September 2000, Tokyo

Deputy Minister for Foreign Affairs of Japan   Ryozo Kato

Deputy Minister for Foreign Affairs   A. Losyukov
of the Russian Federation

42. STATEMENT
by the Prime Minister of Japan
and the President of the Russian Federation
on the Issue of a Peace Treaty
(September 2000)

1. The Prime Minister of Japan and the President of the Russian Federation had thorough negotiations on September 4 and 5 this year in Tokyo on the overall bilateral relationship, including the issue of a peace treaty, with the intention to establish a creative partnership between Japan and Russia consistent with their strategic and geopolitical interests.

2. Both sides confirmed that the following positive results have been achieved since the Japan-Russia Summit Meeting in Krasnoyarsk in 1997, when both sides agreed to make their utmost efforts to conclude a peace treaty by the year 2000 on the basis of the Tokyo Declaration.

   – The Joint Committee on the Conclusion of a Peace Treaty at the level of Foreign Ministers was established.

   – The subcommittee on border demarcation was established, and active negotiations have been held therein.

   – The subcommittee on Joint Economic Activities was established and is actively working. "The Japan-Russia Cooperation Program on the Development of Joint Economic Activities in the islands of Etorofu, Kunashiri, Shikotan and Habomai" (hereinafter referred to as "the Islands") was signed.

   – The Agreement on some matters of cooperation in the field of fishing operations for marine living resources was singed and has been successfully implemented.

   – The Agreement on the so-called free visits to the Islands by procedures, streamlined to the maximum extent possible, has been implemented.

   – The scope of participants in mutual visits between the current residents of the Islands and residents of Japan, which had already been implemented in accordance with the 1991 agreement, has been expanded since 1998.

   – The scope of humanitarian assistance that has been implemented in relation to the earthquake disaster in 1994 now includes those cases which require emergency assistance.

3. Both sides jointly confirmed that it was essential to continue their efforts to realize the Krasnoyarsk Agreement and to promote further strengthening of its positive results to the maximum extent possible.

4. Based upon all the agreements that have been reached up to now, including the Tokyo Declaration on Japan-Russia Relations in 1993 and the Moscow Declaration on Establishing a Creative Partnership between Japan and the Russian Federation in 1998, both sides agreed to continue negotiations to work out a peace treaty "through the solution of the issue of where the islands of Etorofu, Kunashiri, Shikotan and Habomai belong."

   With the intention to raise the efficiency of the negotiation process, both sides instructed their representatives of the Joint Committee on the Conclusion of a Peace Treaty to take the following measures.

   – To develop new measures to further accelerate the works of the Joint Committee on the Conclusion of a Peace Treaty and the subcommittee on border demarcation,

   – To take steps to prepare a new edition of the Joint Compendium of Documents on the History of Territorial Issue between Japan and Russia, especially by inlcouding the materials related to the period after 1993,

   – To activate efforts to explain to each nation the importance of the conclusion of a peace treaty.

5. President Vladimir V. Putin of the Russian Federation invited Prime Minister Yoshiro Mori of Japan to make an official visit to the Russian Federation, with a view to promoting further development of bilateral relations in various fields and the positive advancement of the peace treaty negotiations. Prime Minister Yoshiro Mori of Japan accepted the invitation with appreciation. The time of the visit will be agreed through the diplomatic channels.

   Both sides recognized that it would be beneficial to take advantage of every possible opportunity and to continue an active dialogue.

6. The negotiations were conducted in an atmosphere of honesty, trustworthiness and mutual respect.

5 September 2000, Tokyo

Prime Minister of Japan   Yoshiro MORI

President of the Russian Federation   V.V. PUTIN

Notes

PREFACE

1. I. William Zartman and Macreen R. Berman, *The Practical Negotiator* (New Haven, CT:Yale University Press, 1982), 42–202.

INTRODUCTION

1. For a definition of the term "Globalization," see John Baylis and Steve Smith, eds., *The Globalization of World Politics: An Introduction to International Relations* (Oxford: Oxford University Press, 1997), 14–16.

2. Joseph E. Stiglitz, *Globalization and its Discontents* (New York: W. W. Norton, 2002), 9.

3. Baylis and Smith, *Globalization of World Politics*, 15.

4. Ibid.; Yoshinobu Yamamoto, *Globalism, Regionalism and Nationalism: Asia in Search of its Role in the Twenty-First Century* (Oxford: Blackwell Publishers, 1999), 71.

5. Graham Evans and Jeffrey Newnham, *The Penguin Dictionary of International Relations* (London: Penguin Putnam, Inc., 1998), 201.

6. Baylis and Smith, *Globalization of World Politics*, 14.

7. Robert O. Keohane and Joseph S. Nye Jr., "Globalization: What's New? What's Not? (And So What?)," *Foreign Policy* 118 (spring 2000): 105.

8. Marshall McLuhan and Bruce R. Powers, *The Global Village: Transformation in World Life and Media in the 21st Century* (Oxford: Oxford University Press, 1989); Marshall McLuhan, *The Gutenberg Galaxy: The Making of Typographic* (Toronto: University of Toronto Press, 1962).

9. Keohane and Nye, "Globalization," 108.

10. Ibid.

11. Ibid.

12. Robert J. Holton, *Globalization and the Nation-State* (London: MacMillan, 1998), 84–85.

13. Ibid., 84.

14. Baylis and Smith, *Globalization of World Politics*, 18; Keohane and Nye, "Globalization," 106–7.

15. Stanley Hoffmann classifies "globalization" into three forms: "economic," "cultural," and "political." Stanley Hoffmann, "Clash of Globalizations," *Foreign Affairs* 81,

no. 4 (July/August 2002): 107–8. A joint article by Robert Keohane and Joseph Nye classifies globalism into several forms: "economic," "military," "environmental," and "social and cultural." Keohane and Nye, "Globalization," 106–7, 110–11.

16. Holton, *Globalization and the Nation-State*, 81.

17. Keohane and Nye, "Globalization," 106; Robert Kaplan, *Warrior Politics* (New York: Random House, 2002), 5; cited in Christopher Coker, *Globalisation and Insecurity in the Twenty-first Century: NATO and the Management of Risk,* Adelphi Paper No. 345 (London: The International Institute for Strategic Studies, 2002), 21.

18. Herbert Dittgen, "The End of the Nation-State? Borders in the Age of Globalization," in *Borderlands Under Stress,* ed. Martin Pratt and Janet Allison Brown (The Hague: Kluwer Law International, 2000), 49–68.

19. Marcelo G. Kohen, "Is the Notion of Territorial Sovereignty Obsolete?" in *Borderlands Under Stress.*

20. Coker, *Globalisation and Insecurity,* 20.

21. David Held, ed., *A Globalizing World? Culture, Economics, Politics* (London: Routledge, 2000), 22–24; Takashi Inoguchi and Paul Bacon, "Organizing Hypocrisy and Transforming Sovereignty," *International Relations of the Asia-Pacific* 1, no. 2 (2002): 168–69; for these classifications, I am obliged to the following article: Koichi Tsutsumi, "Gurobaru-ka, Kokka-shuken, Jinken-hosho, Jindo-teki kainyu" [Globalization, state sovereignty, protection of human rights, and humanitarian interference], in *Global-ka to Gendai-Kokka: Kokka, Shakai, Jinken-ron no Kadai* [Globalization and the contemporary states: Tasks of states, society, and human rights], ed. Yoshikazu Nakatani and Norio Yasumoto (Tokyo: Ochanomizu-shobo, 2002), 59.

22. Held, *Globalizing World,* 22; Stiglitz, *Globalization and its Discontents,* 9.

23. Held, *Globalizing World,* 23; Inoguchi and Bacon, "Organizing Hypocrisy and Transforming Sovereignty," 168–69; Tsutsumi, "Gurobaru-ka, Kokka-shuken," 59.

24. Held, *Globalizing World,* 23; Inoguchi and Bacon, "Organizing Hypocrisy and Transforming Sovereignty," 168–69; Tsutsumi, "Gurobaru-ka, Kokka-shuken," 59.

25. Gary Goertz and Paul F. Diehl, *Territorial Changes and International Conflict* (London: Routledge, 1992), 2.

26. Shoichi Inoue, *Ai no Kukan* [Space for love] (Tokyo: Kadokawa-shoten, 1999).

27. Thomas Forsberg, "Explaining Territorial Disputes: From Power Politics to Normative Reasons," *Journal of Peace Research* 33, no. 4 (November 1996): 438.

28. Ibid.

29. Thomas Forsberg, "Theories on Territorial Disputes," in *Contested Territory: Border Disputes at the Edge of the Former Soviet Empire,* ed. Thomas Forsberg (Aldershot, England: Edward Elgar, 1995), 28.

30. Konrad Lorenz, *On Aggression* (New York: Harcourt, Brace & World, 1936), 35. For criticism of Lorenz's theory, see, for example, Samuel S. Kim, "The Lorenzian Theory of Aggression and Peace Research: A Critique," in *The War System: An Interdisciplinary Approach,* ed. Richard A. Falk and S. Kim (Boulder, CO: Westview Press, 1980), 82–115.

31. Lorenz, *On Aggression,* 36.

32. Ibid., 35.

33. Held, *Globalizing World*, 173; Ken'ichi Oomae, *The End of the Nation State: How Region States Harness the Prosperity of the Global Economy* (in Japanese) (Tokyo: Kodan-sha, 1995), 35, 42.

34. Holton, *Globalization and the Nation-State*, 84; Thomas Forsberg, "Beyond Sovereignty, Without Territoriality: Mapping the Space of Late-Modern (Geo) Politics," *Cooperation and Conflict: Nordic Journal of International Studies* 31, no. 4 (December 1966): 368.

35. Hedley Bull, *The Anarchical Society: A Study of Order in World Politics* (New York: Columbia University Press, 1977), 271–73.

36. Samuel P. Huntington, "Transnational Organizations in World Politics," *World Politics* 25, no. 3 (April 1973): 363.

37. Takahiro Yamada, "Globalization to Kokumin-kokka no Henyo: Chikyu Kankyo ni okeru Governance o motomete" [Globalization and transformation of nation-states aiming at governance in the environment of the Earth], *Kokusai Mondai* [International Affairs] (Tokyo: Nihon Kokusai Mondai Kenkyusho [The Japanese Institute for International Affairs]), 497; (August 2001): 18.

38. Stephen D. Krasner, *Sovereignty: Organized Hypocrisy* (Princeton, NJ: Princeton University Press, 1999), 13.

39. Held, *Globalizing World*, 103, 176.

40. Susan Strange, *The Retreat of the State: The Diffusion of Power in the World Economy* (Cambridge: Cambridge University Press, 1996), 60–65.

41. Bull, *Anarchical Society*, 270–71.

42. Stephen D. Tansey, *Politics: The Basics*, 2d ed. (London: Routledge, 2000), 39–40.

43. Strange, *Retreat of the State*, 60–65; Tsutsumi, "Gurobaru-ka, Kokka-shuken," 72.

44. Tsutsumi, "Gurobaru-ka, Kokka-shuken," 59.

45. Hiroshi Kimura, "Kariningurado to Hoppo-ryodo: Sooiten to Ruijiten" [Kaliningrad and the Northern Territories], *Nihon-Kenkyu* [Japan Studies] (Kyoto: Kokusai Nihon Bunka Kenkyu Senter [International Research Center for Japanese Studies]), 24; (February 2002): 25–26.

46. Kohen, "Is the Notion of Territorial Sovereignty Obsolete?" 36, 38.

47. Ibid., 36.

48. *Yomiuri Shimbun* (Tokyo), July 16, 2002, and November 9, 2002.

49. Kohen, "Is the Notion of Territorial Sovereignty Obsolete?" 42.

50. Toshiyuki Akizuki, *Nichiro-kankei to Saharin-Toh: Bakumatu Meiji shoki no Ryodo Mondai* [Japanese-Russian relations and the Sakhalin Island: Territorial problems during the late Bakufu-early Meiji period] (Tokyo: Chikuma-shobo, 1994), 179–99.

51. Kohen, "Is the Notion of Territorial Sovereignty Obsolete?" 44.

52. For details, see Hiroshi Kimura, *Japanese-Russian Relations Under Gorbachev and Yeltsin* (Armonk, NY: M. E. Sharpe, 2000), 191–200.

53. Stephen D. Krasner, "Globalization-ron Hihan: Shuken-gainen no Sai-kento" [Criticism of the theory of globalization: Reexamination of the sovereignty concept], trans. Masaru Kawano, in *Global Governance in Search of Order Without Government* (in Japanese), ed. Akio Watanabe and Jitsuo Tsuchiyama (Tokyo: University of Tokyo Press, 2001), 52.

54. Louise Amoore et al., "Overturning 'Globalization': Resisting Teleology, Reclaiming Politicism," in *Globalization and the Politics of Resistance*, ed. Barry K. Gills (New York: Palgrave, 2001), 22–23.

55. Coker, *Globalisation and Insecurity*, 20.

56. Alvin Toffler and Heidi Toffler, "National Sovereignty: A Myth in Today's Changing World," *Daily Yomiuri* (Tokyo), October 7, 2002.

57. John L. Gaddis, *The United States and the End of the Cold War: Implications, Reconsideration, Provocations* (Oxford: Oxford University Press, 1992), 196.

58. *Economist*, October 6, 1990, 16.

59. Tsutsumi, "Gurobaru-ka, Kokka-shuken," 58.

60. To reach this conclusion I am obliged to John H. Herz, "Rise and Demise of the Territorial State," *World Politics* 9, no. 4 (1957): 490–91.

61. Greg Cashman, *What Causes War? An Introduction to Theories of International Conflict* (New York: Lexington Books, 1993), 143.

62. Paul F. Diehl, "Contiguity and Military Escalation in Power Rivalries 1816–1980," *Journal of Politics* 47, no. 4 (1985): 1206.

63. Lewis F. Richardson, *Statistics of Deadly Quarrels* (New York: The Boxwood Press, 1960), 176–77; Geoffrey Blainey, *The Causes of War* (New York: Free Press, 1973), 231.

64. Richardson, *Statistics of Deadly Quarrels*, 176.

65. Cashman, *What Causes War?* 143.

66. Ibid., 144.

67. Richardson, *Statistics of Deadly Quarrels*, 288.

68. On this point, see, for example, Lloyd Jensen, *Explaining Foreign Policy* (Englewood Cliffs, NJ: Prentice-Hall, 1982), 208; Evan Luard, *Conflict and Peace in the Modern International System* (Boston: Little, Brown and Company, 1968), 111; James Paul Wesley, "Frequency of Wars and Geographical Opportunity," *Journal of Conflict Resolution* 6, no. 4 (December 1962): 387–89; Harvey Starr and Benjamin A. Most, "The Substance and Study of Borders in International Relations Research," *International Studies Quarterly* 20 (December 1976): 581–620; Blainey, *Causes of War*, 231.

69. Former Canadian Prime Minister Pierre E. Trudeau was once quoted as having said (March 1969) that, for Canada, being America's neighbor "is in some ways like sleeping with an elephant. No matter how friendly and even tempered is the beast, if I can call it that, one is affected by every touch and grunt." Quoted in Lois Turner, *Invisible Empires* (New York: Harcourt, Brace, Jovanovich, 1971), 166; and in W. H. Pope, *The Elephant and the Mouse* (Toronto: McClelland and Stewart, 1971), preface, vii.

70. Bruce M. Russett, *International Regions and the International System* (Chicago: Rand McNally, 1967), 200.

71. Forsberg, "Theories on Territorial Disputes," 24; Forsberg, "Beyond Sovereignty, Without Territoriality," 355; Goertz and Diehl, *Territorial Changes and International Conflict*, 20.

72. Forsberg, "Theories on Territorial Disputes," 23.

CHAPTER I

1. Vasilii M. Golovnin, *Zapiski flota kapitana Golovnina v plenu u Iapontsev v 1811, 1812 i 1813 godakh, s priobshcheniem zamechanii ego o Iaponskom gosudarstve i narode* [Notes of captivity in Japan by fleet captain Golovnin in 1811, 1812, and 1813, with his remarks concerning Japanese government and people] (Khabarovsk: Khabarovskoe knizhnoe izdatel'stvo, 1972), 37–40; Captain Golovnin, *Memoirs of Captivity in Japan 1811–1813*, vol. 1 (London: Oxford University Press, 1973), 6, 11.

2. Sten Bergman, *Die Tausend Inseln im Fernen Osten: Reisen und Erlebnisse auf den Kurilen* [Thousand islands in the Far East: Trip to and experiences on the Kuriles] (Stuttgart: Verlag von Strecker und Schroder, 1932), 6–8.

3. John J. Stephan, *The Kuril Islands: Russo-Japanese Frontiers in the Pacific* (Oxford: Clarendon Press, 1974), 36.

4. Toshiyuki Akizuki, "Nichiro-kankei to Ryodo-ishiki" [Japanese-Russian relations and the perception of territory], *Kyosan-shugi to Kokusai-seiji* [Communism and the International Politics] 13, vol. 4, no. 2 (July-September 1979): 6.

5. Ibid., 3.

6. Toshiyuki Akizuki, "Kozuirefusukii-no Tanken to Chishima-chizu" [Kozyrevskii's expedition and the map of the Kuriles], *Hoppo-bunka Kenkyu* [Studies on cultures of the northern regions] (Sapporo: Hoppo-bunka-shisetsu, Hokkaido University) 3 (1968): 141.

7. Ibid., 142.   8. Stephan, *Kuril Islands*, 61.

9. Ibid.   10. Ibid.

11. I am greatly obliged to the late Shinichiro Takakura, professor emeritus of Hokkaido University, for the content of this paragraph.

12. The Japanese and Russian translations of the Joint Compendium (first thirty-five items) are found in appendixes in the following two books: Hiroshi Kimura, *Nichi-Ro Kokkyo Kosho shi* [History of Japanese-Russian border negotiations] (Tokyo: Chuo Koron-sha, 1993), 219–51; Hiroshi Kimura, *Kuril'skaia problema: Istoriia iapono-rossiskikh peregovorov po pogranichnym voprosam* [Kurile question: History of Japanese-Russian negotiations over territorial problems] (Kiev: Iurinskom, 1996), 202–36.

13. George A. Lensen, *The Russian Push Toward Japan: Russo-Japanese Relations, 1697–1875* (New York: Octagon Books, 1971), 71–84; Donald Keene, *The Japanese Discovery of Europe, Honda Toshiaki and other Discoverers 1720–1830* (London: Routledge, 1952), 31–46.

14. Keene, *Japanese Discovery of Europe*, 39–47.

15. Lensen, *Russian Push Toward Japan*, 26; Keene, *Japanese Discovery of Europe*, 56–57.

16. Lensen, *Russian Push Toward Japan*, 25–26.

17. Ibid., 29; Stephan, *Kuril Islands*, 40–41.

18. Lensen, *Russian Push Toward Japan*, 34–35.

19. Ibid., 41–42.

20. Ibid., 96–111.

21. Stephan, *Kuril Islands*, 47.

22. Akizuki, "Kozuirefusukii-no Tanken to Chishima-chizu," 175.

23. Ibid., 149–50, 160–61, 166–75.

24. Stephan, *Kuril Islands*, 42.

25. Lensen, *Russian Push Toward Japan*, 36–38.

26. Ibid., 43–49.

27. Ibid., 46–64.

28. Bernard Pares, *Russia* (New York: Mentor Books, 1943), 15.

29. Vasilii O. Kluchevskii, *Kurs' russkoi istorii* [Course on Russian history] (Moscow: Prosveshchenie, 1993), 13; V. O. Kluchevskii, *A History of Russia* (New York: Russell & Russell, 1960), 2.

30. S. Znamenskii, *V poiskakh Iaponii: Iz russkikh geograficheskikh otkrytii i morekhodstva v Tikhom okeane* [In search of Japan: From Russian geographic discoveries and navigation in the Pacific Ocean] (Blagoveshchensk: Knizhnoe delo, 1929), 164. See also Robert J. Kerner, *The Urge to the Sea: The Course of Russian History* (New York: Russell & Russell, 1971), 84.

31. Znamenskii, *V poiskakh Iaponii*, 152.

32. Ibid.

33. Ibid., 175.

34. Ibid., 164.

35. A. S. Polonskii, *Kurily* [Kuriles] (Saint Petersburg: Tipografiia Maikova, 1871), 89.

36. Znamenskii, *V poiskakh Iaponii*, 164.

37. Anton P. Chekhov, *Sochinenii*, vols. 14–15 (Moscow: Nauka, 1978), 223.

38. Lensen, *Russian Push Toward Japan*, 161–62.

39. Ibid., 167–69.

40. Ibid., 170.

41. Hayao Shimizu, *Nihon-jin no Roshiya Konpurekkusu* [Japanese inferiority complex to the Russians] (Tokyo: Chuo-koron-sha, 1984), iii, 179.

42. Ibid., 178, ii, 118.

43. Lensen, *Russian Push Toward Japan*, 121–76.

44. Ibid., 168.   45. Ibid., 246.

46. Ibid.   47. Ibid.

48. Ibid., 247; Golovnin, *Zapiski flota kapitana Golovnina*, 160.

49. Golovnin, *Zapiski flota kapitana Golovnina*, 258, 291, 303; Golovnin, *Memoirs of Captivity in Japan 1811–1813*, vol. 2, 147, 216; vol. 3, 14–40.

CHAPTER 2

1. John J. Stephan, *The Kuril Islands: Russo-Japanese Frontiers in the Pacific* (Oxford: Clarendon Press, 1974), 80.

2. Esfir' Fainberg, *Russko-iaponskie otnoshenia v 1697–1875 gg.* [Russo-Japanese relations in 1697–1875] (Moscow: Izdatel'stvo vostochnoi literatury, 1960), 113.

3. Yoshimitsu Kōriyama, *Bakumatsu-Nichiro Kankei-shi Kenkyu* [Studies on the history of Russo-Japanese relations toward the end of the Bakufu period] (Tokyo: Tosho-kanko-kai, 1980), 251.

4. Stephan, *Kuril Islands*, 82.

5. Kōriyama, *Bakumatsu-Nichiro Kankei-shi Kenkyu*, 252.

6. Ibid., 252–53.

7. Toshiyuki Akizuki, "Chishima-retto no Ryoyu to Keiei" [Seizure and management of the Kurile Islands], in *Iwanami Kōza: Kindai-nippon to Shokuminchi* [The lecture series of the Iwanami-shoten: Modern Japan and its colonies], vol. 1 (Tokyo: Iwanami shoten, 1992), 126.

8. Kōriyama, *Bakumatsu-Nichiro Kankei-shi Kenkyu*, 252.

9. Leonid N. Kutakov, *Vneshniania politika i diplomatiia Iaponii* [Foreign policy and diplomacy of Japan] (Moscow: Mezhdunarodnye otnosheniia, 1964), 310.

10. P. A. Tihomenov, *Istoricheskoe obozrenie Rossisko-Amerikanskoi kompanii i deistvii ee do nastoiashchego vremeni* [Historical review of the Russian-American company and its activities until the contemporary (or present) days] (Saint Petersburg: Tipografii Eduarda Veimara, 1861), 27.

11. Toshuyuki Akizuki, "Shipanberugu Tanken-tai to Shikotan-to" [The Shpanberg expedition and the island of Shikotan], *Hokkaido Shimbun* (evening edition), July 18, 1989.

12. Stephan, *Kuril Islands*, 84.

13. Kōriyama, *Bakumatsu-Nichiro Kankei-shi Kenkyu*, 255.

14. Gennadii I. Nevel'skoi, *Podvigi russkikh ofitserov na krainem vostoke Rossii 1849–1855* [Achievements of Russian officers on the Russian Far East 1849–1855] (Moscow: Gosudarstvennoe izdatel'stvo geograficheskoi literatury, 1947), 121.

15. Hiroshi Kimura, *Soren to Roshiya-jin* [The Soviet Union and the Russians] (Tokyo: Sōyō-sha, 1981), 153; Morton Schwartz, *The Foreign Policy of the USSR: Domestic Factors* (Encino, CA: Dickenson Publishing Company, Inc., 1975), 75.

16. *Izvestiia*, October 4, 1991. An English translation is available in Graham Allison, Hiroshi Kimura, and Konstantin Sarkisov, eds., *Beyond Cold War to Trilateral Cooperation in the Asia-Pacific Region: Scenario for New Relationships Between Japan, Russia, and the United States* (Cambridge, MA: Strengthening Democratic Institutions Project, Harvard University, 1992), 76–80.

17. *Asahi Shimbun* (evening edition), October 4, 1991.

18. *Asahi Shimbun*, October 15, 1991.

19. *Izvestiia*, October 4, 1991.

20. Seizaburo Satō, *"Shi no Choyaku" o koete* [Beyond the "leap of death"] (Tokyo: Toshi-shuppan, 1992), 141–43, 150, 152.

21. Ivan A. Goncharov, *Fregat "Pallada" (ocherki puteshestviia)* [The frigate "Pallada" (essays about the trip)] (Moscow: Gosudarstvennoe izdatel'stvo geograficheskoi literatury, 1957), 330; Ivan A. Goncharov, *The Frigate Pallada*, trans. Klaus Goetze (New York: St. Martin's Press, 1987), 307.

22. George A. Lensen, "Russia's Expedition of 1852 to 1855" (PhD dissertation submitted to Columbia University) (Ann Arbor, MI: University Microfilms International, 1979), 245.

23. Satō, *"Shi no Choyaku" o koete*, 155.

24. Goncharov, *Fregat "Pallada,"* 424–25; Goncharov, *Frigate Pallada*, 419–20.

25. *Izvestiia*, June 16, 1981.

26. *Pravda*, March 16, 1988.

27. Akizuki, "Nichiro-kankei to Ryodo-ishiki," 18.

28. Fainberg, *Russko-iaponskie otnoshenia*, 174–75.

29. *Izvestiia*, October 4, 1991; Allison, Kimura, and Sarkisov, *Beyond Cold War*, 78–79.

30. Ibid.

31. Akizuki, "Chishima-retto no Ryoyu to Keiei," 128.

32. Ibid.

33. *Izvestiia*, October 4, 1991; Allison, Kimura, and Sarkisov, *Beyond Cold War*, 79.

34. *Izvestiia*, October 4, 1991.

35. Lensen, *Russian Push Toward Japan*, 436, 495–96.

36. William H. Seward, *Travels Around the World* (New York: D. Appleton, 1873), 38; Lensen, *Russian Push Toward Japan*, 439; Shigetada Manabe, *Nichiro Kankei shi 1697–1875* [History of Japanese-Russian relations 1697–1875] (Tokyo: Yoshikawa-kobun-kan, 1978), 322; John J. Stephan, *Sakhalin: A History* (Oxford: Clarendon Press, 1971), 61.

37. Joseph G. Whelan, *Soviet Diplomacy and Negotiating Behavior: Emerging New Context for U.S. Diplomacy*, vol. 1 (Washington, DC: U.S. Government Printing Office, 1979), 31–34.

38. Tsuguo Togawa, "Hoppo-ryodo no Rekishi" [History of the Northern Territories], in *Hoppo-ryodo o kangaeru* [Examining the Northern Territories issue], ed. Hiroshi Kimura (Sapporo: Hokkaido Shimbun-sha, 1981), 45.

39. Ibid.

40. Togawa, "Hoppo-ryodo no Rekishi," 45; Lensen, *Russian Push Toward Japan*, 444–46.

CHAPTER 3

1. Theodore H. von Laue, *Sergei Witte and the Industrialization of Russia* (New York: Columbia University, 1963), 186–87, 149–55.

2. Michael T. Florinsky, *Russia: A History and an Interpretation*, vol. 2 (New York: Macmillan, 1947), 1262–83.

3. Seiichiro Kusunoki, *Kojima Korekata–Ootsu-jiken to Meiji nashonarizumu* [Korekata Kojima: The Ohtsu incident and Meiji nationalism] (Tokyo: Chuo-koron-sha, 1997).

4. Robert K. Massie, *Nicholas and Alexandra* (New York: Atheneum, 1967), 91; Ryotaro Shiba, *Saka no ue no Kumo* [The cloud over the hill], vol. 2 (Tokyo: Bungei-shunju-sha, 1978), 347.

5. Koichi Yasuda, *Saigo no Kōtei, Nikorai-nisei no Nikki* [The diaries of the last Tsar Nicholas II] (Tokyo: Asahi-Shimbun-sha, 1985), 8–9, 18–19.

6. Ian Nish, *The Origins of the Russo-Japanese War* (London: Longman, 1985).

7. John A. White, *The Diplomacy of the Russo-Japanese War* (Princeton, NJ: Princeton University Press, 1964), 310–29; Raymond A. Esthus, *Double Eagle and Rising Sun: The Russians and Japanese at Portsmouth in 1905* (Durham, NC: Duke University Press, 1988), 17, 53, 188; Howard K. Beale, *Theodore Roosevelt and the Rise of America to World Power* (Baltimore, MA: Johns Hopkins University Press, 1956), 312–14.

8. Esthus, *Double Eagle and Rising Sun*, 97, 105.

9. White, *Diplomacy of the Russo-Japanese War*, 252–62.

10. Hisahiko Okazaki, *Senryakuteki-shiko to wa nanika?* [What is strategic thinking?] (Tokyo: Chuo-koron-sha, 1983), 89.

11. Shumpei Okamoto, *The Japanese Oligarchy and the Russo-Japanese War* (New York: Columbia University Press, 1970), 208–13.

12. James W. Morley, *The Japanese Thrust into Siberia, 1918* (New York: Columbia University Press, 1957).

13. George A. Lensen, *Japanese Recognition of the U.S.S.R.: Soviet-Japanese Relations 1921–1930* (Tallahassee, FL: Diplomatic Press, 1970), 131.

14. George F. Kennan, *Russia and the West Under Lenin and Stalin* (Boston: Little, Brown and Company, 1960), 33–48.

15. These are words by Boris I. Nikolaevskii, an emigre historian, who wrote them in regard to the "Basic Convention between Japan and the U.S.S.R.," cited in Lensen, *Japanese Recognition of the U.S.S.R.*, 368.

16. Kennan, *Russia and the West Under Lenin and Stalin*, 208–23.

17. Lensen, *Japanese Recognition of the U.S.S.R.*, 177.

18. I. V. Stalin, *Sochineniia* [Collected Works], vol. 7 (Moscow: Politizdat, 1947), 227.

19. Leonid N. Kutakov, *Japanese Foreign Policy on the Eve of the Pacific War: A Soviet View* (Tallahassee, FL: Diplomatic Press, 1972), 1–68.

20. Georgii K. Zhukov, *Vospominaniia i razmyshleniia* [Recollections and thoughts] (Moscow: Izdatel'stvo agenstva pechati novosti, 1969), 152–78; Otto P. Chaney Jr., *Zhukov* (Norman: University of Oklahoma Press, 1971), 38–59.

21. Kennan, *Russia and the West Under Lenin and Stalin*, 314–33.

22. Boris N. Slavinskii, *Pakt o neitralitete mezhdu SSSR i Iaponiei: Diplomaticheskaia istoriia, 1941–1945 gg.* [Neutrality pact between the USSR and Japan: A diplomatic history, 1941–1945] (Moscow: TOO "Novina," 1995), 50–52, 58–60, 81–83; Slavinsky, *The Japanese-Soviet Neutrality Pact: A Diplomatic History, 1941–1945*, trans. Geoffrey Jukes (London: Routledge Curzon, 2004), 19, 21–22, 26–27, 42–43; Leonid N. Kutakov, *Istoriia sovetsko-iaponskikh diplomaticheskikh otnoshenii* [History of Soviet-Japanese diplomatic relations] (Moscow: Institut mezhdunarodnykh otnoshenii, 1962), 276; Kutakov, *Japanese Foreign Policy*, 184–85.

23. George A. Lensen, *The Strange Neutrality: Soviet-Japanese Relations During the Second World War 1941–1945* (Tallahassee, FL: Diplomatic Press, 1972), 10.

24. Tsuguo Togawa, "Hoppo-ryodo no Rekishi" [History of the Northern Territories], in *Hoppo-ryodo o kangaeru* [Examining the Northern Territories issue], ed. Hiroshi Kimura (Sapporo: Hokkaido Shimbun-sha, 1981), 53.

25. Haruhiko Nishi, *Kaiso no Nihon-gaikō* [My recollections of Japanese diplomacy] (Tokyo: Iwanami-shoten, 1965), 107–8.

26. Lensen, *Strange Neutrality*, 11.

27. Kashima-Heiwa-Kenkyusho, ed., *Nihon Gaikō-shi* [History of Japanese diplomacy], vol. 15 (Tokyo: Kashima-shuppan-kai, 1970), 69–70; Lensen, *Japanese Recognition of the U.S.S.R.*, 127–28.

28. Kutakov, *Istopiia sovetsko-iaponskikh diplomaticheskikh otnoshenii*, 276; Kutakov, *Japanese Foreign Policy*, 186.

29. For the full text of the Neutrality Pact, see Lensen, *Strange Neutrality*, 277–87.

30. Otto D. Tolischus, *Tokyo Record* (New York: Reynal & Hitchcock, 1943), 107; Toshikazu Kase, *Journey to the Missouri* (New Haven, CT: Yale University Press, 1950), 159; Lensen, *Strange Neutrality*, 19.

31. Haruhiko Nishi, *Kaiso no Nihon-gaikō*, 110.

32. Peter Berton, *The Japanese-Russian Territorial Dilemma: Historical Background, Disputes, Issues, Questions, Solutions of A Thousand Scenarios for the Thousand Islands Dispute* (Cambridge, MA: John F. Kennedy School of Government, Harvard University, 1992), 109.

33. James M. Burns, *Roosevelt: The Soldier of Freedom* (New York: Harcourt Brace Jovanovich, Inc., 1970), 575.

34. United States Department of State, *Foreign Relations of the United States, The Conferences of Cairo and Teheran* (Washington, DC: U.S. Government Printing Office, 1961), 868–69.

35. W. Averell Harriman and Elie Abel, *Special Envoy to Churchill and Stalin 1941–1946* (New York: Random House, 1975), 379; Diane Shaver Clemens, *Yalta* (Oxford: Oxford University Press, 1970), 62, 249.

36. Charles E. Bohlen, *Witness to History 1929–1969* (New York: W. W. Norton & Company, 1973), 196.

37. United States Department of State, *Foreign Relations of the United States, The Conferences at Marta and Yalta* (Washington, DC: U.S. Government Printing Office, 1955), 768; Bohlen, *Witness to History 1929–1969*, 196; Herbert Feis, *Churchill, Roosevelt, Stalin: The War They Waged and the Peace They Thought* (Princeton, NJ: Princeton University Press, 1957), 511; Harriman and Abel, *Special Envoy to Churchill and Stalin 1941–1946*, 397.

38. *Crimean Conference Between the Leaders of the Three Allied Powers* (Moscow: Publishing House of Political Literature, 1984), 129.

39. Andrei A. Gromyko, *Pamiatnoe* [Memoir], vol. 1 (Moscow: Politizdat, 1988), 189.

40. Stephan, *Kuril Islands*, 154.

41. Ibid. 240–44, especially, 244.

42. This paper prepared by Blakeslee was not included in the Yalta Briefing Book, and no evidence has been found to indicate that it was brought to the attention of Roosevelt or his secretary of state, Edward Stettinius.

43. Bohlen, *Witness to History 1929–1969*, 196; John L. Snell, ed., *The Meaning of Yalta: Big Three Diplomacy and the New Balance of Power* (Baton Rouge: Louisiana State University, 1956), 160–61.

44. Harriman and Abel, *Special Envoy*, 400.

45. Snell, *Meaning of Yalta*, 154.

46. Lensen, *Strange Neutrality*, 189.

47. Harriman and Abel, *Special Envoy*, 400.

48. Snell, *Meaning of Yalta*, 157.   49. Bohlen, *Witness to History*, 196.

50. Ibid.   51. Ibid., 195.

52. Harriman and Abel, *Special Envoy*, 399.

53. With regard to the position of Winston Churchill and the United Kingdom on the Kurile Islands issue, see Fiona Hill, "A Disagreement Between Allies: The United Kingdom, the United States, and the Soviet-Japanese Territorial Dispute 1945–1956" (an unpublished paper submitted to Professor Irie at Harvard University), 43p+iv.

54. United States Department of State, *Foreign Relations of the United States, 1955–1957*, vol. 23, part I: *Japan* (Washington, DC: U.S. Government Printing Office, 1991), 226.

55. Georgii Kunadze, "V poiskakh novogo myshleniia: O politike SSSR v otono-shenii Iaponii" [In search for the new thinking: With regard to USSR's policy in its relations with Japan] *Mirovaia ekonomika i mezhdunarodnye otnosheniia*, no. 8 (1990): 67.

56. Lensen, *Strange Neutrality*, 192.

57. Ibid., 192–93.

58. John R. Deane, *The Strange Alliance: The Story of Our Efforts at Wartime Cooperation with Russia* (Bloomington: Indiana University Press, 1973), 344.

59. Kutakov, *Istoriia sovetsko-iaponskikh diplomaticheskikh otnoshenii*, 305.

60. Michihiro Kudō, *Nisso-churitsu-joyaku no Kenkyu* [The study on the Japanese-Soviet neutrality pact] (Tokyo: Nanso-sha, 1985), 104–5.

61. Slavinskii, *Pakt o neitralitete mezhdu SSSR i Iaponiei*, 27, 116–18; Slavinsky, *Japanese-Soviet Neutrality Pact*, 26–27, 62–63.

62. Slavinskii, *Pakt o neitralitete mezhdu SSSR i Iaponiei*, 116–18; Slavinsky, *Japanese-Soviet Neutrality Pact*, 62–63; Robert Whymant, *Stalin's Spy: Richard Sorge and the Tokyo Espionage Ring* (New York: St. Martin's Press, 1996), 183, 186, 188, 196.

63. *Stalin's Correspondence with Roosevelt and Truman 1941–1945* (New York: Capricorn Books, 1965), 266–67; Harry S. Truman, *Memoirs by Harry S. Truman*, vol. 1: *Year of Decisions* (New York: The New American Library, 1955), 485–86; Slavinskii, *Pact o neitralitete mezhdu SSSR i Iaponiei*, 305–6; Slavinsky, *Japanese-Soviet Neutrality Pact*, 180.

64. *Izvestiia*, May 12, 1992.

65. Boris N. Slavinskii, *Sovetskaia okkupatsiia kuril'skikh ostrovov (avgust-sentiabr' 1945 goda): Dokumental'noe issledovanie* [The Soviet occupation of the Kurile Islands (August–September 1945): Documentary research] (Moscow: TOO "Lotos," 1993), 22.

66. *Moto Tomin ga kataru Wareware no Hoppo-ryodo* [Former islands residents speak: Our Northern Territories], vol. 1: *Soren Senryo hen* [Soviet occupation] (Sapporo: League of Residents of Chishima and Habomai Islands, 1988), 153, 177.

67. Slavinskii, *Sovetskaia okkupatsiia kuril'skikh ostrovov*, 54–55.

68. Mitsuru Suizu, *Hoppo-ryodo Dakkan eno Michi* [The way to get back the northern islands] (Tokyo: Nihon-kōgyo-shuppan-sha, 1979), 83–85; Mitsuru Suizu, *Hoppo-ryodo Kaiketsu no Kagi* [Keys to solve the Northern Territories issue] (Tokyo: Kenko-sha, 1987), 154–59.

69. Lester Brooks, *Behind Japan's Surrender: The Secret Struggle that Ended an Empire* (New York: McGraw-Hill, 1968), 16.

70. *Moto Tōmin ga kataru Wareware no Hoppo-ryodo (Soren Senryo hen)*, 153, 177.

71. V. N. Berezin, *Kurs na dobrososedstvo i sotrudnichestvo i ego protivniki: Iz istorii normalizatsii otnoshenii SSSR c poslevonnoi Iaponiei* [Course for good-neighborliness and cooperation and its opponents: From the history of normalization of USSR's relations with postwar Japan] (Moscow: Mezhdunarodnye otnosheniia, 1977), 5.

72. I. V. Stalin, *Sochineniia*, ed. Robert H. McNeal, vol. 2 [XV] 1941–1945 (Stanford, CA: The Hoover Institution on War, Revolution and Peace, 1967), 213–15.

CHAPTER 4

1. Masataka Kosaka, *Saisho Yoshida Shigeru* [Prime Minister Shigeru Yoshida] (Tokyo: Chuo-koron-sha, 1968), 69; Kosaka, "Japan as a Maritime Nation," *Journal of Social Political Ideas of Japan* 3 (August 1965): 52.

2. Shigeru Yoshida, *The Yoshida Memoirs: The Story of Japan in Crisis*, trans. Ken'ichi Yoshida (London: Heinemann Press, 1961), 111.

3. Motohide Saitō, "Senryo-ki ni okeru Soren no Tainichi-Seisaku—Kihon-kozo to sono Dotai" [The Soviet policy toward occupied Japan: Its basic structure and evolution], *Soren Kenkyu* [Soviet Studies] (Tokyo: Japanese Institute for International Affairs), no. 6 (April 1988): 126–49.

4. Michael M. Yoshitsu, *Japanese and the San Francisco Peace Settlement* (New York: Columbia University Press, 1983) 31.

5. Hiroshi Kimura, "Soren to Tainichi Kowa" [The Soviet Union and normalization with Japan], in *San-furanshisuko Kowa-jōyaku* [The San Francisco peace treaty], ed. Akio Watanabe and Miyazato Seigen (Tokyo: Tokyo University Press, 1980), 317–46.

6. Nikita S. Khrushchev, *Khrushchev Remembers*, trans. and edit. Strobe Talbott (Boston: Little, Brown, 1970), 36; Peter Lowe, *The Origins of the Korean War* (London: Longman, 1986); David Holloway, *Stalin and the Bomb: The Soviet Union and Atomic Energy, 1936–1956* (New Haven, CT: 1994), 277–81.

7. Boris Slavinsky, "The Korean War that Nearly Led to a World Catastrophe," *New Times* 23 (1990): 38.

8. Louis L. Gerson, *John Foster Dulles* (New York: Cooper Squire, 1967), 65.

9. Leonid N. Kutakov, *Vneshniania politika i diplomatii Iaponii* [Foreign policy and diplomacy of Japan] (Moscow: Mezhdunarodnye otnosheniia, 1964), 251; Dmitrii V. Petrov, *Vneshniaia politika Iaponii posle vtoroi mirovoi voiny* [Japanese foreign policy after World War Two] (Moscow: Mezhdunarodnye otnosheniia, 1965), 60.

10. Graham Allison, Hiroshi Kimura, and Konstantin Sarkisov, eds., *Beyond Cold War to Trilateral Cooperation in the Asia-Pacific Region: Scenario for New Relationships Between Japan, Russia, and the United States* (Cambridge, MA: Strengthening Democratic Institutions Project, Harvard University, 1992), x.

11. *Istoriia Iaponii (1945–1975)* [History of Japan (1945–1975)] (Moscow: Nauka, 1978), 88; Kutakov, *Vneshniaia politika i diplomatiia Iaponii*, 245; Petrov, *Vneshniaia politika Iaponii posle vtoroi mirovoi voiny*, 60.

12. Mikhail Kapitsa et al., eds., *Istoriia mezhdunarodnykh otnoshenii na dal'nem vostoke 1945–1977* [History of international relations in the Far East (1945–1977)] (Khabarovsk: Khabarovskoe knizhnoe izdatel'stvo, 1978), 144.

13. *Pravda*, September 7, 1951.

14. Ibid.

15. Ibid.; Gromyko, *Pamiatnoe*, vol. 2, 138.

16. Akira Shigemitsu, *"Hoppo-ryodo" to Soren Gaikō* ["The Northern Territories" and Soviet diplomacy] (Tokyo: Jiji-tsushin-sha, 1983).

17. United States Department of State, *Foreign Relations of the United States, 1951*, vol. VI, part 1: *Asia and the Pacific* (Washington, DC: U.S. Government Printing Office, 1961), 949.

18. Ibid.

19. *Conference for the Conclusion and Signature of the Treaty of Peace with Japan (San Francisco, California, September 4–8, 1951) Record of Proceedings* (Washington, DC: U.S. Government Printing Office, 1951), 78.

20. Shigemitsu, *"Hoppo-ryodo" to Soren Gaikō*, 39.

21. Gromyko, *Pamiatnoe*, vol. 2, 139.

22. *Conference for the Conclusion and Signature of the Treaty of Peace with Japan*, 119.

23. Kosaku Tamura, "Tainichi Heiwa Joyaku no Seiritsu o meguru Amerika-Gaikō" [U.S. diplomacy concerning the formation of a peace treaty with Japan], *Seikei Ronso* (Kokushikan University) 19–20 (November 1973): 20.

24. Kapitsa et al., *Istoriia mezhdunarodnykh otnoshenii na dal'nem vostoke 1945–1977*, 144.

25. Nikita S. Khrushchev, *Khrushchev Remembers: The Glasnost Tapes*, trans. and ed. Jerrold L. Schecter with Vyacheslav V. Luchkov (Boston: Little, Brown and Company, 1990), 85.

26. Vladimir Eremin, *Rossiia-Iaponiia: Territorial'naia problema: Poisk resheniia* [Russia-Japan: Territorial problem: Search for solution] (Moscow: Respublika, 1992), 33.

27. Boris Slavinskii, *Muchi no Daishō—Soren no Tainichi Seisaku* [The cost of ignorance: Soviet policy toward Japan], trans. Toshiko Sugano (Tokyo: Ningen-no-kagaku-sha, 1991), 259.

28. Petrov, *Vneshniaia politika Iaponii posle vtoroi mirovoi voiny*, 60–61; Kapitsa et al., *Istoriia mezhdunarodnykh otnoshenii na dal'nem vostoke*, 145.

29. Khrushchev, *Khrushchev Remembers*, 83–85.

30. Allison, Kimura, and Sarkisov, *Beyond Cold War*, 11, 17.

31. Hichiro Murayama, *Kuriru-shoto no Bunkengakuteki Kenkyu* [Bibliographical studies on the Kurile Islands] (Tokyo: San'ichi-shobo, 1987), 128–64.

32. Haruki Wada, *Hoppo-ryodo Mondai o Kangaeru* [Examining the Northern Territories issues] (Tokyo: Iwanami-shoten, 1990), 48–96.

33. Ibid., 95.

34. Yuichi Takano, "Hoppo-ryodo no Hōri" [Legal logic on the Northern Territories], in *Hoppo-ryodo no Chii—Chishima Karafuto o meguru Shomondai* [The state of the Northern Territories: Problems on the Kurile Islands and Sakhalin], ed. Kokusai-ho Gakkai [Japanese Association of International Law] (Tokyo: Nanpo-doho-engo-kai [The Association for Assistance of Those Japanese Repatriated from the South], 1962), 236–38.

35. Takane Sugihara, "Kokusai-ho kara mita Hoppo-ryodo" [The Northern Territories seen from international law], in *Hoppo-ryodo o kangaeru* [Examining the Northern Territories issue], ed. Hiroshi Kimura (Sapporo: Hokkaido Shimbun-sha, 1981), 98–103.

36. Wada, *Hoppo-ryodo Mondai o Kangaeru*, 35.

37. Ibid.

38. *U.S. Department of State Bulletin*, vol. 35, no. 900 (September 24, 1956): 484; United States Department of State, *Foreign Relations of the United States, 1955–1957*, vol. 23, part 1: *Japan* (Washington, DC: U.S. Government Printing Office, 1991), 226.

39. Sugihara, "Kokusai-ho kara mita Hoppo-ryodo," 105.

40. Ibid.

41. Slavinskii, *Sovetskaia okkupatsiia kuril'skikh ostrovov*, 24.

42. Allison, Kimura, and Sarkisov, *Beyond Cold War*, 109.

43. See note 38, above.

44. Adam B. Ulam, *Expansion and Coexistence: Soviet Foreign Policy 1917–73*, 2d ed. (New York: Holt, Rinehardt and Winston, Inc., 1974), 564.

45. Ichiro Hatoyama, *Hatoyama Ichiro Kaikoroku* [Memoirs of Ichiro Hatoyama] (Tokyo: Bungei-shunju-sha, 1967), 174–76; Shun'ichi Matsumoto, *Mosukuwa ni kakeru Niji* [Rainbow bridge across Moscow] (Tokyo: Asahi-shimbun-sha, 1966), 17, 180.

46. Matsumoto, *Mosukuwa ni kakeru Niji*, 18–19.

47. Hatoyama, *Hatoyama Ichiro Kaikoroku*, 177.

48. *Asahi Shimbun* (evening edition), January 22, 1955.

49. Matsumoto, *Mosukuwa ni kakeru Niji*, 42–43.

50. Ibid., 43.

51. Ibid., 49.

52. Ibid., 84.

53. Ibid., 98; see also Leonid N. Kutakov, *Istoriia sovetsko-iaponskikh diplomaticheskikh otnoshenii*, 496.

54. *Hokkaido Shimbun*, February 21, 1990.

55. Ibid.

56. Mamoru Shigemitsu, *Zoku Shigemitsu Mamoru Shuki* [Memoires of Mamoru Shigemitsu, continued] (Tokyo: Chuo-koron-sha, 1988), 796.

57. Matsumoto, *Mosukuwa ni kakeru Niji*, 117; Joachim Glaubitz, *Between Tokyo and Moscow: The History of an Uneasy Relationship, 1972 to the 1990s* (London: Hurst & Company, 1995), 42.

58. *Conference for the Conclusion and Signature of the Treaty of Peace with Japan*, 326.

59. Allison, Kimura, and Sarkisov, *Beyond Cold War*, 109–10.

60. Shun'ichi Matsumoto, "Hoppo-ryodo Mondai" [The Northern Territories question], *Kyosan-ken Mondai* [Communist bloc problems] (Tokyo: Japanese Institute for International Affairs) 13 (December 1969): 5.

61. *Asahi Shimbun*, April 22, 1979.

62. Akio Kimura, "Soren-kara mita Hoppo-ryodo" [The Northern Territories problems seen from the Soviet Union], in *Hoppo-ryodo o kangaeru*, 153.

63. Joseph G. Whelan, *Soviet Diplomacy and Negotiating Behavior: Emerging New Context for U.S. Diplomacy*, vol. 1 (Washington, DC: U.S. Government Printing Office, 1979), 571.

64. *Hokkaido Shimbun*, March 2, 1993.

65. Ibid.

66. Ibid.

67. This is a technique that U.S. diplomats call "cherry-picking." Edward U. Rowny, "Negotiating with the Soviet," *The Washington Quarterly* (winter 1980): 61; Leon Sloss and M. Scott Davis, eds., *A Game for High Stakes: Lessons Learned in Negotiating with the Soviet Union* (Cambridge, MA: Ballinger, 1986), 88.

68. Kinya Niizeki, *Nisso-kosho no Butaiura—aru Gaikokan no Kiroku* [Background of the Japanese Soviet negotiations: A diplomat's record] (Tokyo: Nihon-hoso kyokai, 1989), 16.

69. *Asahi Shimbun, Hokkaido Shimbun*, May 27, 1964.

70. Ibid.

CHAPTER 5

1. Kazushige Hirasawa, "Japan's Emerging Foreign Policy," *Foreign Affairs* 54, no. 1 (October 1975): 165.

2. *Le Monde* (Paris), April 9–10, 1972.

3. William E. Griffith, *Peking, Moscow and Beyond* (Beverly Hills, CA: Sage Publications, 1973), 50, 71.

4. Mikhail S. Kapitsa, *Na raznykh paralleliakh: Zapiski diplomata* [Various parallels: Notes of a diplomat] (Moscow: Kiniga i biznes, 1996), 155.

5. Ibid.

6. *Hokkaido Shimbun, Hokkaido Shimbun* (evening edition), *Yomiuri Shimbun* (evening edition), June 27, 1992; *Asahi Shimbun,* June 28 and 30, 1992.

7. Whelan, *Soviet Diplomacy,* 571.

8. Professor Kimie Hara of the University of Waterloo, Ontario, Canada, found the actual document in the Australian Archives, which may prove the following: during the years immediately after the end of World War Two the Japanese Ministry of Foreign Affairs seemed to be aiming at the goal of recovering sovereignty over not necessarily all the four islands but only the two smaller ones. Kimie Hara, *Japanese-Soviet/Russian Relations Since 1945: A Difficult Peace* (London: Routledge, 1998), 23–33.

9. *Asahi Shimbun,* March 7, 1973.

10. Keisuke Suzuki, *Nisso Keizai Kyoryoku* [Japan-Soviet economic cooperation] (Tokyo: Japanese Institute for International Affairs, 1979), 151.

11. Bhabani Sen Gupta, *Soviet-Asian Relations in the 1970s and Beyond: An Interperceptional Study* (New York: Praeger, 1976), 296.

12. Leonid I. Brezhnev, *Izbrannye proizvedeniia (v trekh tomakh), Tom II (1971–1975)* [Selected works (in three volumes)] (Moscow: Politizdat, 1981), 209.

13. Hirokazu Arai, *Mosukuwa–Berurin–Tokyo: Gaikokan no Shogen* [Moscow, Berlin, Tokyo: Witness of a diplomat] (Tokyo: Jiji-tsusin-sha, 2000), 61, 85.

14. Morio Tominaga, "Mosukuwa de mita Hoppo-ryodo" [The Northern Territories question seen in Moscow], *Hoppo-ryodo* (series no. 21) (Sapporo: Japan League for the Return of the Northern Territories, Inc., 1981), 10.

15. *Tanaka Sōri wa kataru—Nisso-Shuno-Kaidan ni tsuite* [Prime Minister Tanaka speaks on the Japan-Soviet summit meeting] (Tokyo: Northern Territories Issue Association, 1974), 16.

16. Arai, *Mosukuwa–Berurin–Tokyo,* 95.

17. *Sankei Shimbun,* November 4, 1980.

18. Andrei A. Gromyko, "Programma mira v deistvii" [Program for peace in action], *Kommunist,* no. 14 (September 1975): 16; A. A. Gromyko, *Vo imia torzhestva leninskoi vneshnei politiki: Izbrannye rechi i stat'i* [In the name of victory of Lenin's foreign policy: Selected speeches and articles] (Moscow: Politizdat, 1978), 419.

19. *Pravda,* June 7, 1977.

20. *Asahi Shimbun* (evening edition), January 26, 1978.

21. *Izvestiia,* February 23, 1978; *Pravda,* February 24, 1978; *Asahi Shimbun,* February 24, 1978.

22. Shigeyoshi Matsumae, *Watashi no Minkan Gaikō Nijunen* [My diplomatic efforts as private individual for twenty years] (Tokyo: Tōkai University Press, 1986), 149–60.

23. Geoffrey Jukes, *Russia's Military and the Northern Territories Issue* (working paper no. 277 of Strategic & Defense Studies Centre, The Australian National University, Canberra, October 1993), 5–10.

24. *Hokkaido Shimbun,* February 6, 1980. See also *Nihon Keizai Shimbun,* January 22, 1980.

25. *Kan-Taiheiyo Rentai Kōso* [Report on the Pacific basin cooperation concept] (Tokyo: Printing Office, Ministry of Finance, 1980).

26. *Izvestiia,* February 24, 1980.

27. *Yomiuri Shimbun* (evening edition), May 9, 1981.

28. *Yomiuri Shimbun,* January 20, 1983.

29. *Washington Post,* January 19, 1983.

30. *Washington Post, Yomiuri Shimbun* (evening edition), May 30, 1983.

31. "Hibernation in May," *Economist,* vol. 291, no. 7432, May 19, 1984, 13–14.

32. *Pravda,* September 7 and 10, 1983.

33. Ibid., September 10, 1983.

34. Kunio Yanagida, *Gekitsui* [Shooting down], vol. 3 (Tokyo: Kodan-sha, 1991), 300.

35. Konstantin Chernenko, *Chernenko Enzetsu, Ronbun Shu* [Collection of speeches and papers by Konstantin Chernenko] (Tokyo: Soren Naigai-seisaku Kenkyu-kai [Study Group of Soviet Domestic and Foreign Policies], 1984), ii.

36. *Japan Times, Mainichi Daily News,* August 28, 1983.

37. *Izvestiia,* March 1, 1982; *Pravda,* March 2, 1982.

38. Konstantin Andreev and Kirill Cherevko, "Vydumka i pravda o 'severnykh territoriiakh'" [Fiction and truth about the "Northern Territories"] *Mezhdunarodnaia zhizn'* [International Affairs], no. 3 (1983): 114–15, 117–18.

CHAPTER 6

1. For one of the best scholarly works on Gorbachev and his policy, see Archie Brown, *The Gorbachev Factor* (Oxford: Oxford University Press, 1997), 406.

2. Mikhail S. Gorbachev, *Perestroika i novoe myshlenie dlia nashei strany i dlia vsego mira* [Perestroika and new thinking for our country and for all the world] (Moscow: Politizdat, 1987), 159.

3. Eduard Shevardnadze, *Moi vybor: V zashchitu i svobody* [My choice: For defense and freedom] (Moscow: Novosti, 1991), 79–80; see also Pavel Palazchenko, *My Years with Gorbachev and Shevardnadze: The Memoir of a Soviet Interpreter* (University Park: Pennsylvania State University Press, 1997), 30; Carolyn McGiffert Ekendahl and Melvin A. Goodman, *The Wars of Eduard Shevardnadze* (University Park: Pennsylvania State University Press, 1997), 33–36.

4. "Vremia perestroiki: Vystuplenie M. S. Gorbacheva v MID SSSR (23 maia 1986 g.)" [Time of Perestroika: Speech by M. S. Gorbachev in the Ministry of Foreign Affairs, USSR, on May 23, 1986], *Vestnik MID SSSR,* no. 1 (August 5, 1987): 6.

5. Robert Legvold, "The Revolution in Soviet Foreign Policy," *Foreign Affairs* 68, no. 1 (1988–89): 83–84, 96.

6. For more details, see chapter 3, "Japan as a Model for Soviet Reform," in Hiroshi Kimura, *Distant Neighbors,* vol. 2: *Japanese-Russian Relations Under Gorbachev and Yeltsin* (Armonk, NY: M. E. Sharpe, 2000), 55–76.

7. *Gaikō ni kansuru Seron-chōsa* [Survey on public opinion concerning foreign policy] (Tokyo: Prime Minister's Cabinet Office, Information Bureau, 1993).

8. The complete assessment of the Reykjavik summit even today remains a subject of speculation and dispute. Though it appeared to end in stalemate, or even failure, paradoxically, the summit was a major turning point in U.S.-Soviet relations, setting a foundation for later success. See, for example, Don Oberdorfer, *From the Cold War to a New Era: The Soviet Union 1983–1991*, updated ed. (Baltimore, MD: Johns Hopkins University Press, 1998), 154–209, particularly, 189–205; Ronald Reagan, *An American Life* (New York: Simon and Schuster, 1990), 683; Ekendahl and Goodman, *Wars of Eduard Shevardnadze*, 113–14; George P. Shultz, *Turmoil and Triumph: My Years as Secretary of State* (New York: Charles Scribner's Sons, 1993), 773–78.

9. Konstantin O. Sarkisov et al., "Vladivostokskie initsiativy: Dva goda spustia" [Vladistock initiatives: Two years after] *Mezhdunarodnaia zhizn'* 7 (July 1988): 147.

10. *Pravda, Asahi Shimbun,* and *Yomiuri Shimbun,* May 4, 1989.

11. Aleksandr N. Panov, *Diplomaticheskaia sluzhba Iaponii i evoliutsiia iapono-sovetskikh i iapono-rossiiskikh otnosheniiv v poslevoennyi period (1945–1955gg.): Uchebnoe posobie* [Diplomatic service of Japan and evolution of Japanese-Soviet and Japanese-Russian relations in the postwar period (1945–1955)] (Moscow: Moskovskii gosudarstvennyi institut mezhdunarodnykh otnoshenii ministerstva inostrannykh del Rossiiskoi Federatsii, 1995), 78.

12. Aleksei Bogaturov and Mikhail Nosov, "Treugol'nik bez uglov?" [Triangle without a corner] *Novoe vremia* [*New Times*], no. 18 [2288] (April 26, 1989): 8–9.

13. Rajendra K. Jain, *The USSR and Japan 1945–1980* (Brighton, Sussex: The Harvester Press, 1981), 310.

14. From a private conversation with Georgii F. Kunadze, then chief of Japanese Politics and Society at the Institute of World Economy and International Relations (IMEMO), Soviet Academy of Sciences.

15. *Vizit M. S. Gorbacheva v Iaponiiu (16–19 aprelia 1991 goda): Dokumenty i materialy* [Visit of M. S. Gorbachev to Japan (April 16–19, 1991): Documents and materials] (Moscow: Politizdat, 1991), 92.

16. Ibid., 106.

17. Ibid., 76.

18. Ibid., 94; *Izvestiia,* May 27, 1991.

19. Comment by Konstantin O. Sarkisov, then head of the Japanese Research Center, Institute of Oriental Studies, Soviet Academy of Sciences, during a private conversation with the author in Kyoto on May 22, 1991.

20. Kazuhiko Tōgō, *Nichiro Shinjidai e no Josō* [An approach toward the new Japanese-Russian era] (Tokyo: Saimaru-shuppan-kai, 1993), 164.

21. *Vizit M. S. Gorbacheva v Iaponiiu,* 93.

22. Geoffrey Jukes, *Russia's Military and the Northern Territories Issue* (working paper no. 277 of Strategic & Defense Studies Centre, The Australian National University, Canberra, October 1993), 7; Derek da Cunha, *Soviet Naval Power in the Pacific* (Boulder, CO: Lynne Rienne Publishers, 1990), 18, 90.

23. The section is based on information provided by Geoffrey Jukes.

24. *Vizit M. S. Gorbacheva v Iaponiiu,* 106; M. K. Gorshkov i V. V. Zhuravlev, eds., *Kurily: Ostrova v okeane problem* [Kuriles: Island of problem in the ocean] (Moscow: ROSSPEN, 1998), 298.

25. *Izvestiia*, April 27, 1991; *Vizit M. S. Gorbacheva v Iaponiiu*, 94.

26. Georgii A. Arbatov, former director of the Institute of the USA and Canada (ISKAN), Soviet Academy of Sciences, stated in an interview in Tokyo in October 1989 that while Japan was dealing with its political problems, the Soviets had decided that "due to the outbreak of ethnic and other domestic problems, we can't even think of broaching the territorial issue with Japan." *Shinju* (an organ of the Anzen-hosho Mondai Kenkyu-kai [Center for National Security Problems], Tokyo), October 1, 1989, 5.

27. Fred Coleman, *The Decline and Fall of the Soviet Union: Forty Years that Shook the World, from Stalin to Yeltsin* (New York: St. Martin's Press, 1996), 323; one suspects, however, that Gorbachev believed that he had visited Japan precisely during the cherry blossom season. In his meeting with the Japanese minister of international trade and industry, Eiichi Nakao, in October 1991, the former general secretary was quoted by Andrei Grachev as having said, "Impressions of my unforgettable trip to your country [Japan] are as fresh as ever. It was a brilliant idea to suggest that I visit Japan during the flowering of the *sakura*" (italics added). Andrei S. Grachev, "A Visit of Understated Expectations," *Moscow News*, no. 42 (October 15, 1993): 68.

28. Vladimir I. Lenin, *Polnoe sobranie sochinenii* [Complete works], 5th ed., vol. 34 (Moscow: Politizdat, 1964), 49.

CHAPTER 7

1. Lev Sukhanov, *Tri goda s El'tsinym: Zapiski pervogo pomoshchnika* [Three years with Yeltsin: Notes of the first assistant] (Riga: VAGA, 1992), 193–94.

2. M. K. Gorshkov i V. V. Zhuravlev, *Kurily: Ostrova v okeane problem* [Kuriles: Island of problem in the ocean] (Moscow: ROSSPEN, 1998), 317–22, 364–66; Vladimir Ovsiannikov, "Boris El'tsin: Izbavliat'sia ot gruza proshlogo" [Boris Yeltsin: Get rid of the past burden], *Novoe vremia*, no. 6 (February 2, 1990): 20–21.

3. Gorshkov i Zhuravlev, *Kurily*, 318.

4. Ibid., 321.

5. *Komsomol'skaia Pravda*, April 25, 1991; Igor' A. Latyshev, *Pokyshenie na Kurily* [Encroachment into the Kuriles] (Iuzhno-Sakhalinsk: Sakhalinskaia Assotsiatsiia "Pressa," 1992), 160.

6. *Sankei Shimbun* (evening edition), September 10, 1991.

7. Cited in Derwent Whittesey, *German Strategy of World Conquest* (New York: Farrar & Rinehard, 1942), 95.

8. Hiroshi Kimura, *Hoppo-ryodo—Kiseki to Henkan eno Josō* [The Northern Territories: Their history and prospects for their reversion] (Tokyo: Jiji-tsushin-sha, 1989), 19–20.

9. Takane Sugihara, "Kokusai-ho kara mita Hoppo-ryodo" [The Northern Territories seen from international law], in *Hoppo-ryodo o kangaeru* [Examining the Northern Territories issue], ed. Hiroshi Kimura (Sapporo: Hokkaido Shimbun-sha, 1981), 97.

10. Gorshkov i Zhuravlev, *Kurily*, 326–27, 330.

11. Robert Legvold, "The Revolution in Soviet Foreign Policy," *Foreign Affairs* 68, no. 1 (1988–89): 83, 84, 96.

12. I. William Zartman and Macreen R. Berman, *The Practical Negotiator* (New Haven, CT:Yale University Press, 1982), 87–146.

13. *Japan Times*, April 22, 1992.

14. *Mainichi Shimbun* (evening edition), January 21, 1992.

15. Strobe Talbott, *The Russia Hand:A Memoir of President Diplomacy* (NewYork: Random House, 2002), 28.

16. *Sovetskaia Rossiia*, September 12, 1992.

17. *Gaikō ni kansuru Seron-chosa* [Survey on public opinion concerning foreign policy] (Tokyo: Prime Minister's Cabinet Office, Information Bureau, 1998), 46.

18. *British Broadcasting Corporation Monitoring Summary of World Broadcasts: Former USSR*, no. 1818 (October 13, 1993), B/18.

19. Boris N. El'tsin, *Zapiski prezidenta* [Memoirs of a president] (Moscow: Ogonek, 1994), 188; *Komsomol'skaia Pravda*, October 10, 1993.

20. Gorshkov i Zhuravlev, *Kurily*, 368–71.

21. *ITAR TASS*, October 13, 1993.

22. Zartman and Berman, *Practical Negotiator*, 87–146.

23. *Asahi Shimbun, Sankei Shimbun*, October 14, 1993; *Far Eastern Economic Review*, October 21, 1993, 13.

24. *Foreign Broadcast Information Service: Soviet Union*, October 13, 1993, 14.

25. Ibid.; *Yomiuri Shimbun, Mainichi Shimbun*, October 14, 1993.

26. *Yomiuri Shimbun* (evening edition), January 22, 1996.

27. *Yomiuri Shimbun* (evening edition), January 20, 1997.

28. *Yomiuri Shimbun*, January 21, 1997.

29. *Yomiuri Shimbun, Asahi Shimbun, Mainichi Shimbun, Sankei Shimbun, Nihon Keizai Shimbun, Hokkaido Shimbun*, July 25, 1997; for an English translation, see *Japan Times*, September 8, 1997; for a Russian translation, see *Nezavisimaia gazeta*, August 12, 1997, and Gorshkov i Zhuravlev, *Kurily*, 371–79.

30. Gorshkov i Zhuravlev, *Kurily*, 374.

31. For the author's analysis, see *Tokyo Shimbun*, August 24, 1997.

32. Andrei I. Kravtsevich, "Russo-Japanese Relations Toward the 21st Century" (an unpublished paper read at the symposium entitled "Russo-Japanese Relations Toward 21th Century," held in Moscow, January 25, 1999).

33. Konstantin Sarkisov, "Russo-Japanese Relations After Yeltsin's Reelection in 1996," in *Japan and Russia:The Tortuous Path to Normalization, 1949–1999*, ed. Gilbert Rozman (NewYork: St. Martin's Press, 2000), 226.

34. *British Broadcast Corporation Monitoring Summary of World Broadcasts: Former USSR*, November 3, 1997, B/7–8.

35. *Yomiuri Shimbun*, February 26 and 27, 1997.

36. *Yomiuri Shimbun, Nihon-Keizai Shimbun*, April 2, 1998.

37. For the most detailed and best analysis of this summit, see Yakov Zinberg, "The Moscow Declaration, the Year 2000 and Russo-Japanese Deadlock over the 'Four Islands,' Dispute," *IBRU Boundary and Security Bulletin* (winter 1998–1999): 86–95.

38. According to *Sankei Shimbun* (November 30, 1998), a high-ranking official of the Russian Ministry of Foreign Affairs made it clear that a letter allegedly by President Yeltsin replying to the Hashimoto proposal was initiated by the leadership under

Russian Foreign Minister Evgenii Primakov. This official added, "From now on, instead of the ailing president, Foreign Minister Primakov will take the lead in negotiations with Japan." Subsequently, another Japanese newspaper, *Asahi Shimbun* (May 22, 2002) disclosed that on the first page of the letter, as received by Japanese Prime Minister Obuchi, the date and time were printed "07/11/98 14:56," which means: 2:56 p.m. on November 7th 1998, one day before Yeltsin returned to Moscow from a Black Sea resort. It was thus crystal clear that the Russian Foreign Ministry had prepared the reply to Hashimoto before Yeltsin's arrival in Moscow, most probably without consulting him.

39. *Yomiuri Shimbun, Sankei Shimbun, Hokkaido Shimbun*, February 22, 1999; *Japan Times, Asahi Evening News*, February 23, 1999.

CHAPTER 8

1. Kazuhiko Tōgō, "Irukutsuku Shuno-kaidan go no Nichiro-kankei" [Japanese-Russian relations after the summit at Irkutsk] (lecture at the Nihon Taigai Bunka Kyokai, April 19, 2001).

2. *Yomiuri Shimbun* (evening edition), December 26, 2000.

3. Hiroshi Kimura, "Politika Rossii v otnoshenii Iaponii: Ego tseli i strategiia iz ust samogo Putina" [Russia's policy toward Japan: Its goal and strategy judging from Putin's words] *Kraevedcheskii biulleteny* (Iuzhno-Sakhalinsk: Sakhalin State University)], no. 2 (2001): 132–39. For criticism of this piece, see "Kimura-san izvolil poshutit," *Pravda*, January 11, 2001.

4. Sumio Edamura, "Nichiro-kosho no 'Wakugumi' o Tatenaose" [Restore the "framework" of Japanese-Russian negotiation], *Chuo-koron* (May 2002): 72.

5. I. William Zartman and Macreen R. Berman, *The Practical Negotiator* (New Haven, CT: Yale University Press, 1982), 87–146.

6. Edamura, "Nichiro-kosho no 'Wakugumi' o Tatenaose," 69.

7. *Mainichi Shimbun*, April 27, 2001.

8. *Nihon-keizai Shimbun* (evening edition), May 7, 2001.

9. "MID Iaponii reshil kuril'skii vopros: Uvoleny spetsialisty po Rossii" [Ministry of Foreign Affairs of Japan decided on the Kuriles question: Specialists on Russia dismissed], *Kommersant*, April 27, 2002: 1.

10. "Makkartizm na Iaponskii lad: V Strane voskhodiashchego solntsa nachalas' 'Okhota na ved'm'—opytnykh spetsialistov po Rossii" [McCarthyism in a Japanese way: In a country of the rising sun with witch-hunting against experiences of Russian specialists has begun], *Rossiiskaia gazeta*, June 20, 2002, 4.

11. Aleksandr G. Iakovlev, *Rossia, Kitai, i mir* [Russia, China, and the world] (Moscow: Pamiatniki istoricheskoi mysli, 2002), 426.

12. "Vystuplenie (13 marta, 2002g.) v Gosudarstvennoi dume v ramkakh pravitel'stvennogo chasa," in Igor' Ivanov, *Vneshniaia politika Rossii v epokhu globalizatsii: Stat'i i vystupleniia* [Russian foreign policy in the days of globalization: Articles and speeches] (Moscow: Olma-press, 2002), 155, 157.

13. Nihon Gaimusho Ōhshukyoku [European Department, Japanese Ministry of Foreign Affairs], *Nichiro Gaisho Kaidan* [Meeting between the Japanese and Russian foreign ministers] (October 12, 2002): 6.

14. Konstantin Pulikovskii, *Vostochnyi ekspress: Po Rossii s Kim Chen Irom* [East express: Around Russia with Kim Jong-il] (Moscow: Gorodets-izdat, 2002).

15. *Yomiuri Shimbun, Sankei Shimbun*, August 12, 2002; Larisa Sayenko, "Putin Wants Korean Rail to Help Russia's Far East," *Reuters*, August 23, 2002.

16. *Kommersant'*, January 11, 2003; *Nezavisimaia gazeta*, January 13, 2003; see also *Itogi*, January 14, 2003.

17. *Nezavisimaia gazeta*, January 13, 2003; see also *Kommersant'*, January 11, 2003.

18. *Kommersant'*, January 11, 2003; *Itogi*, January 14, 2003, 9; see also *Hokkaido Shimbun*, January 12, 2003.

19. *New York Times*, January 13, 2003; *Financial Times*, January 10, 2003.

20. *Nezavisimaia gazeta*, January 13, 2003.

21. http://www.mofa.go.jp/region/europe/russia/pmv0301/plan.html. The Japanese language version is available at the Russian Section of the Japanese Ministry of Foreign Affairs (http://www.mofa.go.jp/mofaj). The Russian version is available at (http://www.mid.ru) *Sovmestnoe zaiavlenie prezidenta Rossii i Prem'er-ministra Iaponii o priniatii rossiisko-iaponskogo plana deistvii Moskva, Kreml', 10 ianvariia 2003 goda* [Joint statement of the Russian president and the Japanese prime minister on the adoption of the Russian-Japanese action plan, Moscow, Kremlin, January 10, 2003].

22. Nihon Gaimusho Ōhshukyoku Roshiaka [Russian Section, European Department, Japanese Ministry of Foreign Affairs], *Nichiro Shuno Kaidan* [Summit meeting between the Japanese prime minister and Russian president], January 10, 2003.

23. Jennifer Andersen, *The Limits of Sino-Russian Strategic Partnership*, Adelphi Paper No. 315 (London: International Institute for Security Studies, 1997), 66, 82.

24. *Itogi*, January 14, 2003, 8.

25. *Izvestiia*, January 11, 2003.

26. Ibid.

27. Paul Klebnikov, *Godfather of the Kremlin: Boris Berezovski and the Looting of Russia* (New York: Harcourt, Inc. 2000), 202–4, 276; Martin McCauley, *Bandits, Gangsters and the Mafia: Russia, the Baltic States and the CIS Since 1992* (London: Longman, 2001), 282–83.

28. McCauley, *Bandits, Gangsters and the Mafia*, 197.

29. *Wall Street Journal*, January 30, 2003.

30. *New York Times*, January 13, 2003.

31. *Nezavisimaia gazeta*, January 13, 2003.

32. Aleksandr Larin, "K voprosu o kitaiskoi 'demograficheskoi ekspansii'" [Concerning the problem of Chinese "demographic expansion"], *Problemy dal'nego vostoka*, no. 6 (2002): 56–57, 60, 65–66.

33. *New York Times*, January 13, 2003.

34. *Nezavisimaia gazeta*, January 13, 2003.

35. Ibid.

36. *Hokkaido Shimbun, Yomiuri Shimbun*, May 17, 2001; *Daily Yomiuri*, May 18, 2002; on May 17, Governor Ishaev, probably under pressure from government in Moscow, denied making such a statement. *Nihon-keizai Shimbun*, May 18, 2001.

37. *Hokkaido Shimbun, Yomiuri Shimbun*, May 17, 2001; *Daily Yomiuri*, May 18, 2001.

38. Ibid.

39. Ibid.

40. *Nezavisimaia gazeta*, January 13, 2003.

41. Olga Kryshtanovskya and Stephen White, "Putin's Militocracy," *Post-Soviet Affairs* 19, no. 4 (October–December, 2003): 289–306.

42. Ibid., 294, 296. 300.

43. Lilia Shevtsova, *Putin's Russia* (Washington, DC: Carnegie Endowment for International Peace, 2003), 81, 131.

44. *Kommersant'*, November 15, 2004; *Vremia Novostei*, November 16, 2004; *Vedomosti*, November 16, 2004.

45. "Rossiia–MID–Kitai–Granitsa," *Novosti Kitaia*, November 15, 2004; "Russian Foreign Minister Views Ties with China, Japan," *BBC International Report* (Asia), November 14, 2004.

46. *Vremia novostei*, November 15, 2004; "Russia: Locals Prepare to Rally to Keep Them," *Asia Africa Intelligence Wire Info Prod Info Prod*, November 15, 2004.

47. *Moscow Times*, November 16, 2004.

48. *Kommersant'*, November 15, 2004; *Trud*, November 16, 2004.

49. *MID RF Soobshchenie dlia pechati*, November 15, 2004.

50. *Nezavisimaia gazeta*, November 14, 2004.

51. *Rossiia-MID-Kitai-Granitsa,* November 15, 2004.

52. "Rossia–Iaponiia–Ostrova–Mnenie," *Novosti Severo-Zapada*, November 15, 2004; *BBC International Report* (Asia), November 14, 2004.

53. Ibid.

54. *Vzgliad 56–go Etazhe Kp. Ru*, November 16, 2004.

55. "Rossia–Iaponiia–Ostrova–Mnenie," *Novosti Severo-Zapada*, November 15, 2004; *BBC International Report* (Asia), November 14, 2004.

56. *Gazeta Ru*, November 15, 2004.

57. Ibid.

58. Ibid.

59. Hiroshi Kimura, "The Russian Way of Negotiating," in *International Negotiation: Actors, Structure/Process, Values*, eds. Peter Berton, Hiroshi Kimura, and I. William Zartman (New York: St. Martin's Press, 1999), 83.

60. *Pravda*, July 29, 1986.

61. Akihiro Iwashita, *A 4,000 Kilometer Journey Along the Sino-Russian Border* (Sapporo: Slavic Research Center, 2004), 17.

62. "Rossiia–MID–Kitai–Granitsa," *Novosti Kitaia*, November 15, 2004; "Russian Foreign Minister Views ties with China, Japan," *BBC International Report* (Asia), November 14, 2004.

63. *Kommersant'*, November 15, 2004.

64. *Izvestiia.Ru*, January 18, 2005; *The Russian Journal*, January 18, 2005.

65. *Sankei Shimbun*, November 17, 2005.

66. "President's Live Television and Radio Dialogue with the Nation," September 27, 2005, The Kremlin, Moscow, *President of Russia Official Web Portal Site*, http://www.president.kremlin.ru/eng/text/speeches/2005/09/27/1955_type82912type829 16type82917type84779_94321.shtml; (in Russian original): http://www.president.kremlin.ru/text/appears/2005/09/94308.shtml

67. *Pravda*, June 7, 1977.

68. Ibid., June 12, 1977. *Nihon-kyosanto to Ryodo-mondai* [The Japanese communist party and the territorial problem] (Tokyo: Shinnihon-bunko, 1981), 63.

69. "Vremia perestroiki: Vystuplenie M. S. Gorbacheva v MID SSSR (23 maia 1986g.)" [Time of Perestroika: Speech by M. S. Gorbachev in the Ministry of Foreign Affairs, USSR on May 23, 1986], *Vestnik Ministerstva inostrannykh del SSSR*, no. 1 (August 5, 1987): 6.

70. See note 66, above.

71. Alexandr Panov, trans. Yasuo Suzuki, *Kaminari nochi Hare* [Thunder then blue skies: The truth of seven years of Japan-Russian diplomacy] (Tokyo: NHK Publications, 2004), 172–73.

CONCLUSIONS

1. Cited in *New York Times*, May 11, 1959; Dan Caldwell, *American-Soviet Relations: From 1947 to the Nixon-Kissinger Grand Design* (Westport, CT: Greenwood Press, 1981), 3.

2. *Pravda*, November 7, 1984.

3. Basil Dmytryshyn, "Current Trends in Soviet Foreign Policy" (paper read for the Japan-U.S. Society at Sapporo in February 1979), 12.

4. *Asahi Shimbun, Sankei Shimbun, Hokkaido Shimbun,* July 19, 1980.

5. *Nihon Keizai Shimbun,* March 27, 1982.

6. John J. Stephan, *The Kuril Islands: Russo-Japanese Frontiers in the Pacific* (Oxford: Clarendon Press, 1974), 208; Yong C. Kim, *Japanese-Soviet Relations: Interaction of Politics Economics and National Security* (Beverly Hills, CA: Sage, 1974), 46.

7. Michael McGwire, "The Rationale for the Development of Soviet Seapower," *United States Naval Institute Proceedings* (May 1980): 181.

8. *The Military Balance 1989–90* (London: International Institute for Strategic Studies, 1990), 42; *The Military Balance 2005–2006,* 167.

9. For this part I rely entirely on research and studies by Geoffrey Jukes. See his "Can the Southern Kuriles be Demilitarized?" a paper presented at the international conference, "New Initiatives for Solving the Northern Territories Issues between Japan and Russia: An Inspiration from the Aland Model," held at Mariehamn/Aland, August 18–20, 2006.

10. *Vizit M. S. Gorbacheva v Iaponiiu (16–19 aprelia 1991 goda): Dokumenty i materialy* [Visit of M. S. Gorbachev to Japan (April 16–19, 1991): Documents and materials] (Moscow: Politizdat, 1991), 106.

11. *Nezavisimaia gazeta,* November 16, 2004.

12. See also John B. Dunlop, *The Rise of Russia and the Fall of the Soviet Empire* (Princeton, NJ: Princeton University Press, 1993), 261; Peter Reddaway and Dmitri Glinski, *The Tragedy of Russia's Reform* (Washington, DC: United States of Peace Press, 2001), 279.

13. *Japan Times, Asahi Evening News,* February 23, 1999.

14. Boris Yeltsin, *Prezidentskii marafon* [Presidential marathon](Moscow: Izdatel'stvo ACT, 2000), 138.

15. Hiroshi Kimura, "The Russian Way of Negotiating," in *International Negotiation: Actors, Structure/Process, Values,* eds. Peter Berton, Hiroshi Kimura, and I. William Zartman (New York: St. Martin's Press, 1999), 83–84.

16. "Rossiia-Iaponia-Ostova-Mnenie," *Novosti severno-zapada,* November 15, 2004; *Gazeta.Ru,* November 15, 2004.

17. Graham T. Allison, *Essence of Decision: Explaining the Cuban Missile Crisis* (Boston: Little, Brown and Company, 1971), 10–14.

18. Igor' A. Latyshev, *Pokyshenie na Kurily* [Encroachment into the Kuriles] (Iuzhno-Sakhalinsk: Sakhalinskaia Assotsiatsiia "Pressa," 1992), 223–24.

19. Hiroshi Kimura, *Distant Neighbors*, vol. 2: *Japanese-Russian Relations Under Gorbachev and Yeltsin* (Armonk, NY: M. E. Sharpe, 2000), 256–57; Roman Solchanyk, *Crimea: Between Ukraine and Russia* (Santa Monica, CA: RAND Corporation, 1996), 4; Leon Aron, "The Foreign Policy Doctrine of Postcommunist Russia and Its Domestic Context," in *The New Russian Foreign Policy*, ed. Michael Mandelbaum (New York: The Council on Foreign Relations, 1998), 42; Igor Kharchenko, "A View from Ukraine," in *NATO Enlargement: Opinions and Options*, ed. Jeffrey Simon (Fort McNair, Washington, DC: 1995), 148, 153.

20. Akihiro Iwashita, *A 4,000 Kilometer Journey Along the Sino-Russian Border* (Sapporo: Slavic Research Center, 2004), 17.

21. "Rossiia-MID-Kitai-Granitsa," *Novosti Kitaia*, November 15, 2004; "Russian Foreign Minister Views Ties with China, Japan," *BBC International Reports* (Asia), November 14, 2004.

22. *Izvestiia.Ru*, January 18, 2005; *Russian Journal*, January 18, 2005.

23. Lisbeth Tarlow Bernstein, *On the Rocks: Gorbachev and the Kurile Islands* (Ann Arbor, MI: UMI, Dissertation Services, 1997), 26, 276.

24. *Pravda*, May 17, 1989. During his second official visit to Japan in December 1988 Eduard Shevardnadze, then Soviet foreign minister, also used the same term. *Pravda*, December 12, 1988.

25. *Sibirskaia Gazeta*, December 9, 1990.

26. Masataka Kosaka, *Options for Japan's Foreign Policy*, Adelphi Paper No. 97 (London: The International Institute for Strategic Studies, 1973), 28. Also see, J. B. Sorensen, *Japanese Policy and Nuclear Arms* (New York: American-Asian Educational Exchange, Inc., 1957), 51.

27. Anatoly Gorev, "Is Russia Ready for a New Economic Development Model?" *RIA Novosti*, March 1, 2007.

28. Roman Dobrokhotov, "Frantsiia ili krizis: Egor Gaidar prognoziruet ekonomicheskii krakh k 2015 godu" [France of crisis: Yegor Gaidar forecast economic crash by 2015], *Novye Izvestiia*, March 6, 2007.

29. "Russia Finance Minister Warns Against Oil 'Euphoria,'" *AFP* in *Johnson's Russia List*, 2006–#274 (December 5, 2006): #31.

30. "Putin Urges Business to Produce More Value-added Products—2," *RIA Novosti*, February 6, 2007; Anna Nikolayeva, "President Putin Comes up with a Spectacular Finale for Himself: Diversifying the Russian Economy," *Vedomosti*, February 7, 2007, in *Johnson's Russia List*, 2007–#30 (February 7, 2007): #9; Anna Smolchenko, "Putin Says Business Must Diversify," *Moscow Times*, February 7, 2007, 1; Stephen Boykewich, "Russia Must Diversify to Profit from Energy: Putin," *AFP*, February 6, 2007.

31. "Opening Address at the Meeting with Representatives from the Russian Union of Industrialists and Entrepreneurs," February 6, 2007, The Kremlin, Moscow, *President of Russia Official Web Portal Site*, http://www.kremlin.ru/eng/text/speeches/2007/02/06/2314_type82912type84779_117945.shtml; (in Russian original): http://www.kremlin.ru/text/appears/2007/02/117926.shtml

32. Ibid.

33. Ibid.

34. Ibid.

35. Ibid.

36. Ibid.

37. Ibid.

38. "Welcome Address by Dr. Kiyohiko Toyama, Vice Minister (Parliamentary) for Foreign Affairs of Japan, to Foreign Policy and Energy Security Seminar (March 1, 2006, Tokyo) http://www.nofa.go.jp/policy/energy/seminar/address0603.html

39. *Regiony Rossii: Sotsial'no-ekonomicheskie pokazateli 2005* [Regions of Russia: Social-economic index 2005] (Moscow: Gasudarstvennyi komitet Rossiiskoi Federatsii po statistike, 2006), tables 2.1 and 4.15, respectively 36–37 and 166–67.

40. *World Development Indicators 2002* (Washington, DC: International Bank for Reconstruction and Development/ World Bank, 2002), 74–76. Figures are not all for the same year, but in politically stable countries they change substantially only for long periods.

41. For writing this paragraph I am entirely obliged to information provided by Geoffrey Jukes.

42. *Regiony Rossii*, 28–31, 575–76.

43. *Yomiuri Shimbun*, June 10, 2005.

44. *Economist*, December 2–8, 2006, 14.

45. Charles W. Kegley Jr. and Eugene R. Wittkopf, *World Politics: Trend and Transformation*, 6th ed. (New York: St. Martin's Press), 40–41.

46. Charles Burton Marshall, "The Problem of Incompatible Purposes," in *Conflict and Cooperation Among Nations*, ed. Ivo Buchaek (New York: Holt, Reinhardt and Winston, Inc., 1960), 519. Sir William Hayter, who served as ambassador to the Soviet Union, also said, summing up the Russian approach to negotiating, "The Russians are not to be persuaded by eloquence or convinced by reasoned arguments. They rely on what Stalin used to call the proper basis of international policy, the calculation of forces." Cited in Dean Acheson, *Present at the Creation: My Years in the State Department* (New York: W.W. Norton & Company, 1969), 275.

47. Fiona Hill and Clifford C. Gaddy, *The Siberian Curse: How Communist Planners Left Russia Out in the Cold* (Washington, DC: Brookings Institution Press, 2003), 200–201.

48. Natalya Alyakrinskaya, "Labor Shortage Puts Russian Economy at Risk," *Moscow News*, March 9, 2007.

49. Ibid.

50. "Isolation of Russian Far East Threat to National Security–Putin," *RIA Novosti*, December 20, 2006.

51. "Opening Remarks at Security Council Session," December 20, 2006, The Kremlin, Moscow, *President of Russia Official Web Portal Site*, http://www.kremlin.ru/eng/text/speeches/2006/12/20/1910_type82912type82913_115719.shtml; (in Russian original): http://www.kremlin.ru/text/appears/2006/12/115650.shtml

52. *Nezavisimaia Gazeta*, October 27, 2003.

About the Author

HIROSHI KIMURA is professor emeritus at Hokkaido University and at the International Research Center for Japanese Studies. After graduating from Kyoto University with a BA in law, he continued his graduate studies at Columbia University, where he earned a PhD in political science (1968). He was a professor and director of the Slavic Research Center at Hokkaido University (in Sapporo), and a professor at the International Research Center for Japanese Studies (in Kyoto). He was a Fulbright-Hays Visiting Professor at the Institute for Sino-Soviet Studies, George Washington University (1977–78), at Stanford University (1982–83), and at Columbia University (1998–99). He was also a special research fellow at the Japanese Embassy in Vienna (1972–73) and in Moscow (1973–75). He served as the Japanese representative, an executive member, and vice president of the International Council for Central and East European Studies (ICCEES).

His recent research has focused on Russian foreign policy in general, and particularly toward Japan. His major publications in English include *Distant Neighbors* (in two volumes): vol. 1, *Japanese-Russian Relations Under Brezhnev and Andropov*; and vol. 2, *Japanese-Russian Relations Under Gorbachev and Yeltsin* (Armonk, NY: M. E. Sharpe, August 2000); *Beyond Cold War to Trilateral Cooperation in the Asia-Pacific Region: Scenarios for New Relationships Between Japan, Russia, and the United States*, coedited with Graham Allison and Konstantin Sarkisov (Cambridge, MA: 1992); and *International Negotiation: Actors, Structure / Process, Values*, coedited with Peter Berton and I. William Zartman (New York: St. Martin's Press, 1999). His publications in Russian include *Курильская проблема: история японо-российских переговоров по пограничным вопросам* (Киев: "Юринком", 1996), and articles for *Коммунист* (Communist), *Мировая экономика и международные отношения* (World Economy and International Relations), and *Проблемы дальнего востока* (Far Eastern Affairs).